JESUS OUR PRIEST

To Donna,
    Every blessing in Eastertide,
        Gerald O'Collins J
        25. iV. 2010.

With prayerful best wishes
Father Michael K. Jones

Jesus Our Priest

A Christian Approach to the Priesthood of Christ

GERALD O'COLLINS, SJ,
AND MICHAEL KEENAN JONES

OXFORD
UNIVERSITY PRESS

OXFORD
UNIVERSITY PRESS

Great Clarendon Street, Oxford OX2 6DP

Oxford University Press is a department of the University of Oxford.
It furthers the University's objective of excellence in research, scholarship,
and education by publishing worldwide in

Oxford New York

Auckland Cape Town Dar es Salaam Hong Kong Karachi
Kuala Lumpur Madrid Melbourne Mexico City Nairobi
New Delhi Shanghai Taipei Toronto

With offices in

Argentina Austria Brazil Chile Czech Republic France Greece
Guatemala Hungary Italy Japan Poland Portugal Singapore
South Korea Switzerland Thailand Turkey Ukraine Vietnam

Oxford is a registered trade mark of Oxford University Press
in the UK and in certain other countries

Published in the United States
by Oxford University Press Inc., New York

British Library Cataloguing in Publication Data

Data available

Library of Congress Cataloging in Publication Data

Library of Congress Control Number: 2009938802

Typeset by SPI Publisher Services, Pondicherry, India
Printed in Great Britain
on acid-free paper by the
MPG Books Group, Bodmin and King,s Lynn

ISBN 978-0-19-957645-6

1 3 5 7 9 10 8 6 4 2

Preface

Ecumenical dialogues between Christian churches and debates within some of those churches have kept alive issues about priesthood: the priesthood of all the faithful (or of all the baptized) and the priesthood of ordained ministers (or ministerial priesthood). All agree that the priesthood of the faithful and ministerial priesthood are closely interrelated. But do they differ in essence and not merely in degree? Through their ordination have the presiding ministers received a special gift for the benefit of the community and so stand in a special relationship to Christ the High Priest? Do that gift and relationship distinguish them from the faithful and from the priesthood received through baptism?

By virtue of their baptism all Christians share in the priesthood of Christ. But does this participation differ from the participation in the priesthood of Christ received through ministerial ordination, so that— for instance—only a validly ordained priest can bring into being the sacrament of the Eucharist? Does ministerial ordination effect such an essential difference?

Any adequate response to these questions depends on a theological understanding of the priesthood of Christ himself. Logically, before tackling any issues concerned with the priesthood of the faithful and the priesthood of the ordained, we need to have reached some clearly worked out conclusions about what is implied by calling Christ a priest or the High Priest of the new covenant (the Letter to the Hebrews).

Perhaps surprisingly, little reflection on Christ's own priesthood is available from modern works in Christology and soteriology. Let us cite three examples. In the closing chapter of *Jesus the Christ* (German original 1974) Walter Kasper briefly examines the 'triple office' of Jesus as priest, prophet (teacher), and king (pastor), and allows less than three pages for a consideration of his priesthood. In *Jesus: God and Man* (German original 1964) and the Christological section of the second volume of *Systematic Theology* (German original 1988) Wolfhart Pannenberg briefly and critically discusses the 'triple office'

of Christ. He denies that we should speak of the earthly Jesus as priest and king or even of his being 'a prophet in the strict sense'. In *Jesus: Symbol of God* (1999) Roger Haight, while ready to talk about Jesus' prophetic role and about his kingly role (at least as 'Saviour' and 'Liberator'), has nothing to say about his priestly function and identity.

If we turn to such landmark documents as *Baptism, Eucharist and Ministry* (*BEM*), published in 1982 by the Faith and Order Commission of the World Council of Churches, and the *Final Report*, published in the same year by the Anglican–Roman Catholic International Commission (ARCIC), we find that they excavate common principles about Christ's priesthood. But they do not say why these principles are true and how they reached such conclusions. Their interest is focused elsewhere: on the ordained ministry and the celebration of the Eucharist.

We can group the convergent statements about Christ's priesthood from *BEM* and ARCIC under ten points. He is (1) the unique priest or high priest (2) of the new covenant, whose (3) once-and-for-all (4) sacrifice (5) for all human beings (6) brought salvation or reconciliation to the world. (7) His priesthood continues through his interceding 'before the Father', by (8) the incorporation into him of the baptized, and by (9) the celebration of the Eucharist, where Christ 'unites' his people and 'gathers, teaches and nourishes the Church' (*BEM*) or 'presides and gives himself sacramentally' (*Final Report*). (10) All other priesthood, whether the priesthood of all the faithful or that of the ordained ministry, is derived from Christ's priesthood.

Although neither document quotes the Letter to the Hebrews or even refers to it, that New Testament text, as we shall see, clearly lies behind points (1) to (7). All of these points call for analysis. Why did Christians apply the language of priesthood to Christ, and in what did they believe his unique priesthood consisted (1)? Can we dive deeper into their language of salvation for all human kind and the expiation of their sins and say more about what his priesthood effected in bringing about a new covenant (2, 5, and 6)? What does the language of sacrifice mean and how can it be justified and maintained (4)? What more did New Testament Christians and their successors maintain, in the light of Hebrews, about a permanent priesthood of Christ (7)?

Both *BEM* and the *Final Report* point to a priesthood of Christ exercised through baptism and the Eucharist (8 and 9). How could they ground such a belief about his priesthood continuing in these sacraments? Does the Letter to the Hebrews allow for a sharing in Christ's priesthood (10)? Is such a participation ruled out by the epistle's emphasis on the once-and-for-all character of his priesthood (3)?

In short, *BEM* and the *Final Report* provide us with a grid of questions that should be raised and explored in the course of this book. Further questions will emerge: when did Christ become a priest? At the incarnation or only at the final sacrifice of his life? Then there are two closely correlated questions: did Christ's priesthood depend essentially on his humanity? Is the priesthood of Christ (and Christian priesthood in any form) a priesthood that will, or even must, be tried and tested by temptations and sufferings?

Then there are questions connected with Christ's 'triple office', championed by John Calvin and John Henry Newman. How might we relate Christ's being priest with his being also prophet (teacher) and king (pastor)? Should we recognize his earthly ministry as an expression not only of his prophetic and kingly function but also of his priestly function? How do baptized and ordained Christians share in Christ's triple office?

Our opening chapter will set out some relevant material on the Jewish priesthood and some aspects of Christ's priesthood to be gleaned from the Gospels. Chapter 2 will present data from Paul's letters (especially 1 Corinthians and Romans), 1 Peter, and the Book of Revelation. Two chapters will then be dedicated to the teaching of Hebrews on Christ's priesthood and the issues it brings up. Chapter 5 will examine what Origen, Cyprian of Carthage, John Chrysostom, Augustine of Hippo, and some other fathers of the Church offer for those who explore the theme of Christ's priesthood.

Chapter 6 will move to what Thomas Aquinas might yield for this theme, before taking up, in Chapter 7, the controversies about the unique priesthood of Christ initiated by the Reformers (in particular, by Luther and Calvin). Chapter 8 will state the positions defended and elaborated by the Roman Catholic response at the Council of Trent, and will gather some reflections on Christ's priesthood from Pierre de Bérulle, Charles de Condren, and other exponents of the 'French

School'. Chapter 9 will retrieve what John Henry Newman, Karl Barth, and others in the nineteenth and twentieth centuries have contributed towards appreciating Christ's 'triple office' and, in particular, his priestly function.

After gathering relevant data from the Scriptures and a range of Christian witnesses, we will be in a position, through two concluding chapters, (1) to describe and define in twelve theses the key characteristics of the priesthood of Christ, and (2) to set out (also in twelve theses) what sharing in that priesthood through baptism and ordination involves.

We are most grateful to many people for their help and encouragement in writing this book and, in particular, to Bishop John Barres, Gerald Bednar, Finbarr Clancy, Robert Draper, James Dunn, Abbot Hugh Gilbert, Mary Grey, Michael Hayes, George Hunsinger, Allan Laubenthal, Brendan Leahy, Philip Moller, Doan Nguyen Kim, Anne Marie Paine, John Ringley, Lawrence Terrien, Anthony Towey, and Jared Wicks. Our warm thanks go to Vicky Rowley (Heythrop College, University of London), who was tireless in tracing and providing on loan books we needed. Unless otherwise noted, all translations from other languages are our own. With much affection we dedicate this work to the staff and members of St Lawrence's Parish, Huntington, Connecticut.

Gerald O'Collins, SJ, and *the Revd Michael Jones*
16 June 2009

Contents

Abbreviations

AA	Vatican II, *Apostolicam Actuositatem*
ABD	D. N. Freedman (ed.), *Anchor Bible Dictionary*, 6 vols. (New York: Doubleday, 1992)
ARCIC	Anglican–Roman Catholic International Commission
BEM	Faith and Order Commission, *Baptism, Eucharist and Ministry* (Geneva: World Council of Churches, 1982)
DzH	H. Denzinger and P. Hünermann (eds.), *Enchiridion symbolorum, definitionum et declarationum* (17th edn., Freiburg im Breisgau: Herder, 1991)
LG	Vatican II, *Lumen Gentium*
LThK	W. Kasper *et al.* (eds.), *Lexikon für Theologie und Kirche*, 11 vols. (3rd edn., Freiburg im Breisgau: Herder, 1993–2001)
LW	J. Pelikan and H. T. Lehmann (eds.), *Luther's Works*, 55 vols. (St Louis and Philadelphia: Concordia Publishing House/ Muhlenberg Press, 1958–67)
LXX	Septuagint
ND	J. Neuner and J. Dupuis (eds.), *The Christian Faith* (7th edn., Bangalore and New York: Theological Publications in India/ Alba House, 2001)
ODCC	F. L. Cross and E. A. Livingstone (eds.), *The Oxford Dictionary of the Christian Church* (3rd edn., Oxford: Oxford University Press, 2005)
par./parr.	parallel passages in the Synoptic Gospels
PG	*Patrologia Graeca*, ed. J. P. Migne (162 vols., Paris, 1857–66)
PL	*Patrologia Latina*, ed. J. P. Migne (221 vols., Paris, 1844–64)
PO	Vatican II, *Presbyterorum Ordinis*
SC	Vatican II, *Sacrosanctum Concilium*
STh.	St Thomas Aquinas, *Summa Theologiae*
TRE	H. Krause and G. Müller (eds.), *Theologische Realenzyklopädie*, 36 vols. (Berlin: Walter de Gruyter, 1977–2004)

1

The Jewish Matrix and the Gospels

Unquestionably, the Letter to the Hebrews (written between 60 and 90 AD) is *the* central New Testament text on the priesthood of Christ and his sacrificial activity. Nevertheless, before examining its witness at length, we need first to take up some strands of teaching in other books of the New Testament and to retrieve something of the Jewish matrix. Hebrews presents Christ's high priesthood against the background of the Jewish priesthood and sacrificial system. Hence we begin with Jewish priests and sacrifices.[1]

JEWISH MATRIX

Abraham and the other patriarchs build altars (e.g. Gen. 12: 7–8; 22: 13) and offer sacrifices (e.g. Gen. 15: 9–11).[2] Even earlier in the narrative of Genesis, Noah, when the flood subsides, builds 'an altar to the Lord' and makes on it 'burnt offerings' of 'clean' animals and birds.

---

[1] On Jewish priesthood see M. D. Rehm, 'Levites and Priests', *ABD* iv. 297–310; H. D. Preuss, *Old Testament Theology*, trans. L. G. Perdue, vol. 2 (Edinburgh: T. & T. Clark, 1996), 52–66; on Jewish sacrifices see ibid. 238–45. On priesthood in general see H. Haag *et al.*, 'Priester. Priestertum', *LThK* viii. cols. 557–70; W. Klein *et al.*, 'Priester, Priestertum', *TRE* xxvii. 379–434.

[2] We are well aware that the place of the Book of Genesis at the beginning of the Bible does not mean that it was composed before the books that follow in the canon. Moreover, the final text of Genesis and other individual books frequently include a variety of traditions that should, or at least can, be dated to various periods. The canonical order does not represent the chronological order of composition of the books of the Old and New Testament, and not even the order of composition of sections within these books.

2 The Jewish Matrix and the Gospels

When 'the Lord smells the pleasing odour', he 'says in his heart' that, despite 'the evil inclination of the human heart', he will never again curse the ground and bring destruction (Gen. 8: 15–22). In building an altar and offering this sacrifice of thanksgiving, Noah does so spontaneously and, obviously, without intending to follow prescriptions about burnt offerings and other offerings understood to have been introduced later by God through Moses (Lev. 1–7).

In the course of the patriarchal narratives, the encounter between Abraham and Melchizedek introduces something startlingly different as regards priestly activity. This priest-king abruptly appears to meet and bless Abraham in the name of 'God Most High (*El Elyon*)' (Gen. 14: 19–20). Like Abraham and Sarah, Melchizedek enjoys intimate contact with God. A priest of a Canaanite sanctuary, he conveys a blessing to Abraham and does so in the name of the deity whom he worships and who is at once identified as 'the maker of heaven and earth' (Gen. 14: 22). Later books will identify 'God Most High' as the Lord (YHWH) or God of Israel (Num. 24: 16; Ps. 46: 4). The brief but startling story of the meeting between Abraham and Melchizedek will be exploited by the Letter to the Hebrews and subsequent Christian tradition.

When we move to the period of the monarchy, we find kings being anointed (e.g. 1 Sam. 9: 16; 10: 1; 16: 12–13; 2 Sam. 2: 4, 7; Ps. 2: 2, 7), even as priests were to be anointed.[3] The new king bore the dignity of priesthood (Ps. 110: 4). At times the king performed some cultic and priestly function (as Solomon did at the dedication of the Temple: 1 Kgs 8: 1–65). During that period there was not yet a 'single priesthood with proper jurisdictional authority';[4] it was only progressively that 'the priests became the only ones who may "draw near" to God at the altar and serve him' (e.g. Lev. 21: 17; Num. 18: 7).[5]

Early priestly activity involved (1) protecting and caring for various sanctuaries (e.g. Bethel) and the Temple in Jerusalem, when Jerusalem as the home of the Temple became the only sanctuary,[6] and

[3] Priests were anointed (e.g. Exod. 29: 7; Lev. 8: 10). The only reference to prophets being anointed comes in Isa. 61: 1–2; see Ps. 105: 15. Elijah was supposed to anoint his successor Elisha (1 Kgs 19: 16), but—*pace* Sir. 48: 8—did not do so.
[4] Preuss, *Old Testament Theology*, ii. 55.
[5] Ibid. 56.
[6] Ibid. 214–24.

(2) instructing people in YHWH's law, as well as blessing people in his name (Deut. 10: 8). Worshippers approached priests to enquire about the divine will, receive oracles, and apply God's revelation to their lives. The opening of Jeremiah's fourth personal lament names 'instruction' as a distinguishing (but not exclusive) feature of the priesthood (Jer. 18: 18). Deuteronomy 'places the priest's role with regard to instructing in the divine law above the sacrificial practice'.[7]

But after the return from exile in Babylon, offering sacrifice gained significance as the primary priestly activity. Even if the Old Testament never provides 'a rationale for sacrifice or a general theory of sacrifice', three kinds of sacrifice (communion sacrifices, sacrifices that were gifts, and sacrifices for sin) became central to the work of priests.[8] They functioned, above all, to lead worship and offer sacrifices. Their privileged vocation involved special access to God: in particular, contact with the altar, the sign of God's numinous presence (Lev. 1–7; 16). Even so, a post-exilic prophet like Malachi, who clearly took a high view of priestly responsibilities, showed deep respect for the 'instruction' (on the Law) priests should impart: 'the lips of a priest should guard knowledge, and people should seek instruction from his mouth, for he is the messenger of the Lord of hosts' (Mal. 2: 7). True 'instruction', mentioned four times, runs like an antiphon through this passage on the duties of priests (Mal. 2: 4–9). Somewhat later, Sirach, in the course of glorifying Aaron (Sir. 45: 6–25) and with an eye on the high priests of Sirach's own time, does not fail to mention Aaron's authority to teach the law (Sir. 45: 17).

Werner Dommershausen sums up the teaching and cultic functions of the priesthood: 'The various priestly duties share the common basis of mediation: in oracles and instruction, the priest represents God to the people; in sacrifice and intercession, he represents the people to God.'[9] In other words, priestly mediation runs in two directions: from God to the people and from the people to God.

---

[7] J. M. Scholer, *Proleptic Priests: Priesthood in the Epistle to the Hebrews* (Sheffield: Sheffield Academic Press, 1991), 18. See also Lev. 10: 10–11 and the priests' role in teaching 'the statutes which the Lord has uttered through Moses'.

[8] Ibid. 238.

[9] W. Dommershausen, '*kōhēn*, priest', in G. J. Botterweck, H. Ringren, and H.-J. Fabry (eds.), *Theological Dictionary of the Old Testament*, trans. D. E. Green, vol. 8 (Grand Rapids, Mich.: Eerdmans, 1995), 66–75, at 70.

St Athanasius of Alexandria, with the Letter to the Hebrews in mind, was to express this two-directional mediatorial work of priesthood as follows: 'He [Christ] became Mediator between God and human beings in order that he might minister the things of God to us and our things to God' (*Contra Arianos*, 4. 6).

After the fall of the monarchy and the return from exile, priests came to the forefront of Jewish life. As the priesthood became more structured and more central to Jewish existence, priestly lineage became essential. Priests belonged to the tribe of Levi and descended from the particular family of Aaron (Aaronites). Aaron himself was deemed to be the first 'high priest' (Ezra 7: 1–5), of royal rank and vestments (Exod. 28–9), and a prophet (Exod. 7: 1–2) who served as the 'mouth' of Moses in transmitting his word (Exod. 4: 14–17): in short, a priest, king, and prophet.

In the post-exilic period we meet for the first time someone who genuinely bore the title of high priest, Joshua (Hag. 1: 1, 12, 14; 2: 2, 4). The high priest 'functioned as the necessary mediator between God and people, for he entered the holy of holies on the Day of Atonement and carried out his cultic rites dealing with sin (Leviticus 16)'.[10] The anointing (Exod. 29: 4–7; Lev. 8: 6–12) and clothing (Exod. 28: 1–29: 9) of the high priest 'continued part of the royal tradition'.[11] As a kind of substitute for the Davidic king, the high priest emerged as a priest-king, but not as a priest, king, *and prophet* (unlike Aaron; see above). Yet John 11: 49–52 pictures Caiaphas, the high priest, as unwittingly expressing a prophecy about the death of Jesus (see below).

At times some Old Testament prophets denounced corrupt priests: for instance, over their drunkenness (Isa. 28: 7) and their murderous plans (Jer. 26: 7–11). Amos recorded a dramatic confrontation between the prophet and the official priest of the royal sanctuary at Bethel (Amos 7: 10–17). Amos warned that the Lord did not delight in religious festivals and sacrifices but in the practice of justice and righteousness (Amos 5: 21–7). Prophets regularly levelled explicit or implicit criticism at empty worship and the way priests and people relied on superficial ritual performance and did not live righteous lives (e.g. Isa. 1: 11–17). In a verse that summed up his message, Hosea declared in

---

[10] Preuss, *Old Testament Theology*, ii. 56.
[11] Ibid. 66.

the name of the Lord: 'I desire steadfast love and not sacrifice, the knowledge of God rather than burnt offerings' (Hos. 6: 6; Matt. cites this verse when portraying Jesus' ministry to sinners: 9: 13; see 12: 7).

Tobit emphasizes the value of almsgiving as 'an excellent offering in the presence of the Most High' (Tob. 4: 7–11). Sirach declares that those who keep the commandments, return kindnesses, and give alms offer acceptable sacrifices to God (Sir. 35: 1–4). The Psalms praise prayer and a 'contrite heart' as sacrifices pleasing to God (Ps. 51: 17; 141: 2). A psalm of judgment on Israel acknowledges that the people have brought God abundant sacrifices, but this is not what God wants. God desires thanksgiving and prayer (Ps. 50: 8–15). In a closing warning the psalmist states on behalf of God: 'those who bring thanksgiving as their sacrifice honour me' (Ps. 50: 23).

Nevertheless, emphasis on right conduct towards God and human beings and denunciations of those who obey the cultic prescriptions of the Law while neglecting its moral commandments does not mean demanding that the sacrificial activity of priests be abolished. In an exchange with Jesus over the greatest commandment, a scribe rightly gives precedence to the practice of love over burnt offerings and other sacrifices (Mark 12: 33). But the exchange does not call for the abolition of the sacrificial system, as we shall see at once in a passage from Isaiah about non-Israelites.

Some strikingly universalist texts about foreign people to whom divine salvation is extended and who join themselves to Israel picture the Temple as being open to all people and Gentiles (seemingly proselytes) being authorized to serve in the Temple and join in its priestly worship. YHWH declares: 'their holocausts and sacrifices will be acceptable on my altar. For my house shall be called a house of prayer for all peoples' (Isa. 56: 6–7). God even intends to select some persons from among the Gentile nations and make them serve in the Temple as 'priests and levites' (Isa. 66: 18, 21)—an expression typical of Israel but now applied to non-Israelites.[12] To make some 'outsiders'

---

[12] For other cases of theological expressions typical of Israel being applied by Old Testament prophets to non-Israelites, see W. Gross, 'YHWH und die Religionen der Nicht-Israeliten', *Theologische Quartalschrift*, 169 (1989), 34–44, at 35. Another (more limited) interpretation is possible here: God intends to select for Temple duty some of the exiled Israelites whom the nations will bring home to Jerusalem.

priests and levites to serve in the Temple alongside the Israelite priests
and levites would be a radical departure from the prescriptions of
Numbers; it limits the exercise of priesthood to the descendants of
Aaron (Num. 4: 1–29; 8: 1–26; 18: 1–23).

Before and after the Babylonian exile, the institution of kingship
stirred various hopes; at times a 'messianic' (anointed) deliverer was
expected as a king. In the post-exilic situation the fourth night vision
of the prophet Zechariah is shaped by an expectation that salvation
was near (Zech. 4: 1–5, 10b–14). This hope was vested in two 'messiahs' or anointed ones: Joshua the high priest and Zerubbabel the
political ruler descended from David. Yet, despite the attention devoted to the rebuilding of the Temple and the growing importance of
the high priest, who was to become a substitute for the Davidic king,
there was little expectation of a Messiah-priest.

There is some evidence from the Dead Sea Scrolls that the Qumran
community, (which, as a whole, was credited with a priestly character),
expected two figures, 'Messiahs of Aaron and Israel'.[13] The *Testaments
of the Twelve Patriarchs* (a Jewish document from the second century
BC), announces in the *Testament of Levi* (no. 18) the coming of one
figure, a wonderful priest-king: 'Then shall the Lord raise up a new
priest, to whom all the words of the Lord will be revealed . . . in his
priesthood the nations . . . shall be illumined by the grace of the Lord.
In his priesthood sin shall cease . . . and he will grant to the saints to eat
of the tree of life.'[14] But this priest-king (like the 'Messiah of David'
and the 'Messiah of Aaron') is not portrayed as a priestly figure who
will bring deliverance from sin and salvation through his own self-
sacrificing death.

Let us sum up some major features of the Levitical priesthood
and, with an eye on the Letter to the Hebrews, set out the points of
continuity and discontinuity between this priesthood and that of
Christ the high priest. (1) In both cases priesthood comes by divine

---

[13] G. Vermes, *Jesus the Jew: A Historian's Reading of the Gospels* (London: Collins,
1973), 136–7; on priesthood according to Qumran documents see Scholer, *Proleptic
Priests*, 35–63.

[14] H. C. Kee (trans. and ed.), in J. H. Charlesworth (ed.), *The Old Testament
Pseudepigrapha*, vol. 1 (New York: Doubleday, 1983), 794–5. Some sections of the
Testaments of the Twelve Patriarchs have been reworked later by Christians, but this
does not appear to be the case in no. 18 of the *Testament of Levi*.

appointment. Priests are chosen by God and not self-appointed. YHWH elected priests (and levites) to serve as his instruments for the benefit of the chosen people (Exod. 25–30, 39–40; Lev. 8–9; Num. 1–10). Jesus also received a divine mandate to serve as high priest of the new covenant. (2) In both cases the divine purpose for priesthood is to bring about the sanctification (through ritual worship) and the instruction of God's people. Priests have both cultic and teaching functions. (3) As the defining and supreme act of worship, sacrifice is *the* specifically priestly function for the Levitical priests and for Jesus. The Letter to the Hebrews, as we shall show, is quite clear about that, even if it firmly contrasts the repeated sacrifices of the Levitical priests with the once-and-for-all sacrifice of Christ. (4) Exercising priesthood did not exclude kingly and prophetic functions, and vice versa. Ezekiel, while ministering as a priest to his fellow exiles, was called around 593 BC to exercise also a prophetic role (Ezek. 1: 1–3). The prophet Elijah, in a contest on Mount Carmel with some priests of Baal, offered a sacrifice that the Lord accepted in dramatic fashion (1 Kgs 18: 17–40). At the time of Jesus the high priest exercised an office that was also kingly. That Jesus was not only a priest (or rather the High Priest) but also king and prophet enjoyed at least partial precedents. A priestly figure could also be a prophet and/or a king.[15]

Five points of discontinuity can be briefly singled out here. (1) Unlike the Levitical priests, Christ did not inherit priesthood through descent from Aaron. Human lineage was not the grounds for his being a high priest 'according to the order of Melchizedek'. (2) Jesus offered his sacrifice once and for all, unlike the yearly and daily sacrifices required from the Jewish priests. (3) Furthermore, he went through his self-sacrifice for the benefit of all people. To be sure, Second Isaiah (see above) associates sacrificial activity in Jerusalem with the universal

---

[15] See also Miriam, a 'prophet' who was associated with the priesthood of her brother Aaron (Exod. 15: 20–1) and led the women in the Song of Miriam, an ancient thanksgiving for what God had done in rescuing the people from the slavery of Egypt. Miriam and Aaron are also remembered as having challenged the prophetic/kingly authority of Moses (Num. 12: 1–16). For another example of a dual role, see Deborah, a prophet and (kingly) judge, who was responsible for Barak's victory over Sisera (Judg. 4: 1–5: 31).

benevolence of God.[16] But the death and resurrection of Jesus, along with the outpouring of the Holy Spirit, brought redemption to all people, Jews and Gentiles alike. (4) By the time of Jesus the cultic activity of the Jewish priesthood had long been confined to one sanctuary, the Temple in Jerusalem. The locale for Jesus' self-sacrifice, however, was no holy sanctuary but a profane place outside the city: a site for crucifixion (Heb. 13: 12–13). (5) Finally, there was something inherently 'conservative' about the Levitical priests. They thought and acted within the framework of an existing order. In exercising his priesthood Jesus aimed at transformation, not mere continuation. His sacrifice initiated a new covenant between God and all human beings.

THE GOSPELS ON OTHER PRIESTS

Concerning priesthood there is much to glean from the Gospels that can illuminate, directly or indirectly, the priesthood of Christ. We begin with Luke's Gospel. In this Gospel the first person to appear is 'a priest named Zechariah, who belonged to the priestly order of Abijah', the eighth of the twenty-four priestly orders (1 Chron. 24: 10). His wife also enjoyed a priestly background, as she was descended from Aaron. Luke opens with the story of the birth of their son, whose life and activity would prove to be prophetic, rather than priestly.

When Zechariah exercises his priestly role by entering the sanctuary to offer incense, while the whole assembly of the people is praying outside, he receives a vision of an angel of the Lord who announces the conception and birth of John the Baptist. Zechariah hesitates to believe this good news, and is struck dumb (Luke 1: 8–20) until his son is born. In the very next chapter the angel Gabriel announces to Mary the conception of Jesus, and she obediently accepts the message (Luke 1: 26–38). Thus Luke sets up a vivid contrast: the priest is reluctant to believe but the girl is willing to do so. Divine manifesta-

---

[16] See further G. O'Collins, *Salvation For All: God's Other Peoples* (Oxford: Oxford University Press, 2008), 42–8.

tions and their reception are by no means limited to priests serving in the Lord's sanctuary in Jerusalem but can extend to a young girl in a minor village.

The opening chapters of Luke tell of Mary and Joseph, after the birth of Jesus, presenting him in the Temple and offering the prescribed sacrifices. The Christ Child was welcomed, not by priests, but by a devout old man (Simeon) and a prophet (the even older Anna), who expressed their faith in him as Saviour, Messiah, and universal Lord (Luke 2: 22–38). Luke adds a story about the 12-year-old Jesus remaining behind in Jerusalem and being found in the Temple engaged in dialogue with 'the teachers', experts in the Jewish religion but not necessarily priests (Luke 2: 41–51).

When the ministry of Jesus begins, Luke follows Mark (1: 40–5) by telling the story of the healing of a leper. Jesus orders the man: 'Go and show yourself to the priest, and, as Moses commanded, make an offering for your cleansing' (Luke 5: 12–14; see also 17: 14–15). Luke and Mark appreciate the respect that Jesus manifests for the role of priest in making judgements about cases of leprosy (Lev. 13–15).[17]

Yet, as far as the Jewish priesthood is concerned, Luke's Gospel contains shadows along with lights. In the parable of the Good Samaritan (Luke 10: 29–37), a priest (representing the highest religious leadership among the Jews) and a levite (a lay associate of priests) do not help a wounded traveller. It is left to a foreigner, a Samaritan who would be expected to be hostile to Jews, to take generous care of the traveller in distress. The priest and the levite may have been like the rabbit in *Alice in Wonderland*: not malicious *per se* but preoccupied or, as that text so succinctly states, 'late for an important date'. Or, as many commentators suggest, the priest and levite fail to look closely, think the man lying on the side of the road is already dead, and do not want to incur ritual impurity by coming in contact with a corpse.

Among a group in the Temple who challenge Jesus about his authority, some were 'chief priests' (Luke 20: 1–8 parr.). The same

---

[17] In an authentic saying Jesus takes for granted the practice of sacrifice in the Temple: 'when you are offering your gift at the altar, if you remember that your brother has something against you, leave your gift there before the altar and go. First be reconciled to your brother, and then come and offer your gift' (Matt. 5: 23–4).

group ('the elders, the chief priests, and the scribes') features in the first prediction that Jesus makes about his passion, death, and resurrection (Luke 9: 22 parr.). In the third passion prediction Luke does not specify those who will hand Jesus over to the Gentiles (18: 20), while Mark names 'the chief priests and the scribes' as those who will do so (10: 33).

As Luke tells the passion story, before the Last Supper Judas confers with 'the chief priests and officers of the temple police' (22: 4) about betraying Jesus. After being arrested Jesus is taken to the house of the (unnamed) high priest (22: 54). The chief priests then play a major role in condemning Jesus, handing him over to Pilate, and securing his execution (22: 66; 23: 4, 13–25). In Mark's passion narrative the chief priests likewise figure prominently (14: 1, 10, 43, 53, 55; 15: 1, 3, 10–11). Without providing his name, Mark highlights the decisive role of the high priest (Caiaphas) (14: 53–4, 60–4). In this passion story the chief priests, along with the scribes, mock Jesus on the cross (15: 31–2).

Matthew adds his own sombre notes in telling how the priests rejected Jesus and were responsible for his death. When Judas repented and 'brought back the thirty pieces of silver to the chief priests and the elders', he threw the money not into the Temple (*hieron*) where all the faithful could attend but 'into the sanctuary (*naos*)', to which only priests, the guardians of the sanctuary, had access.[18] They refuse to put the money into the treasury of the Temple; 'they use it to buy a field, thus inscribing their crime on the soil of Israel'[19] (Matt. 27: 3–10). After the death and burial of Jesus, the chief priests (together with 'the Pharisees') set a guard at the tomb of Jesus and make it 'secure' by sealing the stone. After the

---

[18] When Matthew writes of 'the curtain of the *naos* being torn in two' at the moment of Jesus' death (27: 51; see Mark 15: 38), he apparently refers, not to the Temple in general, but to the Holy of Holies and the inner veil that separated this sanctuary from the holy place. See D. M. Gurtner, *The Torn Veil: Matthew's Exposition of the Death of Jesus* (Cambridge: Cambridge University Press, 2007). Matthew and Mark seemingly understand the rending of the curtain to mean that the death of Jesus has opened up access for all to the Holy of Holies. Previously only the high priest could enter this inner sanctuary and do so only once a year (on the Day of Expiation).

[19] A. Vanhoye, *Old Testament Priests and the New Priest*, trans. B. Orchard (Petersham, Mass.: St Bede's Publications, 1986), 10.

resurrection, the guards tell the chief priests 'everything that had happened'. Thereupon the priests (together now with 'the elders') bribe the soldiers to spread a story that the disciples of Jesus had stolen the body (Matt. 27: 62–6; 28: 11–15).

John's Gospel discredits the hereditary, Temple-centred, religious authorities. They present a collective obstacle to accepting Jesus in faith (9: 22–3). They are mercenary and uncaring shepherds (10: 12–13), and are more concerned with worldly acclaim than the divine favour (12: 43). When the term 'the Jews' (used sixty-nine times by John) refers to those who have an unbelieving or hostile attitude towards Jesus, it refers primarily to the religious authorities: the leading priests involved in the passion story (11: 47; 12: 10; 18: 3; 19: 15, 21) and, in particular, the high priest Caiaphas, who is now named (11: 49–50) and his father-in-law Annas (18: 13, 24).

Nevertheless, with 'paradoxical boldness' (or with brilliant irony?), John presents the high priest as clinching the debate about killing Jesus with words that express simultaneously 'a criminal human calculation and a divine plan of redemption'.[20] What Caiaphas says enjoys a prophetic value rooted in the priestly nature of his office: 'it is better to have one man die for the people than to have the whole nation destroyed'. As John comments, these words reveal a central truth: Jesus was about to die for the sake of and on behalf of the people, and that people would include not only Israel but also all the scattered children of God (John 11: 49–52). The plan of Caiaphas to do away with Jesus had unwittingly set in motion a 'universal plan of salvation to produce one people of God'.[21]

John and the other three Gospels all present the Jewish priesthood and its leadership as directly responsible for Jesus' death. That may well be one of the reasons why early Christians avoided calling their own leaders 'priests' and named them 'apostles', 'evangelists', 'prophets', and, above all, 'overseers (*episcopoi*)', 'presbyters' or elders, and 'deacons'. In our closing chapter we will return to the terminology used for official ministers in early Christianity.

---

[20] Ibid. 14.
[21] A. T. Lincoln, *The Gospel According to John* (London: Continuum, 2005), 330–1.

When the Letter to the Hebrews reflected at length on Jesus' suffering and death, it took up terms that were notorious among Christians of that time ('priest' and 'high priest') and reworked these notions, and, in particular, despite the memory of Caiaphas, it reworked the notion of high priest. Hebrews mentions the crucifixion of Jesus, but never indicates who was responsible for it (Caiaphas, Pilate, or anyone else). It hints at the abuse Jesus endured during his crucifixion (Heb. 13: 13). Yet it portrays the priesthood and, in particular, the high priest in the light of institutions described in the Pentateuch and not in terms of any contemporary figures. It never levels any criticism against specific Jewish priests of the first century, but presents in general the ineffective nature of Jewish sacrifices, which needed to be repeated on a daily or a yearly basis and offered also for the sins of the priests themselves.

THE GOSPELS ON JESUS AS KING AND PROPHET

Not being of the tribe of Levi, Jesus was never called a priest, nor did he ever call himself a priest. That did not stop the author of Hebrews from giving him that title. Yet some writers would deny him that title and even challenge his entire 'triple office'. Thus, Wolfhart Pannenberg declares: 'the historical Jesus . . . was neither priest nor king nor, in the strict sense, prophet.'[22] This blanket denial cries out to be softened, not least because—as we shall see—'priest', 'prophet', and 'king' are used with flexibility. They are analogical, not strictly univocal, terms.

First of all, by his words and actions Jesus claimed, at least implicitly, some kind of *kingly authority*—a claim rejected by the Jewish and Roman authorities. Pontius Pilate had Jesus crucified on the charge of falsely and dangerously pretending to be 'the King of the Jews' (Mark 15: 26 parr.). John's Gospel elaborates the inscription

---

[22] W. Pannenberg, *Systematic Theology,* trans. G. W. Bromiley, vol. 2 (Grand Rapids, Mich.: Eerdmans, 1994), 445; for a brief discussion of the 'triple office' of Jesus, see ibid. 443–8. Years earlier Pannenberg had already challenged the triple office assigned to Jesus: *Jesus: God and Man,* trans. L. L. Wilkins and D. A. Priebe, (Philadelphia: Westminster, 1968), 212–25.

fixed to the cross: 'Jesus of Nazareth, the King of the Jews' (19: 19–20).[23] John also has Pilate questioning Jesus at length over his kingship (18: 33–7), and presenting Jesus 'in the mock insignia of royalty—a crown of thorns and a purple robe' (19: 5).[24] The final exchange between Pilate and the chief priests turns on Jesus' claim to kingship (19: 4–16). Those who play down the historical reliability of the Fourth Gospel explain (or explain away?) this association of Jesus with kingship as mere Johannine theology.

Yet one must reckon with what Mark (along with Matthew and Luke) reports about Jesus as king: (1) the Palm Sunday episode when Jesus dramatized his role as the expected royal figure of Davidic descent by entering Jerusalem in a kingly fashion to restore the fortunes of Israel, and whose action was understood by friends and foes to claim royal authority (Mark 11: 1–10 parr.); (2) Jesus' mysterious language about himself as the Son of David who would be enthroned at God's right hand (Mark 12: 35–7 parr.); (3) Jesus' answer to the high priest about being not only the Messiah and the Son of God but also the Son of Man who will be seated at the right hand of God and will come 'with the clouds of heaven' at the climax of history to gather in the elect (Mark 14: 61–2 parr.); (4) Pilate's question, 'are you the King of the Jews?' (Mark 15: 2 parr.); and (5) the scene in which, after his scourging, Jesus was mocked by the soldiers as 'King of the Jews' (Mark 15: 17–20 par.). Is there nothing that is historically reliable in all this?

One could cite further evidence from the Gospels to establish that the historical Jesus in some sense affirmed his kingly authority, which was accepted by some (e.g. Mark 8: 29) and rejected by others (most significantly by the chief priests). Those who refuse to identify the historical Jesus as king may have succumbed to the notion that one size (of being king) fits all. Kingship has assumed many forms, and not least in the history of Israel and of the whole Middle East.[25]

---

[23] On the historicity and meaning of the inscription, see Lincoln, *The Gospel According to John*, 474–5. For the versions in all four Gospels, see J. Nolland, *The Gospel of Matthew* (Grand Rapids, Mich.: Eerdmans, 2005), 1193–4.

[24] Lincoln, *The Gospel According to John*, 458. Lincoln adds at once: 'For the evangelist, of course, despite all appearances, the one who is on trial actually is the true King of the Jews.'

[25] See K. W. Whitelam, 'King and Kingship', *ABD* iv. 40–8.

While Jesus was the 'King of kings' (Rev. 19: 16), he differed from the kings of this world, including the Hebrew kings. Graham Kendrick's hymn 'The Servant King' catches a specific feature about the kingship of Jesus. Jesus came as a king who wished to serve others (Mark 10: 45 parr.). In its own way John's Gospel understands Jesus to exercise his servant-kingship by witnessing to the truth. Apropos of John 19: 37, Lincoln comments: 'His [Jesus'] kingship is subsumed under and interpreted by his witness to the truth . . . By subordinating kingship to his role as witness, he also subordinates the issue of power to that of truth.' Lincoln adds: 'Jesus does not so much have subjects over whom he rules as followers who accept his witness and who hear his voice as truth.'[26]

Matthew ends his Gospel with the risen Jesus stating that his kingly authority is universal (Matt. 28: 18). The same evangelist understands Jesus to have already revealed his kingly rule from the cross, even to have to taken up that rule on the cross. James and John had asked for places of honour, to sit one on the right hand and the other on the left, in Jesus' coming kingdom (Matt. 20: 21, 23). In the event, the two bandits crucified on either side of Jesus 'get the positions that James and John were after'. Paradoxically, 'Jesus manifests his kingly rule from the cross'.[27]

Pannenberg's hesitations about Jesus' *prophetic identity* are even harder to justify. On several occasions Jesus clearly implied his own prophetic role (e.g. Matt. 12: 41 par.; Mark 6: 4 parr.; Luke 13: 33–4 par.). He links himself to the prophet Jonah (Luke 11: 29–30 par.). Others recognized Jesus as a prophet (e.g. Mark 8: 28; Luke 24: 19; John 4: 19). Luke opens the story of Jesus' ministry by portraying Jesus as being empowered by the prophetic spirit of Isaiah 61: 1–2 (Luke 4: 17–24; see Isa. 58: 6). Pannenberg's language about being or not being a prophet 'in the strict sense' suggests that he presupposes that one size and only one size should fit all who are supposed to be prophets. This is to slide over the major differences between those who are called prophets in the Old Testament: Abraham (Gen. 20: 7; he is the first person in the Bible to be identified as a prophet); Miriam (Exod. 15: 20); Deborah (Judg. 4: 4); the seventy elders who

---

[26] Lincoln, *The Gospel According to John*, 463.
[27] Nolland, *The Gospel of Matthew*, 1194.

prophecy (Num. 11: 25); the prophet like Moses whom God will raise up (Deut. 18: 18–22); Moses himself as the prototype of the true prophet (Deut. 34: 10–11); a band of ecstatic prophets (1 Sam. 10: 6, 10–13); the 'prophets of the Lord' (1 Kgs 22: 5–23); Elijah and Elisha (1 Kgs 17–19; 2 Kgs 2–8); the 'classical' prophets from Isaiah to Malachi.[28]

If the Scriptures allow for a generous diversity in naming some persons as prophets, may we then lay down strict conditions for those whom we will deem to be prophets in some 'proper' sense and deny the title to Jesus? John Schmitt supports some flexibility here when he assesses the evidence and remarks: 'There seems to have been no standard prerequisite for a person to become a prophet in Israel.'[29] As regards Jesus, the vast majority of New Testament scholars may be 'of the most varied theological positions', but they agree that the New Testament's 'picture of Jesus as prophet is historical bedrock'.[30]

As with his kingship, we must allow for Jesus being a prophet in his own particular way. We may not 'simply attribute to him prophecy' as if it were something monolithic; prophecy had been 'understood and practiced' in a thoroughly varied way 'within the Hebrew traditions that were his heritage'.[31] Nor should we approach his being a prophet as if it were rigidly isolated from his other functions of being a king and a priest. We have seen above figures who combine two or even three of these functions: for instance, Melchizedek (priest and king); Aaron (priest, prophet, and king); Deborah (prophet and kingly judge); Solomon (king who also acted as priest); Ezekiel (priest and prophet); John the Baptist (prophet of priestly lineage); and Caiaphas (a high priest with kingly powers who, at least on one occasion, spoke prophetically). Jesus was/is the royal Son of David, the Prophet raised up by God (Deut. 18: 18), and the High Priest

---

[28] On prophets see H. P. Müller, '*nābî*, prophet, prophecy', in G. J. Botterweck, H. Ringren, and H.-J. Fabry (eds.), *Theological Dictionary of the Old Testament*, trans. D. E. Green, vol. 9 (Grand Rapids, Mich.: Eerdmans, 1998), 129–50.

[29] 'Preexilic Hebrew Prophecy', *ABD* v. 482–9, at 482.

[30] M. E. Boring, 'Early Christian Prophecy', ibid. 495–502, at 498.

[31] D. J. Goergen, 'Priest, Prophet, King: The Ministry of Jesus Christ', in D. J. Goergen and A. Garrido (eds.), *The Theology of Priesthood* (Collegeville, Minn.: Liturgical Press, 2000), 187–209, at 199.

according to the order of Melchizedek. He was/is the Shepherd-Priest, the Good Shepherd who was/is the Good Priest.

THE SYNOPTIC GOSPELS ON JESUS AS PRIEST

In the context of this book it is the *priestly office* that is at stake. Let us look first at the Gospels according to Matthew, Mark (the first Gospel to be written), and Luke. Those who disagree with Pannenberg over his refusal to ascribe to Jesus in his earthly ministry the title of priest could be tempted to move straight to the finale of that ministry, the Last Supper, and the priestly gestures and words of Jesus when instituting 'the new covenant in my blood' (Luke 22: 20 par.). Such a move would, however, be premature. In his proclamation of the kingdom or saving rule of God, Jesus' prophetic teaching and miraculous activity should also be characterized as priestly. His public ministry forms an essential part of the exercise of his priesthood. The unstinting self-giving that distinguishes his ministry of service belongs squarely to Jesus' priestly office. His total dedication to the cause of the kingdom and the will of God exemplify what the Letter to the Hebrews says in summing up the priestly work of the incarnate Son: he has come to do God's will (Heb. 10: 7). We can and should recognize Jesus to be priest and to be acting as a priest when he proclaimed the kingdom of God that was breaking into the world.

We shall see in the next chapter how Paul understood his own preaching of the good news to be a priestly, liturgical ministry (Rom. 15: 16). If the apostle could interpret his ministry of evangelization as a priestly service, *a fortiori* one should say this about Jesus' proclamation of the divine kingdom. In a later chapter we will find Origen recognizing teaching and the forgiveness of sins to be priestly activities exercised by 'the ministers and priests of the Church' in imitation of Jesus himself. This obviously presupposes that Jesus, when he taught and forgave sins during his public ministry, was acting in a priestly way.

As we saw above, Jeremiah recognized *instructing* God's people as a distinguishing feature of priesthood. While a priest represented human beings to God through sacrifice and intercession, he *also*

represented God to human beings through 'oracles and instruction'. Not surprisingly, the Gospels report how people repeatedly called Jesus 'rabbi' or 'teacher'.[32] By doing so, they were implicitly recognizing in his activity the work of a priest as teacher/preacher.

When presenting Jesus' message in the synagogue of Nazareth, Luke cites words from Isaiah to picture Jesus not only as bringing good news (in the guise of the anointed preacher/teacher) but also as proclaiming 'release to the captives and recovery of sight to the blind' (Luke 4: 18). In his ministry Jesus was to 'represent God to human beings' *also* through his healing and liberating activity. Like a doctor, Jesus sought out those who were sick, spiritually and physically (Mark 2: 17 parr.).

That Jesus in his earthly ministry healed the sick and delivered people from evil spirits is widely agreed.[33] Experience of life and Christianity in Africa encouraged Donald Goergen to understand and interpret Jesus' healing work as conforming to his priestly identity.[34] Healing sick people of various ailments (e.g. Matt. 11: 2–6 par.) belongs squarely to his priestly function of representing God to human beings. The healing ministry of Jesus, which includes liberating sufferers from evil spirits, forms part of his exercise of priesthood.

Right from the start, Mark understands that being active in proclaiming/teaching is inseparable from Jesus' being active in healing. When Jesus teaches with prophetic/priestly authority, he delivers a man who has been suffering from an unclean spirit. The spectators link his 'teaching with authority' to his power over 'unclean spirits' (Mark 1: 21–8 parr.). Teaching in a house in Capernaum becomes the occasion for Jesus to heal a paralytic (Mark 2: 1–12 parr.). Since Jesus'

---

[32] The title of *didaskalos* (teacher) is applied to Jesus 43 times in all four Gospels. When Jesus is called *rabbi* or *rabbouni* 16 times (in Matthew, Mark, and John, with ten of these occurrences in John), this honorific title has a predominant sense of 'teacher'. However, when Jesus is called *epistatēs* six times in Luke (who does not use *rabbi*), the term is best translated 'Master', with little or no sense of Jesus' authoritative teaching role. As a title applied to Christ, *kathēgētēs* occurs only once (Matt. 23: 10), and can be translated 'Instructor' or 'Master'. See H. Lapin, 'Rabbi', *ABD* v. 600–2.

[33] R. Haight, *Jesus: Symbol of God* (Maryknoll, NY: Orbis, 1999), 71–4.

[34] D. J. Goergen, 'Priest, Prophet, King: The Ministry of Jesus Christ', in Goergen and Garrido (eds.), *Theology of Priesthood*, 193–6.

teaching is priestly, so too is his inseparable activity as healer. Like
Mark, Matthew recognizes how Jesus' teaching and healing cannot be
separated (e.g. Matt. 4: 23; 9: 35), thereby indicating two distinguishable but inseparable facets of his priestly identity and activity.

Both facets emerge in the story of the five thousand being fed
miraculously (Mark 6: 30–44 parr.). When Jesus found a large crowd
of people waiting for him, 'his heart went out to them' and he began
'to *teach* them many things' (vs. 34). In Matthew's version the
compassionate response of Jesus was initially to *heal* the sick (Matt.
14: 14). In Luke's account, Jesus' immediate response took the form
of both teaching the people and healing their sick (Luke 9: 11).
Without explicitly saying as much, the three evangelists illustrate
how teaching and healing inseparably express the priesthood of
Jesus.[35]

On that occasion Jesus feeds a large number of people with a very
small quantity of food. All three Gospels tell the story of the multiplication of the loaves and fishes with language that points ahead to
the priestly action of Jesus at the Last Supper. Mark writes of Jesus
assuming a posture of prayer and seeking the blessing of God: 'Taking
the five loaves and the two fish, he looked up to heaven, and blessed
and broke the loaves, and gave them to his disciples to set before the
people, and he divided the two fish among them all' (6: 41). The
sequence of four verbs ('took', 'blessed', 'broke', and 'gave') recurs in
Mark's account of Jesus' celebration of the Passover meal with his
disciples: 'While they were eating, he took a loaf of bread, and after
blessing it, he broke it, gave it to them, and said: "Take; this is my
body"' (14: 22 parr.). What Jesus does in feeding the five thousand
foreshadows and even anticipates something of his priestly gestures
and words at the final sacrificial and covenant meal that he will
celebrate with his followers.

Before moving to the final Passover meal, we should recall that it
was 'the last supper' or climax of a whole series of meals which had

---

[35] Prior to the feeding of the five thousand, Mark tells of Jesus sending the Twelve
on a trial mission: they are to proclaim and heal (Mark 6: 7–13). This mission of
proclamation and healing means sharing in Christ's priesthood. In a later chapter we
will see how Luther highlighted the preaching of the Word as sharing in the priesthood of Christ. John Chrysostom and Augustine of Hippo, as priestly bishops, were
and remain extraordinarily eminent as ministers of the Word, as we shall see in Ch. 5.

already revealed Jesus' saving and priestly outreach to everyone.[36] Jesus represented God to human beings by forgiving them their sins (e.g. Mark 2: 1–12 parr.). In particular, he conveyed forgiveness to sinners by sharing meals with them (e.g. Mark 2: 13–17 parr.; Luke 19: 1–10). This table fellowship with the sinful and disreputable was a characteristic feature of Jesus' ministry and also a characteristic feature of his exercise of priesthood.

THE LAST SUPPER

Priesthood was a distinguishing rather than a defining feature of Jesus' ministry, which could be defined as more prophetic than priestly. Particularly in Luke's account, Jesus wore the 'garb' of a prophet rather than the 'vestments' of a priest during the ministry. At the Last Supper, however, priesthood became a defining rather than a merely distinguishing feature of what Jesus was about.[37] 'Meal and sacrifice', Pannenberg remarks, 'go together at the Lord's Supper, just as the covenant sacrifice and covenant meal did in Israel.'[38] If the Last Supper is a sacrificial meal, that implies priestly activity on the part of Jesus, since sacrifice is the defining (albeit not exclusive) act of priesthood and priestly ministry. Through the words and gestures of the 'institution narrative' (Mark 14: 22–4 parr.; 1 Cor. 11: 23–5), Jesus offered a covenant sacrifice—a cultic, priestly act which he wanted to be continued as a central practice in the community that he had gathered. His historical, once-and-for-all offering on the cross was to become a

[36] See J. P. Meier, *A Marginal Jew: Rethinking the Historical Jesus*, vol. 2 (New York: Doubleday, 1994), 1035–7.

[37] On the Last Supper see J. A. Fitzmyer, *The Gospel According to Luke X–XXIV* (New York: Doubleday, 1985), 1385–1406; Nolland, *The Gospel of Matthew*, 1069–86; R. F. O'Toole, 'Last Supper', *ABD* iv. 234–41; A. C. Thiselton, *The First Epistle to the Corinthians* (Grand Rapids, Mich.: Eerdmans, 2000), 848–91.

[38] W. Pannenberg, *Systematic Theology*, trans. G. W. Bromiley, vol. 3 (Grand Rapids, Mich.: Eerdmans, 1998), 319. This correct observation can hardly be reconciled with what we noted above: Pannenberg's flat denial that the historical Jesus exercised priestly ministry.

permanently present reality in the celebration of the Lord's Supper. These are the headlines; let us look now at the small print.

Biblical scholars widely agree that the 'bread saying' derives from the historical Jesus. Many argue as well that the 'cup saying' is also traceable to the historical Jesus. The words of institution, if taken at face value, show Jesus defining his death as a sacrifice, which will not only representatively atone for sins but also initiate a new and enduring covenant between God and human beings.

But we must reckon here with the question: how far have the sources of Paul, Mark, Matthew, and Luke been shaped by liturgical usages in the early Christian communities? In 1 Corinthians 11: 23–5 one reads: 'The Lord Jesus on the night when he was handed over took bread, and when he had given thanks, he broke it, and said: "This is my body [which is given] for you. Do this in remembrance of me." In the same way [he took] also the cup, after supper, saying: "This cup is the new covenant in my blood. Do this, as often as you drink it, in remembrance of me."' In Mark's version of the Last Supper, however, the instructions calling for a future repetition of the Eucharist ('Do this in remembrance of me' and 'Do this, as often as you drink it, in remembrance of me') are missing. The qualification of 'my body' as being 'for you' is also missing. Yet, unlike the Pauline tradition, Mark describes the blood as being 'poured out for many'. His version runs as follows: 'He took bread, blessed and broke it, and gave it to them, and said: "Take, this is my body." And he took a cup, and when he had given thanks he gave it to them, and they all drank of it. And he said to them, "This is my blood of the covenant, which is poured out for many"' (Mark 14: 22–4).

Obviously there are differences between (1) the Pauline tradition (to which, apart from adding, apropos of 'my blood', 'which is poured out for you', and not including, apropos of the cup, 'do this in remembrance of me', Luke 22: 19–20 approximates) and (2) the Markan tradition (which is more or less followed by Matt. 26: 26–8, apart from the latter adding that the blood is shed 'for the forgiveness of sins'). In some form the words of institution go back to Jesus. But in what precise form? Admittedly the breaking of the bread, identified as his body, and the pouring out of his blood symbolized forth the sacrificial surrender of his life, the priestly action of total self-giving that was about to take place in his violent death. Clearly those

followers present at the Last Supper shared in his body that was being given up to death and in his blood that would be shed. They were invited to participate in Jesus' destiny and enjoy a new, permanent communion or covenant with him. Whether Jesus spoke of a 'new covenant' (Paul and Luke) or only of a 'covenant' (Mark and Matthew) that was being instituted through his blood, he inevitably evoked key Old Testament passages (e.g. through a cultic link to Exod. 24: 3–8, and through an eschatological link to Jer. 31: 31–3) that illuminated his action and words. In a priestly way he was making a new covenant, sealed and ratified by the shedding of his blood.

But, beyond the group present at the Last Supper, whom did Jesus intend to be the beneficiaries of his death and the new covenant—those who were to share in and profit from his priestly self-sacrifice? The 'for you' of the Pauline and Lukan tradition indicated immediately his disciples who shared the common cup at the Last Supper. Of course, in that case he might well have intended the group who participated in that final, sacrificial meal to represent others, even many others. Since Jesus explicitly called for the *future* repetition of the bread ritual ('do this in remembrance of me'—Paul and Luke) and of the cup ritual ('do this in remembrance of me'—Paul only), he clearly wanted to confer on an indefinite number of others the saving benefits of his life and impending death. Even if Jesus did not literally verbalize the directive, 'do this in remembrance of me', one can reasonably argue that this addition from the Pauline and Lukan churches rendered explicit his intentions. He wanted to establish for countless others his continuing and effective presence in the priestly, sacrificial meal-fellowship that he had instituted with a small, core group of disciples.

Mark (followed by Matthew) has Jesus speaking of his blood poured out 'for many', an inclusive, Semitic expression for a great multitude or countless number (= 'for all'). But in that case did Jesus mean not merely all Jews but also all Gentiles to be the beneficiaries of his priestly activity?

If we understand 'for you' and 'for many' as both pointing to an indefinitely large group, we are still left with the question: did Jesus intend the benefits of his violent death and the new covenant to be conferred on all those and only on all those who were sharing and

would share in the ritual and the fellowship he was creating? Would the benefits of his sacrificial and priestly death 'for many' be passed on only to the new covenant community, the fellowship of those who would share in the saving power of Jesus' death through eating his 'broken body' and drinking from the common cup?

A short answer to those tempted to imagine Jesus limiting the saving impact of the new covenant comes from a practice mentioned above: the meals he shared with all manner of people, not least with the disreputable. That table fellowship conveyed forgiveness to sinners and celebrated in advance the happiness of the heavenly banquet to come, a banquet to which all were invited. Jesus' practice throws light on his priestly intentions at the Last Supper, the climax of a long series of meals that revealed his saving outreach to everyone. Further characteristic activities and attitudes of Jesus also throw light on his priestly intentions at the Last Supper.

In general, characteristic ways in which people act and speak can fill their death with meaning, even when they have no chance at the end to express their motivation and make an explicit declaration of intent. Archbishop Oscar Romero (1917–80), for instance, was abruptly shot dead when celebrating the Eucharist. He had no last-minute opportunity to blurt out some statement interpreting the death that confronted him. Nevertheless, all that he had been saying and doing during his three years as archbishop of San Salvador indicated his basic intentions and filled his martyrdom with significance.

Jesus consistently behaved as one utterly obedient to his Father's will and completely available for the service of those who needed priestly mercy and healing. His words and actions brought divine pardon to those who, in various ways, felt a great need of redemption. He never drove away the lepers, taxation agents, sinful women, children, and all those anonymous crowds of people who clamoured for his love and attention. He valued every individual, and not simply the socially advantaged (e.g. Mark 10: 21 parr.), as unique and irreplaceable.

Now it would be strange to imagine that the threat of the passion abruptly destroyed Jesus' resolution to show himself the servant of all. Rather, a straight line led from his serving ministry to his priestly death. Even if the community or (later) Mark himself added the

sacrificial words, 'to give his life as a ransom for many', there was a basis in Jesus' ministry for the saying, 'the Son of Man came not to be served but to serve, and to give his life as a ransom for many' (Mark 10: 45). He who had shown himself the priestly servant of all was ready to die for all—to release them from various forms of oppressive servitude. As many have insisted, the service of Jesus had been offered especially to the outcasts and the religious pariahs. Part of the reason why Jesus' ministry led to his crucifixion stemmed from the fact that he faithfully and scandalously served the lost, the godless, and the alienated of his society. The priestly physician who came to call and cure the unrighteous (Mark 2: 17 parr.) eventually died in their company. His serving ministry to the reprobates ended when he obediently accepted death between two reprobates. His association with society's outcasts and failures led to his solidarity with them in death. In these terms the passion of Jesus became integrated into the mission of his priesthood as a final act of service. In death, as in life, he served and sacrificed himself for others. Luke 22: 27 ('I am among you as one who serves') is an authentic pointer to this basic pattern in Jesus' priestly behaviour.

Israel was the context for the priestly and prophetic ministry of Jesus. Yet that ministry had a universal dimension.[39] His message of the kingdom reached beyond the frontiers of religious and racial separation. God's reign here and hereafter was for all human beings. The parables of Jesus show this universal horizon. Even in the Parable of the Tax-collector and the Pharisee, the only parable set in the most Jewish of settings, the Temple, this universality showed through. Jesus asserted that the full extent of God's generosity had hitherto been ignored: the divine pardon was offered to all.

By rejecting or at least relativizing dietary laws and merely external regulations of purity (Mark 7: 14–23 par.), which established and preserved boundaries between Jews and Gentiles, Jesus implied that these distinctions had no ultimate significance before God. What mattered was the internal state of the 'heart'—its purity or corruption.[40] Hence Jesus' vision of Israel's future entailed 'many coming from the east and the west to sit at table with Abraham, Isaac, and

[39] See O'Collins, *Salvation for All*, 79–99.
[40] J. Marcus, *Mark 1–8* (New York: Doubleday, 2000), 446–7, 452–61.

Jacob in the kingdom of heaven' (Matt. 8: 11 par.). The priestly ministry of Jesus envisaged salvation for all nations. Having lived and preached such a universal vision, at the end Jesus, one can reasonably suppose, accepted in some sense that he would die for all people.

JOHN ON JESUS AS PRIEST

Unlike the three Synoptic Gospels, John does not tell of the institution of the Eucharist at the Last Supper. This Gospel reports the Last Supper and then a farewell discourse (John 13–16), but no institution narrative. Nevertheless, one finds clear Eucharistic references in Jesus' discourse about 'my flesh for the life of the world' and the invitation to 'eat my flesh and drink my blood' (John 6: 51–8). By 'becoming flesh' and so assuming a complete human nature (John 1: 14), the incarnate Logos could offer himself in death and so surrender his own physical existence 'for the life of the world'.[41] The reality of Jesus' sacrificial death comes through the separation of the 'flesh' to be eaten and the 'blood' to be drunk: 'eating the flesh and drinking the blood entail that the flesh has been broken and the blood shed.'[42] These verses are driven by a sense of a priestly, sacrificial meal and a violent, sacrificial death, even while they contain no explicit reference to the institution of a (new) covenant.

What has been called a 'replacement motif' expresses further aspects of Jesus' priestly identity and function to be gleaned from the Fourth Gospel. In 'fulfilling the significance of the Torah, its symbols and institutions, Jesus can also be said to replace them'. Lincoln explains how the Temple and its sacrifices 'give way to the action and presence of Jesus. Indeed, his crucified and risen body is the new indestructible temple, the new dwelling place of God

---

[41] In *The Gospel According to John*, Lincoln writes: 'As a result of Jesus giving up his life, the world, which is at present alienated from the divine life, will be enabled to experience the gift of this life. A central theme of the Gospel is sounded here—life for the world is at the expense of death for Jesus' (p. 231).

[42] Ibid. 232.

(2.19–21).' 'As the new locus of God's presence, Jesus replaces previous worship arrangements, even those legislated by the law.'[43] Let us explain the grounds for saying all this.

Unlike the other Gospels, John's Gospel links the episode of the cleansing of the Temple with some words of Jesus about the coming destruction of the Temple and its rebuilding. To those who demanded a 'sign' to justify what he had done in cleansing the Temple, Jesus replied: 'Destroy this temple, and in three days I will raise it up.' The evangelist comments: 'he was speaking of the Temple of his body' (John 2: 13–22). Jesus will replace the Temple and its cult with a new, better, and final temple: his risen body.

Two chapters later, when talking with a Samaritan woman (John 4: 21–4), Jesus announces that the time has come when God will be worshipped in 'Spirit and truth', now made available in abundance by Jesus himself who is full of the Spirit (John 1: 33; 2: 34) and truth (1: 16–17). It is no longer appropriate to worship in Jerusalem or on Mount Garizim (where the Samaritans worshipped). Jesus himself is the new place of the divine presence, the new priestly Mediator between God and human beings.

In the Fourth Gospel's portrayal of Jesus, he fulfils the significance of several major festivals: above all, the Passover. The feeding of the five thousand and the discourse on the bread of life occur, as only John observes, at the time of the Passover (John 6: 4). Lincoln writes: 'As the true bread from heaven, Jesus fulfils what was signified not only by the manna of the exodus but also by the unleavened bread of Passover, and Jesus' flesh and blood are now the food and drink of the true Passover meal (6.51–8).'[44] Through his priestly self-gift Jesus has replaced the Passover festival.

At the start of the Fourth Gospel, John the Baptist witnesses to Jesus as 'the lamb of God who takes away the sin of the world' (John 1: 29; see 1: 36). At that point the remark remains mysterious and is left unexplained. But in this Gospel the death of Jesus occurs at the hour when the Passover lambs are being slaughtered (19: 14, 31). Through citing in 19: 31 some words from Exodus 12: 46, John compares the crucified body of Jesus with that of the Passover

---

[43] Ibid. 76–7.   [44] Ibid. 77.

lambs and invests the Jewish 'lamb cult' with new meaning. In his sacrificial death Jesus proves not only the priestly mediator but also *the* acceptable victim who takes away the sins of the world and pours out on the world the superabundant gift of the Holy Spirit (John 7: 37–9; 19: 30, 34; 20: 22–3).

John never calls Jesus a 'priest'. But—in particular, through a replacement motif—his Gospel allows us to glimpse some aspects of Jesus' priesthood. Add too the saying of Jesus about 'consecrating' himself 'for the sake' of his friends (John 17: 19). That could be construed as suggesting how Jesus replaces and goes beyond the activity of the high priest on the Day of Expiation. As priest and victim Jesus is preparing to die for all his friends. When Jesus sanctifies himself for his priestly task, 'this is in line with the way the Gospel portrays him as sharing what would normally be considered divine prerogatives and also as being in control of his own life and mission (John 10: 17–18)'.[45]

Finally, when John specifies that at the crucifixion the clothing for which soldiers cast lots was 'the seamless tunic' of Jesus (John 19: 23–5), some commentators recall Josephus, who described the high priest's tunic in similar terms (*Antiquities*, 3. 161), and suggest that John presents Jesus as dying not only as king but also as priest.[46] But C. K. Barrett considers that this interpretation goes 'too far': 'John's thought was set in motion not by any description of the high priest's vestments but by the fulfillment of Psalm 22.'[47] In any case, we do not depend on a priestly interpretation of Jesus' seamless tunic to recognize the way John's Gospel presents him as priest and victim.

This chapter has set itself to retrieve from the Jewish matrix and the Gospels some data that are relevant to any adequate account of the priesthood of Jesus. Before turning to the major New Testament witness to that priesthood, the Letter to the Hebrews, we take up some themes from the letters of Paul, 1 Peter, and the Book of Revelation. What do they yield for our enquiry into the priestly identity and work of Jesus?

---

[45] Lincoln, *The Gospel According to John*, 438.
[46] So R. E. Brown, *The Gospel According to John*, vol. 2 (Garden City, NY: Doubleday, 1970), 956–7.
[47] *The Gospel According to John* (2nd edn., London: SPCK, 1978), 550.

2

Paul, 1 Peter, and Revelation

As in the case of the four Gospels, we do not find the letters of Paul, 1 Peter, or the Book of Revelation ever expressly calling Jesus a priest. Yet, as with the Gospels, we can find themes that feed into an appreciation of Jesus' priesthood.

PAUL ON JESUS' PRIESTHOOD

In the seven letters that are commonly recognized as coming directly from Paul (Romans, 1 and 2 Corinthians, Galatians, Philippians, 1 Thessalonians, and Philemon), he never speaks of Jesus specifically as a priest. He gives other titles to Jesus: above all, Christ/Messiah, Lord, and Son of God. In the first of the Pastoral Letters (which most scholars would not ascribe in their present form to Paul), Jesus is called the 'one mediator between God and human beings' (1 Tim. 2: 5).[1] Hebrews also calls Christ 'mediator', and does so three times when it presents his priestly work as being that of 'the mediator of a new/better covenant' (8: 6; 9: 15; 12: 24). But what do the seven clearly authentic letters of Paul have to say about the priestly activity and identity of Christ? We begin with three passages in 1 Corinthians.

In dealing with a case for church discipline, Paul cites a principle of Christian belief that seems to have been commonly accepted and

---

[1] On this verse see L. T. Johnson, *The First and Second Letter to Timothy* (New York: Doubleday, 2001), 191–2; J. D. Quinn and W. C. Wacker, *The First and Second Letters to Timothy* (Grand Rapids, Mich.: Eerdmans, 2000), 165–6.

that also sums up a Johannine theme (see our previous chapter): 'Christ, our paschal lamb, has been sacrificed' (1 Cor. 5: 7).[2] Here the death of Christ is understood to correspond to the sacrifice of the Passover lamb. A costly act, the shedding of Christ's blood (see 1 Cor. 11: 25–6), has delivered human beings from bondage and given them a new freedom and purity. This laconic statement, with the associated references Paul makes to unleavened bread used at the Passover (1 Cor. 5: 7–8), recalls the Markan introduction to the Last Supper: 'On the first day of Unleavened Bread, when the Passover lamb is sacrificed, his disciples said to him [Jesus], "Where do you want us to go and make the preparations for you to eat the Passover"' (Mark 14: 12; see 14: 1 and Luke 22: 7). The festival of Unleavened Bread coincided with that of the Passover, which commemorated the deliverance of the people from Egypt through the power of God and under the leadership of Moses (Exod. 12: 1–28). In the Passover festival an unblemished male lamb was slaughtered and eaten with unleavened bread. Some of its blood, regarded as God's portion of the sacrifice (Lev. 1: 5), was smeared on doorposts and lintels, which were reckoned the holy places of a house (Exod. 21: 6; Deut. 6: 9). In the original story from Exodus the blood on the houses of the Israelites protected them against 'the destroyer', who 'passed over' their houses during the plague of the first-born. By the time of Jesus the lambs (slaughtered in the Temple at Passover) and their blood had acquired sacrificial significance.[3]

Thus, early in 1 Corinthians, even before he comes to talk of the Eucharistic meal (10: 16–21) and the Last Supper (11: 23–6), Paul speaks explicitly of the death (and resurrection) of Christ in sacrificial terms. He hints at the blood of Christ shed to purify and deliver sinful human beings. The priestly action of Christ will be explicitly clarified later in 1 Corinthians.

In 1 Corinthians 10 Paul reminds the community of what they do when celebrating the Eucharist: 'The cup of blessing that we bless, is it not a sharing (*koinonia*) in the blood of Christ? The bread that we break, is it not a sharing (*koinonia*) in the body of Christ?' (vs. 16).

---

[2] On this verse see J. A. Fitzmyer, *First Corinthians* (New Haven: Yale University Press, 2008), 230, 241–2.
[3] See B. M. Bokser, 'Unleavened Bread and Passover, Feasts of', *ABD* vi. 755–65.

A cup over which the blessing is offered points to the blood of Christ shed in his passion; the loaf that is broken points to the body of Christ broken on the cross. To drive home what this Christian *koinonia* or communal participation in the body and blood (= sacrificial death) of Christ entails, Paul appeals to what Jewish sacrifices in the Jerusalem Temple (not yet destroyed at that time) imply: 'Consider the people of Israel. Are not those who eat the sacrifices (*thusias*) sharers (*koinonoi*) in the altar (*thusiastēriou*)?' (vs. 18). Then Paul refers to what pagans do in the temples of Corinth: 'they sacrifice (*thuousin*) to demons and not to God' (vs. 20). He would be horrified if his fellow Christians were to share in such pagan sacrifices: 'you cannot drink the cup of the Lord and the cup of demons. You cannot partake of (*metechein*) the table (*tra-pezēs*) of the Lord and the table (*trapezēs*) of demons' (vs. 21). 'Altar' and 'table' seem to be used here as equivalents. Even if they are not strict equivalents, Paul obviously compares the Eucharistic meal to Jewish and pagan sacrifices.

Since the Eucharist derives from what Christ did at the Last Supper, Paul implies that the Eucharist, instituted by Christ on the night before he died, is a sacrifice. By (1) blessing the cup and establishing the new covenant in his blood, and (2) breaking the bread as a sign that his body would be broken on the cross, Christ offered a sacrifice. That also means implying that Christ did something priestly at the Last Supper, since sacrifice entails the exercise of priesthood.[4]

In the previous chapter we have already examined Paul's account of the Last Supper (1 Cor. 11: 23–6), a version that pre-dates the versions provided by Mark, Matthew, and Luke.[5] Just as with the Mosaic covenant (Exod. 24: 8), 'the covenant' was also sealed with blood, the blood of Christ (1 Cor. 11: 25). Paul understands the celebration of the Eucharist to be a sermon on 'Christ crucified' (1 Cor. 1: 23) and risen: 'as often as you eat this bread and drink this cup, you proclaim the death of the [risen] Lord until he comes'

[4] On 1 Cor. 10: 16–21 see A. C. Thiselton, *The First Epistle to the Corinthians* (Grand Rapids, Mich.: Eerdmans, 2000), 755–77; Fitzmyer, *First Corinthians*, 389–94.
[5] On 1 Cor. 11: 23–6 see Thiselton, *First Epistle to the Corinthians*, 866–88, and Fitzmyer, *First Corinthians*, 429–32, 435–45.

(1 Cor. 11: 26). Along with the three Synoptic evangelists, the apostle clearly implies that Christ acted like a priest when instituting the Eucharist and the new covenant and doing so by accepting his violent and bloody death to come.

Several passages in Romans contribute to the theme of Christ's priesthood. The first passage briefly anticipates something that will prove central in the Letter to the Hebrews, the sacrificial ceremony for the Day of Expiation or Atonement (*Yom Kippur*): 'God put forward [Christ] as a means of expiation (*hilastērion*) through his blood' (Rom. 3: 25).[6] Some translate *hilastērion* as a 'place of atonement' or a 'sacrifice of atonement'. Found only here in the Pauline writings, *hilasterion* belongs to a pre-Pauline formula about justification, redemption, and expiation (Rom. 3: 24–6).[7] The term refers to the 'mercy seat' or lid that covered the ark, the chest that contained the covenant or tablets of the Law and that was kept in the Holy of Holies (Exod. 25: 10–22).[8] Paul, along with the tradition he draws on, understands the death of Christ to be a sacrifice and does so with specific reference to the Day of Expiation. The ritual of that festival, still being practised when Paul wrote Romans in the late 50s, involved the high priest entering the Holy of Holies alone and sprinkling sacrificial blood on the mercy seat to make atonement for the sins of the people and his own sins (Lev. 16: 15–17). However, according to Paul, *the* means for expiating sin is not the secret action of the high priest hidden away in the inner sanctum of the Temple on the Day of Expiation, but the public, shameful, and violent death of Christ. Thus *hilastērion* depicts 'Christ as the new "mercy seat" [publicly] presented by the Father [on the cross] as a means of expiating or wiping away the sins of humanity, indeed, as the place of the presence of God, of his revelation, and of his expiating power'.[9] Hebrews will expand at length on details from the ritual of the Day of Expiation.

1 John may also have in mind the ceremony on the Day of Expiation, when it speaks of Christ as 'the *hilasmos* (means of expi-

---

[6] See D. P. Wright, 'Day of Atonement', *ABD* ii. 72–6; G. A. Anderson, 'Sacrifice and Sacrificial Offerings (OT), *ABD* v. 870–6; H.-J. Klauck, 'Sacrifice and Sacrificial Offerings (NT)', ibid. 876–91.
[7] See J. A. Fitzmyer, *Romans* (New York: Doubleday, 1993), 342–3.
[8] On the 'mercy seat' see also Lev. 16: 2, 13–15.
[9] Fitzmyer, *Romans*, 350; italics ours.

ation) for our sins' and 'also for the sins of the world' (1 John 2: 2; see
4: 10). Sometimes *hilasmos* is translated 'atoning sacrifice' or 'means
by which sins are forgiven'. Whatever translation we adopt, at all
events 1 John, by using *hilasmos* rather than *hilastērion*, does not
refer as clearly to the Day of Expiation, nor does it apply to the death
of Jesus the ritual of the Day of Expiation (as Hebrews does). Nevertheless, the reference a few verses earlier to 'the blood of Jesus' that
'cleanses us from all sin' (1 John 1: 7) favours interpreting *hilasmos* in
the light of the ceremony in the Holy of Holies on the Day of
Expiation, and so associating 1 John with the thought of Paul in
Romans 3: 25.[10]

A second central point made by this passage from Paul is that it
'portrays God as offerer of the sacrifice rather than its object'.[11] It was
God who 'put forward' or 'presented' his Son as the 'means for
expiating' sins. This anticipates what Paul will say later in the same
letter about God 'sending his own Son' to deal with sin (Rom. 8: 3)
and 'giving him up for all of us' (8: 32). This prepares the way for
what Hebrews will state, with great elegance, about the Father's
initiative in the incarnation through which the Son 'made purification for sins' (Hebr. 1: 1–3).

Yet, unlike Hebrews, this initiative is expressly associated in Romans 8 (see also Rom. 5: 8) with the divine *love*: 'If God is for us, who
is against us?' If God gave up his Son 'for all of us, will he not with
him also give us everything else?' (Rom. 8: 31–2). Fitzmyer calls
Romans 8: 31–9 a 'hymn to the love of God made manifest through
Christ Jesus'.[12] The love shown both by the Father and the Son runs
like a thread through this passage (vv. 35, 37), and culminates with
the conviction that nothing 'will be able to separate us from the love'

---

[10] On 1 John 1: 7 see S. S. Smalley, *1, 2, 3 John* (Waco, Tex.: Word Books, 1984),
24–6; on 1 John 2: 2 see ibid. 38–41; on 1 John 4: 10, ibid. 243–4. On 1 John 2: 2 see
J. Painter, *1, 2, and 3 John* (Collegeville, Minn.: Liturgical Press, 2002), 146–7.

[11] J. D. G. Dunn, *Romans 1–8* (Dallas, Tex.: Word Books, 1988), 171. With
reference to Exod. 24: 3–8 and commenting on Rom. 3: 25, Dunn writes of the
'public use of sacrificial blood to symbolize the introduction of the new covenant'
(ibid. 170). But the ratification of a covenant at Sinai and now through the violent
death of Jesus does not appear to be envisaged here by Paul; that covenant-theme
turns up rather in 1 Cor. 11: 25.

[12] Fitzmyer, *Romans*, 528–9.

Christ has for us (vs. 39). In another letter Paul puts matters even
more personally: 'the Son of God . . . loved me and gave himself for
me' (Gal. 2: 20). In Hebrews, the divine love revealed in the self-
sacrificing death of Christ is not explicitly as such a theme.[13]

It is in another way that Romans, albeit without introducing the
explicit notion of priesthood, anticipates Hebrews's vision of priesthood: the heavenly intercession of the crucified and risen Christ.
Such intercession had been attributed to angels (e.g. Job 33: 23–6;
Tob. 12: 15). This intercession is now attributed not only to the Holy
Spirit (Rom. 8: 26–7) but also to Christ who sits enthroned at the
right hand of God and constantly 'intercedes for us' (Rom. 8: 34).

Paul describes in various images and metaphors the results of
Christ's priestly work: for instance, adoption as God's sons and
daughters, expiation of sins, justification, reconciliation, and redemption.[14] These benefits are available for all (Rom. 3: 23–4; 11: 32;
2 Cor. 5: 14, 15, 19).[15]

Finally, Paul adds an exhortation that pictures Christian existence
as a priestly participation in the life of Christ: 'through the mercies of
God present your bodies (your selves) [as] a sacrifice (*thusian*),
living, holy, and acceptable to God, and this is your spiritual worship
(*latreian*)' (Rom. 12: 1). In portraying Christian lifestyle, Paul understands that a divine enabling ('the mercies of God') makes possible
personal commitment, and to express this commitment he uses
cultic language. As Fitzmyer comments, 'Christians should live
their lives in "this world" as if they were offering thereby [sacrificial]
worship to God'.[16] This theme has its Jewish antecedents. Fitzmyer
observes: 'The idea of keeping the law as an act of worship or sacrifice
is [already] expressed in Sirach 35: 1–6.' Christians who 'strive to do

---

[13] Hebrews writes rather of the priestly 'obedience' shown by Christ (5: 7–8).
When Romans appeals to Christ's obedience, it does so in the context of a contrast
with the first, disobedient Adam (5: 19).

[14] See G. D. Fee, 'Paul and the Metaphors for Salvation: Some Reflections on
Pauline Soteriology', in S. T. Davis, D. Kendall, and G. O'Collins (eds.), *The Redemption* (Oxford: Oxford University Press, 2004), 43–67.

[15] See further G. O'Collins, *Salvation for All: God's Other Peoples* (Oxford: Oxford
University Press, 2008), 121–41.

[16] Fitzmyer, *Romans*, 639.

what is right give a cultic or sacrificial sense to their lives as they offer themselves and their conduct' to God.[17]

Three adjectives are significant in Romans 12: 1. The consecrated life of believers means presenting themselves to God as a *living* sacrifice, rather than in cultic rituals (whether Jewish or pagan) that present the dead sacrifice of a slain animal. Paul adds further cultic imagery with the term *holy.* What is sacrificed is set apart for God and becomes divine property. The third adjective, 'acceptable/pleasing (*euareston*)', anticipates language in the Letter to the Hebrews about faith and a life of faith being 'pleasing' to God (Heb. 11: 5–6; 12: 28; 13: 16, 21). For Paul in Romans, through their lives Christians offer a living, holy, and pleasing sacrifice, and so give God appropriate 'worship (*latreia*)'. Of the nine occurrences of *latreia* in the LXX, eight refer to Jewish cultic worship.[18] Thus Paul employs cultic, sacrificial language (*thusia* and *latreia*) in an extended sense to picture the 'priestly' existence that God empowers Christians to live.[19]

This exhortation to live a 'priestly' existence recalls what Paul has said about baptism as participating in the death and resurrection of Christ (Rom. 6: 1–14). In particular, talk of a 'living sacrifice' echoes the earlier call to be 'dead to sin and alive to God in Christ Jesus' (Rom. 6: 11). Likewise the exhortation to 'present your bodies (*sōmata*)' as a sacrifice 'acceptable to God' calls to mind the earlier plea that twice uses the same verb ('present, *paristēmi*'): 'do not let sin reign in your mortal body (*sōmati*)', 'do not *present* your members to sin', but '*present* yourselves to God as those who have been brought from death to life' (Rom. 6: 12–13). Thus Christians are called to a 'priestly' existence in their daily life (Rom. 12: 1), and it is an existence made possible by their being united through baptism

<hr/>

[17] Ibid. 640.

[18] H. Strathmann, '*Latreuō, latreia*', in G. Kittel (ed.), *Theological Dictionary of the New Testament*, trans. G. W. Bromiley, vol. 4 (Grand Rapids, Mich.: Eerdmans, 1967), 58–65, at 61.

[19] J. D. G. Dunn comments on Rom. 12: 1: this use of sacrificial imagery 'implies a *replacement* of ritual sacrifice and indicates an assumption that the death of Jesus had been a *final* sacrifice to end all sacrifices' (*Romans 9–16* (Dallas, Tex.: Word Books, 1988), 710; italics ours). One might well make this comment on the Letter to the Hebrews, but I fail to see how it catches the thrust of the verse from Romans in question.

with the crucified and risen Christ (Rom. 6: 1–14). Sharing in Christ's life through baptism entails sharing in a priestly existence that comes from him. Paul's words can be applied to the life (and death) of Christ: in a pre-eminent way he presented his body (himself) as a sacrifice, living, holy, and pleasing to God, and this was his spiritual worship. Hebrews will speak of Christ's perfect obedience to God (4: 15; 5: 7–8) and perfect faith (12: 2).

When interpreting his own apostolic mission and the life of Christians, Paul presses into service a further term that has strong cultic overtones: *leitourgia*, which means offering sacrifice and other priestly service in the Temple (Luke 1: 23), worshipping God (Acts 13: 2), and, in an extended sense, ministry and service to others. Thus the apostle uses the related verb, *leitourgeō* (worship/serve), with reference to the offering that, with a view to furthering Christian unity, he has been collecting for the support of the Christian community in Jerusalem (Rom. 15: 27; see 2 Cor. 9: 12). In this act of generous service, Paul and the contributors share in a priestly way in the sacrificial offering of Christ. In his Letter to the Philippians the apostle (currently in danger of being condemned and executed) writes of being 'poured out [as a libation] over the sacrifice (*thusia*) and offering (*leitourgia*) of your faith' (2: 17; see 2: 30).[20] The Christians of Philippi have supported Paul, and he writes of the gifts they sent as a 'sweet-smelling offering, a sacrifice (*thusia*) acceptable and pleasing to God' (Phil. 4: 18). Once again Paul gives an extended sense to the language of cultic rituals, and applies it to financial help he has received.

A striking use of 'liturgical' language occurs towards the end of Romans. Paul calls himself a 'liturgist' in 'priestly service'; he makes the Gentiles into an acceptable and holy sacrifice by bringing them the good news. 'By the grace given' by God, Paul is a 'minister (*leitourgos*) of Christ Jesus to the Gentiles, in the priestly service (*hierourgounta*) of God's gospel (*euaggelion*), so that the offering (*prosphora*) of the Gentiles might be acceptable and made holy by the Holy Spirit' (Rom. 15: 15–16). Here Paul portrays his role in liturgical, cultic language. In proclaiming the gospel, he functions as a priest who offers his evangelization of the Gentiles as a form of worship or sacrifice. Fitzmyer

---

[20] See R. Meyer and H. Strathmann, '*Leitourgeō, leitourgia, leitourgos, leitourgikos*', in Kittel, *Theological Dictionary of the New Testament*, iv. 215–31.

writes: 'In his mission to the Gentiles Paul sees his function to be like that of a Jewish priest dedicated to the service of God in the Temple. If all Christian life is to be regarded as worship paid to God (12: 1), the spreading of God's gospel is easily compared to the role of a sacred minister in such worship. Paul implies that the preaching of the word of God is a liturgical act in itself.'[21]

Before leaving Paul, we should note some language in Ephesians, a letter that may have come from the 'Pauline school' rather than directly from Paul himself. The letter speaks of believers enjoying through Christ 'access (*prosagōgēn*) in the Spirit to the Father' (Eph. 2: 18). This provides something of a parallel to a repeated theme in Hebrews: the priestly, sacrificial work of Christ has secured access to the presence of God (4: 16; 7: 25; 10: 19–22; 11: 6). If written earlier than Hebrews, Ephesians also anticipates its language of Christ as both priest and victim: 'Christ handed himself over for us, a gift (*prosphora*) [and] a sacrifice (*thusia*) for a sweet-smelling offering (*osmēn euōdias*) to God' (Eph. 5: 2).

Finally, in what is the most personal of the Pastoral Letters and one that may owe something to Paul himself, the apostle is pictured as a veteran missionary giving instruction to a younger and cherished colleague, Timothy. He ends with a moving testimony to Christian hope in the face of impending execution. The time of Paul's departure has come and he is already being poured out as a libation (*spendomai*) or 'offered up' (2 Tim. 4: 6). Sacrificial language is applied to those who suffer martyrdom for the sake of Christ (High Priest and victim), as we will see happen in the case of a second-century martyr, St Polycarp (Chapter 5).

1 PETER ON CHRIST'S PRIESTHOOD

The First Letter of Peter (written by St Peter in the 60s or by someone else as late as the 90s) refers to the sacrificial death of Jesus. It evokes the regulations for the Passover lamb (Exod. 12: 5) when stating that

---

[21] Ibid. 711.

redemption has come through 'the precious blood of Christ like that of a lamb without defect or blemish' (1 Pet. 1: 19). The blood of this sacrificial victim has brought cleansing and forgiveness to believers (1: 2). Yet Jesus is not called a priest; the priestly activity of Jesus is never, or at least never explicitly, named as the source or exemplar for the priestly calling of God's people.[22] Like Paul, 1 Peter uses priestly, sacrificial language for the Christian community but not for Jesus himself. This is so, even though the letter speaks of the suffering of Christ that 'healed' sinners and brought them freedom from sin (2: 24).

Christ is called the 'living Stone' (2: 4), a seeming contradiction, since stones are normally understood to be lifeless and dead. Yet this 'Stone rejected by the builders' (2: 7) has been 'made alive' and 'raised' (to life) by God (1: 3; 3: 22), chosen to be the 'precious Cornerstone' (2: 7) for God's new, 'spiritual house (*oikos*)' (2: 5), and is paradoxically not only the living Stone but also, by implication, a life-giving Stone. Freed from the perishable and dead existence of contemporary paganism, believers have been transformed into 'living stones', who share in the existence of the living Stone and are built together into one 'spiritual house'. The implied agent of this 'construction' is God, who brings the living stones together into a single unit that is joined together and supported by Christ, the foundation of the whole structure.

A 'spiritual house' (or 'household') seems to be 'a metaphor for the community where the Spirit of God dwells, although Peter's intent is not to call attention to the Holy Spirit per se',[23] nor to apply unambiguously temple imagery to represent the Christian community (1 Cor. 3: 16–17; 2 Cor. 6: 16) and the individual Christian (1 Cor. 6: 19). By defining this 'spiritual house' as the place for 'a holy priesthood (*hierateuma*)' (1 Pet. 2: 5) or a 'royal priesthood' (2: 9), the letter implies that it is some kind of temple. A 'spiritual house' defined by priesthood should be a place where sacrifices are offered: after all, 'the

---

[22] Even if 1 Peter invokes baptism (3: 21), it never refers clearly to the Last Supper or to the Eucharist. Possibly the offering of praise and thanksgiving (2: 9) might point to the Eucharist. See J. H. Elliott, *1 Peter* (New York: Doubleday, 2000), 34–5.

[23] J. R. Michaels, *1 Peter* (Waco, Tex.: Word Books, 1988), 100.

work of priesthood is to offer sacrifices'.[24] Hence, not surprisingly, 1 Peter speaks of 'offering spiritual sacrifices (*thusias*), acceptable to God through Jesus Christ' (2: 5). Yet this image of the Christian community as a building (made up of 'living stones') is a metaphorical or extended use of language. In the literal sense, a community is not a building. Furthermore, to write of 'spiritual sacrifices' offered by a 'holy priesthood' is also an extended use of language. Literally speaking, sacrifices are offered by priests through ritual ceremonies conducted in temples. What then are the 'spiritual sacrifices', which—in general—are presumably sacrifices prompted by the Holy Spirit by whom believers have been sanctified (1: 2)? How and where are they offered?

The Hebrew Scriptures, which provide in a covenant formula (Exod. 19: 6) the term 'priesthood (*hierateuma*)' to express the privileged and holy character of God's chosen people, had long used sacrificial language in an extended, metaphorical sense to describe prayer, repentance, and good works (e.g. Ps. 50: 13–14, 23; 51: 17; 141: 2). 1 Peter follows suit by proposing a royal priesthood of Christians that involves prayer (in particular, proclaiming the 'saving acts' of God), holy conduct, and effective witness in their daily lives (1 Pet. 2: 9, 11–12). Motivated by the Spirit, such sacrifices involve praising God and living a holy way of life to the glory of God. The theme of the Christian community's 'spiritual sacrifices' 'acceptable to God through Jesus Christ' (2: 5) recalls what we saw above in Romans 12: 1 and will recur in Hebrews 13: 15–16 (where such 'sacrifices' involve praising God and performing good deeds for those in need).[25]

---

[24] Ibid. 101. Yet, if 1 Peter had intended such cultic connotations, *naos* (sanctuary or temple) and not *oikos* would have been a more appropriate term. Elliott writes: 'When Christians are portrayed as the "Temple" of God in the New Testament [e.g. 1 Cor. 3: 16; 6: 19], *oikos* is never used' (*1 Peter*, 415). He adds: 'The Petrine author manifests no interest in polemicizing against the Jerusalem Temple and its cult or in claiming its replacement by a new "temple" served by the Christian equivalent of the "sons of Aaron"' (ibid.). This observation seems irrelevant. Paul uses temple (*naos*) imagery twice in 1 Cor., but shows no interest in polemicizing against the Jerusalem Temple and its cult, let alone claiming its replacement by a new 'temple' served by the Christian equivalent of the 'sons of Aaron'. Such imagery by itself in no way implies such a polemic or such a claim.

[25] Elliott, *1 Peter*, 423.

1 Peter offers then a priestly and sacrificial vision of the whole Church. Priestly/sacrificial language is employed in an extended, metaphorical way to portray the chosen, covenant people called to a life of holiness (1: 14–15). The priestly property of holiness applies to the entire community, as it did in Exodus 19: 6 and Isaiah 61: 6. Being the living Stone, who communicates life to those who as a royal priesthood constitute together a 'spiritual house(hold)', Christ might have been called a priest (as he is in Hebrews). But he is never given this title. Yet 1 Peter goes beyond Hebrews by picturing the believing community as God's 'covenant people, whose intimate relation to God is like that of holy priests'.[26] Hebrews does not deploy this notion of the Church as God's holy, *priestly* community.

Two metaphors mark the verses we have examined in 1 Peter: the metaphors of growth and construction. While the metaphor of construction is deployed to describe her corporate existence (2: 4–5),[27] the Church is not called 'the body of Christ'. Unlike Ephesians 2: 12–16, 5: 21–32, 1 Corinthians 12: 12–26, and Colossians 1: 18, 1 Peter does not introduce the image of the Church as a body, of which Christ is the living head. In short, we do not find in 1 Peter the images of the Church as the one Body of Christ and the Temple of his Holy Spirit. Christ is called the Cornerstone of a new 'spiritual house(hold)', but 1 Peter does not develop any such 'structural' or spatial image, as Hebrews will do when talking about Christ entering the heavenly sanctuary and ministering there eternally from the right hand of God.

THE BOOK OF REVELATION

Most probably written in the closing years of the reign of the emperor Domitian (81–96 AD), the Book of Revelation repeatedly calls Christ 'the Lamb' but never calls him a 'priest'. He continues to love those

---

[26] Ibid. 437.

[27] See Eph. 2: 19–22, where similar language is used but the conclusion is different: the whole structure of the Church forms a holy temple (*naos*) in which God dwells. The concerns of the two letters differ. 1 Peter looks to a 'consolidation' in Christ of those reborn through baptism; Ephesians emphasizes the integration of both Jewish and Gentile believers into the one Church of Christ.

whom he has freed once and for all from their sins by his sacrificial death. But Revelation portrays that death in terms of his being the victim and not the priest. The book opens with a benediction directed towards Christ: 'To him who loves us and has freed us from our sins through his blood, and has made us to be a kingdom, *priests* for his God and Father, to him be glory and dominion forever and ever' (Rev. 1: 6).[28] The language of priesthood is not applied here to Christ but to the saints on earth (see also 5: 9–10) and to the martyrs already reigning in heaven as 'priests of God and of Christ' (20: 6).

Revelation gives Christ a rich variety of titles or descriptive names. The (slain) 'Lamb' dominates: from 5: 8 to 22: 3, Jesus is twenty-seven times called 'the Lamb', a code-name for the crucified and exalted Lord, now enthroned in heaven but still bearing the signs of his sacrificial death. Mortally wounded while defeating the enemy, this heavenly Conqueror sits now on his Father's throne and rules over the Church and the whole cosmos (3: 21).

In the heavenly liturgy the Lamb sits on the throne of God or stands near it in a setting visualized as a temple, an altar, and a court for the Gentiles (11: 1–2).[29] These and other details—for instance, the smoke of incense (8: 3–4)—show that the author of Revelation was acquainted with the Jerusalem Temple and the ceremonies conducted there. The heavenly sanctuary of Revelation is modelled after the Temple in Jerusalem, while the heavenly ritual is patterned on the liturgy in the Temple.[30] Thus Revelation places the souls of the faithful who have been slain under the altar in the heavenly sanctuary (6: 9–11). They are the 'first fruits (*aparchē*)' redeemed for God and the Lamb (14: 4), with the term derived from the offering of the first

---

[28] The language of 'he has freed us from our sins by his blood' (1: 6) obviously points to Christ's victim role. Yet the active role indicated by 'has freed us' hints at a priestly function: in particular, a priestly activity in the cause of expiation. Rev. 1: 13 depicts the risen Christ as wearing 'a long robe and with a golden sash across his chest'. Some commentators take this description as referring to the robe and sash of the high priest, others as simply indicating the high rank of Jesus, without any specifically priestly connotations (Dan. 10: 5). See G. R. Osborne, *Revelation* (Grand Rapids, Mich.: Baker Academic, 2002), 89; H. B. Swete, *The Apocalypse of St John* (London: Macmillan, 1907), 15–16.

[29] Rev. 11: 1–2 also evokes Ezekiel's vision of the new Temple (Ezek. 40–8).

[30] Revelation, however, places no temple in the New Jerusalem that will come: 'its temple is the Lord God the Almighty and the Lamb' (21: 22).

fruits in the Temple. Their destiny as Christian martyrs has been incorporated into the sacrificial self-giving of the Lamb. Revelation transfers the incense offering (Lev. 16: 13) from the Temple cult to the heavenly liturgy, where incense acquires a metaphorical meaning: the prayers of the saints (Rev. 5: 8; 8: 4).

In the opening chapters of Revelation the glorious Christ *speaks* to the visionary John on the island of Patmos (1: 11, 17, 20), and delivers messages for seven churches of Asia Minor (2: 1–3: 22). The exalted Christ then invites the visionary to enter heaven and enjoy visions of the glory of God and of the Lamb (4: 1–5: 14). But after that invitation the Lamb falls silent. Those who speak or sing in the heavenly liturgy include four 'living creatures', twenty-four 'elders', innumerable angels, and human beings in glory, above all martyrs. We hear the voice of the Spirit from heaven (14: 13) and the voice of God coming from the temple or from the divine throne (16: 1; 19: 5; 20: 3–8).[31] We hear the voice of an eagle flying through the sky (8: 13), the voices of those who worship the beast (13: 4), and of those who mourn the destruction of Babylon (18: 9, 16–20). But Jesus himself speaks again only in the closing vision of the New Jerusalem that comes down from heaven (22: 7, 12–20).

Singing in heaven begins with a hymn (drawn partly from Isa. 6: 2–3) and sung by four 'living creatures' (4: 8). Further hymns come from 'the twenty-four elders' (4: 11), from angels (5: 11), and— eventually—from 'every creature in heaven and on earth and under the earth and in the sea' (5: 13). This universal song of praise is offered to God and to the Lamb (e.g. 5: 13). Revelation recognizes that worship is due only to God (22: 9). The heavenly creatures who glorify God and the Lamb associate with their worship 'the prayers of the saints on earth' and sing a new song to the Lamb.[32]

---

[31] *Thronos* as God's throne occurs 17 times in chs. 4–5, with a total of 38 occurrences in chs. 4–22; judgements issue from God's throne (e.g. 6: 1–8, 16; 8: 3–6; 16: 17). A rainbow around the throne evokes the glory of God, while precious stones intensify the light and reflect the unapproachable brightness/glory that surrounds God himself (4: 3). A group of heavenly figures form an outer circle around the divine throne (5: 11–12) and beyond that comes every creature in the entire cosmos (5: 13–14).

[32] A new song celebrates the defeat of the powers of evil and sin. In the Old Testament a new song 'is always an expression of praise for God's victory over the

He has inaugurated a new era by his sacrificial death, and is found worthy to take a scroll (indicating God's purposes for the future) and open its seven seals: 'You are worthy to take the scroll and open its seals, for you were slain and by your blood you redeemed for God [saints] from every tribe, language, people, and nation. You have made them to be a kingdom and *priests* for our God, and they will reign on earth' (5: 9–10).

The Lamb takes the scroll (5: 8) and opens its seven seals (6: 1–12; 8: 1). The blood of the Lamb cleanses a great multitude of the redeemed, and they worship God within his heavenly temple (7: 9–15). Paradoxically, the Lamb is also called their shepherd: 'the Lamb at the centre of the throne will be their shepherd and will lead them to springs of the water of life' (7: 17). Those human beings, who are already redeemed, the 'first fruits' for God and the Lamb, and who have been purified and made victorious 'by the blood of the Lamb' (7: 14; 12: 11), sing a new song in heaven and follow the Lamb wherever he goes (14: 4). The persecutors of the saints make war on the Lamb, but, being sovereign over all peoples (5: 9–10), he 'will conquer them, for he is Lord of lords and King of kings' (17: 14). Victory is won over the beast and his cohorts (19: 11–21). Here Revelation once again announces something paradoxical: 'the marriage of the Lamb' has come (19: 7, 9), and the blessed elect are invited to the marriage supper. Lambs, of course, do not marry, still less lambs who have been slaughtered.

To sum up: Revelation applies priestly language to the faithful, who have been made fit, even on earth, to join in the heavenly liturgy of praise and worship offered to God and the Lamb. They have been made priestly kings or kingly priests who serve God (5: 9). Right from the start, Revelation makes it clear that, through being identified with the crucified and risen Christ, believers have been constituted kings together with him and share his priestly office (1: 6). In any case, their close proximity to the altar (6: 9–10; 11: 1–2) suggests that they are not only worshippers but also priests.

---

enemy, sometimes including thanksgiving for God's work of creation'. Here Revelation 'associates Christ's redemptive work with the beginning of the new creation' (K. Beale, *The Book of Revelation* (Grand Rapids, Mich.: Eerdmans, 1999), 358; Beale refers to Rev. 21: 1, 2, 5).

This priestly people joins in the heavenly hymns: an activity not found in Romans, 1 Peter, and Hebrews, texts which do not associate priesthood with singing. Where Revelation pictures the priestly people joining before the throne of God in heavenly prayers of praise, in Hebrews heavenly prayer takes the form of intercession coming from Christ, the High Priest seated at the right hand of God. Both priestly singing and priestly prayer enjoy their place and special characteristics in Revelation.

In the central part of Revelation (4: 2–22: 7) Christ himself, as we saw, acts (by opening the seven seals and by leading the heavenly army against the forces of evil), but he never speaks. He is not active as a priestly worshipper through prayer, song, or the offering of incense. Rather, worship is directed towards him. This may be the reason why he is not clearly represented in his priestly role. When Revelation reaches 'the New Jerusalem' (21: 1–22: 5), little is said about any worship (22: 3, 9) and nothing about priestly activity. This contrasts with Hebrews, for which in the 'heavenly Jerusalem' (Hebr. 12: 22) Christ proves a priest forever by permanently interceding for human beings.

REVELATION AND HEBREWS

Before we move in the next chapter to Hebrews, some insights into differences between these two major texts can sharpen our appreciation of their contribution to the theme of priesthood. First, Revelation aims to encourage a persecuted community to persevere to the end in the face of fierce suffering. Martyred Christians can expect a divine vindication. While they will receive their full reward at the last day, they already participate in the promised, priestly kingdom. The addressees of Hebrews have also experienced persecution on account of their faith (e.g. Heb. 10: 32–4; 13: 3). They must imitate the faithful endurance of the great heroes and heroines of the biblical story and the supreme example of Jesus himself (11: 1–12: 11). Yet Hebrews implies that its audience faces other challenges, not least a certain weariness in Christian faith and practice (e.g. 2: 1–3) and a

temptation to return to Old Testament dietary laws (13: 9) and further Jewish practices.

Second, with magnificent poetic imagery Revelation evokes the glory of God and the heavenly entourage around the divine throne: the twenty-four 'elders' (each holding a harp and a golden bowl of incense, 5: 8), four 'living creatures', and various angels. Clearly linked with the twelve tribes of Israel and the twelve apostles, the elders are probably angels, who represent the entire community of the redeemed from both testaments.[33] The four 'living creatures' seem to stand both for all animate life in creation and (along with the twenty-four 'elders') for the servants of the Lamb (5: 6–14). Hebrews can be imaginative and pictorial: for instance, in portraying God as the universal Judge (12: 18–34). But Revelation, from start to finish, draws on the imagery of Daniel, Ezekiel, and other prophetic and apocalyptic sources to produce an unrivalled picture-book that has inspired numerous painters over the centuries.

Third, Revelation, even if it never explicitly mentions baptism and the Eucharist, shows from the start an interest in the worship for which Christians meet (1: 3, 9–10). The Church on earth can model its priestly worship on the heavenly liturgy and the worship of the Lamb. Scenes of heavenly liturgy are woven seamlessly into the text (e.g. chs. 4–5; 7: 9–12; 11: 15–19; 15: 2–8). The 'lamp stands' (1: 12–13, 20) lead on to the angels and saints who worship in the heavenly temple. Not surprisingly, liturgical hymns play an important role in Revelation (from 5: 9 through to 19: 1–10), and are sung by a choir that comprises angels, the elect, and all possible voices in the cosmos (14: 1–3; 15: 2–4). Modelling earthly liturgy on heavenly liturgy is not a theme for Hebrews.

Those who take little notice of Revelation will lose valuable resources for their understanding of Christian worship and priesthood. But Hebrews contains the best-known narrative of Christ's priesthood in the New Testament. It calls for two chapters in this study.

---

[33] See Beale, *Book of Revelation*, 322.

We agree with the overwhelming majority of scholars that Hebrews was not written by Paul himself. Its style, language, and contents differ so markedly from what we read in letters certainly written by the apostle that this treatise is normally attributed to an anonymous author. To say this in no way casts doubt either on its origin as inspired scripture or on its place in the canonical list of books that constitute the Bible.

3

Hebrews on Christ's Priesthood

Our first two chapters have shown how the Letter to the Hebrews (written sometime between AD 60 and 90) does not stand alone in reflecting on Christ's priesthood. Yet it illustrates at length this theme, which the four evangelists, Paul, and other New Testament writers here and there merely touch on implicitly. It is only in the Letter to the Hebrews, which may well have been addressed to a group of former Jewish priests, that the New Testament ever explicitly calls Jesus a 'priest'. The author of this exhortation knows that Jesus belonged to the tribe of Judah (Heb. 7: 14) and thus did not qualify as a priest in the Jewish system. Hebrews breaks new ground by presenting Jesus as the eternal High Priest. Jesus has superseded any priesthood based on membership in the tribe of Levi.[1]

Other books of the New Testament, some of which (e.g. 1 Cor. and Rom.) were written before the earliest possible date for Hebrews, identify Christ with 'my Lord' in Psalm 110: 1: 'The Lord said to my Lord, "sit at my right hand, until I put your enemies under your feet".' Perhaps Jesus himself did so (Mark 12: 35–7 parr.). 1 Corinthians echoes this verse of Psalm 110 by saying: 'He [Christ] must reign until he has put all his enemies under his feet' (15: 25). Ephesians speaks of God raising Christ from the dead and setting him 'at his right hand in the heavenly places' (1: 20). Colossians writes of 'the things that are above, where Christ is seated at the right hand of God' (3: 1). In the previous chapter we noted the

---

[1] On Hebrews' view of priesthood, see J. M. Scholer, *Proleptic Priests: Priesthood in the Epistle to the Hebrews* (Sheffield: Sheffield Academic Press, 1991).

intercessory role that Paul attributes to 'Christ Jesus', who 'was raised', 'is at the right hand of God', and 'intercedes for us' (Rom. 8: 34).[2]

After quoting (at 1: 13) Psalm 110: 1, Hebrews later recalls the place of Christ 'seated at the right hand of the Majesty in the heavens' (8: 1; see also 1: 3; 10: 12–13; 12: 2). But by Chapter 8 the author of Hebrews has already moved the application to Christ of Psalm 110 further by identifying him through what the psalmist goes on to say: 'You are a priest forever according to the order of Melchizedek' (5: 5–8). Hebrews will call Christ 'priest (*hiereus*)' six times and 'high priest (*archiereus*)' ten times.[3] What elements enter this vision of Christ as eternal (High) Priest, which makes its first appearance in Hebrews and seems a self-consciously avant-garde interpretation of Christ's death and exaltation? Let us begin with the 'once-and-for-all' element.

CHRIST'S ONCE-AND-FOR-ALL SELF-SACRIFICE

Priesthood and sacrifice are correlative terms—something taken for granted by the author of Hebrews (8: 3). The priestly practices outlined in the Pentateuch that he recalls involved offering sacrifices of animals. The first time that he mentions the *priestly* identity of Christ, he links it at once to Christ's *sacrificial* activity: he became 'a merciful and faithful high priest to expiate the sins of the people' (2: 17).

Christ proved unlike the Levitical priesthood in two essential features: (1) he offered sacrifice only once, and (2) did so through the sacrifice of himself and not through animal sacrifice (9: 25–6). In his *capacity* as High Priest, Christ sacrificed himself. He was both Priest and Victim, Offerer and Offering.[4] Since the author of

---

[2] Further New Testament texts quote or at least echo Ps. 110: 1: see Mark 14: 62 parr.; Acts 2: 33–5; 5: 31; 7: 55–6; 1 Pet. 3: 22.

[3] See U. Kellerman, '*Archiereus*', in H. Balz and G. Schneider, *Exegetical Dictionary of the New Testament*, trans. V. P. Howard, vol. 1 (Grand Rapids, Mich.: Eerdmans, 1990), 164–5.

[4] St Augustine of Hippo was to call Christ 'the truest priest (*verissimus sacerdos*)' (*Contra Epistulam Parmeniani*, 2. 8. 16) and 'the truest sacrifice (*verissimum sacrificium*)' (*Contra Faustum Manicheum*, 20. 18). In his *Confessions* Augustine addressed God: 'for he was victorious before you and victor because he was victim. For us before

Hebrews knew that Christ died 'outside the camp' (13: 12) and so in a profane place, not *the* place for Jewish cultic sacrifice (the Temple), he had the task of justifying his desire to apply the language and imagery of cultic sacrifice to Christ's priestly identity and activity. We return to this challenge below.

Hebrews insists on the once-and-for-all character of Christ's sacrifice: 'when he offered himself, he did this once and for all' (7: 27; see 9: 12, 28; 10: 10). By a single sacrifice Christ removed the burden of sin for ever. Thus he put an end to any further sacrifices for sin (10: 18). We will need to come back to this issue later, when reflecting on the Christian priesthood that emerged with the practice and doctrine of Eucharistic sacrifice. We will also need to address the issue raised by the language of Christ 'offering himself'. Does this mean that Christ's self-sacrifice was an act of suicide? Furthermore, what of the 'once-and-for-allness' of Christ's sacrificial death being qualified by his ongoing intercession (9: 24)?[5] Obviously the priestly office and activity of Christ extend, in the view of Hebrews, beyond the once-and-for-all event of his crucifixion and resurrection.

QUALIFICATIONS FOR PRIESTHOOD

If Christ did not belong through birth to the Levitical priesthood, what qualified him to be reckoned not only a priest but also the High Priest of the new dispensation? Hebrews lists three qualifications for such high priesthood: 'every high priest is [1] taken from among human beings and [2] appointed on behalf of human beings with respect to the matters pertaining to God, [3] in order to offer gifts and sacrifices for sin' (5: 1). In other words, a high priest is (1) chosen from among human beings, and so (2) not self-appointed but called

---

you he is priest and sacrifice, and priest because he is sacrifice (*pro nobis tibi victor et victima, et ideo victor quia victima; pro nobis tibi sacerdos et sacrificium, et ideo sacerdos quia sacrificium*)' (10. 43).

[5] As we observed in the last chapter, Paul, without naming Christ as priest, says something similar in Romans. He writes of Christ dying 'once and for all' (6: 10) and 'interceding for us' at the right hand of God (8: 34).

by God to represent them (3) in the sacrifices he offers before God (in particular, for the expiation of sins).

Through taking on the human condition in the incarnation (1: 1–4), the Son of God satisfied the first qualification. By itself his eternal, divine status would not have met this requirement. As High Priest he could represent human beings, precisely because he shared their condition, including growth, suffering, and death (5: 7–9). Secondly, he did not 'take for himself the honour' of priesthood but was 'called by God'. To confirm this, the author of Hebrews cites Scripture to portray God appointing Jesus to be High Priest: 'You are my Son; today I have begotten you . . . You are a priest forever, according to the order of Melchizedek' (5: 5–6). One should note that, while Melchizedek who prefigured Christ is called 'a priest', Hebrews repeatedly calls Christ 'High Priest' (3: 1; 4: 14, 15; 5: 1, 5, 10; 6: 20; 9: 11). Thirdly, the Jewish high priests offered sacrifices and did so not only for the sins of the people but also for their own sins (5: 2). Jesus offered his sacrifice, but did not need to offer any sacrifice for his own sins (7: 27), since he was without sin (4: 15).

The opening verses of Chapter 5 address explicitly the (three) characteristics that qualified Christ for his role as High Priest. Elsewhere Hebrews fills out its first priestly requirement of 'being taken from among human beings' (see also 2: 11–13) by detailing Christ's *solidarity* with human limitations. As 'High Priest' he could 'sympathize' with 'our weaknesses' by being tested/tempted in all ways (4: 15). In 'the days of his flesh' he prayed, and did so in painful and threatening situations (5: 7). He grew, was tested, and was made perfect through suffering (2: 10, 18), above all through enduring death (2: 9, 14; 5: 7), a death by crucifixion (6: 6).

In detailing further qualities of Christ's priesthood Hebrews stresses his *obedient fidelity* to God the Father and the divine will (5: 7–9; 10: 7). As 'faithful' High Priest (3: 2, 6), he ran perfectly and to the end the race of faith (12: 2). In his priestly life he proved the supreme model of faith. It was 'through the eternal Spirit' that he was enabled to 'offer himself without blemish to God [the Father]' (9: 14).

Possibly 'the eternal Spirit' is to be read in lower-case ('spirit', not 'Spirit') and denotes here, as Harold Attridge holds, Christ's spirit of self-offering and not the Holy Spirit. Despite references to the Holy Spirit that occur before and after this passage (3: 7–11; 10: 15–17, 29),

Attridge argues that such references 'are too diffuse and ill-focused to support a Trinitarian theology in this context'.[6] To be sure, it would be anachronistic to 'find' here or anywhere else in the New Testament anything like the full-blown, sharply focused 'Trinitarian theology' that emerged only after centuries of prayer, reflection, debate, and controversy. Yet the fact remains that Hebrews looks somewhat Trinitarian (call it 'diffusely Trinitarian', if you like) by presenting words coming from the Father (1: 5–13; 4: 3, 7; 5: 5–6; 8: 8–13), the Son (10: 5–7), and the Holy Spirit (3: 7–11; 10: 15–17; see also 9: 8). Some reference to the consecrating role of the Holy Spirit and to God the Father need not amount to a clearly focused 'Trinitarian theology'. Such a reference to the consecrating role of the Holy Spirit is in any case found elsewhere in the New Testament (notably in Acts 10: 38). Against Attridge's explanation one should question whether listeners could have readily taken 'spirit' in the sense of his proposal: that 'through the eternal spirit' refers not only to 'the spiritual realm' in which Christ's sacrifice takes place but also (and even more) to 'the interior or spiritual quality of his sacrificial death'.[7] Then the verse would fill out further the blameless spirit of self-offering that distinguished Christ's exercise of his priesthood. Beyond question, such an interpretation is possible, but it seems less likely than the 'Trinitarian' one proposed by Craig Koester and others.[8]

BECOMING HIGH PRIEST

Commentators on Hebrews regularly raise the question: when did Christ become High Priest? Did his priesthood begin only with his

---

[6] H. W. Attridge, *The Epistle to the Hebrews* (Philadelphia: Fortress Press, 1989), 250.

[7] Ibid. 251.

[8] C. R. Koester comments: 'Prior to [Heb.] 9: 14 all references to the "spirit" in the singular, except 4: 12, have been to the Holy Spirit. Listeners could have been expected to identify "the eternal Spirit" in 9: 14 with the Holy Spirit (cf. "the Spirit of grace," 10: 29). Calling the Spirit "eternal" connects it to "eternal redemption" (9: 12)': *Hebrews* (New York: Doubleday, 2001), 410.

death (9: 11–14) and exaltation to the right hand of God?[9] Or did his
priesthood originate with his coming into the world (10: 5), when he
'appeared for all at the end of the age' (9: 26)?

Even if Hebrews never expressly asks and answers our question,
from the start it relates the incarnation of the Son of God to his
priestly activity of purifying sin (1: 2–4). Divine sonship and a
human priesthood, made possible through the incarnation, belonged
together and qualified as priestly activity the whole history of Jesus,
even if *the* defining moment of his priesthood came with his death
and exaltation. Hebrews deployed vivid priestly imagery to depict
what came at the end. Yet a priestly self-offering characterized his
entire human existence (10: 5–7).

THE ORDER OF MELCHIZEDEK

The four Gospels tell of Christ moving from the Last Supper to the
Garden of Gethsemane, where he allowed himself to be trapped by
the forces that came to destroy him. The four evangelists take their
readers through the savagery of the passion without stopping to
dwell on its terrible pain. In a terse, laconic fashion they write of
Jesus being bound, spat upon, scourged, crowned with thorns, and
hustled to his death on Calvary. Nailed to a cross, he died a death by
slow torture. Some readers of the passion narratives would have
presumably witnessed the dreadful sight of people condemned to
die by crucifixion. Other readers could fill in for themselves the
horrific vision of a human being *in extremis.* Either way, crucifixion
presented the human condition pushed into terrible pain beyond
bearable limits.

In the previous chapters we noted two attempts to respond imaginatively to the story of the crucifixion by transcribing it into the

---

[9] Koester, *Hebrews*, 109–10.

language and ritual of priestly activity. The theology of the cross is central to Paul; yet he can also express the crucifixion by evoking Exodus (12: 3–8, 21) and the sacrifice of lambs: 'Christ, our paschal lamb has been sacrificed' (1 Cor. 5: 7). John's Gospel embraces a similar approach by placing the crucifixion on 'the day or preparation' when Passover lambs were slain in the Temple, and by presenting Jesus as the Lamb of God (1: 29, 36) who in death fulfilled and replaced the Passover ritual (19: 31, 36).

The sustained reflection that Hebrews offered on the sacrificial death took, however, another route, one that Paul had adumbrated in passing. The apostle called Christ the *hilastērion* or 'means for expiating [sins]' (Rom. 3: 25), thereby hinting at the function of the Levitical high priest on the Day of Expiation (Lev. 16: 12–15). The author of Hebrews imaginatively transcribed the death and exaltation of Christ through images drawn from the ceremonious ritual of Yom Kippur. But the cornerstone for this sustained reflection came from another source: the priest-king Melchizedek, who blesses Abraham (Gen. 14: 17–20) and is called a 'priest forever' (Ps. 110: 4). The mysterious person of Melchizedek served the purposes of Hebrews, providing a figure who was both prior to and superior to the Levitical priesthood.

After three times attributing to Christ an eternal priesthood 'according to the order of Melchizedek' (5: 6, 10; 6: 20), the author of Hebrews comes clean, so to speak, with his strategy: the priesthood of Melchizedek was earlier and greater than the Levitical priesthood (7: 1–28). Since the Bible does not mention Melchizedek's ancestors, his birth, or his death, he 'remains' a priest forever (7: 3), unlike the Levitical priests who all died and could not continue in office forever. Abraham gave Melchizedek a tenth of the spoils from a victory over 'the kings' and received a blessing from him, thus showing how Melchizedek was greater than Abraham and his descendant Levi (the head of the priestly tribe). With the cornerstone of Melchizedek in place, Hebrews presses on to argue that, being a 'priest forever according to the order of Melchizedek', Christ is superior to any Levitical high priest. He 'holds his priesthood permanently', and 'always lives to make intercession' for those who 'approach God through him' (7: 24–5).

For good measure, Hebrews throws in two further arguments to support the unique superiority of Christ's high priesthood. First, unlike the Levitical priesthood, he was appointed by a divine oath: 'The Lord has sworn and will not change his mind' (7: 20–1, citing Ps. 110: 4). Second, unlike all the other high priests, Christ had 'no need to offer sacrifice *day after day*, first for his own sins, and then for those of the people' (7: 27). On the Day of Expiation the high priest offered sacrifice first for himself and his household (Lev. 16: 6–14) and then for the people (Lev.16: 15–16). These sacrifices were offered, as the author of Hebrews knows, only once a year (Heb. 9: 7, 25). Yet seemingly he fuses here the sacrifices on the Day of Atonement with other sacrifices.

Later on the author of Hebrews will add further details when contrasting the Jewish priests with Jesus. They 'stand day by day' at their service, 'offering again and again the same sacrifices that can never take away sins'. Christ, however, 'offered for all time a single sacrifice for sins' that was effective, and then 'sat down at the right hand of God' (10: 11–12). There was a unique finality to the sacrifice of Christ, the High Priest who is seated for ever on the throne of God in heaven (8: 1).

TEMPLE AND PRIESTLY IMAGERY

The superiority of Christ's high priesthood involves differences in kind, and not merely in degree, from the Levitical priesthood and its high priesthood. Yet Hebrews shapes its vision of Christ's priesthood by appropriating principles and images taken from the rituals of Jewish priesthood. Without ever mentioning as such the Temple in Jerusalem, Hebrews draws on what the Pentateuch prescribes for the Jewish sanctuary (in the wilderness) and priestly practices. Our text uses categories familiar to its audience (especially Lev. 16) in depicting Christ as the new High Priest engaged in the ritual of the Great Day of Expiation (Heb. 9: 7).

Hebrews portrays Christ's passage through death to heaven as being like the Jewish high priest moving behind the curtain or veil (Exod. 26: 31–5) right into the Holy of Holies (Heb. 9: 3). Christ has passed through the heavens (4: 14) and entered the inner shrine of God (6:

19–20). The author of Hebrews knows that Christ died by crucifixion (6: 6), yet imagines the body of Christ moving into the heavenly sanctuary and not onto the cross. He knows also that Christ died in a profane place 'outside the camp' (13: 12), and yet he appropriates the imagery of Israel's sacred sanctuary and its Holy of Holies.

The author of Hebrews appreciates that the earthly sanctuary erected by Moses (Exod. 25: 40) was only a 'sketch and shadow' of the true, heavenly 'tabernacle' set up by God (Heb. 8: 2, 5; see 9: 23–4). Nevertheless, he draws in detail (9: 1–28) on the regulations for Jewish worship and its setting (Exod. 25: 10–40) to picture the characteristic features of Christ's priestly sacrifice. The Mosaic regulations for worship and an earthly sanctuary involved a tent or tabernacle called the 'Holy Place', which contained a lamp stand, a table, and 'the bread of the Presence' (Lev. 24: 5–9). Then behind a second curtain was the tabernacle called the Holy of Holies. In it stood the golden altar of incense (Exod. 30: 6), the ark of the covenant or chest that contained the tablets of the Law (Exod. 25: 10–22), an urn with manna from the wilderness (Exod. 16: 32–4), and Aaron's rod (Num. 17: 1–13). Hebrews cites all these details prescribed for the 'first covenant': 'a tent was constructed . . . in which were the lamp stand, the table, and the bread of the Presence; this is called the Holy Place. Behind the second curtain was a tabernacle called the Holy of Holies. In it stood the golden altar of incense and the ark of the covenant overlaid on all sides with gold, in which there were a golden urn holding the manna, Aaron's rod that budded, and the tablets of the covenant' (9: 1–4).

The priests went 'continually into the first tabernacle to carry out their ritual duties' (9: 6). But only the high priest went into the Holy of Holies, and did so only once a year (on the Day of Expiation), taking with him blood from the sacrifice of a bull and a goat to sprinkle on the mercy seat and to expiate the sins committed by himself and the people (9: 7; see Lev. 16: 11–19).

The self-sacrifice in which Christ offered his own blood (9: 25), Hebrews argues, was incomparably superior to sacrifices using the blood of goats and bulls (9: 12–14). Christ's sacrifice involved the life of a person and not that of irrational animals (10: 4). Unlike the Levitical high priest, he was both priest *and* victim (9: 12), and he did not make this offering every year but once and for all (9: 12, 25–6; 10: 11–12). When he made it, he did not enter into a 'sanctuary con-

structed by human hands' but into 'heaven itself' to appear in the very presence of God (9: 24). Unlike the ritual of Yom Kippur and other offerings, Christ's once-and-for-all offering and his blood proved efficacious in 'purifying' and 'perfecting' the conscience of human beings (9: 9, 14), and was efficacious for all time (10: 11–12).[10]

Apropos of blood, Hebrews recalls that the blood of bulls and goats was used not only for the ritual of Yom Kippur (9: 6, 10: 4) but also when the covenant was inaugurated by Moses (9: 18–21). Rituals involving blood were understood either to effect cleansing or to unite in a covenantal relationship (or both). The author of Hebrews observes that under the Mosaic Law almost everything is purified 'with blood', given the premise that 'without the shedding of blood there is no forgiveness of sins' (9: 22). Forgiveness, however, was not available through the Law, which was 'only a shadow of the good things to come' (10: 1). The sacrifices, offered year by year, did not make worshippers perfect by cleansing them once and for all from sin. The author of Hebrews states matters firmly: 'it is impossible for the blood of bulls and goats to remove sin' (10: 4) and cleanse the human conscience (9: 9, 13–14).

The sin offering of the Law (10: 8) could never take away sin, but Christ's own blood did so and 'perfected for all time those who are sanctified' (10: 11–14). It was the new covenant, made effective through Christ's blood, that brought a full and final remission of sins (10: 16–17, citing Jer. 31: 33–4; see also Heb. 12: 24; 13: 20).

CHRIST'S PRIESTLY IMPACT

The last paragraph brings us to the question of the redemptive work of Christ the High Priest. At times Hebrews expresses it generically as 'eternal redemption' (9: 12) and 'eternal salvation' (5: 9), or speaks of Christ destroying 'the one who has the power of death: that is, the

---

[10] Hebrews does not, however, attempt to explain *how* Christ's blood actually purifies sinners. Does it do so by revealing to them the full extent of God's mercy and grace and cleansing their consciences (9: 9, 13–14), whenever the proclamation of Christ's death evokes faith in them and empowers them to serve the living God (9: 14)? Or does the cleansing power of Christ's blood work also for those who have never heard of his self-sacrificing death?

devil' (2: 14). This language of deliverance *from* (death and the power of the devil) and deliverance *for* (eternal salvation) takes a more precise form elsewhere.

Negatively, Christ's priestly work is a sacrifice of expiation that purifies human beings defiled by sin. Their 'hearts' are now 'sprinkled clean'. Their 'conscience' is now 'purified from dead works' (9: 14). Positively, with their 'bodies washed with pure water' in baptism (10: 22; see 1: 3), they can 'worship the living God' by sharing in the new covenant established by Christ's sacrificial death. As High Priest, he functions above all as the 'mediator of a new covenant' (9: 15; 12: 24). The new covenant forms a linchpin, without which Hebrews would fall apart. This definitive commitment of God is interpreted against the background of the Mosaic covenant but stands in contrast with it as the 'better' or fully efficacious covenant (8: 7–13).

Christ's sacrifice has opened a new and living way into the presence of God (10: 19–20), and allows his followers to move in hope towards the inner shrine of heaven, where Jesus their 'forerunner' and High Priest belongs forever (6: 19). They can continue to appropriate Christ's self-offering, knowing that he constantly 'appears in the presence of God' on their behalf (9: 24; see 6: 20).

Christ's priestly journey into the heavenly sanctuary has ended with his sitting at the right hand of God (1: 3). But his priesthood continues forever, inasmuch as he 'lives always' to 'make intercession' for those who 'approach God through him' (7: 25). Paul too had written, as we saw, of the risen Christ 'who intercedes for us' at the right hand of God (Rom. 8: 34). Hebrews agrees but goes further by interpreting this permanent intercession as characterizing Christ's role as 'a priest forever' (7: 22, 24).

SACRIFICE OF PRAISE

The final chapter of Hebrews, in which commentators have regularly detected elements that bring Paul's letters to mind, contains a certain parallel, albeit a richer one, to what we examined in Romans 12: 1. The author of Hebrews exhorts his addressees: 'through him [Christ] let us continually offer a sacrifice (*thusian*) of praise to God: that is, the fruit (*karpon*) of lips that confess his name. Do not neglect to do

good and to share what you have, for God is pleased (*euaresteitai*) with such sacrifices (*thusiais*)' (13: 15–16). Christians are to offer in sacrifice not the fruit of the fields but the 'fruit' of their lips in confessing and praising God.

Without saying that they share in Christ's own priesthood, Hebrews uses cultic, sacrificial language to depict the appropriate lifestyle of believers.[11] They are called to a priestly existence that involves ongoing sacrifice not only through their prayers of praise and confession of faith but also through 'doing good' and generously sharing with others.[12] Such doing good has been clarified a few verses earlier: it entails mutual love, hospitality to strangers, care for those in prison, fidelity in marriage, and avoiding avarice (13: 1–5). One should also recall the exhortation at the end of the preceding chapter to 'offer God a pleasing worship (*latreuōmen euarestōs*)' (12: 28). What the closing chapter says about the daily sacrifice of Christian life fills out what such 'pleasing worship' involves. Hebrews echoes the Old Testament's conviction about what a true 'sacrifice of thanksgiving' means (e.g. Ps. 50: 14, 23).

Interestingly, the final chapter of Hebrews seems to refer to the Eucharist in which Christians shared on a weekly basis: 'we have an altar (*thusiastērion*) from which those who officiate in the tent [= Jewish priests] have no right to eat' (13: 10). In the last chapter we saw what Paul wrote in 1 Corinthians 10 about communal participation through the Eucharist in the sacrificial death of Christ. Something similar seems to be intended at the end of Hebrews. As the spiritual food available on an altar, the Eucharist commemorates and sacramentally perpetuates for Christians the bloody death of Christ on the cross (Heb. 13: 12). Through Eucharistic eating believers share in the covenant established by Christ's death and find in him 'the altar' where they can offer to God the sacrifices of their daily lives. Inevitably this verse in Hebrews (13: 10) played a role in later attempts to find further references to the Eucharist elsewhere in the letter.[13]

---

[11] In *Proleptic Priests*, Scholer illustrates in much detail how three verbs, already used in the LXX with cultic-priestly meaning (*proserchesthai, eiserchesthai,* and *teleioun*) are applied to the addressees of Hebrews. It is then in cultic-priestly language that Hebrews describes Christian access to God through prayer and worship.

[12] It is obedience expressed in praise of God and service of others (rather than animal sacrifices) that 'pleases' God (Heb. 10: 5, 8).

[13] On interpretations of this verse see Koester, *Hebrews*, 568–70.

4

Four Questions for Hebrews

Having spelled out some major aspects of Christ's priesthood according to Hebrews, we are still left with at least four central questions: (1) Who, according to Hebrews, are the beneficiaries of Christ's priestly work? (2) Was the exercise of his priesthood limited to the end of his life? Could the years of his public ministry *also* be interpreted in priestly terms? (3) Does the language about Christ 'entering into the Holy Place' with 'his own blood' imply that he directly took his own life? Were we saved then by an act of (priestly) suicide? (4) Finally, from the second century Hebrews began to be read, interpreted, and applied in the light of an emerging ministerial priesthood and a doctrine of Eucharistic sacrifice. Does the text of Hebrews allow for or even justify such developments?[1]

THE BENEFICIARIES

Sometimes Hebrews seems comprehensive, even universalist, in its proposals about the beneficiaries of Christ's priestly work. Jesus, it announces, 'tasted death for everyone' (2: 9).[2] Yet it can also propose that Jesus 'became the source of eternal salvation for all who obey him' (5: 9).[3] Salvation is a gift, but receiving this gift prompts people

---

[1] On the interpretation of Hebrews in Christian history, see C. R. Koester, *Hebrews* (New York: Doubleday, 2001), 19–63.
[2] See ibid. 22–3, 218.
[3] See ibid. 290, 299.

to follow him obediently on the journey of faith. But what then of
those who, through no fault of their own, have never heard of Jesus
and thus are not in a position to repent of their sins, 'obey him' on
the journey of faith, be delivered from death, and enjoy in glory the
presence of God? It seems that salvation is available only to those
who know of Christ's priestly work and can approach God's 'throne
of grace' to 'receive mercy' for past sins and find 'grace' for present
and future 'need' (4: 16). Is the possibility of salvation then restricted
to those who consciously approach the royal throne of God through
Jesus the High Priest (7: 25)? The language of what has been done 'on
our behalf', of 'we', 'us', and 'for us' (6: 19–20; 9: 24) might lend
credibility to this restrictive interpretation.

Nevertheless, a classic roll-call of heroes and heroines of faith
(11: 1–12: 1) does not list any Christians but only those who lived
before Christ and hence could not consciously have accepted redemption coming through his priestly work. Significantly, a remark
about 'we' being 'among those who have faith and so are saved' (10: 39)
introduces that list. Followers of Jesus may enjoy privileged helps (yet
with their corresponding duties), but still belong among the wider
group of 'those who have faith and are saved'.

Not surprisingly, Hebrews proposes in Chapter 11 an 'open'
version of faith: 'the reality of things hoped for' and 'the proof of
things not seen. By this [faith] the elders [our ancestors] received
approval. By faith we understand that the universe was fashioned by
the word of God, so that from what cannot be seen that which is
seen has come into being' (11: 1–3). A further verse adds two
(rather general) requirements to this 'open' account of faith: 'without faith it is impossible to please God; for whoever would approach him must believe that he exists and that he rewards those
who seek him' (11: 6).[4]

The opening three verses of Hebrews 11 describe faith but say very
little about its content. The passage hints at the future. Divine
promises (presumably of some eternal inheritance) have aroused
the hope of human beings and their trust that God will keep these
promises, which concern future things which are 'not seen'. Faith also

---

[4] On these and other relevant verses on faith see ibid. 468–553.

involves a conviction about the past. One understands by faith the unseen origin of the world: it was 'fashioned by the word of God'. Just as people of faith rely on the word of God about the *genesis* of the universe, so too do they rely on the word of God's promise when considering the *goal* of the world and their existence. Both in their view of the past and their hope for the future, the lives of those who have faith are intertwined with the life of the invisible God.

This description of faith makes no mention of Christ. He will appear later, when the list of heroes and heroines of faith reaches the figure of Jesus, 'the pioneer and perfecter of faith' (12: 2). The opening verses of Hebrews 11 invoke 'the elders' or 'ancestors', people who have been approved and honoured by God for their perseverance in faith. Then follow examples of those who have lived on the basis of faith, with particular attention paid to Abraham, Sarah, and Moses. Some of those who exemplify faith (Abel, Enoch, and Noah) existed prior to Abraham, Sarah, and the formation of the chosen people. One figure of faith is 'Rahab the prostitute', an outsider who belonged to the story of the conquest of the promised land (Jos. 2: 1–24; 6: 22–5).

Hebrews 11: 6 lets us glimpse the shape that the faith of outsiders can take. 'Pleasing God' means doing the divine will, in particular, through deeds of kindness and service to others (13: 16, 20–1). Such conduct does not depend upon a conscious relationship with Christ the High Priest. A faith that 'pleases' God is a possibility open to all. Likewise, 'approaching' God in prayer does not necessarily depend on an awareness of the priestly intercession of the exalted Christ. That intercession functions, whether or not worshippers are conscious of the priestly presence of Christ when they approach God in prayer. These and further aspects of Hebrews 11: 6 spell out an 'open' account of faith. Salvation through such faith is offered to all people and offered on the basis of the self-sacrificing priesthood of Christ, even if they are not (or not yet) in a position to follow him in *conscious* obedience on the pilgrimage of faith.[5]

[5] See further G. O'Collins, *Salvation for All: God's Other Peoples* (Oxford: Oxford University Press, 2008), 248–59.

A PRIESTLY MINISTRY

Happily, the years Jesus spent on his teaching and healing activity
have been commonly called his 'public ministry'. Should we, or may
we, in the light of Hebrews also describe those years as his 'priestly
ministry'? The imagery deployed in Hebrews might encourage a
negative answer: after all, that imagery evokes the inauguration of
the Mosaic covenant, the cultic rituals of Yom Kippur, and the daily
sacrifices offered by the Levitical priesthood. Nevertheless, some
exhortations towards the close of Hebrews open up the possibility
of interpreting the public ministry of Jesus not only in a prophetic/
teaching and kingly/pastoral mode but also in a priestly mode.

First, Hebrews speaks of receiving the divine *kingdom*, the central
theme of Jesus' ministry of service to God and others, and doing so
with a gratitude that amounts to offering God reverential worship.[6] It
exhorts the addressees: 'since we are receiving an unshakable kingdom, let us be grateful and thereby offer God pleasing worship'
(*latreuōmen euarestōs*) with 'reverence and awe' (12: 28). Then
Hebrews encourages its readers to live lives of self-sacrificing love
by 'continually offering to God a sacrifice of praise' (*thusian aine-
seōs*), which is the 'fruit of lips that confess his name', and by serving
others (13: 15–16).

In his public ministry Jesus confessed constantly the name of God:
through his parables, his teaching on prayer ('may your name be
made holy': Matt. 6: 9 par.), and other items that made up his
proclamation of the divine kingdom that was breaking into the
world and should be received with intense joy. Furthermore, Jesus
constantly went about doing good (see Acts 10: 38) and shared
everything that he had, so that his whole life became a sacrifice
pleasing to God. To be sure, Hebrews does not relate to the public
ministry of Jesus its closing exhortations. Yet what these admonitions
encourage the community to do finds its perfect example in what

---

[6] The proclamation by Jesus of the divine kingdom highlighted both its present
reality (the 'already') and its future consummation (the 'not yet'). Hebrews likewise
speaks of receiving the divine kingdom (already present) and waiting for the heavenly
'city [still] to come' (13: 14).

Jesus had said and done in his ministry of the kingdom. The priestly language of worship and sacrifice that Hebrews uses to describe a proper Christian existence fits what we know of the public life of Christ presented by the Gospels.

Beyond question, when describing Christ the High Priest Hebrews sets out very little about 'the days of his flesh' (5: 7)[7] beyond his being born of the tribe of Judah (7: 14) and dying on a cross (6: 6) outside Jerusalem (13: 12). Nevertheless, the author of Hebrews is concerned to insist that the *entire life* of Jesus was without sin (4: 15) and that, while tested by suffering, he behaved with unshaken obedience (5: 7–8; 13: 12). As High Priest he never needed to offer sacrifices of expiation for his own sins (7: 27). When the pre-existent Son came, he came to do the will of God (10: 5–7); he proved himself to be 'holy, blameless, undefiled' (7: 26) and so at the end could offer himself to God 'without blemish' (9: 14). This was a blameless, priestly life that involved, from beginning to end, completing the race of faith perfectly (12: 1–2). Christ remains the unsurpassable source and model of faith for others.

In short, his suffering, death, and exaltation formed the defining moment of Christ's priesthood. But that priesthood embraced his whole story, and not least the years about which we know most: his public, priestly ministry, when he obediently gave himself totally to the service of the kingdom. The earthly and heavenly priesthood of Christ may be distinguished but belong inseparably together.

DEATH BY SUICIDE?

By telling of his scourging and crucifixion, the Gospels imply that Jesus died a bloody death, even if it is only John who literally mentions the shedding of Jesus' blood (19: 34). Hebrews introduces the blood of Christ seven times, and states that it was with his own blood that he entered the Holy Place (9: 12, 25). This language has long prompted many interpreters to speak of Christ as priest *and*

---

[7] 'The days of his flesh' comprised in fact the entire life of Jesus, even if Hebrews focuses on his passion and death (see 10: 19–20).

victim. Did he deliberately and directly make a victim of himself by
literally slaying himself? Were human beings, then, saved by an act of
suicide?

In two ways Hebrews rules out such a thesis of priestly suicide.
First, it knows that others crucified Jesus (6: 6; 12: 2). There is no
suggestion that he died by self-crucifixion. Second, a long section on
faith and the life of faith begins with the violent death of Abel (11: 4).
It concludes by comparing Abel with Jesus, whose 'sprinkled blood
speaks in a manner superior to Abel' (12: 24). By bringing together
the (mythical) figure of Abel and the (historical) figure of Jesus, the
author of Hebrews knows that they both died not by suicide but as
victims of violence perpetrated by others.

For Hebrews, 1 Peter (e.g. 2: 22–4), Revelation (e.g. 1: 5), the
evangelists, and the New Testament witnesses in general, it was important that Christ voluntarily 'gave himself for our sins' (Gal. 1: 4).
His priestly death came about through human malice (represented
and personified above all by Caiaphas, Judas, and Pilate), yet it also
embodied Jesus' free decision. Murderous human calculations converged with the unswerving obedience of Jesus to bring about his
death 'outside the city gate' (Heb. 13: 12).

Neither the author of Hebrews nor any other New Testament
witness develops a 'theoretical' framework to 'explain' this 'convergence' of motives and actions, but they provide elements to let us do
so. One can speak of Jesus' willing his death by accepting it. His self-
sacrificing death was not due to his *direct* and positive will (or to that
of his Father) but to the abuse of human freedom on the part of
political and religious authorities. The New Testament captures this
mysterious convergence of divine and human decisions and actions
involved in Christ's death by applying the same verb (1) to the
human perpetrators and (2) to the divine protagonists: 'hand over
(*paradidōmi*)'. (1) Judas agreed to hand Jesus over at a price (Mark
14: 10–11); the religious authorities handed Jesus over to Pilate the
Roman governor (Mark 15: 1, 10); and then Pilate handed Jesus over
to be crucified (Mark 15: 15). Thus Jesus became the victim of
human sinfulness. (2) Paul writes about the faithful love of Jesus
who would not run away: 'he loved me and handed himself over for
me' (Gal. 2: 20). By allowing his only-begotten Son to become and
remain vulnerable to the malicious decisions of human beings, God

too was involved in the 'handing over': 'He did not spare his own Son but handed him over for us all' (Rom. 8: 32; see 4: 25). Human malice and divine love astonishingly 'joined forces' in effecting a 'handing over' to death (and resurrection), which brought our redemption.[8] Along such lines we can endorse and make sense of Hebrews' picture of Jesus the High Priest as being a willing priest *and victim*, without that leading to the false conclusion that Jesus' death was an act of suicide.

BAPTISM, EUCHARIST, AND PRIESTHOOD

In the preface we cited two ecumenical documents that both appeared in 1982: the Faith and Order Commission's text *Baptism, Eucharist and Ministry* (*BEM*) and the *Final Report* of the Anglican–Roman Catholic International Commission (ARCIC). Without ex-plicitly citing Hebrews but with that letter obviously in mind, both texts characterized the priesthood of Christ as the 'unique priesthood of the new covenant'. 'Unique' denotes something that is the only example of its kind, but does not necessarily exclude the possibility of others somehow, albeit secondarily, participating in what is unique. This allows both documents, which came from an ecumenical dia-logue and consensus, to recognize some participated priesthood that 'derives from' Christ's priesthood and 'is wholly dependent upon it' (*Final Report*, 36; see *BEM* 17, both text and commentary). God established a new priesthood, but its 'uniqueness' does not mean that it can in no way be shared in.

Baptism and the Eucharist are key to the issue here. Do these two basic sacraments, which historically have been understood as the grounds for the common priesthood of the faithful (baptism) and for the ordained ministry of the priests who celebrate the Eucharist, feature at all in Hebrews and its account of Christ's unique priest-hood?

---

[8] See further G. O'Collins, *Jesus Our Redeemer: A Christian Approach to Salvation* (Oxford: Oxford University Press, 2007), 169–72.

Repentance and faith are understood in Hebrews to lead to baptism, a rite of initiation that includes a laying-on of hands (6: 2), cleanses hearts, and brings a life of faith, hope, and love. The grace of baptism means 'approaching' God in *faith* (10: 22), 'holding fast' to the confession of *hope* (10: 23), and 'considering' how to help others through *love* and good deeds (10: 24).

Hebrews does not at this point characterize as priestly such a picture of the life of the baptized. However, the letter goes on, as we have seen, to express in sacrificial language both the continual praise and confession of God and the practical exercise of love (13: 15–16). This Christian life on the part of the baptized takes place 'through Christ' (13: 15). He makes possible the sacrificial and self-sacrificing life of baptized Christians. Since 'sacrifice' (and sacrificial language) and 'priest' (and priestly language) are correlative terms (see 8: 2), Hebrews is in fact speaking, equivalently, of the common priesthood of all the baptized.

As regards the Eucharist, Koester finds in Hebrews no clear allusions to the Lord's Supper.[9] Yet he recognizes the real possibility of such an allusion: 'When Hebrews invites the baptized to draw near to God through the flesh and blood of Christ (10: 19–25), one may imagine that the context is a Eucharistic celebration, where the faithful "eat" and receive "grace" from the "altar" (13: 9–10).'[10] For Koester, while 'altar' might refer to the Eucharist, it more probably alludes to the cross or sacrificial death of Jesus.[11] The reference to '*eating* from the altar', however, seems to make a Eucharistic sense more plausible. It seems less plausible to take 'eating' in the sense of believing in Jesus' cross or sacrificial death.

What we find more decisive are the references in Hebrews to Christ as mediator of the new covenant (9: 15; 12: 24; see 8: 6), to the 'blood of the covenant', and to 'the blood of the eternal covenant' (13: 20). According to Paul and Luke, Jesus said at the Last Supper: 'This cup is the new covenant in my blood' (1 Cor. 11: 25; Luke 22: 20). Mark and Matthew cite a slightly different liturgical tradition: 'this is my

---

[9] Koester, *Hebrews*, 127–9.
[10] Ibid. 128.
[11] Ibid. 568–9.

blood of the covenant' (Mark 14: 24; Matt. 26: 28).[12] The four accounts
derive from two slightly different traditions for celebrating the Eucharist (on the one hand Paul and Luke, and on the other Mark and
Matthew). Hebrews pushes beyond all these accounts of the Last
Supper and makes it clear that, just as the covenant at Mount Sinai
was established by a sacrifice (9: 18–21), so the sacrificial death of Jesus
established a new, superior covenant. Around the Mediterranean world
Christians heard at their Eucharistic celebrations the language of 'the
covenant' and 'the blood of the covenant'. In using such language the
author of Hebrews and his audience would, one can confidently pre-
sume, share an obvious reference to the celebration of the Eucharist.

We are not arguing that the Eucharist was 'integral' to the 'argument'
being developed by the author of Hebrews.[13] The celebration of the
Eucharist, still less some special group of ministers to preside at Eucharistic celebrations, is simply not an issue raised by Hebrews. Yet, like some
other themes (e.g. baptism), the Eucharist could be present without
playing a major role in the text. The choice should not become: either
the Eucharist is integral to the argument of Hebrews or it is not there at all.

Early Christianity pressed the relationship between the Eucharist,
the ordained ministry, and Christ's priesthood on different grounds.
First, Clement of Alexandria (d. around AD 215) judged Melchizedek's
offering of bread and wine (Gen. 14: 18) to be a 'type' foreshadowing
what Christ did at the Last Supper (*Stromata*, 4. 25). Since the priest-
king Melchizedek 'resembles' and foreshadows the Son of God (Heb.
7: 3), he can be seen to do this in ways not explicitly considered by
Hebrews: for instance, when he offers Abraham bread and wine.

Then, in the third century, St Cyprian of Carthage (d. 258) put all
this firmly in the context of Christ's priesthood and Christian priests
who participate in that priesthood. A Christian priest who offers
bread and wine in the Eucharist serves to perpetuate the offering of
Christ the High Priest at the Last Supper: 'If Christ Jesus is himself
the great High Priest (*summus sacerdos*) of God the Father and if he
offered himself as a sacrifice to the Father and directed that this
should be done in remembrance of him, then without a doubt that

---

[12] Heb. 9: 20 ('saying this [is] the blood of the covenant') intriguingly echoes Mark
14: 26 ('he said then, "this is my blood of the covenant"').
[13] Koester, *Hebrews*, 128, n. 269.

priest (*sacerdos*) truly serves in Christ's stead who imitates what
Christ did.' Cyprian draws the conclusion: 'he [the priest] offers up
a true and complete sacrifice to God the Father in the Church when
he proceeds to offer it just as he sees Christ himself to have offered it'
(*Letters*, 63. 14. 4).[14] The authority of the Letter to the Hebrews
obviously supported calling Christ 'the High Priest' and speaking
of his self-offering in sacrifice. The Christian leader of the liturgical
assembly, who celebrated the Eucharist in 'memory' of Christ, was
understood to 'act in Christ's stead' and offer 'a true and complete
sacrifice to God'.

Furthermore, the psalm that Hebrews cited several times when
insisting that Christ is a priest 'forever' encouraged such teaching
about the Eucharist and Christian priests. The continued offering of
the Eucharist corresponded to, and was even required by, Christ's
eternal priesthood. Acting on the mandate to 'do this in memory of
me' (1 Cor. 11: 24; Luke 22: 19) was understood to express *visibly* the
permanent priesthood of Christ that was expressed *invisibly* in his
interceding constantly for all at the right hand of the Father. By
connecting the bread and wine offered by Melchizedek with the eternal
priesthood of Christ, Cyprian and others supported the permanent,
even daily, celebration of the Eucharist. They did not inaugurate such a
permanent celebration. Paul, the evangelists, and Acts, usually without
a hint as to who presided, indicate that such Eucharistic celebration
was already taking place from the very start of Christianity. What
Cyprian and others did promote, however, was a sense that those
who presided at the Eucharist shared in the one high priesthood of
Christ that Hebrews presented.

CHRIST AS PRIEST AND VICTIM: A SUMMARY

Before moving beyond the Scriptures to examine subsequent developments in beliefs (and connected practice) about the priesthood of
Christ, let us summarize what we have gleaned from the New Testament,

---

[14] Trans. G. W. Clarke, *The Letters of St. Cyprian of Carthage*, vol. 3 (Mahwah,
NJ: Paulist Press, 1986), 106.

or at least argued for on its basis. We can set out our findings schematically:

- Christ was/is a priest or rather the unique High Priest (Hebrews).
- Christ's priesthood began with the incarnation (Hebrews probably), and was deployed in his public (priestly) ministry (the Gospels; Hebrews implicitly).
- This sacrifice was motivated by obedience (Hebrews) and love (Paul: Gal. 2: 20; see Rom. 5: 8).
- By his priestly sacrifice he expiated sin (the Gospels; Paul: Rom. 3: 25; Hebrews; Revelation).
- By his sacrifice he inaugurated the new covenant (the Gospels; Paul: 1 Cor. 11: 25; Hebrews).
- His sacrifice occurred once and for all; it is unrepeatable (Hebrews and Paul: Rom. 6: 10).
- All human beings were/are the beneficiaries of his sacrifice (the Gospels; Paul: Rom. 3: 23–5; Hebrews).
- His sacrifice brought salvation (Hebrews), access to God (Ephesians; Hebrews), and reconciliation (Paul: Rom. 5: 10–11, 2 Cor. 5: 18–20).
- In his sacrifice Christ was also victim (John; Paul: 1 Cor. 5: 7; 1 Peter; Hebrews).
- His sacrifice is prefigured and illustrated by the ceremonies of Yom Kippur (Paul: Rom. 3: 25; Hebrews; 1 John 2: 2 probably) and by the Passover Lamb (John; Paul: 1 Cor. 5: 7; Revelation).
- His priestly intercession continues permanently (Paul: Rom. 8: 34; Hebrews).
- Even if Christ's priesthood is unique, the baptized share in the priesthood of Christ (Paul; 1 Peter; Revelation; Hebrews).
- The baptized also share in that priesthood through the Eucharist (Paul; the Gospels; Hebrews probably; 1 Pet. 2: 9 possibly).
- They also share by anticipation in the heavenly liturgy, centred on the Lamb and on God (Revelation).

5

Some Church Fathers
on Christ's Priesthood

The first millennium of Christianity provides some but not much explicit teaching about the priesthood of Christ. The references to him as priest are scattered and yield little by way of systematic thought. The major New Testament document on his priesthood, the Letter to the Hebrews, was acknowledged as canonical in the East from the second century. But in the West, despite its being quoted and echoed by St Clement of Rome in a letter written to the Corinthian Christians around AD 96, Hebrews was not clearly accepted as canonical before the fourth century.[1] In any case the fathers of the Church, East or West, rarely wrote commentaries on Hebrews.[2] The earliest seems to have been one by Origen (d. c. 254). Only four fragments survive from that commentary. But some of his extant homilies on Leviticus (not to mention a few other works) deal with the priesthood of Christ, where he examined the new high priest in the light of the old and quoted or echoed Hebrews.[3] Let us begin with Clement, St Ignatius of Antioch, and St Polycarp, and then move to Origen.

---

[1] For a summary of the early 'reception' of Hebrews, see 'Hebrews, Epistle to the', in F. L. Cross and E. A. Livingstone (eds.), *Oxford Dictionary of the Christian Church* (3rd edn., Oxford: Oxford University Press, 2005), 747; hereafter *ODCC*. See ibid. for entries on the Church fathers who will be mentioned in this chapter.

[2] For lists of early and later commentaries on Hebrews, see H. W. Attridge, *The Epistle to the Hebrews* (Philadelphia: Fortress Press, 1989), 413–15; C. R. Koester, *Hebrews* (New York: Doubleday, 2001), 135–9.

[3] On Origen's use of Hebrews in his extant works, see R. A. Greer, *The Captain of Our Salvation: A Study in the Patristic Exegesis of Hebrews* (Tübingen: Mohr (Siebeck), 1973), 7–64.

CLEMENT, IGNATIUS OF ANTIOCH,
AND POLYCARP

In a letter to the Church of Corinth, where some younger individuals (who may also have been 'presbyters') had pitted themselves against a group of older 'presbyters', Clement aimed to heal this division. Whatever was the exact nature of the leadership problem among the Corinthian Christians, one of the central tasks of the older presbyters was the sacrifice they offered. Clement referred three times to Christ as 'high priest', described at length the Levitical priesthood (in particular, the relationship of Aaron the priest with the other tribes), and defended the 'approved officers (*dedokimasmenoi*)' (most likely 'presbyters, *presbuteroi*') who had 'offered sacrifices with innocence and holiness' and 'fulfilled a ministry (*leitourgia*) with honour and integrity'.[4]

Notoriously, the meaning of 'presbyters' and 'officers', along with their functions, is less than totally clear in this letter, written at a time of transition to settled ministerial order. How were these presbyters appointed? Did the 'sacrifices' they 'offered' point to their presiding at the celebration of the Eucharist? Despite the ambiguities, 1 Clement has its value in being the first post-New Testament example of a controversy concerning the nature of ministry that examines Christian priesthood by returning to its major source, the High Priest of Hebrews. Down the centuries this pattern will recur: a crisis over priests and their function will lead to some clarifying of priesthood in the light of the original priesthood of Christ himself.

Clement closes his letter with liturgical language that invokes Christ as the High Priest:

May the all-seeing God and Master of spirits and Lord of all flesh [Num. 16: 22; 27: 16] who chose the Lord Jesus Christ and us through him to be his own people [Deut. 14: 2] grant to every soul over whom his magnificent and holy name has been invoked [in baptism] faith, fear, peace, patience, long-suffering, self-control, purity, and sobriety. So may we win his approval through our

---

[4] Clement's *First Letter*, 44. 4–6; trans. C. C. Richardson, *Early Christian Fathers*, vol. 1 (London: SCM Press, 1953), 64. For striking parallels and allusions to Hebrews in *1 Clement*, see D. A. Hagner, *The Use of the Old and New Testaments in Clement of Rome* (Leiden: Brill, 1973), 179–95.

High Priest and defender Jesus Christ. Through him be glory, majesty, might and honour to God, now and forevermore. Amen.[5]

St Ignatius of Antioch, in a letter written to the Christians of Philadelphia ten or fifteen years after 1 Clement, also grapples with division in the early Church. He praises 'presbyters (*presbuteroi*)' and 'deacons (*diakonoi*)' who have proved loyal to their bishop (*episcopos*) by remaining 'on his side'.[6] The bishop does not owe his ministry to the Christian people but to the 'Father and the Lord Jesus Christ'.[7] Once again, controversy in a particular community (here Philadelphia rather than Corinth) over those who minister in Christ's name occasions an appeal to his priesthood. The cluster of characteristics mentioned by Ignatius blend some themes from Hebrews (High Priest, Holy of Holies, and access to God's presence) with the Johannine theme of Christ as 'door' (John 10: 7, 9). He is even the door for all, including the patriarchs and prophets who preceded him in history: 'Priests (*hiereis*) are a fine thing, but better still is the High Priest (*archiereus*) who was entrusted with the Holy of Holies. He alone was entrusted with God's secrets. He is the door to the Father. Through it there enter Abraham, Isaac, and Jacob, the prophets and the apostles and the Church. All find their place in God's unity.'[8]

Human priests and problems connected with them bring to mind Christ and the superiority of his high priesthood. Even though the high priests of the old covenant could enter into the Holy of Holies, Christ alone was 'entrusted with God's secrets'; only through Christ can one enter the heavenly sanctuary and enjoy the presence of the Father.

In this particular controversy Ignatius reminds his addressees that it was Jesus the High Priest who has effected their unity ('place in God's unity'). At once he relates this unity to the Eucharistic meal (celebrated on an altar and understood as a sacrifice) and to the monarchical episcopate (in place in Asia Minor by the early second century): 'Be careful, then, to observe a single Eucharist. For there is one flesh of our Lord, Jesus Christ, and one cup of his blood that

---

[5] *1 Clement*, 64; Richardson, 79.
[6] *To the Philadelphians*, proem; Richardson, 107–8.
[7] *To the Philadelphians*, 1; Richardson, 108.
[8] *To the Philadelphians*, 9; Richardson, 110.

makes us one, and one altar just as there is one bishop along with the
presbytery [or presbyterate] and the deacons.'[9]

In a letter, sent to the Philippians in connection with Ignatius and
a desire to make a collection of his letters, St Polycarp of Smyrna
blends the high priesthood of Christ into his prayer: 'May God and
the Father of our Lord Jesus Christ, and the eternal High Priest
himself, the Son of God, Jesus Christ, build you up in faith, truth,
and in all gentleness.'[10]

When Polycarp came, many years later, to be martyred around AD
155, his prayer was more clearly Trinitarian by including twice the
Holy Spirit. He prayed to God the Father in terms that went beyond
Hebrews by suggesting that in his martyrdom he shared in the self-
sacrifice of Christ the High Priest: 'I bless you because you have
deemed me worthy of this day and hour, to take my part in the
number of the martyrs, in the cup of your Christ [Mark 10: 38–9 par.,
along with the 'cup' at the Last Supper], for resurrection to eternal
life of soul and body in the immortality of the Holy Spirit' ['the
eternal Spirit' of Heb. 9: 14?].' Polycarp added: 'May I be received in
your presence this day as a rich and acceptable sacrifice.' He ended by
saying: 'for this and for everything, I praise you, I bless you, I glorify
you, through the eternal and heavenly High Priest in heaven, Jesus
Christ, your beloved Servant, through whom be glory to you with
him and the Holy Spirit, now and for all ages to come. Amen.'[11]
'Through our eternal High Priest in heaven' evokes, of course, the
repeated language of Hebrews about Christ being the High Priest
forever (according to the order of Melchizedek), who has entered
into heaven itself (Heb. 9: 24), where he lives always to make intercession for those who approach God through him (Heb. 7: 25). It
also evokes the closing exhortation of Hebrews to 'offer continually
through him [Christ] a sacrifice of praise to God' (13: 15).

Once we move into the third century we find that more reflection
on Christ's priesthood and participation in it begin to appear. Related developments were taking place on three other fronts. First,
baptismal creeds evolved, and would eventually be replaced by

[9] *To the Philadelphians*, 4; Richardson, 108.
[10] Polycarp, *To the Philippians*, 12; Richardson, 136.
[11] *Martyrdom of Polycarp*, 14. 2–3; Richardson, 154.

the Nicene Creed (325), at least in its fuller form as the Nicene-
Constantinopolitan Creed (381). Second, Eucharistic prayers developed in the third century: the Liturgy of Addai and Mari, the
Egyptian form of the Liturgy of St Basil, and (if it does belong
there and not to the fourth century) the *Apostolic Tradition* of St
Hippolytus. Third, we find the earliest rites of ordination: for instance, in the *Apostolic Tradition*. Origen witnesses to the way in
which, at least in the East, 'bishop (*episcopos*)', 'presbyter', and 'dea-
con' had become the standard arrangement and names for ordained
Christian ministers. Origen himself applies Old Testament language
for 'priests (*hiereis*)' to the Christian 'bishops' and 'presbyters'.

ORIGEN ON CHRIST'S PRIESTHOOD

Origen understood Christ to be the source and archetype of all
priesthood and to exercise an impact on every rational being. In
the course of his homilies on Leviticus, Origen echoed and extended
New Testament language about Christ as 'King of kings' and 'Lord of
lords' to call him not merely the Priest of priests but 'the High Priest
of the high priests'.[12] Encouraged by the theme of 'all things, whether
on earth or *in heaven*' being reconciled to God through Christ's
sacrifice (Col. 1: 20), Origen declared: 'He [Christ] is the great
High Priest not for the sake of humankind alone but for every
being, offering himself as a sacrificial offering once and for all' (*In
Ioannem*, 1. 40; *PG* 14. 93). Where Hebrews wrote of Christ 'tasting
death for all' (Heb. 2: 9), Origen interpreted 'all' to include angels
and even the whole cosmos. In his all-embracing priestly role, Christ
has graced the angelic spirits, expiated the sins of human beings, and
restored the entire universe.

In his homilies on Leviticus, often cited for their contribution
towards understanding Jewish and Christian self-definition in the
third century, Origen offers an extended commentary on Christ the
High Priest, especially in relation to the Aaronic priesthood and their

---

[12] *Hom.* 6. 2. 6; see Origen, *Homilies on Leviticus 1–16*, trans. G. W. Barkley
(Washington, DC: Catholic University of America Press, 1990), 119.

functions.[13] While there are genuine debates about Origen's treat-
ment of Jewish issues in his works, he saw the Synagogue and the
Church as 'standing side by side to face the pagan attack', and
'Christianity as the fulfillment of the best elements in Judaism'.[14]

The homilies of Origen scrutinize the root meaning of issues for
Christians, and do so by finding allegories. He prefaces his homilies
by drawing attention to the foolishness of those Christians who want
to follow literally the meaning and practice of Old Testament texts.
Such a literal approach would lead them to 'sacrifice calves and lambs
and to offer fine wheat flour with incense and oil'.[15] Origen himself
presents Christ as the new High Priest in the light of an allegorical
approach to the old covenant. Thus he interprets the first of the two
sanctuaries found in the Tent of Witness as the Church,[16] and the
second as the heavenly sanctuary and divine throne where Christ
continues to exercise his work as High Priest.[17]

In an earlier (fifth) homily Origen moves beyond any literal meaning in the physical act of eating when he explains the priestly action
of Christ in offering himself to God (Heb. 9: 14) for the sins of the
world. (He refers to the author of Hebrews as 'the apostle', reflecting
the Eastern belief that Paul was the author of the letter.) Origen starts
from statements in Leviticus about sacrificial offering (6: 16, 18): 'the
priest who offers it will eat it.' Origen finds this 'hard to understand',
since 'that which it says must be eaten seems to be referring to the sin;
just as in another place the prophet says concerning the priests that
"they will eat the sins of my people" [Hos. 4: 8]'. This 'shows that the
priest ought to eat the sin of the one who is offering'. What, then, of
Christ who is both 'the sacrifice which is offered for the sin of the
world and the priest who brings the offering? The apostle explains
this by one word when he says, "who offered himself to God" [Heb.

[13] On Origen see J. A. McGuckin (ed.), *The Westminster Handbook to Origen*
(Louisville, Ky.: Westminster John Knox, 2004). For Origen's reflections on Christ
as High Priest, see id., 'Origen's Doctrine of Priesthood', *Clergy Review*, 70 (1985),
277–86, 318–25; and Greer, *The Captain of Our Salvation*, 58–60.
[14] N. R. M. de Lange, *Origen and the Jews: Studies in Jewish–Christian Relations in
Third-century Palestine* (Cambridge: Cambridge University Press, 1976), 73.
[15] *Hom.* 1. 1. 2; Barkley, 30.
[16] *Hom.* 9. 9. 3; Barkley, 196.
[17] *Hom.* 9. 9. 5; Barkley, 197.

9: 14] . . . This is the priest who eats and consumes "the sins of the people", about whom it is said, "You are a priest forever after the order of Melchizedek" [Heb. 5: 6, citing Ps. 110. 4]. Therefore, my Lord and Saviour eats "the sins of the people".'

This conclusion leaves Origen with the question: how could Christ the High Priest eat the sins of the people? He finds an answer by introducing another passage of Hebrews: 'our God is a consuming (*katanaliskon*) fire' (12: 29, citing Deut. 4: 24). 'What does the "God of fire" consume?' Origen sweeps aside any literal answer by asking: 'will we be so senseless as to think that God consumes the firewood, straw, or hay [1 Cor. 3: 12]? The "God of fire" consumes human sins. He consumes them, devours them, and purges them, as he says in another place, "I will purge you with fire for purity" [Isa. 1: 25].'[18]

Thus Origen draws on instructions concerning sacrifices for the Levitical priests and a verse of Hebrews about God as a 'consuming fire' to illustrate how Christ's self-offering 'eats up' the sins of human beings. Thus far in his fifth homily he has provided some vivid reflections on what Hebrews states about Christ's priestly self-offering removing human sin (e.g. Heb. 9: 26). But then, once again citing Leviticus, Origen moves beyond anything we find explicitly in Hebrews to focus on the ministry of ordained Christian priests.

As well as being called to a life of holiness and wisdom, they share in the *priesthood Christ gave to the Church* by conveying like him divine forgiveness to sinners. A prophetic text illuminates what Christian priests do in imitation of Christ the High Priest: 'the ministers and priests of the Church receive "the sins of the people" [Hos. 4: 8] according to the example of the One who gave the priesthood to the Church. Imitating their Teacher, let them grant the people forgiveness of sins.'[19] Origen refers here to the priestly activity of Jesus during his public ministry when he not only taught but also conveyed forgiveness to sinners. He refers also to the sacramental practices of reconciliation that are emerging in Origen's own priestly ministry.

---

[18] *Hom.* 5. 3. 2; Barkley, 93–4.

[19] We do not have the Greek original of Origen's text; in the Latin translation by Rufinus of Aquileia (d. 411) 'the ministers and priests' are called *ministri* and *sacerdotes* (presumably translations of the original *hiereis*).

Origen takes it for granted that some Christians ('the ministers and priests') participate in a specific way in the priesthood of Christ through their role in forgiving and reconciling sinners. His concern is to highlight the spiritual qualities required of such ministerial priests. To that end he echoes a text from Leviticus about the Aaronic priests eating what remains of the sacrifices 'in a holy place', the Tent of Witness: 'these priests of the Church ought to be so perfected and learned in the priestly duties that they consume "the sins of the people in a holy place, in the court of the Tent of Witness [Lev. 6: 16]", not sinning themselves.'[20] Origen transfers this 'holy place' from any geographic location in a cultic sanctuary to the holy way of life required of priests: 'a sound faith and holy conduct are "a holy place"'.[21]

Origen concludes this fifth homily by declaring that a 'pure heart and good work' will enable priests to 'have a part in the divine sacrifice through the eternal High Priest, our Lord and Saviour, Jesus Christ'.[22] When encouraging ministerial priests to live a holy way of life in the service of Christ and the Church, Origen might have cited appropriate texts from Hebrews about the unblemished, sinless life of Jesus the High Priest. Instead he appropriates, as we have seen, a phrase from Leviticus (about 'eating the sins of the people') to develop his reflections on Christ and those who through ordination share in his priesthood.

Given Origen's propensity for gleaning Christian meaning from Old Testament texts, it is not surprising that he focuses at length on something not taken up by Hebrews: the vestments worn by the priests (Exod. 28: 1–43). In its outer, visible form this clothing represents the inner character and virtues embodied, supremely, in the priestly activity of Christ, 'the one great High Priest'.[23] In his sixth homily Origen detects rich moral significance in the washing of the Old Testament priests and the various vestments with which they

---

[20] *Hom.* 5. 3. 3; Barkley, 94–5.
[21] *Hom.* 5. 3. 4; Barkley, 95.
[22] *Hom.* 5. 12. 9; Barkley, 115.
[23] *Hom.* 6. 2. 6; Barkley, 119. Exploiting a possibility suggested by Heb. 10: 5, Origen calls 'the flesh' of Christ his 'priestly robe' (*Hom.* 9. 2. 3; Barkley, 178).

were clothed: for instance, in the cape, belt, breastplate, and mitre of the Jewish high priest. Interior qualities give meaning to an array of garments.

To conclude: Origen understands all Christians, and not merely ministerial priests, to share in Christ's priesthood. Ministerial priesthood, for Origen, seems to differ only in function and not in nature from the common priesthood that comes through faith and baptism. As McGuckin puts it, for Origen 'any rigid distinction between priesthood of the faithful and priesthood of the clergy leads in the end to a devaluation of both notions'.[24] The baptized have the dignity of being able to participate in the high priesthood of Christ by serving as high priests themselves: 'you too can function as a high priest before God within the temple of your spirit if you would prepare your garments with zeal and vigilance; if the word of God has washed you and made you clean, and the anointing and grace of your baptism have remained uncontaminated.' Origen pictures the high-priestly holiness of Christian life as being 'clothed with two garments, of the letter and the spirit', being 'girded twice' so as to be 'pure in flesh and spirit', being 'adorned "with a cape" of works and "a breastplate" of wisdom'.[25] This remarkable picture of the high-priestly possibilities for all baptized Christians goes beyond anything we have examined in Paul, 1 Peter, Revelation, and Hebrews. Those New Testament witnesses, as we have seen, exhorted all the faithful to live united with Christ a 'priestly' existence. Origen calls it a 'high-priestly' existence.

ST CYPRIAN OF CARTHAGE ON CHRIST'S PRIESTHOOD

In the last chapter we saw how Cyprian understood the Christian *sacerdos* (by which he usually meant a bishop) to make Christ and his

---

[24] McGuckin, 'Origen's Doctrine of Priesthood', 324.
[25] *Hom.* 6. 5. 2; Barkley, 125.

sacrifice present and effective through the celebration of the Eucharist. This presupposed that the priesthood of Christ was somehow
shared with bishops (and other *sacerdotes*). In other words, the
priesthood of Christ, while unique, was open to some kind of
secondary, ministerial participation. How does Cyprian understand
this participated priesthood? A major letter (no. 63), 'the first extant
study on the nature of the Eucharist', offers some lines for a reply.
This letter, while addressed to an episcopal colleague, Caecilius, 'is
more in the nature of a circular pastoral letter directed to Cyprian's
fellow bishops generally'.[26]

The main aim of the letter is to expound and defend the traditional practice of using a cup of wine mixed with water for the
Eucharist. Apparently some non-orthodox groups of Christian were
using water alone in the Eucharistic cup.[27] Once again we have an
example of some aberration or crisis among ministers in the Church
provoking a reaction, which expounded and defended appropriate
priestly activity and in so doing clarified something of Christ's own
priesthood.

The sacrifice of Christ, Cyprian insists, was linked to the past,
through being 'foreshadowed in mystery' by a 'priest of the most
high God', Melchizedek and the sacrifice he offered of bread and
wine. 'Who', Cyprian asks, 'is more truly a priest of the most high
God than our Lord Jesus Christ, who offered sacrifice to God the
Father and made the very same offering as Melchizedek had done, viz.
bread and wine, that is to say, his own Body and Blood?'[28] Thus
Cyprian goes beyond the way that the Letter to the Hebrews construed
the Melchizedek story (Gen. 14: 18–20) by adding a further detail: the
bread and wine that Melchizedek offered to Abraham was a sacrifice
which made present in advance 'a symbol of Christ's sacrifice'. When
'the Lord brought to fulfillment and completion that symbolic action,
he offered bread and a cup mixed with wine, and so he who is Fullness
itself fulfilled the truth of that prefigured symbol'.[29]

[26] G. W. Clarke, *The Letters of St. Cyprian of Carthage*, vol. 3 (Mahwah, NJ: Paulist Press, 1986), 288.
[27] Ibid. 288–90.
[28] *Letters*, 63. 4. 1; Clarke, 99.
[29] *Letters*, 63. 4. 3; Clarke, 100.

Cyprian thus links tightly together the (foreshadowing) offering of Melchizedek with the (completed) offering at the Last Supper, which committed Christ to his death on Calvary. At the Last Supper Christ ritually expressed his sacrificial intentions and made present his self-sacrifice, which was fully achieved and consummated on Calvary. His followers share in this sacrificial action of Christ the High Priest. Cyprian witnesses to the common faith of Christians that 'at every sacrifice [every celebration of the Eucharist]' the 'passion of our Lord is the sacrifice we offer... As often as we offer the cup in remembrance of the Lord and his passion, we are doing what all are agreed the Lord did before us.'[30] Speaking as a bishop and addressing his episcopal colleagues, Cyprian testifies to their inherited belief that when celebrating the Eucharist they offer a sacrifice, the passion of the Lord. The high priesthood of Christ is a priesthood in which others share. His priesthood was not confined to the temporal limits of his earthly life: it was both anticipated in advance by Melchizedek and participated in subsequently.

Commentators on Cyprian debate various issues: what were the precise links for him between the Levitical priesthood, Christ, and Christian priesthood? Whom did Cyprian consider a *sacerdos*?[31] What was the bishop's role as *sacerdos*? Scholarly replies vary. But there is little dispute over Cyprian's call to his episcopal colleagues to walk in the light of Christ, follow him, and to observe his commandments.[32] In another letter he insists that 'bishops (*sacerdotes*) ought to be humble because both the Lord and his apostles were humble'.[33] The humble character of Christ the High Priest proposes a model for imitation. The theme of Christ's high-priestly humility and the humility expected from those who share in his priesthood will

---

[30] *Letters*, 63, 17. 1; Clarke, 107.

[31] On Cyprian's use of *sacerdos*, see L. F. Bacchi, *The Theology of Ordained Ministry in the Letters of Augustine of Hippo* (San Francisco: International Scholars Publications, 1998), 58–9. J. D. Laurance points out that 'Cyprian was the first Latin writer to use *sacerdos* of the leader of the Eucharist' (*Priest as Type of Christ: The Leader of the Eucharist in Salvation History According to Cyprian of Carthage* (New York: P. Lang, 1984), 220).

[32] Cyprian, *Letters*, 63, 18. 3–4; Clarke, 108–9.

[33] Cyprian, *Letters*, 66. 3. 1; Clarke, 117.

recur in the writings of St John Chrysostom, bishop of Constantinople (d. 407), and St Augustine, bishop of Hippo (d. 430).

ST JOHN CHRYSOSTOM ON
CHRIST'S PRIESTHOOD

In the thirty-four homilies that he delivered on the Letter to the
Hebrews during his last years in Constantinople, Chrysostom nat-
urally had much to say about the priesthood of Christ. Like many of
his contemporaries, he believed that Paul was the author of Hebrews
and at times quoted the apostle's undoubtedly authentic letters to
develop or reinforce arguments in Hebrews.

Shaped by the more literal approach of the School of Antioch
(rather than the allegorical approach of the School of Alexandria),
Chrysostom normally stays close to the drift of Hebrews, even if he
gives some conclusions his own twist. For instance, the author of
Hebrews takes it for granted that priesthood and sacrifice are correlative terms: 'every high priest is appointed to offer gifts and
sacrifices; hence it is necessary for this priest [Christ] also to have
something to offer' (8: 3). As Chrysostom paraphrases the statement,
'there is no priest without a sacrifice. It is then necessary that he
[Christ] also should have a sacrifice.' And that is 'why he died'.[34]
Chrysostom puts more bluntly than Hebrews the 'necessity' of
Christ's self-sacrificial death. Quoting Hebrews 5: 8–9, Chrysostom
also highlights obedience as a key ingredient in his priesthood but
presses beyond Hebrews by invoking 'the exceeding greatness of his
[Christ's] love' (*Hom.*, 8. 3). This is a love that invites imitation: 'let
us imitate him, let us look on him so as to love and to be loved. For
from Love good works proceed . . . out of love all good things arise.
For nothing is good which is not done through love' (*Hom.*, 19. 3).

---

[34] *Hom.* 14. 2; from St John Chrysostom, *Homilies on Hebrews*, trans. F. Gardiner, in
P. Schaff (ed.), *A Select Library of the Nicene and Post-Nicene Library of the Christian
Church*, vol. 15 (Grand Rapids, Mich.: Eerdmans, 1989), 333–555. We use Gardiner's
translation, making occasional corrections; for the original text of the homilies see J. P.
Migne (ed.), *Patrologia Graeca*, vol. 63 (Paris: L. Migne, 1862), 9–236.

In Chapter 3 we saw how Hebrews never explicitly raises (and answers) the question: when did Christ become High Priest? It implies that his entire human existence was priestly. Chrysostom is quite clear about this: Christ's high priesthood began with the incarnation: 'He did not come first and then become [High Priest], but came and became at the same time' (*Hom.*, 15. 4). In other words, through the human condition that he assumed, right from the outset high priesthood was an essential characteristic of the earthly existence of the incarnate Son of God.

In enunciating Christ's high-priestly role, the Letter to the Hebrews also calls him 'mediator,' and does so three times when presenting his priestly work as 'the mediator of a new/better covenant' (8: 6; 9: 15; 12: 24). But Hebrews does not take time to put the question, as Chysostom does: 'What is a mediator?' He replies: 'A mediator is not lord of the thing of which he is mediator, but the thing belongs to one person, and the mediator is another: as for instance, the mediator of a marriage is not the bridegroom but one who aids him who is about to be married.' Chrysostom, when applying this scheme, moves from a mediation that takes place in an interpersonal situation of attraction and love to a mediation that deals with a situation of alienation and a breakdown in interpersonal relations. 'The Son', he writes, 'became mediator between the Father and us. The Father . . . was angry against us, and was displeased [with us] as being estranged [from him]. [The Son] accordingly became Mediator between us and him, and prevailed with him' (*Hom.*, 16. 2).

Here Christ's high-priestly mediation is portrayed with accents not found in Hebrews: it worked to placate and win over a 'displeased' and even 'angry' God the Father. In another homily Chrysostom makes this even more explicit when commenting on the language of Hebrews about Christ 'entering heaven' and 'appearing for us/on our behalf in the presence of God' (Heb. 9: 24, 26). According to Chrysostom, the 'for us' means that Christ went up 'with a sacrifice which had the power to *propitiate* the Father' (*Hom.*, 17. 2; italics ours). This fateful development in interpreting Christ's high-priestly mediation turns up, as we will see, in Augustine, Aquinas, and among Catholics and Protestants in the aftermath of the Reformation.

Chrysostom picks up and expands the image Hebrews introduces of hope as 'a sure and steadfast anchor of the soul, a hope that enters

the inner shrine behind the curtain, where Jesus, a forerunner on our behalf, has entered' (Heb. 6: 19–20). Chrysostom pictures Christ as an anchor pulling believers from the rough sea into the heavenly harbour (*Hom.*, 11. 3). Christ is not 'merely' interceding for human beings at the right hand of the Father (e.g. Heb. 7: 25); he is hauling them into the heavenly sanctuary. He has gone ashore, pushing through the curtain of the Holy of Holies and pulling with him the anchor line attached to humanity, the ship in the outer court. Christ the High Priest is the anchor, now secure at the right hand of God and hauling a storm-tossed vessel closer and closer to port.

Chrysostom invokes here 'forerunner', a word with which the author of Hebrews supported the picture of a close link between this world and the heavenly sanctuary. Yet in making his point Chrysostom switches images—from a ship being hauled into port to a group of people following a lead runner on the same road: '[The author] did not simply say, "He is entered in", but "where he is entered in, a forerunner for us", as though we also ought to arrive. For there is no great interval between the forerunner and those who follow: otherwise he would not be a forerunner; for the forerunner and those who follow ought to be on the same road and to arrive after [each other]' (*Hom.*, 11. 4).

In Chapter 3 we showed how Hebrews 13: 15–16 parallels Romans 12: 1 by using cultic, sacrificial language to depict the appropriate lifestyle of believers. Without literally speaking of them as sharing in Christ's own priesthood, Hebrews implies this. When he treats the priesthood of all the baptized, Chrysostom does so quite explicitly and cites Romans rather than the final chapter of Hebrews: 'Let us bring such sacrifices as can be offered on that [heavenly] altar, no longer sheep and oxen, no longer blood and fat. All these things have been done away with; and there has been brought in their stead "the reasonable service" [Rom. 12: 1]. But what is this "reasonable service"? The offerings made through the soul; those made through the Spirit.' Such offerings, Chrysostom explains, 'have no need of a body, no need of instruments, nor of special places'. '*Each one is himself the priest*' of such offerings as 'moderation, temperance, mercifulness, enduring ill treatment, long suffering, humbleness of mind' (*Hom.*, 11. 5; italics ours). The altars and animals used for sacrifice in the old dispensation have given way to the new covenant. All believers can actively share now in the priesthood of Christ through acts of virtue

and the suitable interior disposition that accompanies them. Such are the sacrifices to be offered by all.

Chrysostom insists so much on a sacrificial lifestyle, a kind of priesthood of daily life, that he even states that if believers acted in such a manner they would not need the mediation of ordained priests. 'Mortify your body', he says. 'Let not the love of wealth burn or possess you . . . This is an excellent sacrifice, *needing no priest but him who brings it.* This is an excellent sacrifice, performed indeed below, but forthwith taken up on high.' Chrysostom uses sacrificial imagery to drive home the point: 'Do we not wonder that in former times fire came down and consumed all [e.g. 1 Kgs 18: 38]? It is possible now also that fire may come down far more wonderful than that, and consume all the offerings presented: nay rather, not consume but bear them up to heaven. For it does not reduce them to ashes, but offers them as gifts to God' (*Hom.*, 11. 6; italics ours).

In various subsequent homilies Chrysostom returns to the positive vision of priestly holiness of daily life that he draws from Hebrews: 'it is not merely freedom from sins which makes a man holy, but also the presence of the Spirit and the wealth of good works.' He hears a herald for Christ saying: 'I do not merely wish that you should be delivered from the mire, but also that you should be bright and beautiful' (*Hom.*, 17. 8).[35]

Chrysostom takes up 'heaven', a theme that recurs in Hebrews, and pictures it not so much as a 'place' but as the way of life worthy of Christians. 'If we are near to God', he says, 'we are in heaven. For what do I care about heaven, when I see the Lord of heaven, when I myself am become a heaven? . . . Let us then make our soul a heaven' (*Hom.*, 16. 7). This lovely invitation, 'let us then make our soul a heaven', could sum up Chrysostom's message to the people of Constantinople—his vision of what the one sacrifice of Christ the High Priest could and should mean in their lives.

---

[35] In the same passage Chrysostom draws on the story of King Nebuchadnezzar choosing handsome young Jewish captives for his royal court (Dan. 1: 3–6): 'if the Babylonian king, when he made choice of the youths from his captives, chose those who were beautiful in form and of fair countenance, much more is it needful that we, when we stand by the royal table [at the Eucharist], should be beautiful in form [I mean] that of the soul, having adornment of gold, our robe pure, our shoes royal, the face of our soul well-formed, the golden ornament put around it, even the girdle of truth.'

None of this emphasis on the Christian holiness and priestly self-sacrifice of daily life is intended to underplay the superiority and centrality of Christ the High Priest. Citing the dignity Hebrews assigns to Melchizedek, Chrystostom exclaims: 'If he who bears a type of Christ is so much better not merely than the [Aaronic] priests but even than the forefather himself of the priests [Aaron], what should we say of the reality [Christ]? You see how abundantly he shows his superiority' (*Hom.*, 12. 4). Christ surpasses even the best of the Jewish high priests: his priesthood (1) benefits all people and (2) lasts forever: (1) 'He is able to aid all men'. (2) In the Old Testament, 'the high priest, although he were worthy of admiration during the time in which he was [high priest], as Samuel, for instance, and any other such, but after this, no longer, for they were dead. But here [with Christ] it is not so' (*Hom.*, 13. 6).

Chrysostom also follows Hebrews (e.g. 5: 1) by assigning Christ's priesthood to his humanity, but adds a further twist concerning his kingship. In the whole sweep of Old Testament history kings performed cultic and priestly functions; it was only progressively, as we saw in Chapter 1, that priests became the only ones who could serve God at the altar. Chrysostom has noticed this shift and remarks: 'First it [the Old Testament priesthood] was royal and then it became sacerdotal, therefore also in regard to Christ: for King indeed he always was [through his divinity], but he has become priest from the time he assumed the flesh and offered the sacrifice [of himself]' (*Hom.*, 13. 2).[36]

Chrysostom likewise follows Hebrews when expounding the new covenant inaugurated by Christ's self-sacrifice, but he deals more explicitly with the link between that sacrifice and partaking in the Eucharist, 'the immortal Table' (*Hom.*, 13. 9). Like Origen, he recognizes the inseparable association of Christ's priesthood with the Eucharist. He emphasizes that the Eucharist is 'not another sacrifice'. 'We offer always the same [Sacrifice], or rather we perform a remembrance of a Sacrifice' (*Hom.*, 17. 6). Chrysostom introduces a medical analogy to account for the once-and-for-all sacrifice of Christ being repeatedly 'remembered' and applied. It is both a powerful medicine that has been 'applied once and not often' and that brings or should

[36] On Chrysostom attributing priesthood to Christ the man, see Greer, *The Captain of Our Salvation*, 284–5.

bring good health; yet it needs to be applied repeatedly because of the 'wounds' of human sin (*Hom.*, 17. 5).

In Chapter 2 we remarked on the Book of Revelation inviting the faithful on earth, already graced as a priestly people, to join in the heavenly liturgy, those hymns of praise and worship offered by angels and redeemed human beings to God and to the Lamb. Commenting on 'the heavenly things' (Heb. 11: 16) mentioned by the author of Hebrews, Chrysostom thinks of the 'heavenly hymns' already sung here on earth and asks: 'Do not we also who are below utter in concert with them the same things which the divine choirs of bodiless powers sing above?' (*Hom.*, 14. 3). In the same homily he cites the vigilance shown by combatants and their heralds as they prepare through the night to compete at the Olympic Games, and argues: 'If then he who is about to strive before men uses such forethought, much more will it befit us to be continually thoughtful and careful, since our whole life is a contest. Let every night then be a vigil, and let us be careful that when we go out in the day we do not make ourselves ridiculous.' Christ the High Priest is then portrayed as the divine Judge of those who sing on earth: 'the Judge of the contest is seated on the right hand of the Father, hearkening diligently that we utter not any false note, anything out of tune' (*Hom.*, 14. 10).

In portraying the High Priest of Hebrews, Chrysostom offers a range of rich images to encourage personal love for him. He directs the women in his audience to think of Christ as a perfect husband:

Tell me now, if you had a husband, a great and admirable man, who thoroughly loved you and cared for you, and you knew that he would live always and not die before you, and would give you all things to enjoy in security as your own, would you then have wished to possess anything [else]? Even if you had been stripped of all, would you not have thought yourself the richer for this [love of your husband]? (*Hom.*, 20. 7)

For parents Chrysostom pictures the search for God through Christ the High Priest as a desperate search for a son they have lost:

suppose that any among us has lost his son, what do we not do? What land, what sea do we not make the circuit of? Do we not reckon money, houses, and everything else as secondary to finding him? And should we find him, we cling to him, we hold him fast, we do not let him go. And when we are going to seek anything whatever, we busy ourselves in all ways to find what is

sought. How much more ought we to do this in regard to God, as seeking what is indispensable.

Chrysostom pleads in a pastoral way when he adds: 'But since we are weak, at least seek God as you seek your money or your son. Will you not leave your home for him? Have you never left your home for money?' (*Hom.*, 22. 6).

'Leaving your home' evokes a central theme in Hebrews: life is a 'horizontal' pilgrimage to a better, heavenly country and 'the city' God has prepared for us (Heb. 11: 14–16). Chrysostom gives this image a 'vertical' twist. Christian life means 'stretching' or lifting ourselves up from earth to heaven:

I myself know many men almost suspended apart from the earth, and beyond measure stretching up their hands . . . and praying with earnestness. Thus I would have you always, and if not always, at least very often; and if not very often, at least now and then, at least in the morning, at least in the evening prayers. For, tell me, can you not stretch forth the hands? Stretch forth the will, stretch forth as far you will, yes, even to heaven itself. (*Hom.*, 22. 7)

Let us sum up under eight headings what Chrysostom says about Christ's high priesthood when expounding the text of Hebrews. First, in some places he embellishes the images he finds. For instance, Christ becomes the *anchor* hauling human beings from rough seas into the heavenly port. Second, Chrysostom answers some questions not expressly answered in Hebrews: Christ was High Priest from the *first moment of his incarnate existence*. Third, his self-sacrifice is identified with the sacrifice of the Eucharist ('not another sacrifice'). Fourth, picturing Christ as both King and High Priest, Chrysostom unambiguously states that his priesthood benefits or can benefit all people. Fifth, Chrysostom moves beyond Hebrews by specifying the *loving* quality of Christ's self-sacrificing obedience. As we observed in Chapter 2, Paul also interpreted Christ's death in terms of love.

Sixth, Chrysostom takes from Hebrews the motif of Christ's high priesthood involving mediation, but develops this mediating role as *propitiating* a 'displeased' God. Seventh, as the bishop of a city where many Christians seem to have become lethargic in practising their faith, Chrysostom goes further than Hebrews in spelling out the priestly behaviour required of believers. At times he becomes lyrical

in his exhortations, when urging his audience, 'let us then make our soul a heaven', and encouraging them to join the heavenly choirs in the heavenly liturgy. Eighth, his rhetorical powers become fully deployed through his images of a perfectly loving husband, a lost son, and Christian life as stretching up one's hands to heaven.

ST AUGUSTINE ON CHRIST'S PRIESTHOOD

Augustine's reflections on the priesthood of Christ emerged (1) as he reacted to the old pagan rites (still part of the religious and social fabric of urban and country life,[37] even after the emperor Theodosius I had outlawed pagan worship in 386 and the emperor Honorius had closed down in 399 a pagan temple in Carthage),[38] and (2) as he was forced by the Donatist controversy to examine the place of the ministerial priesthood within Christian life.[39] Thus Augustine's account of Christ as priest was constructed, at least partly, in a polemical context. He used Christ's priesthood to establish and support a Christian community and language that would promote true conversion of heart and reconciliation over and against pagan and Donatist forms of religious community and language, which could

---

[37] Roman public officials often served also as priests; see M. Beard, 'Priesthood in the Roman Republic', in M. Beard and J. North (eds.), *Pagan Priests: Religion and Power in the Ancient World* (London: Duckworth, 1990), 19–48.

[38] Much of Augustine's teaching and preaching belonged to a world in which he still had to react to pagan cults: see R. Dodaro, '*Christus Sacerdos*: Augustine's Preaching against Pagan Priests in the Light of S[ermon] Dolbeau 26 and 23', in *Augustin prédicateur 395–411*, Actes du Colloque International de Chantilly 5–7 septembre, 1996 (Paris: Institut d'Etudes Augustiniennes, 1998), 377–93, at 383. Theodosius' action in forbidding sacrifices to idols helped push such worship underground; it certainly produced serious resentment. In response to the emperor's edict a famous orator, Libanius of Antioch, wrote: 'to snatch from a region the temple which protects it is like tearing out its eye, killing it, annihilating it' (quoted by H. D. Saffrey, 'The Piety and Prayers of Ordinary Men and Women in Late Antiquity', in A. H. Armstrong (ed.), *Classical Mediterranean Spirituality: Egyptian, Greek, Roman* (London: Routledge & Kegan Paul, 1986), 195–213, at 200.

[39] On the Donatist controversy see 'Donatism', *ODCC* 503.

not genuinely promote these spiritual goods. At the heart of the matter lay the question: what was 'it to be a Christian?'[40]

Apropos of (1), Robert Dodaro has shown how Augustine's appeal to Christ as *sacerdos* in *De Civitate Dei* (*The City of God*) was 'a critique of Roman pagan priesthoods and of the pivotal role which they played in legitimating Roman political ideology and imperialism'.[41] In Book 10 of *The City of God* Christ as true priest was understood in contrast to the function of pagan priests. In particular, as Dodaro points out, 'the Word made flesh' represented an 'antidote to the neurotic social consequences of the "religious" denial of death at the centre of Roman heroic ideal'.[42]

Apropos of (2), Donatism arose in the early fourth century over the episcopal consecration performed by a bishop, who was accused of being a traitor during the persecution of Diocletian. The Donatists seem to have denied the validity of baptism and other sacraments administered by unworthy ministers, and to have required the 're-baptism' of Christians who had fallen back into sin. Augustine's view of Christ's priesthood, along with his reaction to pagan cults, also stemmed from his opposition to the Donatist view that a priest was a true source rather than simply a mediator of holiness. The underlying principle upheld by Augustine (with some roots in the teaching of Cyprian and Chrysostom) was that 'Christ is the only true minister of the sacraments that are administered in his name'.[43]

Augustine developed for all the sacraments what Cyprian (see above) had written about the saving work of Christ in the Eucharistic context. For Augustine, in 'the sacraments of baptism and the Eucharist' the 'saving work of Christ, who is both priest and sacrifice, is actualized for the individual'.[44] To 'rebaptize' those already bap-

---

[40] R. Markus, *The End of Ancient Christianity* (Cambridge: Cambridge University Press, 1990), 20.

[41] R. Dodaro, '*Christus Sacerdos*: Augustine's Polemic Against Roman Pagan Priesthoods in *De Civitate Dei*', Festschrift B. Studer, *Augustinianum*, 33 (1993), 101–35, at 102.

[42] Ibid. 113.

[43] G. Bonner, '*Christus Sacerdos*: The Roots of Augustine's Anti-Donatist Polemic', in A. Zumkeller (ed.), *Signum Pietatis*, Festschrift for C. P. Mayer (Wurzburg: Augustinus-Verlag, 1989), 325–39, at 338.

[44] Ibid. 331.

tized in heretical or schismatic groups was abhorrent for Augustine: it meant ignoring the primary role of Christ in the administration of baptism and the other sacraments.

It was probably his opposition to Donatist views of ordained ministers that prompted Augustine to be reticent about using *sacerdos* for either a bishop or a presbyter and normally to apply the term only to Christ. Applying *sacerdos* to a human minister could have encouraged the Donatist position that the ordained minister was the source rather than the merely visible mediator of holiness. Thus Augustine was more reluctant about using *sacerdos* than Cyprian (to whose authority the Donatists appealed to justify their position on 'rebaptism'); Cyprian had no qualms about applying *sacerdos* to bishops. It is only occasionally that we find Augustine using the term of anyone other than Christ, applying it to bishops occasionally and only now and then to 'simple' priests.[45]

For Augustine, pagan views and practices about the cult of heroes have a certain counterpart among the Donatists. They wrongly interpret 'the roles of priesthood and sacrament in a manner which exaggerates human accomplishment and fixates upon an obsessive need for exemplary heroes'.[46] Over against both groups Augustine sets Jesus as the supreme martyr, whose priesthood was distinguished above all by the virtue of humility. When thinking about Jesus, Augustine finds the heart of the matter not in his human accomplishments but in his humility. The figure of the humble Christ stands at the very centre of Augustine's Christology in general and of his view of Christ's high priesthood in particular. It is precisely 'in the form of a [humiliated] slave' that Christ is Mediator, Priest, and Sacrifice (*The City of God*, 10. 6).

Augustine saw pride to be the heart of sinfulness and humility to be the central virtue for all Christians. While humility should characterize everyone, it should distinguish in a special way ordained

---

[45] D. Zahringer, *Das kirchliche Priestertum nach hl. Augustinus* (Paderborn: Schöningh Verlag, 1931), 115–19.

[46] Dodaro, '*Christus Sacerdos*', 389. For Augustine's criticism of the cult of heroes among Donatists and pagans and the self-deceiving pride it involved, see *Sermons III/ 11: Newly Discovered Sermons*, 198. 44–5; trans. E. Hill (Hyde Park, NY: New City Press, 1997), 213–15; *Sermons III/8*, 273. 3, trans. E. Hill (Hyde Park, NY: New City Press, 1994), 18.

ministers. For them, in particular, through his incarnation, passion, and death Christ is the model and teacher of humility: we see this in the *sacrificial*, '*medical*', and *ecclesial* aspects of his priesthood.[47]

As did the author of Hebrews and Chrysostom, Augustine understands 'priesthood' and 'sacrifice' as correlative realities: 'he [Christ] is priest in that he offered himself as a holocaust for expiating and purging away our sins.'[48] This priest is also the victim: 'he alone is priest in such a way as to be also the sacrifice. He offered to God a sacrifice that was nothing other than himself. He could not find a totally pure victim, endowed with reason, apart from himself.'[49] Christ was both the offerer and the sacrifice offered. Augustine clarifies this further in one of his sermons: 'this sacrifice, in which the Priest is also the Victim, has redeemed us by the shedding of the Creator's blood.'[50] He explains the role of the blood shed 'by the one true victim' as the 'price' that 'cancelled' the 'bond' of sin: 'Previously blood used to be shed by animal victims, because the blood was being foretold that was to be shed by the one true victim, the blood of your Lord, the blood that is the price paid for you, the blood by which the bond of your debt would be cancelled, by which, that is, the old

---

[47] See Bacchi, *The Theology of Ordained Ministry in the Letters of Augustine of Hippo*, 116–23.

[48] *Newly Discovered Sermons*, 198. 50; Hill, 219. The classic passages where Augustine expounds the nature of sacrifice come in *The City of God*, 10. 5–6, and *De Trinitate*, 4. 14; both passages need to be supplemented by other texts from Augustine to illustrate the full scope of his interpretation of sacrifice. See E. C. Muller, 'The Priesthood of Christ in Book IV of the *De Trinitate*', in J. T. Lienhard, E. C. Muller, and R. J. Teske (eds.), *Augustine: 'Presbyter Factus Sum'* (New York: Peter Lang, 1993), 135–49.

[49] Augustine, *Expositions of the Psalms*, 26. 2; trans. M. Boulding, vol. 1 (Hyde Park, NY: New City Press, 2000), 275.

[50] *Sermon* 342. 1; in *Sermons III/10*, trans. E. Hill (Hyde Park, NY: New City Press, 1995), 34. Note the paradox, which can be justified on the basis of the *communicatio idiomatum* ('interchange of properties'): to say that the divine Creator of the world has shed his blood recalls the words of St Melito of Sardis in 'On the Pasch': 'He who hung up the earth is himself hung up; he who fixed the heavens is himself fixed [on the cross]; he who fastened everything is fastened on the wood. The Master is reviled. God has been killed' (no. 96). On the 'interchange of properties' see G. O'Collins, *Christology: A Biblical, Historical and Systematic Study of Jesus* (2nd edn., Oxford: Oxford University Press, 2009), 172–4; and G. Strzelczyk, '*Communicatio idiomatum*', *lo scambio delle proprietá. Storia, 'status quaestionis' e prospettive* (Rome: Gregorian University Press, 2004).

staleness of your sin would be eliminated. It has happened, it has been shed, he himself is being offered.'[51]

For Augustine the unique identity of the victim (the Son) and of the price paid (the Creator's blood) meant that Christ's self-sacrifice 'placated' or 'appeased' God. Commenting on Psalm 95, Augustine tells his audience that Christ is a 'priest' through whom 'you can placate your God'.[52] Yet we should notice that Augustine questions the view of those Christians who misinterpret atonement as if it means the Son appeasing the Father's anger and thus winning back the divine love for humanity. So far from this being the truth, right from the outset the Son was sent by the Father to forgive and save fallen human beings. Augustine asks: should we 'think that God the Father was angry with us, saw his Son die for us, and thus abated his anger against us?' Augustine recalls the question put by St Paul (Rom. 8: 31–2): 'if God is for us, who is against us?' 'Unless the Father had already been "appeased", would he have handed over his only Son for us?' Basing himself on Ephesians 1: 4 ('he [God] chose us in him [Christ] before the foundation of the world'), Augustine concludes: 'The Father loved us previously, not only before his Son died for us, but also before he founded the world' (*De Trinitate*, 13. 11. 15).

Wherever we place Augustine on the issue of Christ as priest and victim 'placating' an angry God by his self-sacrifice, this idea is foreign to Paul's letters[53] and to the Letter to the Hebrews. It does not speak of Christ's priestly work involving placation, and only twice of God's anger, but never of this anger in connection with Christ and his suffering. The divine 'anger' comes up when Hebrews quotes Psalm 95 on the rebellion of Israel in the wilderness, a rebellion that stopped the people from enjoying immediately a peaceful settlement in the promised land of Canaan (Heb. 3: 7–11).

Apropos of Christ's self-sacrificial death, Augustine touches on the issue of this *one* sacrifice and the 'many' sacrifices apparently involved when priests repeatedly offer the Eucharist. What is the

---

[51] *Newly Discovered Sermons*, 374. 20; Hill, 405.

[52] *Sermon*, 176. 5; in *Sermons III/5*, trans. E. Hill (Hyde Park, NY: New City Press, 1992), 276.

[53] On Paul see G. O'Collins, *Jesus Our Redeemer: A Christian Approach to Salvation* (Oxford: Oxford University Press, 2007), 153–6.

relationship between the 'many' sacrifices offered on many altars and the once-and-for-all sacrifice of Christ? Reflecting on Psalm 19: 10 ('Lord, save the king'), Augustine recalls the passion of Christ: 'he who by his suffering gave us an example to do battle may offer our sacrifices also, as our Priest risen from the dead and established in heaven... Christ now offers sacrifice on our behalf.'[54] Here the plural, 'our sacrifices', refers to the (singular) Eucharist (just as it does in 'these holy and pure sacrifices (*haec sancta sacrificia illibata*)' of the ancient Roman Canon). It is the one High Priest who now makes the Eucharistic offering for Christians everywhere; it is not a case of many priests offering many sacrifices.

The prayer to 'save the king' has led Augustine to consider the role of the High Priest in the offering of the Eucharist—a striking example of the kingly and priestly offices being intertwined in a relationship that seems closer with each other than with the prophetic office.[55] At the time of David, Augustine remarks, 'only kings and priests were anointed; at that time only they were anointed persons. In these two was prefigured the one future King and Priest, the one Christ with both functions; and he was given the title "Christ" in virtue of his anointing.' As usual, Augustine relates all this to the life and practice of Christians: 'not only was our Head anointed, his Body was too, we ourselves. He is King because he reigns over us and leads us; Priest because he intercedes on our behalf.'[56]

By their baptismal anointing all Christians are incorporated into Christ, the Priest and Victim, and become one with him. 'He is like a spotless lamb', Augustine writes,

who redeemed us by his own spilt blood, uniting us into one body with himself making us his members, so that in him we too are Christ. This is why anointing is proper to all Christians, even though in earlier times under the old covenant it was given to two kinds of persons only. From this it is

---

[54] *Expositions of the Psalms*, 19. 10; Boulding, 217.
[55] In Revelation the elect are made priests in a kingdom as they serve God (Rev. 1: 6; 5: 10)—another striking example of the ease with which kingly and priestly offices are joined.
[56] *Expositions of the Psalms*, 26. 2. 2; Boulding, 274–5.

obvious that we are the Body of Christ, being all anointed. In him all of us belong to Christ, but we are Christ too, because in some sense the whole Christ is Head and Body.[57]

To express this union with Christ the High Priest, Augustine develops what Hebrews says about the Jewish high priest going into the 'secret sanctuary', the Holy of Holies (Heb. 9: 3, 7). Augustine asks:

What is that [secret inner room at the heart of the Temple]? The place where the high priest alone used to enter. But perhaps our High Priest is himself this hidden part of God's tabernacle. He received flesh from this tabernacle, and made an inner recess of the tabernacle for us. This was so that others of his members, by believing in him, might be the tabernacle, and he himself be its inner recess.[58]

Obviously this imagery goes beyond anything envisaged by Hebrews. Yet it beautifully evokes the outcome of Christ's sacrifice and the new union it has created: one embodied 'tabernacle' of all Christ's followers, with the High Priest himself constituting the 'secret sanctuary', the very Holy of Holies.

Along with the sacrificial theme, Augustine elaborates a *medical* image of Christ's priestly work: 'It was by the divine Physician's humility that mankind was cured from the deadly tumour of pride, which had caused the fall of the first parents . . . the redemption was nothing else than the neutralization of man's pride by God's humility.'[59] To express vividly Christ's humility in curing human pride, Augustine imagines the boasts of the devil: 'he has the audacity to boast that he is stronger and mightier than Christ because he was not born of a woman in the flesh, not arrested, not scourged, not spattered with spittle, not crowned with thorns, not hung on a cross, not dead and buried.' Augustine adds: 'these are all things

[57] *Expositions of the Psalms*, 26. 2. 2; Boulding, 275.

[58] *Expositions of the Psalms*, 26. 2. 10; Boulding, 281.

[59] R. Arbesmann, 'The Concept of "Christus Medicus" in St. Augustine', *Traditio*, 10 (1954), 1–28, at 9. In well over 40 texts Augustine develops or at least alludes to the healing activity of Christ the divine Physician; see ibid. 2–3. See also B. E. Daley, 'A Humble Mediator: The Distinctive Elements in Saint Augustine's Christology', *Word and Spirit*, 9 (1987), 100–17.

that the proud deride, which the humble Mediator underwent . . . in order to heal them of the tumour of pride.'[60]

This 'humble priest (*sacerdos*)' is simultaneously a 'humble doctor (*medicus*)'. It is the medicine (of humble suffering) he provides that alone can heal the sickness of human pride, which is the very heart of our sinfulness. As a humble doctor, Christ encourages us by drinking the medicine first: 'he came to us in our sickness as a doctor . . . The cup of suffering is bitter, but the doctor drinks it first, in case the sick patient should hesitate to drink it.'[61] Christ as priest and sacrificial victim is, for Augustine, our doctor and even our medicine: 'he himself is the doctor, the medico, he himself the medicine: the medico because he is the Word, the medicine because "the Word became flesh" [John 1: 14]. He himself the priest, himself the sacrifice.'[62] Augustine uses the theme of Christ 'the doctor' and 'the medicine' to picture the change from the old covenant to the new: 'all those sacrifices' were done away with and 'one sacrifice' was provided—'the body of Christ purging away sins'.[63]

We quoted Augustine above on Christ as 'the Head' of 'the Body', which is the Church. He utilizes this *ecclesial* theme to portray Christ performing his priestly function precisely as Head of the Church (with the Church being constituted through the very event of the incarnation): 'your Savior took flesh to himself; your Mediator took flesh to himself, and by taking flesh he took the Church to himself. He was the first to make a libation, as coming from the Head, of what he would offer to God, a High Priest forever [Heb. 5: 6] and the propitiation for our sins [1 John 2: 2].'[64] When he draws on Ephesians, Augustine uses the language of 'Head' in a priestly way: 'He himself [Christ], you see, is the Head of the Church [Eph. 5: 23], the One who has already ascended into heaven and is seated at the right hand of the Father, showing us in his whole burnt offering of himself what we should also be hoping for where our flesh is concerned.'[65]

---

[60] *Newly Discovered Sermons*, 198. 41; Hill, 211.
[61] *Newly Discovered Sermons*, 299A. 5; Hill, 268.
[62] *Newly Discovered Sermons*, 374. 23; Hill, 407.
[63] *Newly Discovered Sermons*, 374. 19; Hill, 403.
[64] *Newly Discovered Sermons*, 198. 43; Hill, 212. In the same sermon Augustine will also say: 'The one and only Priest is the Mediator himself, the sinless Head of the Church, through whom is effected the purging away of our sins' (198. 51; Hill, 220).
[65] *Newly Discovered Sermons*, 198. 44; Hill, 213.

The image of head and body allows Augustine to picture a priest-hood that characterizes the whole Church: 'it is the whole universal Church which is the Body of that one Priest. To that Priest belongs his Body. That, after all, is why the apostle Peter says to the Church itself, "a holy people, a royal priesthood" [1 Pet. 2: 9].'[66] This 'con-gregation or communion of saints' has been offered 'as a universal sacrifice to God through the High Priest'. He 'offered himself in his passion for us that we might be the Body of so glorious a Head' (*The City of God*, 10. 6). He made those for whom his sacrifice was offered one with himself.

TWO MAJOR CONTRIBUTIONS

Two contributions that Augustine made to Christian thinking about Christ's priesthood stand out: the first concerns the link between sacrifice and humble obedience, and the second involves recognizing Christ to be the invisible minister of baptism and the other sacra-ments.

First, as we saw above, Origen, Cyprian, and even more Chrysos-tom built on Hebrews' teaching about Christ's priestly obedience (Heb. 4: 15; 5: 7–9) and the virtuous 'sacrifices' required of his followers (Heb. 13: 16) to insist on the spiritual qualities and holiness of life that count far more with God than any external, merely ritual performance of sacrifice. Augustine cites Hosea 6: 6 ('I desired mercy and not sacrifice') and Hebrews 13: 16 ('do not forget kindness and charity, for by such sacrifices God's favour is obtained') to conclude that 'what is commonly called a sacrifice is a symbol of the true sacrifice . . . mercy is the true sacrifice'. In short, all authentic sacri-fices refer to and depend on 'the love of God and neighbour' (*The City of God*, 10. 5).

For Augustine, the reality of sacrifice inheres in every work that unites human beings with God: 'a man who is consecrated in the name of God and vowed to God is a sacrifice, inasmuch as he dies to

---

[66] *Newly Discovered Sermons*, 198. 49; Hill, 218.

the world that he may live for God.' 'True sacrifices', he declares, 'are works of mercy done to ourselves or our neighbour and directed to God' (ibid. 10. 6). Hence Augustine prized so highly the humble obedience of Christ, which set him poles apart from the proud heroes worshipped by the pagans.[67]

A holiness of life and total, loving dedication to God and neighbour characterized the earthly activity of Jesus. He worshipped in the synagogues and attended the festivals in Jerusalem. But what above all defined the teaching, healing, table fellowship with sinners, and other aspects of his public ministry, was 'the true sacrifice' of mercy. In this way Augustine's account of the heart of sacrifice allows us to understand the whole life of Christ as eminently self-sacrificial and priestly.

Second, the Donatists accused the Catholic Church of being 'traitors' and real schismatics. Hence, so they argued, its ministers, like Judas Iscariot himself, were incapable of validly administering baptism or the other sacraments. Here we should recall that in the patristic era baptism (that included confirmation) was deemed the primary sacrament. It was only centuries later that the Eucharist became clearly acknowledged as the centre of the sacramental system, 'the sacrament of sacraments', for St Thomas Aquinas (d. 1274).[68] Hence baptism touched the heart of the controversy between the Donatists and Augustine.

Against the Donatists, Augustine insisted that the invisible Christ himself is the real minister of baptism (*In Ioannis Evangelium*, 5. 18). Hence a traitor like Judas Iscariot could administer a 'valid' sacrament, provided he used the required elements (water for baptism) and words (the invocation of the Holy Trinity for baptism). Since the invisible Christ, not the visible minister, is the 'origin, root, and head' of the baptized, even sacraments administered by those in schism (e.g. the Donatists) should be recognized as valid (*Contra Epistulam Petiliani*, 1. 5. 6). Elsewhere Augustine put this point more forcefully: baptism, 'consecrated by the words of the Gospel', is 'holy', however shameless and unclean [its human ministers] may be, since its

---

[67] See e.g. *Newly Discovered Sermons*, 159B. 9–13; 198. 38–9, 60; Hill, 155–9; 208–10, 225–6.
[68] See his *STh.* 3a. 65. 3; 3a. 75. 1 resp.

[inherent] sanctity cannot be polluted and the divine power supports the sacrament, whether for the salvation of those who use it aright or for the destruction of those who use it wrongly' (*De Baptismo*, 3. 15).

In other words, the efficacy of the sacrament—in particular, baptism—does not depend on the personal holiness of its visible minister. This is because it is primarily the invisible Christ (made visible in his Body, which is the Church) who performs the baptizing, the ordaining, and whatever would later be called the dispensing of all sacramental graces. Christ is actively and personally present in the administration of all the sacraments. They are things that God constantly does for the faithful through Christ, not vice versa.

Here Augustine's recognition of Christ's permanent, priestly activity moves beyond what Paul (Rom. 8: 34) and Hebrews (7. 25; 9: 24) say about the High Priest's permanent intercession at the right hand of God on behalf of human beings. One might interpret Augustine's view of Christ's active presence in the administration of all the sacraments as developing and applying what Hebrews said about human beings 'approaching God' through the High Priest. Yet Augustine initiated here a lasting development in the appreciation of what Christ's permanent, (invisible) priestly activity involves in the daily life of the Church.

OTHER FATHERS ON CHRIST'S PRIESTHOOD

Other fathers of the Church add little to the interpretation of Christ's priesthood that we have found in Clement, Ignatius of Antioch, Polycarp, Origen, Cyprian, Chrysostom, and Augustine. We begin with St Athanasius of Alexandria (d. 373).

Like the Letter to the Hebrews, Chrysostom, and Augustine, Athanasius understands Christ's priesthood as rooted in the humanity that he assumed: the Word became High Priest once he was robed in the 'vestment' of his flesh (*Contra Arianos*, 2. 8). Or more fully: 'when he assumed flesh like ours and himself offered this flesh, he was called High Priest (*archiereus*), and he was made faithful and merciful: merciful, because when he offered himself for us, he had mercy on us; faithful . . . because he offers [present tense] a faithful

sacrifice, enduring, not ceasing.' Perhaps with reference to its perpetuation in the Eucharist and, certainly, by way of contrast with the
Old Testament sacrifices, Athanasius emphasizes the permanent nature of this 'faithful sacrifice': 'nothing was faithful or constant in the
sacrifices of the Law; they came and passed day by day, so that a new
cleansing was necessary. But the sacrifice of our Saviour once it had
taken place accomplished all things; it was made faithful in that it
endures forever' (*Contra Arianos,* 2. 9).

Since Athanasius finds difficulty in treating fully the humanity of
Christ, he has little to say about Christ's priesthood. What he does say
highlights the Word more than the 'flesh' that was assumed. As Greer
puts matters: 'for Athanasius the High Priest of Hebrews is the Word
at the Incarnation. He identifies the priestly vestments, as well as the
offering, with the body taken by the Word.'[69]

More than two centuries later St Gregory the Great (d. 604) also
clearly links the priesthood of Jesus with the incarnation. Like Origen
and others, Gregory highlights the cleansing of sins as a major result
of Christ's priestly work: 'He [Christ] unceasingly presents his incarnation to the Father for us. For his incarnation is truly the offering
of our cleansing; and seeing that he presents himself as man, his
presence wipes out the sins of man' (*Moralium,* 1. 24. 32). Such
language, unlike that of Hebrews, seems to name the incarnation
and the new divine 'presence' it brought, rather than the passion,
crucifixion, and resurrection, as the defining moment of Christ's
priesthood. Yet it opens up the possibility for understanding his
whole life and, in particular, his public ministry as truly priestly.

Eusebius of Caesarea (d. *c.* 340), the 'Father of Church History', in
Book 5 of his *Demonstration of the Gospel* followed Clement of
Alexandria, Cyprian, and others in interpreting the bread and wine
offered by Melchizedek as foreshadowing the Eucharist. Eusebius
even claimed that this 'priest of the pagans was never known to
offer flesh in his sacrifices but only bread and wine'. On the basis of
one encounter between Abraham and Melchizedek, how did Eusebius know about the constant sacrificial practice of the latter: never
flesh but only bread and wine? Eusebius also went far beyond the text

<hr/>

[69] Greer, *Captain of Our Salvation,* 96.

of Genesis by crediting Melchizedek with an inspired, 'prior knowledge' of the Eucharistic 'mysteries'. More importantly, Eusebius followed Cyprian and anticipated Chrysostom by connecting the celebration of the Eucharist with the one sacrifice of Christ the High Priest: 'all the priests sent out to all nations offer a spiritual sacrifice [the Eucharist] in accord with ecclesiastical regulations, signifying by wine and bread the mysteries of his Body and saving Blood' (*Demonstration of the Gospel*, 5. 3; *PG* 22, cols. 367–8).

In a work attributed to St Damasus (d. 384), the pope left a soaring litany of titles for Christ and the reason for each: for instance, 'Priest, because he offered himself as a sacrifice' and 'Lamb because he suffered'.[70] In this terse fashion Damasus, like so many others, witnessed to the inseparable link between priesthood and sacrifice.

In his *Catecheses*, St Cyril of Jerusalem (d. 386) explained two items that concerned the priesthood of Christ: 'He is called by two names, Jesus because he bestows salvation, and Christ because of his priesthood' (10. 11; *PG* 33, col. 676). The name of 'Christ' came from his heavenly anointing by the Father: 'He is called Christ, not as having been anointed by human hands, but as anointed eternally by the Father to his High Priesthood over human beings' (10. 4; *PG* 33, col. 664).

With an eye on the Letter to the Hebrews, St Ambrose of Milan (d. 397) explained why it was necessary for Christ the High Priest to shed his blood. A high priest was obliged to enter the holy place with something bloody to offer, but God had rejected the blood of animals: 'the priest must have something to offer, and according to the Law he must enter into the Holy of Holies, not without blood [Heb. 9: 22]. Therefore, because God rejected the blood of bulls and goats [Heb. 9: 12–13], it was necessary for this High Priest ... penetrating the highest heavens, to enter into the Holy of Holies by his own blood, in order to become an eternal offering for our sins' (*De Fide*, 3. 11. 87). Through stating that God 'rejected' the blood of animals, Ambrose put more strongly what Hebrews wrote about such sacrifices being incapable of removing sin (Heb. 10: 4). He also went beyond Hebrews by claiming that it was 'necessary' for Christ the

[70] *The Decree of Damasus*, PL 19, cols. 787–90; trans. W. A. Jurgens, *The Faith of the Early Fathers* (Collegeville, Minn.: Liturgical Press, 1970), 404.

High Priest to shed his own blood if he were to become 'an eternal offering for our sins'. The necessity of Christ's self-sacrificing death would become a recurrent theme in theology (e.g. with St Anselm of Canterbury) and popular piety.

St Cyril of Alexandria (d. 444) famously spent much of his energy in elaborating language that would account for the union between divinity and humanity in the one Christ. Hence it is not surprising to find him reflecting on Christ as human standing to offer priestly sacrifice and as divine seated to receive it. Commenting on Hebrews 8: 1–2, Cyril wrote: 'as God, he is seated on the throne of his divinity', but 'by the divine dispensation made sharer in human nature he bears the name of priest (*hiereus*) and minister (*leitourgos*)' (*De Recta Fide ad Reginas*, 111). Rooting Christ's priesthood and its exercise in his humanity was common doctrine that went back to the Letter to the Hebrews. What Cyril did not observe here was something made clear from the opening chapter of Hebrews, the divine identity of Christ. It was this identity that conferred a unique value on the priestly sacrifice which he performed inasmuch as he was human.

When expounding the Eucharist, Cyril does, of course, insist that the life-giving body and blood offered are those of the Word: 'in order for humankind to be redeemed, the body must belong to none other than the Word of God himself, the Word of God become a human being.' Precisely because it is the flesh of the Word of God himself, the Eucharist is a life-giving sacrament. Acknowledging the divine identity of the One received in the Eucharist necessarily involves acknowledging the divine identity of the One responsible for human salvation in general: 'if Christ did not suffer and die as God in the flesh, then he has not provided salvation to those he came to save.'[71] In developing his doctrine of the Eucharist and, more broadly, his Christology (including Christ's sacrificial death), Cyril does not, however, tend to articulate matters in terms of Christ's priesthood.[72]

[71] S. A. McKinion, *Words, Imagery and the Mystery of Christ: A Reconstruction of Cyril of Alexandria's Christology* (Leiden: Brill, 2000), 93. On the life-giving 'flesh of the Word himself', see e.g. Cyril's *Third Letter to Nestorius* (no. 7) and his *Twelve Anathemas* (no. 11).
[72] In their works on Cyril's Christology, neither McKinion nor J. A. McGuckin, *St Cyril of Alexandria: The Christological Controversy. Its History, Theology, and Texts*

Finally, we should mention three works on the priesthood of ordained ministers: *De Fuga* (*On Flight*) by St Gregory of Nazianzus (d. 389/90), which explains his own unusual vocation and reflects on the responsibilities and privilege of priesthood; *On the Priesthood* by Chrysostom, a work that, despite the title, is more concerned with bishops than with priests; and the *Pastoral Rule* by Gregory the Great, which describes how bishops should deal pastorally with different types of people in the Church. One might have expected some reflections on Christ's own priesthood, albeit in a different register, in these three works. But there is little to report, even from Chrysostom. Apropos of the celebration of the Eucharist, he expresses his wonder at Christ the High Priest, 'who sits above with the Father' and yet is 'held in our hands, and gives himself to those who wish to clasp and embrace him'.[73]

CONCLUSIONS

Right from Clement at the end of the first Christian century down to Augustine in the early fifth century, we saw how issues about ministry in the Church repeatedly prompted reflection on Christ's own priesthood. But what did that reflection contribute to those who wish to understand and interpret the figure of Jesus as priest? In the light of what we gleaned in the first four chapters about the priesthood of Christ and, especially, what we drew from the Letter to the Hebrews (which reinvented, at least for Christians, the notion of priesthood), we might ask: do the fathers of the Church add a wider range and richness for those who ponder Jesus as priest? In reply we might distinguish three areas: first, various points where the fathers repeat,

---

(Leiden: Brill, 1994) include 'priesthood' in their index of subjects. Nor, for that matter, does a more general book on Cyril: T. G. Weinandy and D. A. Keating (eds.), *The Theology of Cyril of Alexandria: A Critical Appreciation* (London: Continuum, 2003). For Cyril on Christ's priesthood, see Greer, *Captain of Our Salvation*, 332–7, and T. F. Torrance, *Theology in Reconciliation: Essays Towards Evangelical and Catholic Unity in East and West* (Eugene, Oreg.: Wipf & Stock, 1996), 156–85.

[73] Chrysostom, *On the Priesthood*, 3. 4; trans. G. Neville (London: SPCK, 1964), 70–1.

more or less, what they find in Hebrews on Christ's high priesthood and what they find about the priestly lifestyle of believers in Hebrews, Romans 12: 1, and 1 Peter; second, some points where they restate with embellishments what they read in their scriptural sources; and third, some points over which they develop an understanding of Christ the priest that takes us beyond what we find explicitly in Hebrews or elsewhere in the New Testament. We will refer to the fathers in the order in which they appear above.

First, our authors follow Hebrews in recognizing that the priest-hood of Christ involved his sacrificial (or, more precisely, self-sacrificial) activity (see e.g. Cyprian, Origen, Chrysostom, Augustine, Damasus, and Ambrose). Offering sacrifice forms the bedrock of his being a priest and his being acknowledged as such. Christ's sacrifice has expiated human sin; it has, in Origen's striking language, 'eaten up human sins'. Or, as Chrysostom put matters, this sacrifice has proved a powerful medicine to heal the wounds of sin. The fathers also follow Hebrews by attending to Melchizedek as foreshadowing the priestly figure of Christ (e.g. Cyprian, Chrysostom, and Eusebius of Caesarea) and, even more importantly, by acknowledging that the priesthood of Christ depends on his assuming the human condition. Without his humanity he would not be a priest (e.g. Chrysostom, Augustine, Athanasius, and Cyril of Alexandria). They vigorously agree with Hebrews about the unique superiority of Christ's priest-hood. Chrysostom endorses and explains what Hebrews proposes about this priesthood as mediation. Finally, in various ways the fathers take up not only from Hebrews but also from Paul and 1 Peter the theme of a sacrificial lifestyle that should characterize all the baptized (and especially, so Cyprian and others add, the lives of bishops and presbyters). Sharing in the priesthood of Christ raises very high the bar for the holy conduct and generously self-sacrificing love expected from his followers (e.g. Chrysostom).

Second, our authors at times restate in vivid ways the New Testa-ment witness to Christ's priesthood. Chrysostom's rhetorical powers lead him to portray the High Priest of Hebrews in different registers: for instance, as a perfect husband. When he expounds 'the heavenly things' of Hebrews 11: 16 as 'heavenly hymns' sung on earth in harmony with the heavenly choirs above, Chrysostom, without say-ing so, introduces from Revelation something of its theme of the

heavenly/earthly liturgy. The obedience of Christ belongs essentially
to the picture Hebrews and the Gospels paint of his priesthood.
Several of the fathers use different tones in producing what is essentially the same picture. For Origen, the vestments worn by Old
Testament priests represent the inner character and virtues of Christ.
Cyprian, Chrysostom, and (especially) Augustine highlight the
humility of Christ, the Priest and Victim. Chrysostom insists (like
Paul in Romans and Galatians) that love inspired the priestly actions
of Christ. This theme was to shape the way Thomas Aquinas presents
the passion and death of Christ. Chrysostom and Augustine associate
Christ's priesthood with his kingship, a link implied by Hebrews
when repeatedly picturing the exalted Christ as seated in majesty at
the right hand of God the Father.

Some of these restatements open up attractive lines of thought.
When Ignatius represents Christ the High Priest as the unique centre
of Christian unity, he may prompt us to enlarge the 'one Lord, one
faith, one baptism, one God and Father of all' by adding 'and
one High Priest', who calls us to 'maintain the unity of the Spirit in
the bond of peace' (Eph. 4: 3–6). One restatement is less than happy.
Where Hebrews writes of Christ's priestly self-sacrifice purifying
human beings from the defilement of sin, Chrysostom and Augustine
(with qualifications) harness this sacrifice to the cause of appease-
ment. Christ's sacrifice placates an angry God the Father. This 'narrative' of Christ's suffering and death, endorsed in passing by
Aquinas, was to flourish at the time of the Reformation and beyond.

Then, third, some of the narratives of Christ's priesthood answer
questions seemingly left open by Hebrews or else apply what they
find there (and elsewhere in the New Testament) to developments in
the life of the Church.[74] We can cull three examples from what we
have reported above. (1) Chrysostom, Augustine, and others (e.g.
Gregory the Great) understand Christ's priesthood to have begun
with the incarnation. This responds to an issue that Hebrews does
not clearly settle and, even more significantly, allows us to interpret
the whole life of Christ, including his public ministry, as priestly

---

[74] Hebrews refers to the angels in order to demonstrate Christ's superiority to
them (1: 5–2: 18). Origen, as we saw above, understands Christ to be High Priest also
for the angels.

activity. Augustine's cherished theme of Christ exercising his priestly ministry as a 'humble doctor' can also be applied to the earthly ministry of Jesus. When he cured the sick, forgave sins, and in other ways practised a healing ministry, he was already revealing himself to be a 'humble doctor' for a wounded and sinful humanity.

(2) Like Romans 12: 1, Hebrews articulates in sacrificial language the appropriate lifestyle of believers. Origen, Chrysostom, and Augustine endorse this but develop in their own ways the grounds for this participation in Christ's priesthood. Given his built-in propensity for allegory, Origen exploits allegorical possibilities offered by the garments of Old Testament high priests—something that Hebrews does not do—in order to exhort the baptized to put on such vestments and live with Christ a 'high-priestly' existence. Through acts of virtue and the appropriate inner dispositions, believers, according to Chrysostom, can themselves become 'the priest' of such offerings. 'Fire' will 'come down' from above, not to reduce such offerings 'to ashes' but to bear them up to heaven 'as gifts to God'. Augustine develops a narrative of priesthood in the light of Christ performing his high-priestly functions precisely as Head of the Church. Christ shares his priesthood with those who are incorporated through baptism into his Body, the Church. The image of head and body allows Augustine to account for the way priesthood characterizes the entire Church and all its members.

Finally (3), how did our authors understand the relationship between Christ's priesthood and that of ordained ministers in his Church? We saw how Origen took it for granted that some Christians ('the ministers and priests') shared in a special way in the priesthood of Christ and its exercise in forgiving sins. Ignatius, Cyprian, and Chrysostom invested energy in relating Christ's priesthood to the permanent celebration of the Eucharist in the Church. Cyprian and others (e.g. Eusebius of Caesarea) followed Clement of Alexandria by interpreting Melchizedek's offering of bread and wine as prefiguring the Eucharist. The author of Hebrews, as we saw in Chapter 3, seems to have referred to the Eucharist, but did not spot any foreshadowing of the Eucharist in the two gifts offered by Melchizedek. Cyprian, however, links together Melchizedek's offering with Christ's offering at the Last Supper, which was fully achieved and consummated on Calvary. When they celebrate the Eucharist, bishops (who are the

prime addressees of Cyprian) offer the passion of Christ, the one sacrifice that Christ himself offered. As we saw, Chrysostom insisted that the Eucharist was 'not another sacrifice' but the same sacrifice once offered by Christ and now performed/offered in 'remembrance'. Augustine put matters this way: 'as our Priest risen from the dead and established in heaven . . . Christ now offers sacrifice on our behalf.' It is the one High Priest who now offers the Eucharist for Christians everywhere.

This might have led Augustine to develop further the relationship between the invisible Christ offering permanently his self-sacrifice on the cross and the visible bishop or priest who celebrates the Eucharist. That relationship would feature prominently in the theology and spirituality of the Middle Ages and later. Christians at the time of Augustine understood baptism to be the primary sacrament, the sacrament that had become controversial with Donatists and others. Against the Donatists, Augustine affirmed that the invisible Christ was the real minister of baptism. Many later Christians acknowledged the great debt they owe to Augustine when he developed what Hebrews had said about human beings permanently 'approaching God' through Christ the High Priest. Augustine applied this to baptism (and other sacraments), through which Christ's priestly activity is constantly exercised in an invisible but powerful way.

A second major contribution that we drew from Augustine can set the agenda for a question that will be raised at the end of this study: what does one mean by sacrifice when one speaks of Christ's priestly self-sacrifice? Can we be helped today by Augustine's broad account of true sacrifices as 'works of mercy done to ourselves or our neighbour and directed to God'?

6

Aquinas on Christ's Priesthood

One might have expected the middle member of a classic, triple 'A' team (who lived after Augustine and before Aquinas) to have contributed some reflection on the priesthood of Christ. However, St Anselm of Canterbury (d. 1109), while establishing with his theory of 'satisfaction' an enduring expression for Christ's redemptive work, did not appeal to, let alone interpret, his high-priestly role. A recent study of Anselm's Christology dedicates pages to the suffering and death of Christ but has nothing to report on his priesthood.[1] Indirectly, however, the theory of redemption as satisfaction, at least in the way it was received and modified by later theologians, was to influence versions of Christ's priesthood. Hence we need to set out briefly this theory before moving on to examine the account of this priesthood provided by St Thomas Aquinas (d. 1274).[2]

ANSELM ON SATISFACTION

From the time of Augustine, Western theologians were encouraged to think of Christ vicariously ransoming human beings by paying the penalty for their sins. The Vulgate translation (completed in 404 by

---

[1] D. Deme, *The Christology of Anselm of Canterbury* (Aldershot, Hampshire: Ashgate, 2003).

[2] Priesthood belonged to the triple scheme, priest–prophet–king, which characterized Christ's saving function as mediator between God and human beings. He fulfilled this role not only through his priesthood but also through being a prophet (*Summa Theologiae*, 3a. 7. 8) and king (ibid. 22. 1 ad 3; 31. 2 ad 2); hereafter *STh*.

St Jerome) was interpreted as Christ himself speaking in Psalm 69: 4: 'I paid back what I never took (*quae non rapui, tunc exsolvebam*).' Augustine put this more fully: 'I had not stolen, yet I paid the price. I did not sin, and I paid the penalty [for sin] (*non rapui, et exsolvebam; non peccavi, et poenas dabam*)' (*Expositions of the Psalms*, 68. 1. 9). This verse was to provide a key text for Aquinas on Christ's passion effecting our salvation by way of satisfaction.[3] The notion of a penalty paid for human sins (along with some other versions of redemption) had been around before Anselm, but he developed his own characteristic thinking on the need for reparation.

Anselm argued that 'every sin must be followed either by satisfaction or by punishment' (*Cur Deus Homo*, 1. 15). Anselm ruled out the latter solution for undoing the past and preparing a new future. God does not wish to punish but to see the good work of creation 'completed' (ibid. 2. 5). Now satisfaction, Anselm maintained, requires from human beings not only that they should stop sinning and seek pardon but also that they do something over and above existing obligations towards God: namely, a work of supererogation that will satisfy for the offence. However, since all sin offends the divine honour of the infinite God, the reparation must likewise have infinite value—something of which finite human beings are incapable. Moreover, they have nothing extra to offer God, since they already owe God everything (ibid. 1. 19–20, 23). Thus Anselm concluded to the 'necessity' of the incarnation. Only the *God*-man can offer something of infinite value; the hypostatic union or personal union with the Word of God confers such value on the human acts of Christ. Only the God-*man* has something to offer; being without sin, Christ is exempt from the need to undergo death, and hence can freely offer the gift of his life as a work of reparation for the whole human race (ibid. 2. 6–7, 11, 14, 18–19).

Anselm laid fresh stress on the humanity and human freedom of Christ, who spontaneously acted as our representative and in no way is to be construed as a penal substitute who passively endured sufferings to appease the anger of a 'vindictive' God. Anselm's theology of satisfaction had its cultural roots in monasticism and the

---

[3] *STh*. 3a. 48. 2.

feudal society of northern Europe. The 'honourable' service owed by monks to their abbots and of vassals to their lords was a religious and social factor that guaranteed order, peace, and freedom. Denying the honour due to superiors meant chaos. Anselm's thoroughly logical account of redemption, which stood far apart from the thought-world of the Letter to the Hebrews, looks vulnerable on some grounds: for instance, his non-biblical version of justice and sin—something obviously linked to the readership he envisaged. Quite unlike the author of Hebrews (who addressed Christian believers suffering from both persecution and lethargy), Anselm aimed to present a rational case for the coherence and even 'necessity' of the incarnation to readers who were not Christians or were Christians with doubts. Apropos of justice, the commutative sense of justice Anselm adopted for his argument seems to picture God as so bound to a fair and balanced order of compensation that it would be 'unthinkable' simply to grant forgiveness without requiring reparation. Likewise, instead of interpreting sin very clearly as infidelity and disobedience that ruptures a personal relationship with an all-loving God or as 'crucifying again the Son of God' (Heb. 6: 6), Anselm pictured sin as an infinite dishonour that upset the proper order of things. Although elsewhere he richly recognized the merciful love of God, *Cur Deus Homo* contains only a brief closing reference to the divine mercy.

Given its scope, intended audience, and focus on reparation and not on sinners' new relationship with God, the book omits some notable items: (1) the resurrection (with the gift of the Holy Spirit and that major patristic theme, the divinization of the redeemed), (2) the full significance of Jesus' life and public ministry, and (3) his high-priestly mediation. For the scheme of satisfaction it was enough that the incarnation occurred and that Christ (not characterized in the light of Hebrews as priest and victim) freely gave his life to make reparation for human sin. *Cur Deus Homo* turns Christ's life into a mere prelude to death.

Along with its limitations, Anselm's theory of satisfaction still retains its grandeur and fascination.[4] It continues to be wrongly

---

[4] See P. Gilbert, H. Kohlenberger, and E. Salmann (eds.), *Cur Deus Homo*, Studia Anselmiana 128 (Rome: S. Anselmo, 1999).

presented as the first articulation of the 'theory of penal substitution'.[5] But, as we saw above, Anselm explicitly rejected the notion of
God exacting retribution by *punishing* his Son in the place of sinful
human beings. Such penal ideas crept in later. We will indicate the
early stages of this change in the *Summa Theologiae* of Aquinas.

PRIESTHOOD AND SATISFACTION

It is in the third part of the *Summa* that Aquinas writes about Christ
the High Priest and, when doing so, often draws biblical support
from the Letter to the Hebrews, a text on which he had commented
shortly before (*Commentary on the Epistle to the Hebrews*). Like
Origen, Chrysostom, and—as we shall see—Luther and Calvin,
Thomas wrote a separate work on Hebrews. Their study of this key
New Testament text obviously strengthened their reflections on
Christ's priesthood.

In the perspective of Thomas's theology, Christ and his sacraments
form a bridge between human activity and God. In particular, the
Eucharist provides a sacramental means of entry into the offering
and fruits of Christ's priestly sacrifice. Hence we will examine not
only what Aquinas says directly about Christ's priesthood in question
22 of the third part of the *Summa* but also what he says about the
closely related notion of Christ's mediation (question 26) and in later
questions about the sacraments, especially about the Eucharist.[6]

We grasp Aquinas's understanding of Christ's priesthood by setting it within the broader framework of the way he follows and
modifies Anselm's theory of redemption as satisfaction. Before he

---

[5] See P. F. Carnley, *Reflections in Glass* (Sydney: HarperCollins, 2004), 4; see also
75, 76, 84, 132.

[6] A modern classic study of Aquinas's interpretation of Christ's priesthood is
E. J. Scheller, *Das Priestertum Christi im Anschluss an den hl. Thomas von Aquin.
Vom Mysterium des Mittlers in seinem Opfer und unserer Anteilnahme* (Paderborn:
Schönigh, 1934). We have made our own translations of passages from the *STh.*,
albeit with an eye on the sixty-volume edition and translation produced by Domin-
icans of English-speaking provinces and their friends (London: Eyre & Spottiswoode,
1964–76).

reaches the passion and death of Jesus, Aquinas has already taken up the Anselmian notion of redemptive satisfaction effected by the incarnate Son of God. But he does not endorse here an unqualified necessity: 'the incarnation was not necessary for the restoration of human nature, since by his infinite power God had many other ways to accomplish this end' (*STh*. 3a. 1. 2). In detailing reasons for the 'fittingness' of the incarnation, Aquinas highlights the destructive-ness of sin and the 'repairing' of human beings themselves more than the 'repairing' of a moral order disturbed by sinful offences against God (3a. 1. 2, 4). He mitigates Anselm's position by maintaining that God could pardon sin even though adequate satisfaction was not made, and by stressing the way love makes satisfaction valid: 'in satisfaction one attends more to the affection of the one who offers it than to the quantity of the offering' (3a. 79. 5).

Christ's sacrifice is expounded as a meritorious sacrifice, under-gone by him and truly accepted by God as being inspired by love (*STh*. 3a. 48. 3 resp.).[7] For Aquinas, as it was for the Letter to the Hebrews, the sinlessness of Christ was a further indispensable quali-fication in making this sacrifice acceptable to God: 'no one other than Christ was able to satisfy for the sin of the whole human race, since he alone was free of every sin' (*Super ad Romanos*, 3. 1). We return below to Aquinas's notion of sacrifice, which shades his portrayal of Christ as priest.

The Anselmian approach to redemptive satisfaction shows up in a biblical commentary composed some years before Aquinas began the *Summa Theologiae* around 1266. When commenting on Isaiah, he associates Christ being a priest with his work of satisfying for human sin. Following a long tradition of understanding as a prophetic fore-telling of Christ's coming the words 'to us a child is born, to us a son is given' (Isa. 9: 6), Aquinas lists various titles of Christ that are based upon the Scriptures: 'brother', 'teacher', 'watchman', 'defender', 'shep-herd', 'example for our activities', and 'food for wayfarers'. Then he adds that Christ is given to us 'as a price of redemption' and 'as price of remuneration'. The same verse from Isaiah promises that 'the

---

[7] In his *Summa Contra Gentiles* Aquinas stated in an unqualified way: 'the offence is cancelled only by love' (3. 157). It was the quality of Christ's love (rather than the quantity of his suffering or of the blood he shed) that counted with Aquinas.

government/authority will be upon his [the child's] shoulders'. This draws from Aquinas the reflection: 'God placed upon the shoulders of Christ first sins, as upon one who *satisfies* [Isa. 53: 6]; second a key, as upon a priest [Isa. 22: 22] . . . third, principality, as upon a conqueror [Isa. 9: 6] . . . fourth, glory as upon one who triumphs [Isa. 22: 24]' (*Super Isaiam*, 9. 1. 1; italics ours). Here Aquinas already interprets human redemption as the work of satisfaction performed by Christ as priest.

To support his understanding of 'satisfy', 'key', 'principality', and 'glory', Aquinas alludes to a range of verses in Isaiah, which we indicate in square brackets. The 'key' 'as upon a priest' seems to indicate the key of his palace that the Davidic king entrusted to his major-domo. The notion of 'major-domo' does not, of course, by any means cover all that Aquinas will say about the priesthood of Christ. As we have already seen, it entails much more (above all, the unique love exercised by this priest) than God's 'placing' human sins upon 'the shoulders of Christ'.

PRIESTLY SACRIFICE

Let us now take up Aquinas's most significant treatment of Christ's priesthood as found in *STh.* 3a. 22. Divided into six articles, this question maintains a theme that reaches back through Augustine to Hebrews: Christ achieved his priestly work by offering a sacrifice— namely, himself. His priesthood and sacrifice are inseparably linked. As regards sacrifice, Augustine, as we recalled in the last chapter, understood 'sacrifice' to inhere in every work that unites human beings with God. Aquinas offers a similar description: 'anything placed before God with the purpose of raising the human spirit to him may be termed a sacrifice' (22. 2 resp.). Thus Hebrews (on which Aquinas wrote a commentary) and Augustine remain very much present in question 22.

Aquinas leads off in the first article by maintaining that Christ eminently exemplifies the 'characteristic function' of a priest, 'to be a mediator between God and the people'. That function means that a priest both (1) 'communicates to the people the things of God' or

'divine gifts', and (2) 'offers to God the prayers of the people and to some degree (*aliqualiter*) makes reparation to God for their sins'. To illustrate the first characteristic task of the priestly office, Thomas cites Malachi 2: 7 (see Chapter 1 above) about the duty of priests to teach the divine law to the people (22. 1 resp.). This description of the two-way function of priesthood recalls the summary account of priestly mediation in the Old Testament provided by Werner Dommershausen (Chapter 1 above). The mediation of priests runs in two directions: from God to the people and from the people to God.

Aquinas firmly bases himself here (and in the subsequent five articles) on the witness to Christ's priesthood provided by the Letter to the Hebrews. He also argues here that, while other human beings possess only particular graces, Christ, as the Head of humanity, must possess 'the fullness of all graces' (22. 1 ad 3). Hence Christ is not only king and prophet but also priest. Elsewhere Aquinas pushes the same principle of perfection—Christ must have the best of every-thing available—when providing similar, triple schemes about the *grace* of Christ (the grace of the hypostatic union, habitual or super-natural grace, and the grace of 'headship' or of being Head of the Church) and about the *human knowledge* of Christ (the beatific vision, infused knowledge, and experimental knowledge).[8]

The second article follows Hebrews by maintaining that Christ was priest *and* victim, but not in the sense of his committing suicide: he 'did not slay himself'. Two distinct intentions converged to bring about Christ's death: 'in the intention of his executioners there was no question of Christ being a sacrificial victim; for his executioners are not said to have offered a sacrifice to God; on the contrary, their action was gravely sinful.' But if we refer 'the slaying of Christ to the will of the one who suffered and who freely gave himself up to his passion, then he takes on the character of a victim' (22: 2 ad 2). Aquinas makes a crucial distinction between the will of those who put Jesus to death and the will of Jesus in accepting his death.

Aquinas deftly evokes Hebrews (and the Jewish Law) by proposing three reasons for sacrifice: to obtain remission for sins (Heb. 5: 1;

---

[8] See *STh.* 3a. 7–12; G. O'Collins, *Christology: A Biblical, Historical, and Systematic Study of Jesus* (2nd edn., Oxford: Oxford University Press, 2009), 208–9, 264–9, 274, 284–5.

10: 12), to cause saving grace (Heb. 5: 9), and to bring perfect unity with God in glory (Heb. 10: 19). It was precisely through the humanity of Christ that these three benefits were conferred: 'Christ as man was not only a priest but also a perfect victim, being at the same time a victim for sin, a peace victim, and a holocaust' (22. 2 resp.). The Old Law prescribes three principal sacrifices: the sacrifice for sin, the peace offering, and the holocaust. The purpose of these multiple and repeated sacrifices was achieved once and for all by Christ's sacrifice of himself.

Article 3 examines how Christ's priestly work expiates sin: by removing 'the stain of guilt' and fully removing liability to punishment by 'satisfying' God. While Christ was a priest 'inasmuch he was human', nevertheless, it was 'one and the same' person who was priest and God: his divine identity made his sacrifice 'most efficacious in blotting out sins' and truly capable of 'satisfying fully'. Thus his priesthood had 'full power to expiate sins' and bring about 'a perfect cleansing from sins'. One hears an echo here of Anselm's argument about Christ's divine identity conferring an infinite value on his human act of satisfaction for sins. Yet Aquinas reaches further back to cite Augustine in his support: 'four things are to be considered in every sacrifice—to whom it is offered, *by whom it is offered*, what is offered, for whom it is offered. One and the same true Mediator reconciling us to God by the sacrifice of peace remained *one with him to whom it was offered*, united in himself those for whom he offered it, and at the same time offered it himself and was himself that which he offered' (*De Trinitate*, 4. 14; italics ours). In developing Augustine's argument, Aquinas succeeds in justifying theologically the full and perfect value that the Letter to the Hebrews acknowledged in Christ's self-sacrifice (22. 3 resp. and ad 1).

Against the sufficiency of Christ's high-priestly sacrifice Aquinas wonders whether such sufficiency is put in question by the Church's Eucharistic practice of a daily sacrifice for sins—an issue that could not be controversial for Hebrews, which at best barely touches on the Eucharist (see Chapter 3 above). Aquinas argues that the enduring nature of human sinfulness is reason enough that Christ's sacrifice to remove those continual sins continues as well. But, once again appealing to Augustine, he adds: 'the sacrifice that is offered every day in the Church is not distinct from the sacrifice that Christ himself

offered, but is a commemoration of it. As Augustine [*The City of God*, 10. 20] says: "Christ himself is both the priest who offers it [the sacrifice] and the offering: he wished the daily sacrifice of the Church to be the sacrament of this reality"' (22. 3 ad 2).

To support further the daily offering of the Eucharist for the atonement of sins, Aquinas recalls an argument that Origen (*In Ioan.* 6. 32) drew from the particular animal, a lamb, prescribed by the Old Law for morning and evening sacrifice every day (Num. 28: 3–4). This daily offering of a lamb prefigured Christ's sacrifice, which was 'the consummation of all other sacrifices'. For good measure, Thomas quotes John 1: 29: 'behold the Lamb of God who takes away the sins of the world' (22. 3 ad 3). His exegesis obviously goes beyond any 'authorial' intention of the evangelist. John's Gospel has in mind, the annual (not daily) Passover ritual when lambs were offered and eaten (see Chapter 1 above).

In the fourth article Aquinas raises the question: 'did the effect of Christ's priesthood benefit Christ himself as well as others?' On the basis of one of the twelve 'anathemas' appended to Cyril of Alexandria's third letter to Nestorius (read at the Council of Ephesus in 431 but apparently not officially approved by the Council fathers), Aquinas replies: since Christ was innocent of sin, he did not derive any benefit from the exercise of his priesthood (see DzH 261; ND 606/ 10). Along with an explicit and non-controversial argument, 'the offering of sacrifice is the principal act of the priestly office' (22. 4 resp.), Aquinas endorses Cyril's implicit position that sacrifice for oneself is necessarily a sacrifice for one's sins. Here a small quibble seems in order. To be sure, Old Testament's sacrifices 'for oneself' were regularly understood and prescribed as sacrifices to expiate one's own sins. But what of the second and third principal types of sacrifices mentioned by Aquinas in article 2: 'the peace offering' and 'the holocaust'? The Letter to the Hebrews recognizes effects of Christ's sacrifice that go beyond the expiation of sins. Surely being the Mediator of the new covenant who has opened the way to God's presence could be understood to be Christ's priesthood *also* benefiting himself?

In the course of his discussion Thomas qualifies his position. Christ, while having no need to offer a sacrifice of satisfaction for his own sins, 'gained the glory of the resurrection from his act of

worship, by which, under the influence of love, he bore with humility his passion' (22. 4 ad 2).

As well as acknowledging the love that was the driving force of Christ's self-sacrifice and the glory gained by resurrection, Aquinas presses beyond Hebrews and even Augustine by introducing a philosophical/theological axiom he uses elsewhere (e.g. *STh.* 1a. 2. 3): the most perfect representative of any kind exercises a causal influence on all participants in that kind. Thus Christ communicates priesthood and its benefits to others, because he is 'the source of all priesthood'. Just as 'the sun gives light but is not illuminated [by anything else] and a fire heats but is not heated [by anything else], so Christ is "the first agent" in the genus of priesthood who does not "receive" but rather "influences" others in that genus' (22. 4 resp.). The principle enunciated here converges somewhat with the tenth point we gleaned in our Preface from *BEM* and the *Final Report*: all other priesthood is *derived* from Christ's priesthood.

In the same paragraph Aquinas adds a phrase that would be repeated frequently in modern times: the ordained 'priests of the new law' 'act in the person of Christ'.[9] He cites in support the Vulgate translation of Paul's words in 2 Corinthians 2: 10: 'what I have given . . . I have done for your sake in the person of Christ (*in persona Christi*).' In post-New Testament times the Greek term *prosōpon* was to pick up the sense of 'person', but in Paul's phrase it is more accurately translated as 'in the presence of Christ'. Thomas was to speak of ordained priests acting 'in the person of Christ' when celebrating the Eucharist (*STh.* 3a. 82. 1 resp.; 3. 82. 5 resp.). But he also proposes some important, alternative language in his commentary on Hebrews: 'only Christ is the true priest, the others being only his ministers' (*Hebreos* 8. 4).[10]

---

[9] See e.g. the 1947 encyclical on the sacred liturgy by Pius XII, *Mediator Dei*, who speaks of 'ministers at the altar' acting 'in the person of Christ' (DzH 3852; ND 1736). The Second Vatican Council's Dogmatic Constitution on the Church (*Lumen Gentium*) teaches that it is 'in the person of Christ' that the 'ministerial priest effects the Eucharistic sacrifice' (no. 10).

[10] The 1992 *Catechism of the Catholic Church* (no. 1545) quotes this sentence from Thomas, evidently wishing to emphasize the unique status of Christ's priesthood and to avoid applying to ordained ministers the controversial term 'sacrificing priests'.

In his fifth article Thomas reflects on the eternal nature of Christ's priesthood and might have drawn on the Creed ('and his kingdom will have no end') to state: 'just as his kingship lasts forever, so too does his priesthood.' Rather, he distinguishes the once-and-for-all event of redemption (the actual offering of the sacrifice) from its results (or its 'consummation'): while 'the passion and death of Jesus are never to be repeated', the 'efficacy' of his sacrifice lasts forever (22. 5 ad 2). The offering at the Last Supper, with its outcome in the death on Calvary, is over and done with and not repeatable, but it remains an eternal sacrifice as being permanently the source of eternal union between God and human beings.

Citing the prescriptions in Leviticus 16: 11–12 for the Great Day of Expiation, Aquinas observes that the precise place for the sacrifice of two animals was outside and not within the Holy of Holies. This allows him to make the analogy: Christ's passion and death set the stage for his entrance *into* the Holy of Holies, where his priestly activity continues but no longer as it did on earth—on the altar outside the Holy of Holies. Christ 'entered into the Holy of Holies— that is, into heaven—providing a way of entry for us by the power of his own blood', which was 'shed for us on earth' (22. 5 resp.).

The shedding of Christ's blood took place only on earth. Here, despite their substantial convergence on other points, Aquinas's theology contrasted with some strands of devotion in the late Middle Ages. Various visions and depictions of heaven included graphic accounts of Christ bleeding in heaven.[11] The *Adoration of the Lamb*, painted in the early fifteenth century by the brothers Hubert and Jan van Eyck, shows angels and saints in heaven adoring the Lamb. He stands enthroned on an altar, but his blood flows into a chalice on

---

[11] See C. W. Bynum, 'The Power in the Blood: Sacrifice, Satisfaction and Sub-stitution in Late Medieval Soteriology', in S. T. Davis, D. Kendall, and G. O'Collins (eds.), *The Redemption* (Oxford: Oxford University Press, 2004), 177–204, at 183–6. When commenting on Heb. 10: 19, John Calvin offers a certain counterpart to the 'vision' of the van Eyck brothers: 'the blood of Christ . . . flows continually in un-adulterated purity; it will suffice for us to the end of the world . . . the blood of Christ is continually being shed before the face of the Father to spread over heaven and earth' (*The Epistle of Paul the Apostle to the Hebrews*, trans. W. B. Johnston (Edin-burgh: Oliver & Boyd, 1963), 140–1).

that altar. This may be justified in terms of the faithful still on earth appropriating, especially through the Eucharist, the redemption achieved by Christ's suffering and death. But by representing the continuing shedding of blood the imagery departs from the way in which the heavenly adoration of 'the Lamb who was slain' is depicted in the Book of Revelation. As we recalled in Chapter 2, right from its opening verses (1: 6) this book speaks of the blood of Christ, but always as blood that has been shed (once and for all in the past) to cleanse and free human beings from their sins.

Throughout question 22 it is only in the fifth article that Aquinas cites the Book of Revelation. Here he does so to good effect when considering the impact of Christ's priesthood on the saints in heaven. Since they have arrived in heaven, they 'will not need any further expiation through the priesthood of Christ', but 'they will need consummation through Christ'. Their 'glory will depend on him', 'the Lamb' who will be 'the lamp' of the heavenly Jerusalem (Rev. 21: 23).

The sixth and final article of question 22 addresses the issue: how can Christ be a 'priest according to the order of Melchizedek'? Such language suggests that, since a part is less than a whole, Christ's priesthood is somehow a subset of the priesthood of Melchizedek. As Christ is 'the source of all priesthood' and 'the principal/supreme priest', he cannot follow 'the order of others' and be a 'priest according to the order of Melchizedek' (22. 6, *videtur quod non*). Christ's priesthood seems to have been more clearly prefigured by the 'order' of Levitical priesthood, in which, unlike what was said about Melchizedek, there were sacrifices that entailed the 'shedding of blood' (22. 6 ad 2).

Yet Aquinas follows Hebrews 7: 4–10 by insisting that the priesthood of Melchizedek prefigured 'the pre-eminence of Christ's priesthood' over the Levitical priesthood. Melchizedek received tithes from Abraham, in whose 'loins' the Levitical priesthood was already present. The meeting between Melchizedek and Abraham showed the superiority of the former because he received tithes from the latter, and, as Hebrews but not Aquinas notes, Melchizedek blessed Abraham. To say then that Christ's priesthood is according to the order of Melchizedek indicates 'the pre-eminence' of Christ's 'true priesthood over its symbol, the priesthood of the Law' (22. 6 resp.).

Unlike the Letter to the Hebrews, but like the patristic tradition that followed Clement of Alexandria, Thomas understands Melchizedek's offering of bread and wine to have foreshadowed the Eucharist and thus to have prefigured more explicitly 'the pre-eminence of Christ's priesthood over that of the Law'. The 'true sacrifice of Christ is communicated to the faithful under the appearance of bread and wine'. In this way Christ the High Priest never ceases to offer through the Eucharist his one sacrifice. Thus Melchizedek's offering of bread and wine pointed to this constant offering and to the Eucharistic fellowship and 'ecclesiastical unity' that 'sharing in the sacrifice of Christ establishes' (22. 6 ad 2).

We can add a few footnotes to this central account of Aquinas on Christ's priesthood by examining some points in what he wrote about Christ as Mediator, the sacraments, and the ascension, as well as in the liturgical texts that he composed for the feast of Corpus Christi (instituted in 1264). But before doing that, we need to reflect further on a theme that runs right through the six articles of question 22: the sacrifice of Christ and its effects. As we saw, Thomas expounded the following aspects of this central theme: sacrifice is a central act of priestly mediation (art. 1); in Christ's case the priest was also the sacrificial victim (art. 2); his priestly sacrifice expiated sins and is commemorated in the Eucharist, the daily sacrifice of the Church (art. 3); Christ's sacrifice was motivated by love and gained him the glory of the resurrection (art. 4); while the passion of Christ is never repeated, the efficacy of his priestly sacrifice lasts forever (art. 5); Melchizedek's offering of bread and wine prefigured the sacrifice that Christ communicated to the faithful 'under the appearance of bread and wine' (art. 6).

We saw how Thomas, in the light of Psalm 51: 19 and of what Augustine wrote in *The City of God* (10. 5), endorsed a broad, non-cultic account of sacrifice: 'anything placed before God with the purpose of raising the human spirit to him may be termed a sacrifice' (22. 2 resp.). Yet in the very same response Aquinas proposed a more cultic reading of sacrifice, or at least of the priestly sacrifice of Christ, who was 'a perfect victim, being at the same time a victim for sin, a peace victim, and a holocaust'. Thomas drew here on the Letter to the Hebrews, which lavishly used imagery from sacrificial rituals in the Old Testament, with the aim of showing both (1) the superiority of

Christ's priesthood to that of the Levitical priesthood and (2) the superiority of the sacrifice Christ offered once and for all (Heb. 9: 12, 26–8). But, then, Hebrews recalled that Christ did not die in the sacred setting of an altar in the sanctuary of the Temple but in a profane setting: his bloody death on a cross took place 'outside the city gate' (Heb. 13: 11–13). Not unlike Hebrews, Thomas proposes a non-cultic, as well as a cultic, reading of Christ's priestly sacrifice. The tension between these two readings will surface dramatically in Reformation debates over the ministry of those ordained to share in Christ's priesthood.

It was outside question 22 and its account of Christ's priestly sacrifice that Aquinas allowed himself to interpret the specific purpose of sacrifice; it was that of 'placating' God: 'in the proper meaning of the term one calls sacrifice something which is done to render God due honour with a view to placating him' (*STh*. 3a. 48. 3 resp.). Earlier in the *Summa Theologiae* Thomas dedicated an entire question to sacrifice (2a2ae. 85). There he stressed the obligation to offer sacrifice and to do so to God alone, but he never introduced in that context the purpose of placating God. When he dealt with Christ's passion and sacrifice, however, Aquinas did so in the light of satisfaction which he saw as the act of a particular form of justice: namely, penance that involves a penal or punitive element (3a. 47. 3), an element expressly excluded by Anselm. This change Aquinas introduced into the Anselmian view of satisfaction helped to prepare the way for the idea of Christ being punished and so propitiating an angry God by paying a redemptive ransom. Aquinas held that, by offering his blood, Christ paid this price to God (3a. 48. 4 ad 3).

To be sure, Thomas did not hold that Christ's priestly work of reconciliation meant that God began to love sinful human beings again only after the punishment was effected and the ransom paid. God's love for human beings, he insisted, is everlasting; it is we who are changed by the washing away of sin and the offering of a suitable compensation (*STh*. 3a. 49. 4 ad 2). Yet, despite some improvements (e.g. the stress on Christ's *loving* acceptance of his passion), the way Aquinas adjusted Anselm's theory of satisfaction helped open the door to an unfortunate version of redemption: Christ as a penal substitute who was personally burdened with the sins of humanity, judged, condemned, and deservedly punished in our place. Thus,

through his death he satisfied the divine justice, paid the required price, and propitiated an angry God. In this way Anselm's theory about Jesus offering satisfaction to meet the requirements of commutative justice and set right a moral order damaged by sin acquired, quite contrary to Anselm's explicit statements, elements of punishment and vindictive (or retributive) justice.[12] But any such talk about Christ being punished and so placating an angry God seems irreconcilable with what the Letter to the Hebrews proposed about Christ's priesthood and the inseparable reality of his sacrifice.[13]

PRIESTLY MEDIATION

Since the Letter to the Hebrews calls Christ 'mediator' when it presents his priestly work as 'the mediator of a new/better covenant' (8: 6; 9: 15; 12: 24), it is to be expected that Thomas would take up the notion of mediation as a subset discussion of Christ's priesthood, as John Chrysostom did (see Chapter 5 above). He does dedicate one question (of two articles) to the theme of mediation (*STh.* 3a. 26. 1–2), but without ever mentioning Hebrews and its account of Christ as High Priest. The key text, cited three times in the two articles, is 1 Timothy 2: 5, which acknowledges Christ as 'the one mediator between God and human beings'. We should note that this text does not say either that Christ is 'the one and only mediator' or that he is 'unique mediator'.

Aquinas is concerned to show that this mediatorship of Christ does *not* mean that others (priests and prophets in the Old Testament and Christian priests) cannot be called 'in a qualified sense (*secundum quid*) mediators between God and human beings: namely, inasmuch as they co-operate in uniting human beings with God, either as preparing the way or as ministers.' The 'prophets and priests of the Old Law' can, therefore, be called 'mediators', since they 'announced and prefigured the perfect Mediator between God and

[12] For difficulties about theories of penal substitution, see G. O'Collins, *Jesus Our Redeemer* (Oxford: Oxford University Press, 2007), 133–60.

[13] Ibid. 162–5.

men'. In their turn, 'the priests of the New Law can be called mediators between God and men inasmuch as they are ministers of the
true Mediator, administering in his place (*vice ipsius*) the sacraments
of salvation' (26. 1 resp. and ad 1).

Speaking of 'the priests of the New Law' who, in the place of
Christ, visibly minister the sacraments injects some priestly environment into question 26, but—to be fussily accurate—Thomas never
calls Christ a 'priest' in this question. As we saw above, Aquinas
begins his account of Christ's priesthood in question 22 by calling
him 'a mediator between God and the people'. Yet here in question 26
he does not state that, being a mediator, Christ was/is a priest. In any
case, mediation is a broader category than priesthood. All priests are
mediators, but not all mediators are priests.

Thomas sets himself to interpret and restate the classic text from
1 Timothy about Christ as 'mediator'. In doing this, he glosses the text
by calling Christ 'the good Mediator who reconciles enemies' (26. 1 ad
2; see Augustine, *The City of God*, 9. 13) and 'the perfect Mediator
between God and human beings, inasmuch as through his death he
reconciled the human race with God' (26. 1 resp.). In expounding here
the text from 1 Timothy, Aquinas consciously borrows the language of
'reconciliation' from 2 Corinthians 5: 19. But he does not cite what
Hebrews had to say about Christ's 'more excellent', high-priestly 'ministry (*leitourgia*)' *mediating* 'a better covenant' (Heb. 8: 6).

Nevertheless, Christ's office as mediator and that as priest share
inseparably a central and necessary presupposition: the Son of God
took on the human condition. Thomas's stress on Christ's humanity
as a priest parallels his reasoning about mediation. He firmly follows
Augustine (*The City of God*, 9. 15) by insisting that 'it is as man' that
Christ was and is 'Mediator'. Aquinas writes:

we may consider two things in a mediator: first, his role as intermediary;
second, his office of bringing [others] together. Now the role of being an
intermediary involves being distinct from both extremes, while the mediator's
office of bringing these extremes together involves bearing what belongs to
one over to the other. Now, neither of these [conditions] can be applied to
Christ inasmuch as he is God but only inasmuch as he is a human being.

Both conditions are realized in Christ as human being. 'Inasmuch as
he is a human being, he is distinct from God in nature and from

[other] human beings in the eminence of both grace and glory. Inasmuch as he is a human being, his office is to bring together God and human beings, which he does by communicating to human beings the commandments and gifts of God and by offering satisfaction and prayers to God for human beings.' Hence Aquinas concludes: Christ 'is most truly called Mediator, inasmuch as he is a human being' (26: 2 resp.).

Christ's function as priestly Mediator depended, then, upon his becoming incarnate. The defining moment of this mediation was his passion, death, and resurrection. Aquinas is well aware how Hebrews understands that Christ, by mediating through his passion a new covenant (Heb. 9: 15; 12: 24), offered human beings eternal life by a new way into the presence of God (Heb. 10: 19–20). It was then that, 'through his death the perfect Mediator between God and human beings reconciled the human race to God' (26. 1 resp.).

THE SACRAMENTS AND CORPUS CHRISTI

As regards the sacraments, Aquinas endorses an unqualified statement: 'the whole liturgy (*ritus*) of the Christian religion is derived from the priesthood of Christ' (*STh.* 3a. 63. 3 resp.). Since the defining moment of that priesthood came in the passion, Thomas maintains: 'through his passion' Christ 'initiated the liturgy (*ritus*) of the Christian religion' (3a. 62. 5 resp.). Thus he holds tightly together Christ's priesthood and passion with the sacramental life of Christians.

Those who become the 'members' of the crucified and risen Christ (through baptism and confirmation) or who become his ministers (through ordination) receive a 'sacramental character' that 'indelibly' marks them. Such sacramental characters (that can never be repeated or received a second time), Aquinas remarks, 'are nothing else than certain kinds of participation in Christ's priesthood derived from Christ himself' (*STh.* 3a. 63. 3 resp.). Those who receive such a 'character' or seal are 'deputed' not only 'firstly and principally to the enjoyment of glory', but also, secondly, 'to receive or hand on to others what pertains to the worship of God'. In this way, 'those who

are deputed to Christian worship, of which Christ is the author, receive a character by which they become like Christ', the High Priest himself (ibid.).

Two articles later, when defining the permanent or 'indelible' nature of sacramental 'characters', Thomas returns to the 'configuration' to Christ the Priest that the sacramental character effects: 'a sacramental character is a certain participation in Christ's priesthood ... just as Christ has the full power of spiritual priesthood, so his faithful are shaped like him [literally, 'configured to him'] in that they share in some spiritual power relating to the sacraments and the things pertaining to divine worship.' On the one hand there is 'the power (*potestas*)' of Christ's priesthood, and on the other, the sacramental character by which the faithful (all the baptized faithful) share in his priesthood. The relationship is comparable to what holds between 'that which is full and perfect' and 'something that participates in it'.

This general principle allows Thomas to press on and argue for the enduring nature of sacramental characters: just as Christ's priesthood is eternal,[14] so 'every sanctification brought by his priesthood is perpetual'. Hence, 'the character remains indelibly' in/on the human soul of the baptized (*STh.* 3a. 65. 5 resp.). In expounding further the indelible nature of the sacramental character, Aquinas introduces the scheme of principal and instrumental causes and powers. The baptismal character remains 'indelibly in the soul, not by reason of its own perfection, but by reason of the perfection of Christ's priesthood, from which the character is derived as a certain kind of instrumental power (*virtus*)' (3a. 65. 5 ad 1).

In general, Aquinas connects the power of all the sacraments (in their full scope and not merely in the 'character' imparted by three sacraments) to Christ's sacrifice in the passion and to faith in the power of Christ's passion and its effects. It is 'the power (*virtus*) of Christ's passion that operates in the sacraments' (*STh.* 3a. 64. 1 ad 2). To illustrate that 'the sacraments of the Church derive their power from the passion of Christ', Thomas endorses an ancient reflection on

---

[14] To establish the eternity of Christ's priesthood, Aquinas cites Ps. 110: 4 ('you are a priest for ever according to the order of Melchizedek'), rather than the text of the Letter to the Hebrews itself.

the blood and water that issued from the side of Christ (John 19: 34). It was from the side of Christ asleep on the cross that there flowed the sacraments (in particular baptism and the Eucharist, symbolized respectively by the water and the blood) that brought salvation to the Church (*STh*. 3a. 62. 5 resp.).

Yet, when reflecting on the sacraments and their ministers, Thomas hardly ever invokes Christ's priesthood as such. Since 'the whole liturgy of the Christian religion is derived from the priesthood of Christ' (see above), one might expect Thomas to invoke that priesthood more frequently, but this is not the case. He declares that 'the whole power of the sacraments flows from Christ's passion, which belongs to him as a human being' (*STh*. 3a. 64. 7 resp.). One might have expected Aquinas to say: 'the whole power of the sacraments flows from Christ's passion, which belongs to him as a human being *and High Priest.*' In theory, he links together Christ's (1) passion, (2) priesthood, and (3) the sacraments. But in practice, the second theme is sometimes omitted or at least quietly assumed.

Like Augustine, he distinguishes the principal, invisible agent (Christ) from the instrumental (visible) agents in the administration of the sacraments (even if, unlike Augustine, he uses the terminology of principal and instrumental causes). Ordained ministers are like 'an instrument' that 'acts not by reason of its own form, but by the power of the one who moves it'. Hence, 'ministers of the Church can confer sacraments, though they be wicked' (*STh*. 3a. 64. 5 resp.).

Unlike Augustine, Thomas explicitly recognizes that 'God did not bind his power to the sacraments [and the ordained ministers of the Church], in such a way as to be unable to confer the effect of the sacraments without [conferring] the sacrament themselves' (*STh*. 3a. 64. 7 resp.). This conviction underlies the view Thomas expresses when treating the sacrament of penance (or reconciliation). In case of emergency a non-ordained Christian could receive the confession and, while unable to absolve the sins confessed, can be confident that Christ 'the High Priest' will supply the necessary absolution. Aquinas writes: 'when there is reason for urgency, the penitent should fulfill his own part, by being contrite and confessing to whom he can, and although this person [presumably another Christian] cannot perfect the sacrament, so as to fulfill the part of the priest by giving absolution, yet this defect is supplied by the High Priest' (3a. Supplement, 82. ad 1).

Thomas's specific discussion of the Eucharist (*STh.* 3a. 73–83) also introduces very occasional references to Christ as priest. Let us cite two of them. First, when arguing that the Eucharist is the greatest of the sacraments, he remarks that it is even greater than those three sacraments that confer an indelible 'character' (baptism, confirmation, and holy orders): 'the sacramental character, as stated above [3a. 63. 3], is a kind of participation in Christ's priesthood. Hence the sacrament that joins Christ himself to human beings is more sublime than a sacrament that [merely] imprints a character of Christ' (3a. 65. 3 ad 3). Second, when examining 'defects' in the celebration of a sacrament, Thomas cites the (far-fetched) case of a priest who, in the course of celebrating the Mass, recalls that he is under 'some excommunication': 'he ought [to continue] while resolving humbly to seek absolution; and so he will receive absolution from the invisible High Priest for his act of completing the divine mysteries' (3a. 83. 6 ad 2).

The prose of Thomas's Eucharistic theology was translated into poetic and liturgical texts that he composed for the office (known as '*Sacerdos in eternum* (priest for ever)'), and Mass of the Feast of Corpus Christi, works that seem to be correctly attributed to him. The priesthood of Christ is explicitly invoked in the opening antiphon for the first vespers of the feast; it begins with the words, 'Christ our Lord, a priest forever according to the order of Melchizedek (*sacerdos in eternum Christus Dominus secundum ordinem Melchisedech*)'.[15] But that seems to be the only explicit naming of Christ's own priesthood in the texts composed by Thomas for the new feast of Corpus Christi.

For matins he wrote *Sacris solemniis* (best known for its penultimate strophe, which begins '*Panis angelicus*'), for lauds *Verbum supernum prodiens* (best known for its last two strophes, which begin '*O salutaris hostia*'), for vespers *Pange lingua gloriosi* (best

[15] On the office of Corpus Christi, see P. M. Gy, 'L'Office du Corpus Christi, oeuvre de S. Thomas d'Aquin. État d'une recherche', in *Revue des Sciences Philosophiques et Théologiques*, 64 (1980), 491–507; reprinted in id., *La Liturgie dans l'histoire* (Paris: Cerf, 1990), 223–46. See also J. Lamberts, 'The Origins of the Corpus Christi Feast', *Worship*, 71 (1996), 432–46; M. Rubin, *Corpus Christi: The Eucharist in Late Medieval Culture* (Cambridge: Cambridge University Press, 1991); J. A. Weisheipl, *Friar Thomas D'Aquino: His Life, Thought, and Works* (rev. edn., Washington, DC: Catholic University of America Press, 1983).

known for its last two strophes, which begin '*Tantum ergo*').[16] For the Mass he composed the propers, the wonderful sequence, *Lauda Sion salvatorem*, and apparently *Adoro te devote* (used as a hymn of thanksgiving after Mass). But in all these hymns and propers the only explicit reference to anyone's priesthood comes in the third-to-last strophe of *Sacris solemniis*. With reference to the Last Supper, this strophe acknowledges that Christ performed a priestly action ('that sacrifice') and committed to priests the function of continuing this priestly office, but does not literally call Christ a priest: 'thus he instituted that sacrifice, the celebration of which he wished to commit only to priests, to whom it thus belongs to receive and to give to others (*sic sacrificium istud instituit, cuius officium committi voluit solis presbyteris, quibus sic congruit, ut sumant et dent ceteris*)'.[17] In the hymns Thomas composed, Christ is named as 'saving victim (*salutaris hostia*)' and as 'the paschal lamb (*agnus Paschae*)' (in *Lauda Sion*).

The office and Mass composed (most likely) by Aquinas leave us with a puzzle. He wrote about Christ's priestly institution of the Eucharist at the Last Supper and the consummation of this priestly offering on Calvary. He spoke of Christ's 'sacrifice' and called him 'victim' and 'Paschal lamb'. He mentioned his will that only 'priests' should subsequently celebrate the Eucharist. But, apart from the opening antiphon of the first vespers (see above), Thomas never explicitly names Christ himself as 'priest'. One does not find that title alongside 'shepherd (*pastor*)', 'king (*rex*)', leader (*dux*)', and 'saviour (*salvator*)', titles that occur in *Lauda Sion*, to which one can add 'loving pelican (*pie pellicane*)', an address to Christ that comes in *Adoro te devote*.

This reticence seems part of a larger phenomenon. In *Poetry of the Passion* Jack Bennett studies twelve centuries of English verse, from *The Dream of the Rood*—he prefers to give this untitled work the name of 'A Vision of a Rood'—in the early eighth century down to

---

[16] These three hymns have their antecedents in older liturgies, but none of them can be found complete before the thirteenth-century office of Corpus Christi. At the very least, Thomas reworked these texts.

[17] In the Mass the offertory verse applies to the priests of the New Law some words from Lev. 21: 6: 'the priests of the Lord offer incense and loaves to God, and therefore they shall be sacred to their God and not profane his name.'

the twentieth.[18] About half the book deals with the period of Thomas Aquinas and the centuries that preceded and followed him. Poetic texts of all kinds studied in this volume call Christ 'king', 'lord', 'hero', 'warrior', 'knight', 'man of sorrows', 'saviour', 'lover', but never 'priest'. Since these poetic texts of the Middle Ages deal with Christ's priestly sacrifice on Calvary (including such details as his five wounds) and sometimes with his priestly offering at the Last Supper, their 'failure' to call Christ priest or the new High Priest also seems surprising, but it puts Thomas's reticence in a larger cultural setting. Passion narratives abound, but they are not articulated precisely and explicitly in terms of Christ's priesthood. Here one can also cite the two classic volumes of Gertrud Schiller, *Iconography of Christian Art*.[19] She gathers many kinds of images of Christ that picture him as judge, lord of the cosmos, ruler of the world, saviour, teacher, victor, and so forth. But images of Christ as priest are hardly ever to be found.

THE ASCENSION

His close study of the Letter to the Hebrews prompted Aquinas into a further footnote to his (relatively brief) account of Christ's priesthood: the significance of the ascension, by which 'he prepared a way for us into heaven' (*STh.* 3a. 57. 6 ad 1).

In the old dispensation the entry of the high priest once a year into the Holy of Holies prefigured a key moment in Christ's role as priest: his ascending into heaven to sit at the Father's right hand. Aquinas saw that entrance into heaven as a final step in the process of human salvation. 'As the high priest in the Old Testament', he wrote, 'entered the sanctuary to stand before God for the people, so also Christ entered heaven "to make intercession for us" [Heb. 7: 25].' Thomas insists on Christ's humanity as central to his priestly role, including the definitive, heavenly stage (or point of arrival) of that priestly role: 'The showing (*repraesentatio*) of himself in the human nature, which he took with

---

[18] J. A. W. Bennett, *Poetry of the Passion: Studies in Twelve Centuries of English Verse* (Oxford: Clarendon Press, 1982).
[19] London: Lund Humphries, 1971–2.

him to heaven, is itself a pleading for us.' God, who 'exalted the human nature in Christ, will also show mercy towards those for whose sake the Son of God assumed human nature' (*STh*. 3a. 57. 6 ad 2).

In the twentieth century Tom Torrance also attended to the priestly implications of the ascension and did so under the rubric of 'the three-fold office of Christ in the ascension'.[20] In this discussion, Christ as priest drew much more attention than Christ as prophet and king. Torrance understood that, 'through the Spirit, Christ's own priestly ministry is at work in and through the Church which is his body'.[21] Torrance built his account of the ongoing priestly ministry of the ascended Christ around three themes: 'eternal self-oblation', 'eternal intercession or advocacy for us', and 'eternal benediction'.[22] Aquinas showed a similar interest in the second theme. But his treatment of the priestly face of Christ's ascension might have been enriched by Torrance's first and third themes: the ascended Christ eternally offers himself to the Father on our behalf and eternally imparts to us his blessing.

CONCLUSION

In this chapter we have been concerned to expound and evaluate Aquinas's reflections on Christ's priesthood. As we recalled in note 2 above, Aquinas also recognized Christ's functions as prophet and king. In at least one passage of the *Summa* he also drew the three offices together, substituting 'legislator' for 'prophet': 'the legislator is one figure, the priest another, and the king another. But all of these come together in Christ as the fountain of all graces (*alius est legislator et alius sacerdos et alius rex; sed haec omnia concurrunt in Christo tanquam in fonte omnium gratiarum*)' (*STh*. 3. 22. 1 ad 3).

We will see in later chapters how others developed their thinking about Christ's priesthood within a view of his triple office as priest, prophet, and king.

---

[20] T. F. Torrance, *Space, Time and Resurrection* (Edinburgh: Handsel Press, 1976), 112–22.
[21] Ibid. 118.
[22] Ibid. 112–18.

7

Luther and Calvin on Christ's Priesthood

Contemporary debates did not disturb very much the narrative that Thomas Aquinas developed about Christ's priesthood. Open to biblical voices (especially the Letter to the Hebrews) and later voices (especially Augustine of Hippo), he embraced a world of Catholic theology in reflecting, albeit not very extensively and explicitly, on that priesthood and what it entailed. The complex theological legacy of the thirteenth century, while weakened in the following two centuries, clearly came unstuck in the controversies of the sixteenth. The intense religious fervour of Martin Luther (1483–1545) and John Calvin (1509–64) measured and reinterpreted Christ's priesthood in an environment they saw to be marked by widespread corruption.[1]

MARTIN LUTHER

Luther, the earlier Reformer, restated the spiritual or interior aspect of Christ's priesthood, seemingly as an antidote to the external disarray and worse that he saw in the sixteenth-century Church. In *On the Papacy in Rome*, a treatise from 1520, he wrote: 'Christ is a

[1] For background material on Luther see D. K. McKim (ed.), *The Cambridge Companion to Martin Luther* (Cambridge: Cambridge University Press, 2003); on Calvin, see id. (ed.), *The Cambridge Companion to John Calvin* (Cambridge: Cambridge University Press, 2004). For extensive material on the Reformation see H. J. Hillerbrand (ed.), *The Oxford Encyclopedia of the Reformation*, 4 vols. (Oxford: Oxford University Press, 1996). Luther will be quoted from J. Pelikan and H. J. Lehmann (eds.), *Luther's Works*, 55 vols. (St Louis and Philadelphia: Concordia Publishing House/Muhlenberg Press, 1958–67); hereafter *LW.*

spiritual, internal priest; for he is seated in heaven and intercedes for us as a priest; he teaches internally, in the heart, and does what a priest is supposed to do between God and us.'[2] Here, alongside two themes common to Hebrews (Christ's priestly intercession for us and his being mediator), Luther introduced the theme of his being 'a spiritual, internal priest', one who 'teaches us internally in the heart'. This account of Christ's priestly activity privileged his inward teaching over something highlighted by Augustine and Aquinas: Christ's role as the primary (invisible) minister of the visible sacraments and Christian worship. Nevertheless, Luther's spirituality of Christ's priesthood was to enjoy its later, fruitful echoes among Catholics—especially in the French School that will feature in the next chapter.

Christ's Priesthood and Christian Life

For Luther, priesthood is a kind of law of Christian community life. For Luther, mutual bearing of burdens (Gal. 6: 2) and taking the place of another in order to bear the other's burden is priestly activity at its best: 'if you followed this teaching of the apostle, you would know that it is not benefits but burdens that you have to bear.'[3]

Baptism, not holy orders, is the gateway to this universal priesthood. Reborn by water and the Holy Spirit, all Christians become priests. Luther leaves aside ministerial ordination to frame an account of Christ's priesthood being shared through baptism: 'Christ is a priest, therefore all Christians are priests . . . We are priests, as he is Priest'.[4] In reinstating here the common priesthood of all the baptized,[5] Luther shows his interest in what Christ's priesthood does 'for us (*pro nobis*)' and what it calls us to do, more than in examining what that priesthood is 'in itself (*in se*)'.

---

[2] *LW* xxxix. 80.
[3] *LW* xxvii. 392.
[4] *LW* xl. 19–20.
[5] Like Chrysostom and other fathers of the Church, Aquinas upheld the common priesthood of the baptized. Citing Ps. 51: 19, Rom. 12: 1, and 1 Pet. 2: 5, he wrote: 'devout lay people are united with Christ by a spiritual union through faith and charity . . . They have a spiritual priesthood for offering spiritual sacrifices' (*STh.* 3a. 82. 1 resp.).

Luther understands three functions above all to be established through sharing by baptism in Christ's priesthood. All Christians have the power and should take up the mandate (1) to preach, (2) to come before God with their intercessions for one another, and (3) 'to sacrifice themselves to God'. When listing the functions of the universal priesthood, Luther follows the same order. He puts (1) teaching and preaching the word of God at the head of the list, ahead of (2) praying for others and (3) sacrifice.[6]

By characterizing (1) preaching as a primary function of priests, he stands in some continuity with the tradition of Jeremiah and Malachi. They insisted on 'instruction' in the Law as an essential duty of priests (see Chapter 1 above). For Luther, the priesthood of all believers means that they have the right and duty to teach and spread God's word. This is their highest priestly office.[7] By highlighting in this way the priestly nature of preaching, he encourages those who interpret the public ministry of Jesus as essentially priestly.

The permanent, heavenly activity of Christ the High Priest is defined by (2): intercessory prayer. Hence praying for one another and, indeed, for the whole world looms large among the duties brought by sharing in his priesthood. One should beware of reading Luther's view of universal priesthood in the light of later individualism. As Paul Althaus comments, 'Luther never understands the priesthood of all believers merely in the "Protestant" sense of the Christian's freedom to stand in direct relationship to God without a human mediator. Rather he constantly emphasizes the Christian's evangelical authority to come before God on behalf of the brethren and also of the world.' Hence Althaus can conclude: 'The universal priesthood expresses not religious individualism but its exact opposite, the reality of the congregation as a community.'[8] In that sense universal priesthood is a necessary condition for establishing authentic Christian community which prays for the people of the world that God might also give faith to them.

---

[6] *LW* xl. 21.

[7] Although he held teaching and spreading God's word to be the highest priestly office of all the baptized, Luther limited the public preaching of the word within the Church to those who had been called by the community.

[8] P. Althaus, *The Theology of Martin Luther*, trans. R. C. Schultz (Philadelphia: Fortress Press, 1966), 314.

As Christian priesthood is derived from Christ's priesthood, and since all priesthood involves the correlate of sacrifice (see the Letter to the Hebrews, Augustine, and Aquinas above), so Christian sacrifice (3) is rooted in Christ's sacrifice. Althaus explains:

For Luther, Christ's priesthood and the Christian's priesthood belong together ... In the final analysis, the Christian's priestly sacrifice is nothing else than Christ's own sacrifice. For the life of Christians is Christ's life. All sacrifice through which the community exists is an offering with and in Christ in that one sacrifice which took place once but is yet everywhere present, which cannot be repeated but lives on in the reality of the community.[9]

Since through his sacrifice Jesus the High Priest has gained for all the forgiveness of their sins, the baptized, now become priestly members of the Christian community, can forgive the sins of one another. In a 1519 sermon on 'the Sacrament of Penance', Luther maintains that, because the 'whole Church is full of the forgiveness of sins',[10] each of its members (and not merely the ordained priest) has received authority to proclaim and bring the gift of forgiveness to his or her neighbour from Christ himself. Luther declares: 'Any Christian can say to you, "God forgives you your sins, in the name" etc., and if you can accept that word with confident faith, as though God were saying it to you, then in that same faith you are surely absolved.' Luther adds later in the same sermon: 'this authority to forgive sins is nothing other than what a priest—indeed, if need be, any Christian—may say to another when he sees him afflicted or affrighted in his sins.'[11] Within the community of believers everyone can speak the Gospel's word of forgiveness to those in trouble.

As for the Eucharist, rather than being a sacrifice (or perpetuation of Christ's priestly sacrifice), it is for Luther 'a sure sign' of solidarity between all the faithful (or 'saints'), a common self-sacrificing love that, united with Christ's passion, bears one another's sufferings. In a 1519 sermon on the Eucharist Luther writes: 'In this sacrament' a

[9] Ibid. 315.
[10] *LW* xxxv. 21.
[11] Ibid. 12, 21.

suffering believer is 'given a sure sign from God himself that he is
thus united with Christ and his saints and has all things in common
with them, that Christ's sufferings and life are his own, together with
the lives and sufferings of all the saints.'[12] Those who receive the
Eucharist are called to share lovingly the misfortunes of others and
support anyone in need: 'When you have partaken of the sacrament,
therefore, or desire to partake of it, you must in turn share the
misfortunes of the community... Your heart must go out in love
and learn that this is the sacrament of love. As love and support are
given you, you in turn must render love and support to Christ and
his needy ones.'[13]

Three Treatises and Christ's Priesthood

Three treatises that Luther wrote between 1520 and 1523 addressed
his contemporary concerns about the Church and the world, and
yield interesting material for those attempting to assess his understanding of Christ's priesthood. We can then turn to the lectures on
the Epistle to the Hebrews that Luther gave in the years 1517–18. This
commentary pre-dates by a few years the three treatises, but it is
illuminating to take it up *after* the treatises. Once we have presented
their theological conclusions on Christ's priesthood, we will be better
able to grasp some scriptural positions that fed into those conclusions.

In *The Freedom of a Christian* (published in November 1520)
Luther addressed Pope Leo X ('most excellent Leo') about his concerns, most of which revolved around the behaviour of the clergy. He
contrasted the lifestyle of contemporary priests with that of Jesus,
who lived in unconsecrated places, ate and drank with sinners, went
alone to pray in the desert, and died, not adorned with sacred robes,
but naked on a cross. He had been sent into the world for no other
priestly ministry than that of the word. In their turn, Christ's bishops

---

[12] *LW* xxxv. 52.
[13] Ibid. 54. For an insightful contemporary reflection on the Reformation controversies over the Eucharist, see G. Hunsinger, *The Eucharist and Ecumenism*
(New York: Cambridge University Press, 2008).

and priests are 'called and instituted' only for that ministry.[14] Here Luther once again stood firmly with those who associate priesthood with the years when Jesus was fully engaged in preaching the kingdom of God. Luther also stood in a long line, which stretched back to Origen and Cyprian in the third century (see Chapter 5 above), of all those who had called on ministerial priests to let the example of Christ's priestly holiness shape their own lives and priestly activity.

Christ's kingship was seamlessly linked to his priesthood.[15] He was 'true king, but not after the fashion of the flesh and the world, for his kingdom is not of this world. He reigns in heavenly and spiritual things.' The humble, spiritual way Christ exercised his kingly priesthood involved the three functions of (1) preaching/teaching, (2) interceding, and (3) self-sacrifice. Luther insisted: 'His priesthood does not consist in the outer splendour of robes and postures like those of the human priesthood of Aaron and our present-day church. But it consists of spiritual things through which he by an invisible service intercedes for us in heaven before God, there offers himself as a sacrifice, and does all the things a priest should do . . . he teaches us inwardly through the living instruction of the Spirit, thus performing the two real functions of a priest, of which the prayers and the preaching of human priests are visible types.'[16] Besides restating what he understood to be the three central functions of Christ's priesthood and of those who by ministerial ordination shared in that priesthood, Luther clearly implied in such passages that the priests and bishops of his time, dwelling 'in sacred places' and

[14] 'It does not help the soul if the body is adorned with sacred robes of priests or dwells in sacred places or is occupied with sacred duties or prays, fasts, abstains from certain kinds of food . . . on the other hand, it will not harm the soul if the body is clothed in secular dress, dwells in unconsecrated places, eats and drinks as others do, does not pray aloud, and neglects to do all the above-mentioned things which hypocrites can do . . . Nor was Christ sent into the world for any other ministry except that of the word. Moreover, the entire spiritual estate—all the apostles, bishops, and priests—has been called and instituted only for the ministry of the word' (*LW* xxxi. 345–6).

[15] In fact, Luther reflected more on Christ's office of priest and king ('munus duplex'), whereas Calvin elaborated more effectively the doctrine of Christ's threefold office as prophet/teacher, priest, and shepherd/king (the 'munus triplex'). See K. Bornkamm, *Christus—König und Priester. Das Amt Christi bei Luther im Verhältnis zur Vor- und Nachgeschichte* (Tübingen: Mohr Siebeck, 1998).

[16] *LW* xxi. 354.

indulging a 'splendour of robes and postures', had returned to the practices of that past priesthood of Aaron abrogated by the true priest of Hebrews.

Luther looked beyond ordained ministers and stated: 'all of us who believe in Christ are priests and kings in Christ.' The High Priest of Hebrews has made all believing Christians 'his fellow priests' and, like him, they will 'appear before God' as 'priests forever':

Not only are we the freest of kings, we are also priests forever, which is far more excellent than being kings, for as priests we are worthy to appear before God [2] to pray for others and [1] to teach one another divine things...Thus Christ has made it possible for us, provided we believe in him, to be not only his brethren, co-heirs, and fellow kings, but also his fellow priests. Therefore we may boldly come into the presence of God in the spirit of faith, cry 'Abba, Father!', [and] [2] pray for one another.[17]

Without wanting to rid the Church of ordained ministers,[18] Luther insisted on the royal priesthood of all believers: 'we Christians are all kings and priests and therefore lords of all.'[19] He protested against the word 'priest' and its equivalents being monopolized by a clerical caste: 'Injustice is done by those words "priest", "cleric", "spiritual", [and] "ecclesiastic", when they are transferred from all Christians to those few who are now by a mischievous usage called "ecclesiastic".' 'Holy Scripture', he added, 'makes no distinction between them, although it gives the names "ministers", "servants", [and] "stewards" to those who are now proudly called popes, bishops, and lords, and who should, according to the ministry of the Word, serve others and teach them the faith of Christ and the freedom of believers.'[20]

The priestly service of Christ remains paradigmatic for ministry in his Church. Protesting against a clerical world, which had become

---

[17] *LW* xxi. 354–5.

[18] 'A bishop, when he consecrates a church, confirms children, or performs some other duty belonging to his office, is not made a bishop by these works. Indeed, if he had not first been made a bishop, none of these works would be valid. They would be foolish, childish, and farcical' (ibid. 360).

[19] Ibid. 357.

[20] Ibid. 356.

fascinated with putting on 'sacred robes', Luther longed to encourage his contemporaries to 'put on Christ and neighbour':

[A priest] puts on his neighbour and so conducts himself toward him as if he himself were in the other's place . . . He [Christ] has so put on us and acted for us as if he had been what we are. I should lay before God my faith and my righteousness that they may cover and intercede for the sins of my neighbour, which I take upon myself and so labour and serve in them as if they were my own. This is what Christ did for us.[21]

To imitate Christ's priestly activity by praying for one another and bearing one another's burdens is uncontroversial. But is it possible literally to 'take upon' oneself the sins of others? And, more significantly, is this what Christ the priest 'did for us'? We return to this issue below.

In *The Babylonian Captivity of the Church*, published in the autumn of 1520, Luther criticized trenchantly an ecclesiastical system that had led many Christians away from true, biblically based faith, just as the Jews were carried away from Jerusalem into slavery. Inevitably this protest had things to say about Christ's priesthood and ordained ministers.

The tract deals first with the reception of Holy Communion under both 'kinds'. At the time the practice was for lay persons to receive the Eucharist under the 'species' of bread alone, whereas priests also received from the chalice of consecrated wine. Luther argued that Christ's command at the Last Supper was for all (not merely ordained priests) to do both—to eat *and* drink: 'the word and example of Christ stand unshaken when he says, not by way of permission, but of command: "drink of it, all of you" [Matt. 26: 27]. For if all are to drink of it, and the words cannot be understood as addressed to the priests alone, then it is certainly an impious act to withhold the cup from laymen when they desire it.' Luther went on to say of the Eucharist: 'The sacrament does not belong to the priests but to all men. The priests are not the lords, but servants in duty bound to administer both kinds to those who desire them, as often as they desire them. If they wrest this right from the laity and deny it to them by force, they are tyrants.'[22]

---

[21] Ibid. 371.
[22] *Captivity*, LW xxxvi. 21, 27; hereafter references to this volume will be made within our text.

What Luther called 'the most wicked abuse of all' was the notion that what Christ mandated at the Last Supper was a priestly sacrifice. The Mass, for Luther, was not a sacrifice but the last will and testament of one who was about to die. It promised forgiveness of sins, a promise then confirmed by the death of the Son of God: 'the Mass or Sacrament of the Altar is Christ's testament, which he left behind him at his death to be distributed among his believers'. Here 'Christ says "the new testament in my blood" [Luke 22: 20; 1 Cor. 11: 25], not somebody else's but his own, by which grace is promised through the Spirit for the forgiveness of sins, that we may obtain the inheritance' (pp. 37, 40). Here Luther departed from the Christian tradition, witnessed to in the first extant work on the Eucharist, a third-century letter by Cyprian of Carthage, that what Christ said and did at the Last Supper was sacrificial, a sacrificial offering that would be consummated on Calvary. Hence, when celebrating the Eucharist in memory of what Christ did at the Last Supper, Christian priests, in the words of Cyprian, 'offer a sacrifice, the passion of the Lord' (see Chapter 5 above). Modern ecumenical dialogues were to suggest that the Eucharist could and should be understood as both testament (or covenant) and sacrifice.

Yet one can appreciate Luther's strong protests. In his day, defective ways of understanding the Eucharist as sacrifice included regularly celebrating Masses for stipends and without congregations.[23] Problematic and simply scandalous practices had built up over the centuries. From the sixth or, at the latest, from the seventh century the custom had grown of priests celebrating Mass alone, and in the same period 'side altars' (which enabled priests to 'say Mass' by themselves) began to be built in churches (for instance, around 550 in the church of San Vitale in Ravenna). In the Western Church the Mass often became an exercise of personal devotion, and from the ninth century so-called 'private Masses' entered common usage, and

---

[23] Even apropos of this practice of a priest celebrating 'private' Masses, Luther, at least initially, showed some sensitive consideration: 'he should take pains to refer all this to the prayers which he offers for the dead or the living, saying to himself, "Lo, I will go and receive the sacrament for myself alone, and while doing so I will pray for this one or that one"' (ibid. 55). But soon he published vehement criticisms of such practices: e.g. *The Misuse of the Mass* (1521) and *The Abomination of the Secret Mass* (1525).

so too did 'multiple' Masses. It was said of the devout Pope Leo III (pope 795–816), who crowned Charlemagne Roman emperor on Christmas Day 800, that he celebrated Mass seven or even nine times a day. In monasteries Masses were celebrated almost continuously at side altars, with ordained monks obliged to seek through the Mass many material and spiritual benefits not only for themselves but also for living and dead benefactors. A Mass could also take the place of a severe penance that had been imposed: for example, one Mass offered on payment of a stipend could substitute for a year of fasting. Foundations paid for numerous Masses, and some monasteries guaranteed to say a thousand or more Masses for the imperial family or other powerful families. Priests were ordained simply to offer Masses for such intentions and not to serve the pastoral needs of the faithful. Some monastic rules prescribed that an ordained monk should not say more than seven Masses a day, but in obligatory cases not more than twenty a day. One rule stated: 'not more than thirty a day.' Along with such sad misuse of the Eucharist, it became rarer for the faithful to receive Holy Communion. The Fourth Lateran Council (1215) tried to remedy the situation by making it obligatory to receive Holy Communion at least once a year. The saintly King Louis IX of France (d. 1270) communicated only six times a year.[24] It seemed like a situation of 'more Masses and less Communion'.

Quite understandably, Luther and other Reformers were deeply concerned at the number of Masses that were being celebrated every day in many places and had nothing to do with the pastoral needs of the people. They railed against such 'Private Masses', in which only the priest communicated and at which sometimes no one else participated. Since the Eucharist is a banquet, they argued, it lacks meaning unless some participants are present and communicate. Moreover, such multiplication of Masses looked like an attempt to 'earn' salvation for oneself and others—or, in other words, a lapse

[24] See C. Vogel, 'Une mutation cultuelle inexpliqué: le passage de l'eucharistie communautaire à la messe privée', *Revue des Sciences Religieuses*, 54 (1980), 231–50; id., 'La Multiplication des messes solitaires au moyen age. Essai de statistique', ibid. 55 (1981), 206–8.

into justification by good works that told against the unique sacrifice of Christ that was all-sufficient for human salvation.

From a theological point of view, Luther argued that a sacrifice is something offered to God, whereas a testament and promise are things we receive. Hence, at the Eucharist we cannot offer to God and receive from God simultaneously:

distributing a testament or accepting a promise differs diametrically from offering a sacrifice . . . for the former is something that we receive and the latter is something that we give. The same thing cannot be received and offered at the same time, nor can it be both given and accepted by the same person, any more than our prayer can be the same thing as that which our prayer obtains, or the act of praying be the same thing as the act of receiving that for which we pray. (p. 52)

When championing the need to hear Christ's 'testament' and 'promise' of forgiveness, Luther denounced the practice (in Western Christianity) of priests reciting in a whisper the Eucharistic Prayer (the Roman canon or what is called today the First Eucharistic Prayer). This perversion prevented the faithful from hearing the words of Christ's instituting his testament and promise:

nowadays they take every precaution that no layman should hear these words of Christ, as if they were too sacred to be delivered to the common people. So mad are we priests that we arrogate to ourselves alone the so-called words of consecration, to be said secretly, yet in such a way that they do not profit even us. For we too fail to regard them as promises or as a testament for the strengthening of the faith. Instead of believing them, we reverence them with I know not what superstitious and godless fancies. (p. 41)

The need to hear the words of Christ led Luther not only to reject the custom of the Eucharistic Prayer being whispered and a silent 'elevation' of the Host, but also to opt for the liturgy being celebrated in the vernacular. Both changes would finally let the people hear again the words that awaken faith:

For it is faith that the priest ought to awaken in us by this act of elevation. And would to God that as he elevates the sign, or sacrament, openly before our eyes, he might also sound in our ears the word, or testament, in a loud, clear voice and in the language of the people, whatever it may be, in order

that faith may be more effectively awakened. For why may Mass be said in Greek and Latin and Hebrew, but not in German or any other language? (pp. 53–4)

Luther's 1523 treatise, *Temporal Authority: To What Extent It Should Be Obeyed*, defended rulers and governments against the prevailing notion that the Church was the source of all earthly authority. Since this discussion of secular authority links it to and separates it from Christ's kingly and priestly roles, the treatise has some relevance for our study of Christ's priesthood.

Luther distinguishes between two kingdoms or two 'swords': that of this world and that of God. Unlike those who belong to the kingdom of this world, 'those who belong to the kingdom of God are all the true believers who are in Christ and under Christ, for Christ is King and Lord in the kingdom of God . . . For this reason he came into the world, that he might begin God's kingdom and establish it in the world. Therefore he says before Pilate, "My kingdom is not of this world" [John 18: 36–7].'[25]

Luther argues that Christ's 'own office and vocation' did not discredit the many other 'offices' and 'vocations' of the secular world: in particular, the 'sword' of earthly rulers. He writes:

If an office and vocation were to be regarded as disreputable on the ground that Christ did not pursue it himself, what would become of all the offices and vocations other than the ministry, the one occupation he did follow? Christ pursued his own office and vocation, but he did not thereby reject any other. It was not incumbent upon him to bear the sword, for he was to exercise only that function by which his kingdom is governed and which properly serves his kingdom. (p. 100)

People perform all sorts of roles in this world, which are not essential to Christ's kingdom. It is through 'God's Word and Spirit' (Eph. 6: 17) that he rules his followers 'inwardly'. As Luther says, 'nor is it essential to his kingdom that he be a married man, a cobbler, tailor, farmer, prince, hangman, or constable. Neither is the temporal sword or law essential to it, but only God's Word and Spirit. It is by these that his people are ruled inwardly' (p. 100).

---

[25] *Temporal Authority*, *LW* xlv. 88; hereafter references to this volume will be made within our text.

The preaching of the word is central to Christ's spiritual realm and his kingly/priestly office and to the apostles and 'all spiritual rulers' who followed him:

This is the office which he also exercised then and still exercises now, always bestowing God's Word and Spirit. And in this office the apostles and all spiritual rulers had to follow him. For in order to do their job right they are so busily occupied with the spiritual sword, the Word of God, that they must perforce neglect the temporal sword and leave it to others who do not have to preach. (pp. 100–1)

To show that his kingdom 'exists solely by God's Word and Spirit', Christ did not take up vocations involving matrimony, earthly authority, 'and similar externals'. This vocational limit 'had to be Christ's peculiar function as the Supreme King in this kingdom'. Christians, while following this Supreme King by 'God's Word and Spirit', have in their lives 'some other external office by which God may also be served' (p. 101).

The main part of the treatise sets out the limitations of earthly authority, and reminds readers that 'we are not baptized into kings, or princes, or even into the mass of mankind, but into Christ and God himself' (p. 106). Through baptism believers share in Christ's priestly kingship. Baptism joins them to Christ and the essence of his vocation as king and priest. Luther's view of temporal authority shades his view of those who share in Christ's priesthood through ordination: 'What, then, are the priests and bishops? Answer: Their government is not a matter of [secular] authority and power, but a service and an office, for they are neither higher nor better than other Christians.' Once again, Luther insists, preaching constitutes the heart of the office of priests and bishops: 'Their ruling is nothing more than the inculcating of God's word, by which they guide Christians and overcome heresy' (p. 117).

In the final part of this treatise Luther considers how a prince should use the authority given to him. Here we see that, like Calvin a decade later, the qualities of kingship are very much the proper qualities of priesthood. In relation to either office, any individual, in this case the ruling prince, should examine himself in the light of the royal Christ. Luther writes: 'He [the prince] should picture Christ to himself and say, "Behold, Christ, the supreme ruler, came to save

me. He did not seek to gain power, estate, and honour from me, but considered only my need, and directed all things to the end that I should gain power, estate, and honour from him and through him"' (p. 120). In sketching the proper disposition of a prince, Luther even introduces Paul's language about Christ's 'emptying himself' (Phil. 2: 7), even if it is only to encourage a self-emptying 'in the heart': 'In such a manner should a prince in his heart empty himself of his power and authority, and take unto himself the needs of his subjects, dealing with them as though they were his own needs. For this is what Christ did to us; and these are the proper works of Christian love' (p. 120).

Commentary on the Letter to the Hebrews

As we stated above, Luther's commentary on Hebrews pre-dates by a few years the three treatises we have just discussed. Yet his lectures on the scriptural basis of Christ's priesthood throw further light on the positions he was to espouse in the treatises.

Initially, Luther compares Christ 'our Priest' in his 'one sanctuary' with the actions of creatures that provide protection in nests and other safe sanctuaries. Christ's 'humanity alone' is a refuge 'where we are protected and saved from a judgement of this kind [eternal judgement]'. To bolster this image Luther quotes some words from Christ himself and from the Old Testament: 'how often would I have gathered your children together as a hen' (Matt. 23: 37); 'he [God] will cover you with his pinions, and under his wings you will find refuge' (Ps. 91: 4). Luther likens this motherly embrace to the protection of a tabernacle: 'You have protected me in the secret place of your tabernacle' (Ps. 27: 5). Luther concludes by maintaining that the author of Hebrews intends to present Christ as more 'a Priest than as a Lord and Judge, in order that he may console those who are frightened'.[26]

---

[26] *Hebrews*, LW xxix. 167; Luther also cites here Mal. 4: 2 ('for you who fear my name the Sun of righteousness shall rise, with healing in his wings'), and Ps. 63: 7 ('I will exult in the cover of your wings'). Hereafter references to this volume will be made within our text.

Above we recalled what Luther says (in *The Freedom of a Christian* and elsewhere) about the consolation that Christians should offer to one another through bearing each other's burdens and offering each other forgiveness. Commenting on Hebrews, Luther uses a touching image to picture such consolation coming from Christ himself, as if he were a hen gathering her chickens and protecting them in a 'heavenly' nest. As we saw in Chapter 2 when comparing Hebrews with Revelation, the Letter to the Hebrews can be imaginative and pictorial. Even so, it never pictures the heavenly sanctuary (where Christ sits at the right hand of the Father and intercedes for humanity) as if it were like a 'nest' in which, in a motherly way, Christ protects frightened human beings from judgement. Luther's characteristically vivid image presents in a new and consoling way Christ's priestly activity in the heavenly sanctuary.

More controversial is something we already spotted in *The Freedom of a Christian*: Luther's notion that literally taking on the sins of others was a principal aspect of Christ's priesthood. In support of this position, Luther goes back behind the Letter to the Hebrews 5: 1 and introduces a text from Numbers 18: 1: 'The Lord said to Aaron: "You and your sons and your father's house with you shall bear the iniquity of the sanctuary, and you and your sons with you shall bear the sins of your priesthood".' Luther recognizes that these sins were not necessarily committed by the Old Testament priests themselves. But they were called to bear the sins of others, 'because it is the nature and duty of priesthood to be the bearer and carrier of sins' (p. 168). 'Christ', Luther argues, was 'the true Aaron and "the Lamb of God who takes away the sins of the world [John 1: 29]"'. The priesthood of Christ 'reached its peak and accomplished its work when he cried out for us on the cross' (pp. 168–9).

Beyond question, exegetical difficulties emerge here. It is one thing to say, as Hebrews does, that it is the nature and duty of priesthood to offer sacrifice for sins and for the cleansing of guilty human consciences (see Chapter 3 above). It is another to maintain that such sacrifices for the expiation or cleansing of sins involve priests in personally 'carrying and bearing the sins of others'. The text quoted from John does not establish this conclusion, even if over the centuries numerous Christians have shared Luther's interpretation. The imagery of the Passover Lamb, deployed at the start of John's Gospel

and then reappearing at the crucifixion (19: 34–7), points to Christ removing or doing away with the 'stain' of sins by shedding his blood, but not to his personally 'shouldering' such sins and bearing them off.[27] Furthermore, the narrative of Christ's priesthood that we read in the Letter to the Hebrews hardly supports the unqualified statement that it was on the cross that this priesthood 'reached its peak and accomplished its work'. Hebrews understands Christ's priesthood to have 'reached its peak' when he entered the heavenly sanctuary, and to have 'accomplished its work' when he sat at the right hand of God to intercede permanently for human beings.

The theme of Christ's having taken upon himself the guilt of human sins, which we read here in this commentary on Hebrews from 1517–18, will flower in Luther's later works. Christ would be pictured as if he had personally committed all these sins himself and so incurred the anger of God the Father. The crucifixion became a 'war' against the crucified Son. He was punished and suffered as our substitute on the cross, and his atrociously painful death placated the anger of God and so made justification available for us. This view of what constituted the 'peak' of Christ's priestly work was regularly 'supported' by Luther and many others by several texts from Paul (Rom. 8: 3–4; 2 Cor. 5: 21; Gal. 3: 13), by three passages from the Hebrew Scriptures (Lev. 16; Ps. 22; Isa. 53), and by expanding

---

[27] In *The Gospel According to John* (London: Continuum, 2005) Andrew Lincoln may toy with the idea of John 1: 29 meaning that Christ 'bears the sins of many', but the evidence from the whole Gospel seems to make him come down firmly on the passage pointing to Jesus' sacrificial death that 'removes' the sin of the world. He writes: 'the identification of Jesus with the lamb of God who takes away the sin of the world . . . appears to combine the imagery from Deutero-Isaiah (Isa. 53.4–12) of the servant-witness who *bears the sins of many* and is led as a lamb to the slaughter with that of the Passover lamb, which did not, of course, deal with sin (Exod. 12.1–11). The latter colours the description of Jesus' death, which, in this narrative, occurs at the same time as the slaughter of the Passover lambs (cf. 19.14, 31) and is seen as that of an unblemished Passover lamb (cf. 19.36, citing Exod. 12.46). The cause of the world's hostility to the Creator's purposes, manifesting itself in the refusal to acknowledge the Logos (cf. 1.10), is sin. If Jesus' mission of saving the world (3.17) and of giving life to it (6.35, 51) is to be accomplished, then the world's sin has to be dealt with, and one of the ways in which this Gospel's narrative portrays Jesus is as the sacrificial victim, whose death *removes* the primary obstacle to the world's reception of the divine gift of life' (p. 113; italics ours).

Christ's cry of abandonment on the cross (Mark 15: 34 par.) in terms of divine punishment.

In the last chapter we saw how Thomas Aquinas modified Anselm's theory of satisfaction by introducing talk of Christ's priestly sacrifice 'placating' God. This was to open the way to language about Christ as penal substitute setting right a moral order damaged by sin. In place of Anselm's commutative version, God's justice was interpreted as vindictive—with the divine anger venting itself on Christ, the substitute for sinners, whose suffering on the cross was the rightful punishment imposed on human sin. Such changes in Anselm's theory did not remain a Protestant monopoly. Catholic preachers, like J. B. Bossuet (1627–1704) and L. Bourdaloue (1632–1704), spoke of God's vengeance and anger being appeased at the expense of his Son. As victim of the divine justice, Christ even suffered the pains of the damned. French religious eloquence, both in the seventeenth century and later, turned God into a murderer who carried out a cruel vendetta before being appeased and then exercising divine mercy.[28] This version of Calvary plays down the active, self-sacrificing role of Christ as priest (see Hebrews in Chapters 3 and 4 above) and reduces him, more or less, to being the passive victim of God's displeasure.

Luther's engagement with Hebrews brings out, at least as much as the author of that text, what Christ the High Priest does 'for us (*pro nobis*)', and inculcates even more the need for faith in the efficacy of the passion.

Only the blood of Christ that was shed makes the conscience clean through faith in the Word of Christ...One should think of his passion with the desire that faith be increased: namely, that the more frequently one meditates, the more fully one believes that the blood of Christ was shed for one's own sins. For this is what it means to eat and drink spiritually: namely, to be enriched and incorporated into Christ by means of this faith. (pp. 210–11)

---

[28] On Luther and others who pictured Christ as a penal substitute for human sin, see B. Sesboüé, *Jésus-Christ l'unique médiateur. Essai sur la rédemption et le salut,* i (Paris: Desclée, 1988), 67–83, 360–5. On problems with this view and difficulties about its use of various scriptural texts, see G. O'Collins, *Jesus Our Redeemer* (Oxford: Oxford University Press, 2007), 133–60.

In Chapter 3 we saw that any reference to the Eucharist in the Letter to the Hebrews is minor and, for all intents and purposes, implicit. Luther, however, since he primarily interprets the Last Supper and the Eucharist as Christ bequeathing a last will and testament to his followers, readily links Hebrews 9: 17 ('a will/testament takes effect only at death') to the Eucharist and quotes Matthew 26: 28–9: 'this is my blood of the new testament, which will be shed for many for the remission of sins. But I tell you I shall not drink again of this fruit of the vine until that day when I drink it new with you in my Father's kingdom.' 'With these most delightful words,' Luther comments, 'he [Christ] bequeaths to us, not the riches or the glory of the world, but once and for all absolutely all the blessings: that is, as I have said, the remission of sins and possession of the future kingdom' (p. 213).

Notably, Luther associates the permanent but hidden presence of Christ the High Priest in the Holy of Holies with the cleansing of conscience and hope for heaven. He quotes from John Chrysostom a passage that we cited above in Chapter 5: 'If we draw near to God, we are in heaven. For what do I care about heaven when I see the God of heaven?' For Luther, the heavenly dimension of Christ's priesthood bulks large, and to drive home this point he quotes 1 Corinthians 15: 47–9: 'The first man was from the earth, earthly . . . the second man is from heaven. As was the earthly man, such also are the earthly; and as is the heavenly, such also are the heavenly. Therefore, just as we have borne the likeness of the earthly, let us also bear the likeness of the heavenly' (p. 215).

To use this passage from 1 Corinthians to inculcate a hope for heaven and heavenly things may go a little beyond what Paul intended to convey.[29] Luther might have pressed into service some passages from the Letter to the Hebrews itself about 'desiring a better country, a heavenly one' (Heb. 11: 16). Yet, like Hebrews, he is concerned with the invisible, divine blessings: 'since these divine blessings are invisible, incomprehensible, and deeply hidden, nature cannot attain or love them unless it is lifted up through the grace of God.' Luther calls such life 'hidden in the invisible God' a 'heavenly' existence: 'Christ's believers are most properly called heavenly because if "the soul is present more where it loves than where it lives",

---

[29] See A. C. Thiselton, *The First Epistle to the Corinthians* (Grand Rapids, Mich.: Eerdmans, 2000), 1285–90.

and if it is the nature of love to change one who loves into what is
loved, it is true that those who love heaven and God are called
heavenly and divine, though not because they are heavenly by nature
or in a metaphysical sense' (pp. 216–17).[30]

As heavenly priest Christ now exercises his priesthood in the
presence of God and in a hidden, interior way. For their part,
believers must exercise confident faith: 'a Christian must be sure,
yes, completely sure, that Christ appears and is a priest before God on
his behalf. For as he will believe, so it will happen to him' (p. 217).

When commenting on Hebrews 10: 19–20 ('we have confidence to
enter the sanctuary by the blood of Christ', for he 'has opened the way
for us') Luther expounds Christ's priesthood in a passage full of
evocative images. He calls this 'Priest' a 'leader', 'companion', 'helper',
'ferryman', 'eagle', and by implication 'bridegroom'. Luther shows
himself at his best in describing Christ's priestly work as effecting a
'crossing over' from the earthly to the heavenly. Christ 'crossed over
first of all', and he 'not only gave an example by crossing over, but he
also holds out his hand to those who follow'. As a kind of marvellous
Charon, Christ ferries believers across from earth to heaven:

while others can teach and exhort to cross over, this Christ alone is not only
the Companion but also the One who leads the way, not only the Leader but
also the Helper, yes, the Ferryman, as we read in Deuteronomy 32: 11: 'As an
eagle incites its nestlings forth by hovering over its brood, so he spread his
wings to receive them and bore them up on his pinions.' For he who relies on
Christ through faith is carried on the shoulders of Christ. He [Christ] will
cross over successfully with the bride, of whom it is written that 'she comes up
through the desert leaning on her beloved' [Song of Solomon 8: 5]. (p. 226)

Summary

At a time of widespread abuses in the clerical culture Luther emphasized the hidden dimension of the priesthood of Christ, 'the spiritual
priest for the inner man'. He 'sits in heaven and makes intercession

[30] The quotation probably comes from St Bernard of Clairvaux, *Liber de Precepto
et Dispensatione*, 20. 60.

for us', teaching 'us inwardly in the heart'. Such language, which we recalled at the start of this chapter, privileges the interior function of his priesthood over its public function in the sacramental life of the Church.

Yet Luther's view of Christ's priesthood and human participation in it does not (or should not) result in an individualism that ignores the community of believers. On the one hand, through baptism Christians become priests of Christ, the great High Priest, and share in his kingly office. This participation in his priesthood and kingship gives them the spiritual freedom to approach God without other human mediators. But, on the other hand, they are called to bear one another's burdens and share as a community of heirs in celebrating the testament left them through the Last Supper. They should preach the word to each other, forgive the sins of others, and come before God with their intercessions for one another (and the world).[31]

Luther highlights the priestly activity of Christ during his earthly ministry of preaching. Christ taught the word of God, and that priestly ministry of the word continues now as he 'teaches us inwardly through the living instruction of the Spirit'. He ate and drank with sinners, and at the Last Supper left us his last will and testament, the promise of the forgiveness of sins.

Many (but obviously not all) Christians will distance themselves from Luther's interpretation of the Last Supper and the Eucharist, which denies its sacrificial import. What the Gospels report from the Last Supper shows us Christ, through his words and gestures, acting in a priestly, sacrificial way. He commits himself to his self-sacrificing death that will be consummated on Calvary (see Chapter 1 above). Many Christians will also part company with a view of the crucifixion that seems to play down the active role of Christ's self-sacrifice and make him only the passive victim of the divine displeasure.

Finally, as Roman Catholics we treasure above all four items in Luther's exposition of Christ's priesthood: (1) its recognition that Christ acted as a priest in his public ministry of preaching; (2) its

---

[31] On Luther's view of the priesthood of all believers, see W. Pannenberg, *Systematic Theology*, trans. G. W. Bromiley, ii (Grand Rapids, Mich.: Eerdmans, 1994), 126–9.

insistence that all the baptized share in his priesthood, with its duties
of proclaiming the word, interceding for others, and bearing each
other's burdens; (3) its plea that preaching and humble service
should distinguish the ministry of ordained priests at least as much
as their cultic activity; and (4) the charming imagery with which
Luther depicts Christ the priest as a kind of heavenly Charon and, in
another passage, as a motherly hen who protects and consoles her
little ones in a heavenly nest.

JOHN CALVIN

While hiding in Basle, Calvin spent some months (January–August
1535) composing (in Latin) his *Institutes of the Christian Religion*
(*Christianae Religionis Institutio*), which was published in March
1536.[32] With other Protestants, he had fled from Paris to Basle
when it had become dangerous for them to remain in France. King
Francis I had reacted with considerable hostility to the incident of the
'Placards' on 18 October 1534. During the night copies of a handbill
attacking the Mass were attached to public buildings; a copy was even
thrust into the royal bedroom. In exile Calvin wrote his *Institutes*, a
work that came to be recognized as one of the most significant
theological and literary works of the sixteenth century.[33]

The work outlines the necessary ingredients for salvation, and
speaks frequently of 'piety (*pietas*)'. This word, which Calvin
would use in other works, might happily be called today 'spirituality'.
E. A. McKee explains how the Reformer understood 'piety' to cover
primarily 'the attitude and actions directed to the adoration and
service of God. It also includes in a subordinate place some related
themes that he often associates with that word, especially the filial
piety of human relationships and, more loosely, respect and love for

---

[32] Trans. F. L. Battles, ed. J. T. McNeill, 2 vols. with continuous pagination
(Philadelphia: Westminster Press, 1960); hereafter references to these volumes will
be made within our text—indicating (in this order) the book, chapter, and page(s) in
the trans. by Battles.

[33] On Calvin and his life see B. Cottret, *Calvin: A Biography*, trans. M. Wallace
McDonald (Grand Rapids, Mich.: Eerdmans, 2000).

the image of God in all human beings.' McKee sums up what this involves in terms of unity with the Trinity: 'Calvin's piety is the ethos and action of people who recognize through faith that they have been accepted in Christ and engrafted into his body by the sheer grace of God. By this adoption, this "mystical union", the Lord claims them as belonging solely and wholly to God in life and in death, as God's people and members of Christ, by the power of the Holy Spirit.'[34]

In Book 2 of his *Institutes* ('The Knowledge of God the Redeemer in Christ, First Disclosed to the Fathers Under the Law and Then to Us in the Gospel'), Calvin expounds Christ's priestly mediation in Chapter 15: 'To know the purpose for which Christ was sent by the Father and what he conferred upon us, we must look above all at three things in him: the prophetic office, kingship and priesthood' (2. 15/1, 494). Calvin closely associates the prophetic and kingly offices of Christ with his priestly function. As he writes, 'I recognize that Christ was called Messiah especially with respect to, and by virtue of, his kingship. Yet his anointings as prophet and as priest have their place and must not be overlooked by us' (2. 15/2, 496). Calvin was the first Christian to treat in an extended way this tripartite manner of presenting the ministry of Jesus, and he applied it to all the baptized faithful.

Prophet, King, and Priest

In defining Christ's prophetic office, Calvin understands Christ to have 'made an end of all prophecies'. He gathers from Old Testament texts that witness to the expectation of the final prophet, as well as a statement from the Samaritan woman in John's Gospel: 'When the Messiah comes, he will teach us all things' (John 4: 25) (2. 15/1, 495). Calvin understands Daniel to be the final Old Testament prophet who would seal 'both vision and prophet [Dan. 9: 24]': 'not only that the prophetic utterance there mentioned might be authoritatively established, but also that believers might patiently go without the prophets for a time because the fullness and culmination of all revelations was at hand' (2. 15/1, 495).

---

[34] J. Calvin, *Writings on Pastoral Piety*, ed. E. A. McKee (Mahwah, NJ: Paulist Press, 2002), 5.

This leads Calvin to the opening two verses of Hebrews and its privileging of the prophetic office over other possible ways for describing God's envoys: 'In many and various ways God spoke of old to our fathers *by the prophets* but in these last days he has spoken to us through a beloved Son' (ibid.; italics ours). In his 'prophetic dignity' Christ conveys to us 'all parts of perfect wisdom': 'outside Christ there is nothing worth knowing, and all who by faith perceive what he is like have grasped the whole immensity of heavenly benefits . . . And in the prophetic dignity Christ leads us to know that, in the sum of doctrine as he has given it to us, all parts of perfect wisdom are contained' (2. 15/2, 496).

Like Luther before him, Calvin notes emphatically the spiritual characteristic of Christ's *kingship*: 'it is spiritual in nature' (ibid.) and, like Christ's eternal priesthood, also eternal in nature. Calvin follows the author of Hebrews in using the figure of Melchizedek to establish the eternal nature of Christ's priesthood. He turns to the divine promise in Psalm 89: 35–7 to demonstrate the eternity of Christ's kingship: 'Once for all I have sworn by my holiness I will not lie to David. His line shall endure forever, his throne as long as the sun before me. Like the moon, it shall be established forever, the witness of heaven is sure.' From this Calvin concludes to an eternal kingship exercised vis-à-vis the coming Church: 'God surely promises here that through the hand of his Son he will be the eternal protector and defender of his Church. We find the true fulfillment of this prophecy in Christ alone' (2. 15/3, 497).

Christ's kingship, much the same as his priesthood, works spiritually and with eternal results:

we see that whatever is earthly is of the world and of time, and is indeed fleeting. Therefore, Christ, to lift our hope to heaven, declares that his 'kingship is not of this world' [John 18: 36]. In short, when anyone of us hears that Christ's kingship is spiritual, aroused by this word let him attain to the hope of a better life; and . . . protected by Christ's hand, let him await the full fruit of this grace in the age to come. (2. 15/3, 498)

To drive home the spiritual, eternal nature of Christ's kingship, Calvin cites Luke and Paul:

This is the purport of Christ's reply to the Pharisees [Luke 17: 20–1]: because the Kingdom of God is within us, it will not come with observation. Probably because he professed himself King under whom God's highest

blessing was to be expected, the Pharisees jestingly asked Christ to furnish his tokens. But he enjoined them to enter into their own consciences, because the Kingdom of God . . . is righteousness and peace and joy in the Holy Spirit [Rom. 14: 17]. This he did to prevent those otherwise too much inclined to things earthly from indulging in foolish dreams of pomp. These words briefly teach us what Christ's kingdom confers upon us. For since it is not earthly or carnal and hence subject to corruption, but *spiritual*, it lifts us up even to *eternal* life. (2. 15/4, 499; italics ours)

Like Christ's priesthood, his kingship does not allow for 'foolish dreams of pomp' and 'earthly or carnal' objectives; it brings rather the interior gifts of 'righteousness and peace and joy'. These gifts of Christ the King arm believers with the necessary spiritual weaponry, so as to 'pass through this life with its misery, hunger, cold, contempt, reproaches, and other troubles—content with this one thing: that our King will never leave us destitute, but will provide for our needs until, our warfare ended, we are called to triumph' (ibid.). Exile from the kingdom of his birth (France) fed this vision of the kingdom of Christ. The man, who had been a priest and had to strip himself of his (worldly) ecclesiastical benefices shortly before beginning to write the *Institutes*, could find consolation in a spiritual kingdom and a spiritual priesthood. Calvin's reforming views had led him not only to flee a kingdom of this world but also to give up an earthly priesthood with its 'beneficial' advantages.

The anointing of this spiritual King came with his baptism and the descent of the Holy Spirit. The Spirit now provides the King's followers with 'spiritual' and 'heavenly' riches: 'For the Spirit has chosen Christ as his seat, that from him might abundantly flow the heavenly riches of which we are in such need. The believers stand unconquered through the strength of their King, and his spiritual riches abound in them' (2. 15/5, 500). As King and lawgiver of the Church, Christ reigns by divine power, and the final 'act of his reign' will come at the Last Judgement (2. 15/5, 501).

When Calvin turns to focus on Christ's *priestly office*, he declares Christ to be necessary, because 'God's righteous curse bars our access to him, and God in his capacity as judge is angry toward us'. Christ's priestly mediation serves to 'obtain God's favour for us and appease his wrath' (2. 15/6, 501). Hence, Calvin argues, 'the priestly office belongs to Christ alone because by the sacrifice of his death he

Luther and Calvin

blotted out our own guilt and made satisfaction for our sins'. The death of Christ emerges as utterly central in this vision of his priesthood: 'we or our prayers have no access to God, unless Christ, as our High Priest, having washed away our sins, sanctifies us and obtains for us that grace from which the uncleanness of our transgressions and vices debars us. Thus we see that we must begin from the death of Christ in order that the efficacy and benefit of his priesthood may reach us' (2. 15/6, 502).

This language about Christ 'appeasing the anger of God' and so making 'propitiation' for human sin turns up in Calvin's commentary on Hebrews. He translates *hilaskesthai tas hamartias tou laou* (Heb. 2: 17) as 'to make propitiation for the sins of the people'. Nowadays attention to the meaning(s) of *hilaskesthai* and its cognates in the LXX has led many scholars to accept the translation 'to expiate', 'to make expiation for' (REB), 'to make a sacrifice of atonement' (NRSV), or 'to make atonement for' (Craig Koester, see below). Hebrews intends a cleansing or expiating of sin and guilt, not an appeasing of the divine anger. Where Hebrews later speaks of 'offering (*prospherein*) sacrifices (*thusias*) for sins' (Heb. 5: 1), Calvin once again takes this to mean 'appeasing the wrath of God'.[35] But one must insist that the idea of Christ in his once-and-for-all sacrifice appeasing, placating, or propitiating an angry God seems quite foreign to Hebrews and its teaching. Hebrews never speaks of 'propitiation' and in only one context of God's 'anger', but never of the divine anger in connection with Christ and his suffering. The divine 'anger' comes up when Hebrews quotes Psalm 95 on the rebellion of Israel in the wilderness, a rebellion which stopped people from enjoying immediately a peaceful settlement in the promised land of Canaan (Heb. 3: 7–4: 13).

Commenting on Hebrews 2: 17, Craig Koester suggests that 'the idea of propitiation' might be 'appropriate', since 'the author assumes

---

[35] J. Calvin, *The Epistle of Paul the Apostle to the Hebrews*, trans. W. B. Johnston (Edinburgh: Oliver & Boyd, 1963), 33, 59. Surprisingly, when he comes to Heb. 9: 28 ('*to pollōn anenegkein hamartias*'), Calvin translates the phrase 'to bear the sins of many' and explains it (in a way that recalls Anselm) as meaning 'to free those who have sinned from their guilt by his *satisfaction*' (ibid. 131; italics ours). One might have expected him to take here a Lutheran line and comment in terms of Christ's 'personally taking upon himself the sins of many'.

that divine wrath threatens his listeners, just as it threatened Moses' generation (3: 7–4: 13; 10: 26–31; 12: 29)'. But this is to slide over the fact that only the first of these three passages mentions divine anger. Even more importantly, the first passage has nothing to do with Christ in his self-sacrificing death. It is concerned with Israel's rebellion in the desert, a failure the audience of Hebrews risks repeating. Koester is on better ground when he recognizes that 'the dominant element in Hebrews' is 'expiation' or 'the removal of sin', as 'indicated earlier by the comment that Christ "made purification for sins"' (1: 3). Koester appreciates how the Day of Atonement, which 'included rites for purifying' objects, people, and the whole community, is very present in the thought of Hebrews. It 'argues that such rituals may purify people physically, but the death of Christ purifies the conscience'.[36]

Calvin refers to the faithful as sharing in Christ's priesthood: 'Christ plays the priestly role not only to render the Father favourable and propitious toward us by an eternal law of reconciliation, but also to receive us as his companions in this great office.' Sharing in Christ's priesthood enables believers to gain entrance into the heavenly sanctuary: 'we who are defiled in ourselves, yet are priests in him, offer ourselves and our all to God, and freely enter the heavenly sanctuary that the sacrifices of prayers and praise [Heb. 13: 15] that we bring may be acceptable and sweet-smelling [Rom. 12: 1; Eph. 5: 2] before God.' We are 'imbued with his [Christ's] holiness insofar as he has consecrated us to the Father with himself [John 17: 19], although we would otherwise be loathsome to him' (2. 15/6, 502). Calvin makes such references to the priesthood of believers, but, unlike Luther, he does so only rarely.

Calvin ends this section of his *Institutes* by striking out at 'the fabrication of those who, not content with Christ's priesthood, have presumed to sacrifice him anew! The papists attempt this each day, considering the Mass as the sacrificing of Christ' (ibid.). Below, we return to Calvin's understanding of the Eucharist. He was right to protest against views that wrongly interpreted the Mass as if it meant repeating the sacrifice of Christ. Later we will take up the question

---

[36] C. R. Koester, *Hebrews* (New York: Doubleday, 2001), 241.

and, in the light of the New Testament (in particular, the Letter to the Hebrews) and what we glean from the tradition (starting with what we found in the writings of Cyprian of Carthage), will propose language that acceptably expounds the relationship between the once-and-for-all sacrifice of Christ the High Priest and the celebration of the Eucharist by ordained ministers.

The Indictments

It is in his treatment of the governance of the Church and of the Eucharist that we find not only some of Calvin's strongest indictments of contemporary Christendom but also certain insights into the priesthood of Christ and ministerial priesthood.

First, in the course of Book 4 ('The External Means or Aims by which God Invites Us into the Society of Christ and Holds Us Therein'), Calvin targets scandals in the contemporary *governance* of the Church: abuses connected with clerical benefices, ordinations being 'travestied', princes intervening in the affairs of the Church, and other 'monstrous abuses' (4. 5/4–10, 1087–95). He appeals to a purer past in the hope of fashioning a better future. He denounces bishops for having 'strenuously' fled from 'the office of preaching' and deeming 'the bishopric nothing but a title of splendor and magnificence'. As for most 'rectors of churches', they 'no more think of feeding the flock than a shoemaker of plowing'. He indicts the moral failures of priests in vivid and, many would argue, somewhat exaggerated terms: 'there is scarcely a bishop, and not one in a hundred parish priests, who, if his conduct were to be judged according to the ancient canons, would not be subject either to excommunication or at least deposition from office' (4. 5/13–14, 1096–7).

When addressing the primacy of the Roman See, Calvin engages those who claim that the office of high priest in the old covenant had been transferred to the pope. They argue: 'because the Jews were hedged about on all sides with idolaters, in order to prevent their being distracted by the variety of religions, God put the seat of his worship at the midpoint of the earth; there he appointed one high priest, to whom all should look, the better to preserve unity among

them' (4. 6/2, 1103).[37] While agreeing that the high priests in the Old
Testament prefigured Christ and that their priesthood had been
transferred, Calvin rejects any transference to a vicar of Christ and,
in so doing, sets out four aspects of Christ's priesthood. He asks:

> To whom was it [the Jewish high priesthood] transferred? Obviously not to
> the pope (as he dare shamelessly boast) when he takes the title unto himself,
> but to Christ, who, as he alone keeps that office without vicar or successor,
> consequently resigns that honour to no one else. For this priesthood consists
> not in teaching[38] only but [also? above all?] in appeasing God, which Christ
> by his death has accomplished, and in that intercession which he now makes
> in his Father's presence. (4. 6/2, 1104)

Thus Christ's high priesthood (1) is untransferable, because it
consists not only (2) in his teaching but also (3) in his death that
'appeased' God, and (4) in the permanent intercession that Christ
makes in his Father's presence.

Those who follow Hebrews in accepting that Christ died for all and
once and for all and intercedes permanently for all in heaven should
agree (1) that *this* high-priestly office of Christ cannot be transferred.
(2) Many, including the authors of this book, are happy to find
Calvin maintaining that the priestly office of Christ *also* involved
his teaching. In fact, Calvin holds that the incarnate Son of God was a
priest from the beginning: 'His birth includes his priesthood.'[39]
(3) But the notion that Christ's self-sacrifice 'appeased' God's anger
against sinners, while widely influential, does not find support in the
New Testament (see above). Yet the idea of Christ as the 'expiatory
victim' who 'appeased God' (4. 18/6, 1435) or propitiated an angry
God is central to Calvin's interpretation of Christ's priestly activity.
(4) In the history of Christianity no one seemed to have emphasized
more than Calvin the ascension of Christ into heaven, his 'sitting at

---

[37] Calvin addresses here an argument developed by Johann Eck (1486–1543) in *De Primatu Petri* (Paris, 1521). Medieval and some later Christians pictured Jerusalem as being '*in medio terrae*' (at the centre of the earth).

[38] In fact Calvin holds that the incarnate Son of God was priest not merely from the baptism that initiated his public ministry but right from the beginning: 'His birth includes his priesthood' (*The Epistle to the Hebrews*, 62, commenting on Heb. 5: 5).

[39] Ibid.

the right hand of the Father', his interceding for us, and the benefits it brings.[40]

Second, when indicting the Church of Rome's teaching on *the Mass* and *the ministerial priesthood*, Calvin intersperses remarks on the priesthood of Christ. In a way that recalls Augustine's sense of Christ as the invisible but real minister of the sacraments, Calvin insists that the sacraments 'must show forth Christ' and 'attest him as already given and revealed' (4. 14/20, 1297).

As regards the Eucharist, Calvin rejects, as we saw above, any talk of it being a sacrifice. Rather, it is a 'working' out of the one sacrifice of Christ that enables the faithful to 'feed upon' it: 'We now understand the purpose of this mystical blessing [the Lord's Supper]: namely, to confirm for us the fact that the Lord's body was once for all so sacrificed for us that we may now feed upon it, and by feeding feel in ourselves the working of that unique sacrifice' (4. 17/1, 1361). In another passage Calvin calls this confirmation that 'the Lord's body was once for all sacrificed for us' a 'form of representation' in which 'the effectiveness of Christ's death is today shown to us in the Supper' (4. 18/12, 1440). In other words, he understands the Eucharist to be a confirmation, representation, and 'showing to us' of Christ's once-and-for-all sacrifice. In the next chapter we will examine how far this differs from the account the Council of Trent offered when dealing with 'the sacrifice of the Mass'.

Since Christ was 'consecrated priest and pontiff by his Father' and enjoys an 'immortal' priesthood, he 'needs no vicar' or 'partners' to replace him. Hence Calvin denounces contemporary Christendom's ministerial priesthood and daily Mass as attempting to usurp Christ's eternal priesthood:

those who sacrifice daily are required to appoint for their oblations priests whom they put in Christ's place as successors and vicars. By that substitu-

---

[40] These benefits are threefold. First, Christ's ascent opens to human beings the way into the heavenly kingdom that had been closed through Adam: 'we do not await heaven with a bare hope, but in our Head already possess it' (2. 16/6, 524). Second, Christ 'appears before the Father's face as our constant advocate and intercessor ... thus he turns the Father's eyes to his own righteousness to avert his gaze from our sins' (ibid.). Third, Christ rules as king and 'daily lavishes spiritual riches' upon the members of his kingdom (2. 16/6, 525).

tion they not only deprive Christ of his honour and snatch from him the prerogative of that eternal priesthood but [also] try to cast him down from the right hand of his Father, where he cannot sit immortal without at the same time remaining eternal priest. (4. 18/2, 1430)[41]

Calvin next dismisses as 'too flimsy and foolish to need refutation' the idea, developed from the second century (see Chapter 5 above), that ministerial priests are like Melchizedek, because they offer bread and wine in the Eucharist: 'Melchizedek gave bread and wine to Abraham and his companions, to refresh them, wearied by their journey and battle. What has this to do with a sacrifice?' Calvin denounces the Roman liturgy (see the First Eucharistic Prayer) for 'perversely' introducing the notion of sacrifice when the author of Hebrews thought only of Melchizedek blessing and supporting Abraham and his companions: 'if Melchizedek's offering were a figure of the sacrifice of the Mass, would the apostle [presuming Paul to be the author of Hebrews], I ask you, who sifts even the least things, have forgotten a matter so serious and grave?' (4. 18/2, 1431).

Calvin rejects any notion of the daily 'sacrifice of the Mass' (or 'sacrifice of Christ in the Mass') as implying that Christ's one sacrifice has to be repeated and 'ratified by new oblations every day'.[42] Rather, it is through 'the preaching of the gospel and the administration of the Sacred Supper'[43] that the benefit of the self-sacrificing oblation

---

[41] Calvin understands the ordained priests of his day to be attempting to usurp Christ's priestly function: through the offering of the Mass they pretend to 'intercede before God for the people and, having appeased God, obtain atonement for sins'. This is impossible, since 'Christ is the sole Pontiff and Priest of the New Testament, to whom all priesthoods have been transferred and in whom they have been closed and terminated' (2. 18/14, 1442). Since earlier in the *Institutes*, as we saw above, Calvin recognized the priesthood of believers, we should understand him to argue here that 'all *ministerial/ordained* priesthoods have been terminated'.

[42] Calvin insists on a scheme of one victim, one sacrifice, and one cross: 'it is not enough to understand that Christ is the sole victim, unless we add that there is only one sacrifice, so that our faith may be made fast to his cross' (4. 18/6, 1435).

[43] His concern for the preaching and teaching the good news—often neglected in sixteenth-century Christendom—sometimes leads Calvin to subsume everything under teaching: 'Priests are set up by the pope and his followers to sacrifice Christ, not teach the people. But Christ offered himself as a sacrifice for men's eternal redemption and he alone officiated in that priestly act. He simply orders the fruit of his sacrifice to be brought to us in the teaching of his gospel' (*Calvin: Commentaries*, trans. J. Haroutunian and L. P. Smith (London: SCM Press, 1958), 373).

of Christ is communicated: 'Christ did not once for all offer himself up on condition that his sacrifice should be ratified by new oblations each day, but that the benefit of it should be communicated to us by the preaching of the gospel and the administration of the Sacred Supper.' Calvin adds: 'Thus Paul says, "Christ, our paschal lamb, has been sacrificed" [1 Cor. 5: 7], and he bids us feast [1 Cor. 5: 8]. This, I say, is the means whereby the sacrifice of the cross is duly applied to us, when it is communicated to us to be enjoyed, and we receive it in true faith' (4. 18/3, 1432). In other words, the once-and-for-all priestly sacrifice of Christ and its benefits are to be applied, communicated, received, and enjoyed. By 'partaking of the body of Christ', Christians 'celebrate the remembrance of the sacrifice already made' (4. 18/10, 1438).[44]

Calvin distinguishes two kinds of sacrifice: a 'sacrifice of propitiation or of expiation' and a 'sacrifice of praise and reverence' (or 'a sacrifice of thanksgiving') (4. 18/13, 1441).[45] Christ, the true priest and victim, offers the first sacrifice, while believers are called to exercise the second kind of sacrifice, which includes 'all the duties of love'. Calvin writes: 'when we embrace our brethren with these [duties of love], we honour the Lord himself in his members. Also included are all our prayers, praises, thanksgivings, and whatever we do in the worship of God. All these things finally depend upon the greater sacrifice [offered by Christ], by which we are consecrated in soul and body to be a holy temple to the Lord' (4. 18/16, 1443–4).

To support and explain the second kind of sacrifice, Calvin, not surprisingly, cites Romans 12: 1 ('offer your bodies as a living sacrifice, holy, acceptable to God, your reasonable worship'): 'he [Paul] had in mind the spiritual manner of worshipping God, which he tacitly contrasted with the carnal sacrifices of the Mosaic law. Doing good and sharing are called sacrifices that are pleasing to God [Heb. 13: 16]. Thus the generosity of the Philippians in relieving Paul's poverty is a fragrant sacrifice [Phil. 4: 18]; and thus all the good works of believers are spiritual sacrifices' (4. 18/16, 1444).

---

[44] Calvin quotes here Augustine, *Contra Faustum Manichaeum*, 20. 18.

[45] Notice how Calvin takes here 'propitiation' and 'expiation' as equivalents, and prioritizes the first synonym, 'propitiation'.

Preaching, the Lord's Supper, and Priesthood

Calvin uses the New Testament term 'presbyter' to set out his vision of ordained ministry as entailing (1) preaching the gospel, (2) a 'feeding the flock' that included administering the sacraments, and (3) governing the community, but as excluding any alleged sacrifice to 'make atonement for sins'. He derives this vision of ordained ministry from the express will of Christ: 'Christ commanded that stewards of his gospel and sacraments be ordained, not that sacrificers be installed. He gave a command to preach the gospel and feed the flock, not to sacrifice victims. He promised the grace of the Holy Spirit, not to enable them to make atonement for sins but duly to engage in and maintain the government of the church' (4. 19/28, 1476). In his support Calvin cites some classic New Testament texts in which the risen Christ commissions his followers (Matt. 28: 19–20; Mark 16: 15; John 21: 15).

More broadly, in both the Old and New Testaments such ministry centres on preaching and teaching the Word of God: 'whatever authority and dignity the Spirit in Scripture accords to either priests or prophets [in the Old Testament], or apostles or successors of the apostles [in the New Testament], it is wholly given not to the men personally, but to the ministry to which they have been appointed or (to speak more briefly) to the Word, whose ministry is entrusted to them' (4. 8/2, 1150). It is from their fidelity to the Word of God that the doctrinal authority of Moses, the Old Testament priests, the prophets, and the apostles derives: 'they are to speak nothing but his Word' (4. 8/2, 1151). Calvin invokes Malachi 2: 7: '"The lips of a priest should guard knowledge, and men should seek the law from his mouth, for he is the messenger of the Lord of Hosts." Therefore, if the priest wishes to be heard, let him show himself to be God's messenger: that is, let him faithfully communicate the commands which he has received from his Author' (ibid.).

Not surprisingly, in this context Calvin reminds his readers of the example of Christ himself in being faithful to the Word, and quotes John 7: 16: 'My teaching is not mine but his who sent me.' Christ, 'because he performs the ministry of teaching, by his own example prescribes for all his ministers what rule they ought to follow in teaching' (4. 8/4, 1152).

The Last Supper celebrated by Christ and the Eucharist celebrated by Christians ought to be 'received with thanksgiving' for 'continually reviving' them and teaching them to 'cleave together' in *communion*: 'the Supper itself is a gift of God, which ought to have been received with thanksgiving... The Sacrament promised that by Christ's death we are not merely once restored to life, but are continually revived... The Supper was to have been distributed in the public assembly of the church to teach us of the communion by which all cleave together in Christ Jesus' (4. 18/7, 1435). The Lord's Supper means, in short, a 'breaking of bread for the communion of believers' (4. 18/8, 1437).[46]

Given his stress on communion, Calvin argues that the altar must give way to the table, which expresses the communal feast or banquet. Since sacrifice and sacrificing priests were done away with by the one sacrifice of Christ, it follows that there is no need for an altar. 'After Christ's sacrifice was accomplished', Calvin writes, 'the Lord [God] instituted another method for us, that is to transmit to the believing folk the benefit of the sacrifice offered to himself by his Son. He has therefore given us a Table at which to feast, not an altar upon which to offer a victim. He has not consecrated priests to offer sacrifice, but ministers to distribute the sacred worship' (4. 18/12, 1440).

His view of the Lord's Supper as communal thanksgiving and praise allows Calvin, in the light of Hebrews 13: 15 ('let us continually offer a sacrifice of praise to God, that is, the fruit of lips that confess his name'), to name the Eucharist as a kind of sacrifice, a sacrifice in an extended sense of that term: 'The Lord's Supper cannot be without a sacrifice of this kind, in which, while we proclaim his death [1 Cor. 11: 26] and give thanks, we do nothing but offer a sacrifice of praise' (4. 18/17, 1445). In this way Calvin answers a question we raised in Chapter 4 about any possible reference to Eucharistic sacrifice in the Letter to the Hebrews.

[46] In his *First Catechism* of 1538, Calvin was to highlight the 'communication' of the faithful in the Lord's body and blood as 'food and protection' for their spiritual life and as a call to mutual love among those to whom Christ gave himself in communion. See I. J. Hesselink, *Calvin's First Catechism: A Commentary* (Louisville, Ky.: Westminster John Knox Press, 1994), 34–5, 145–7.

Since sacrifice and priesthood mutually require and define each other, Calvin draws on 1 Peter and Hebrews (understood to be authored by Paul) to conclude: 'from this office of sacrificing, all Christians are called a royal priesthood [1 Pet. 2: 9], because through Christ we offer the sacrifice of praise to God of which the apostle speaks: "the fruit of lips confessing his name".' Like Luther, Calvin accepts that Christ's priesthood and his self-sacrifice empower believers to share in this priestly self-sacrifice:

The Mediator interceding for us is Christ, by whom we offer ourselves and what is ours to the Father. He is our Pontiff, who has entered the heavenly sanctuary [Heb. 9: 24] and opens a way for us to enter [Heb. 10: 20]. He is the altar [Heb. 13: 10] upon which we lay our gifts, that whatever we venture to do we may undertake in him. He it is, I say, that has made us a kingdom and priests unto the Father [Rev. 1: 6]. (ibid.)

Calvin puts this more briefly elsewhere: 'every one of us ought to offer himself and all his possessions to God in sacrifice, and so to perform his priestly office.'[47]

Calvin understands this priesthood of believers to have been prophesied by Isaiah: 'you shall be named the priests of the Lord' (Isa. 61: 6). Calvin interprets this verse as predicting a more glorious future: 'Up to now the Lord has chosen you for his own but in the future he will honour you with much more splendid gifts, for he will elevate you all to priestly honour.' At the coming of Christ, 'all the faithful were honoured and exalted with priestly dignity'. Believers share in Christ's priesthood, since it is they (and not animals, as in the Old Testament) who 'are to be brought as sacrifice': that is to say, 'brought to obedience in Christ'. Calvin cites Paul's words about his priestly service of the gospel through which 'he made an offering of the Gentiles that they might obey God [Rom. 15: 16]'.[48]

Both in what he says here about the 'sacrifice' of obedience to Christ and in what he says above about the priestly (self-)sacrifices of all Christians, Calvin follows faithfully the teaching of Romans 15: 16 and Hebrews 13: 15, respectively. Yet his comments stand in some tension with what he has written earlier in an unqualified manner: 'the apostle [understood to be the author of Hebrews] maintains

---

[47] *Calvin Commentaries*, 373.
[48] Ibid.

without exception that death is necessary to make a sacrifice.'[49] Sacrificial obedience to Christ and offering oneself and all one's possessions to God 'in sacrifice' do not as such involve death. Calvin, as we shall see in the next chapter, does not like the adjective 'bloodless'. Yet obedience to Christ and 'performing' the 'priestly office' of sacrifice in daily life do not include a literal and repeated being slain in 'bloody' sacrifice. Recognizing some variations in the use of the term 'sacrifice' and the (somewhat) various realities to which it points is needed. In a sense Calvin himself acknowledges that, when he talks of 'two kinds' of sacrifice (see above). Calvin's own usage, based on the Scriptures, conflicts with his insistence that, 'without exception', 'death is necessary to make a sacrifice'.

THE CHALLENGES

Obviously, Luther and Calvin challenged much in the contemporary Roman Catholic understanding and practice of the ordained priesthood and its connection with Christ's priesthood. Calvin, in particular, vigorously objected to ministerial priests taking it upon themselves to offer the daily sacrifice of the Mass. He also dismissed anointing with oil in ordination as belonging with 'the outworn ceremonies' of the Old Testament prescriptions for the priesthood (4. 19/31, 1478–9). Luther, however, took up this anointing at ordination to move beyond Eucharistic celebration and encourage gentleness in the priestly ministry: 'they [priests] are anointed on their fingers, not so much for the purpose of being worthy to touch the sacrament of the body of Christ as to deal gently with the matter of the same sacrament: that is, with the people of Christ.'[50]

---

[49] *The Epistle to the Hebrews*, 139, summing up matters about Christ's priesthood after Heb. 10: 18. What the author of Hebrews, in fact, affirms is that under the Law 'the shedding of blood' (death) is necessary for 'the forgiveness of sins' (Heb. 9: 22). He does *not* affirm that death is necessary to make any sacrifice. How could he? He exhorts his readers to a 'continual sacrifice of praise' (Heb. 13: 15), which does not involve repeatedly dying.
[50] *Hebrews, LW*, xxix. 170.

As well as issues about the ordained priesthood, the Reformers put wider questions on the agenda for the Council of Trent (1545–63). How should Christians understand the priesthood of Christ and his redemptive, once-and-for-all sacrifice? Specifically, what links can be recognized between his priestly sacrifice (the Letter to the Hebrews) and the celebration of the Last Supper (Paul and the Gospels)? Then—more broadly—what did and does Christ's 'triple office' as priest, prophet, and king involve? In particular, did Christ exercise a priestly office during his public ministry?

How should one express the sharing in this triple office that baptism brings and express, especially, the common priesthood of all the baptized? Does such a common priesthood leave room for any special participation in Christ's priesthood through ministerial ordination? Above all, does the exercise of the ordained ministry in celebrating the Eucharist entail offering a sacrifice, or is it simply a 'remembrance' of Christ's historical sacrifice and a communion through a shared meal?

8

Trent and the French School on Christ's Priesthood

This chapter will examine first the response of the Council of Trent to challenges coming from the Reformers. In four different decrees the Council addressed issues that, at least implicitly, bore on the priesthood of Christ: the decrees on justification (1547), on 'the most holy Eucharist' (1551), on 'the most holy sacrifice of the Mass' (1562), and on 'the sacrament of order' (1563). As we shall see, explicit references to the priesthood of Christ were rare; his 'triple office' as priest, prophet, and king lay beyond sight (to be taken up vigorously only in the twentieth century by the Second Vatican Council, 1962–5); no mention was made of Christ's priesthood being exercised during his public ministry, when preaching God's kingdom and teaching. Nor was there any reference to the common priesthood (and prophetic kingship) of all the baptized—a theme developed centuries later by the Second Vatican Council.

Disputes with the Reformers had moved the Eucharist, the ordained priesthood, and its connection with Christ's priesthood to the forefront of issues for the Council of Trent when it finally opened in 1545. This resulted in a one-sided stress on priesthood as cultic and hierarchical—with, for instance, preaching the Word of God as a priestly function left out of the picture.

In the aftermath of Trent, many leaders (e.g. St Charles Borromeo, d. 1584; St Philip Neri, d. 1595; and St Vincent de Paul, d. 1660) dedicated themselves to reforming and renewing the ministerial priesthood—not least in its 'office' of preaching and teaching. So too did various religious institutes, including the Society of Jesus,

officially approved in 1540. The new or renewed stress on preaching had its impact on church buildings.

Pulpits (elevated stands made of wood or stone) were first introduced in the later Middle Ages, and spread rapidly in the sixteenth century and later. In early Christianity bishops, like Augustine of Hippo, preached from their 'cathedra' or chair. Later the 'ambo' or elevated step, from which cantors led the singing and readers proclaimed the biblical texts, was also used for preaching. But the concern with preaching that came at the Reformation and its aftermath prompted the construction of elaborate and even dominant pulpits, from which preachers announced the word of God and true doctrine.

A school of spirituality, examined in the second half of this chapter, was inspired by Pierre de Bérulle (d. 1629) and understood sacrifice and mediation to belong to every aspect of priestly ministry (and, indeed, to every act of faithful Christians), and not merely to those activities that are cultic and liturgical. This spirituality was based on the incarnation, which it viewed as an essentially priestly act, initiating Christ's life of service on earth and eternal ministry in heaven. This view did not limit the priestly activity of Christ to the first Holy Thursday and Good Friday, but saw it unfolding through the resurrection and ascension as further 'states' of the Lord's incarnation.

When examining this French school we will consider the work not only of Bérulle but also of Charles de Condren (d. 1641) and Jean-Jacques Olier (d. 1657), whose spirituality centred on a special union between ministerial priests and Christ, priest and victim. We conclude this chapter with the teaching of St John Eudes (d. 1680) on the priesthood. He understood preaching the word to be an integral part of Christ's priesthood. He also composed a liturgy (no longer in use) in honour of 'Jesus Christ the high priest and all holy priests and levites'.

THE COUNCIL OF TRENT

The Council of Trent is almost a misnomer, in that it might suggest a cohesive set of meetings taking place over a relatively short period of

time and attended by the same participants.[1] In fact, the Council met over almost twenty years (1545–63), stopping and starting again because of various political, ecclesial, and doctrinal jolts. By the time it opened many of the writings of Luther and other Reformers had appeared more than twenty-five years earlier, and by the time the Council closed the unity of the Church that it desired had become a fading memory. What then does it say, explicitly or implicitly, about the priesthood of Christ?

The Decree on Justification

This decree, coming from the sixth session of the Council, published on 13 January 1547, and arguably the most important decree of the entire Council, expounds the doctrine of grace—and, in particular, the reception of the grace of justification by adults, its preservation and increase, and the recovery of justification if it has been lost by grave sin.[2] The document makes no specific mention of Christ's priesthood. Where it quotes or echoes, albeit rarely, the Letter to the Hebrews, it has nothing to say about Christ the High Priest but deals with other issues: for instance, the impossibility of 'pleasing God' without faith (Heb. 11: 6) (DzH 1532; ND 1935).

From start to finish, the decree makes it quite clear that there is no self-justification or self-redemption. All human beings, inasmuch as they are sinners, need the grace of Christ and 'the merit of his passion' (DzH 1523; ND 1927)—or, in equivalent terms, his priestly mediation, through which they can be 'reborn' and 'become just' (ibid.).

---

[1] On Trent and its context see R. Bireley, *The Refashioning of Catholicism* (Basingstoke: Macmillan, 1999); M. A. Mullett, *The Catholic Reformation* (London: Routledge, 1999); J. W. O'Malley, *Trent and All That: Renaming Catholicism and the Early Modern Age* (Cambridge, Mass.: Harvard University Press, 2000). R. Po-Chia Hsia, *The World of Catholic Renewal 1540–1770* (Cambridge: Cambridge University Press, 1998).

[2] Nowadays this decree should be read in the light of the 1999 *Joint Declaration on the Doctrine of Justification*, the fruit from thirty years of Catholic–Lutheran dialogue and a text officially accepted by the Catholic Church and the Lutheran World Federation (ND 527, 940, 2000k-s).

When clarifying the causes of the sinner's justification, the Council mentions four such causes: final, efficient, meritorious, and instrumental. It is in explaining the third of these causes that the decree comes closest to drawing explicit attention to Christ's priesthood: 'the meritorious cause [of justification] is the beloved, only-begotten Son of God, our Lord Jesus Christ, who "while we were yet sinners" [Rom. 5: 10], "out of the great love with which he loved us" [Eph. 2: 4] merited for us justification by his most holy passion on the wood of the Cross and made satisfaction for us to God the Father' (DzH 1529; ND 1932). The scheme of four causes recalls in general the Aristotelian language of Thomas Aquinas. In particular, the great 'love' that was shown in Christ's passion and 'merited' justification for sinners echoes Thomas's understanding of redemption and his modification of Anselm's theory of 'satisfaction' (see Chapter 6 above).[3] Aquinas went on to treat explicitly the priestly mediation of Christ, but this 1547 decree from the Council of Trent did not follow suit.

The Decree on the Most Holy Eucharist

Aspects of Christ's priesthood were to emerge in Trent's 1562 decree on 'the most holy sacrifice of the Mass'. We see a hint of these things to come in a preliminary 1551 decree on 'the most holy Eucharist', even if here again there is no explicit mention of Christ's priesthood. He is called 'the/our Lord' (frequently), 'our Saviour' (twice), 'our Redeemer' (twice), and 'only begotten Son of God' (once), but never 'Priest'.

The 1551 decree did not purport to offer a complete doctrinal account of the Eucharist but to affirm clearly important points that were being challenged, misinterpreted, or flatly denied: above all, the presence of Christ's body and blood in the Eucharist. While doing that, it also recalled the institution of the Eucharist at the Last Supper (DzH 1637–8; ND 1514–15), as well as 'the most excellent love of our Lord Jesus Christ, who laid down his precious life as the price of

---

[3] Calvin also maintained Anselm's language about Christ making *satisfaction*: see his *Institutes*, 2. 15/6, 502; 4. 18/7, 1435; 4. 18/13, 1441.

our salvation' (DzH 1649; ND 1524). Although the decree thus evoked what many Christians consider to be the two defining moments in the exercise of Christ's priesthood (his self-offering at the Last Supper and its consummation on Calvary), it did not draw explicit attention to that priesthood.

Given this silence about Christ's priesthood, it is not surprising that the decree never quotes the Letter to the Hebrews. It does, however, evoke the language of Hebrews about Christ sitting 'at the right hand of the Father in heaven', yet without calling him 'Priest' and acknowledging his permanent priestly intercession. Rather, the decree is concerned that the heavenly presence of Christ does not exclude the innumerable instances of his presence in the Eucharist: 'there is no contradiction in the fact that our Saviour always sits at the right hand of the Father in heaven according to his natural way of existing and that, nevertheless, in his substance he is sacramentally present to us in many other places' (DzH 1636; ND 1513).

The decree contains a touching plea for 'all who bear the name of Christians' to become of 'one heart' by meeting in the Eucharist, 'this symbol of concord', or—in the words of Augustine—this 'sign of unity' and 'bond of charity' (DzH 1649; ND 1524). Here, at least, the Council joins with Luther and Calvin in understanding the Eucharist to be the great sign and expression of mutual Christian love and communion.

The Decree on the Most Holy Sacrifice of the Mass[4]

In upholding the sacrificial value of the Eucharist and its relationship to (or identity with) the sacrifice of the cross, this 1562 decree was likewise aimed against positions held by the Reformers, albeit without naming them. Calvin, as we saw in the previous chapter, restricted Christ's sacrifice to the cross and leaves aside the Last Supper when associating Christ's priestly 'office' with his sacrificial death. In general, the Reformers highlighted the 'memorial' dimension of the Eucharist, understanding it to be a sacred meal or communion

---

[4] See D. N. Power, *The Sacrifice We Offer: The Tridentine Dogma and Its Reinterpretation* (Edinburgh: T. & T. Clark, 1987).

instituted by Christ but without sacrificial value in itself. For our purposes the first two chapters of the decree (on the historical institution of the Mass at the Last Supper and the value of the Mass as sacrifice) are the most significant.

These two chapters quote, or at least echo, the Letter to the Hebrews six times. Twice they follow Hebrews by explicitly calling Christ 'a priest forever according to the order of Melchizedek' (DzH 1739–40; ND 1546).

The first chapter firmly connects the celebration of the Last Supper with Christ's impending death on the cross: 'He ... was once and for all to offer himself to God the Father by his death on the altar of the cross, to accomplish for them [all who are to be sanctified] an ever-lasting redemption.' But, since 'his priesthood was not to end with his death', through the celebration of the Last Supper he left to the Church 'a visible sacrifice'.[5] Christ 'offered his body and blood under the species of bread and wine to God the Father'. He thus instituted a 'new Pasch': namely, 'himself to be offered by the Church through her priests under visible signs in order to celebrate the *memory* of his passage from this world to the Father' (italics ours).

Trent, while agreeing here with the Reformers that the Eucharist was a 'memorial', went beyond them in adding that it was a sacrifice with two major effects over and above its value as 'memorial'. Christ, the Council taught, instituted this 'visible sacrifice', by which 'the bloody sacrifice that he was once and for all to accomplish on the cross would [1] be present, [2] its memory perpetuated until the end of the world, and [3] its salutary power applied for the forgiveness of sins which we daily commit' (DzH 1740–1; ND 1546). The Reformers (for instance, Calvin in what we recalled in the previous chapter) would accept (2) and (3). The sticking-point was Trent's claim that Christ exercised his priesthood at the Last Supper and did so not only by offering himself (and so beginning the sacrifice of the passion) but also by instituting a ritual through which his priestly sacrifice on the cross would remain present as a visible sacrifice offered through ordained priests. Holding such a participation in

---

[5] Thus the Council of Trent proposed an inseparable link between 'priest', 'sacrifice', victim ('to offer himself'), and 'altar'. The texts we cite from ch. 1 of Trent's decree on the sacrifice of the Mass are found in DzH 1740–2; ND 1546–7.

the priesthood of Christ marked an essential parting of the ways between the Catholic Church and the Reformers (or at least the vast majority of them). According to the Council's decree, through this participation Christ's *visible* priesthood did not end with his death, even while his *invisible* priesthood continues 'at the right hand of the Father' through his eternal intercession for human beings.

Before ending chapter 1 of the decree on the sacrifice of the Mass, Trent proposed *four biblical reasons* for regarding the Last Supper as a sacrifice. Today commentators argue from the very words and gestures of Christ in the institution narrative. The cup over which a blessing was offered pointed to the blood of Christ shed in his passion; the loaf that was broken pointed to the body of Christ broken on the cross. His words and gestures show Christ offering a covenant sacrifice ('my body for you' and 'the (new) covenant in my blood')—a cultic, priestly act that he wished to be continued as a central practice in the community that he had gathered.[6] The Last Supper was a sacrificial meal, something that involved priestly activity on the part of Jesus. Contemporary exegesis prompts us to endorse what a Lutheran theologian, Wolfhart Pannenberg, writes: 'Meal and sacrifice go together at the Lord's Supper, just as the covenant sacrifice and the covenant meal did in Israel.'[7] The first reason given by Trent comes close to what Pannenberg and others, with different nuances, argue. For its second and third reasons Trent appealed, respectively, to the prophet Malachi and to Paul. The fourth appeal is biblical but more general.

First, the Council recalled that 'the old Pasch' was a ritual that 'the multitude of the children of Israel offered (*immolabat*) to celebrate the memory of the departure from Egypt'. Modern scholars develop the sacrificial and priestly implications of 'offered'. Whatever the festival of the Passover meant initially (see e.g. Exod. 12: 1–13), by the time of Jesus (and his contemporary Philo of Alexandria) the slaughter of the lambs under the supervision of priests and levites in

---

[6] On the priestly, sacrificial intentions of Jesus at the Last Supper, see G. O'Collins, *Salvation For All: God's Other Peoples* (Oxford: Oxford University Press, 2008), 111–14.

[7] W. Pannenberg, *Systematic Theology*, trans. G. W. Bromiley, iii (Grand Rapids, Mich.: Eerdmans, 1998), 319.

the Temple and other elements in the ritual had long given the celebration sacrificial significance. Robert Daly writes: 'Regardless of whether or to what extent the Passover was or was not regarded as a sacrifice in its origins, the Jewish tradition by the time of Philo had long looked upon the rite as sacrificial—indeed as one of the foundation sacrifices of Judaism.'[8] John Scholer quotes with approval this statement, and adds that in Philo's view of universal priesthood the whole nation acted as priests at the Passover: 'The Passover festival is the one occasion when the people of Israel are explicitly characterized as functioning priests.'[9] In such terms the argument of Trent stands up well: if 'the old Pasch' should be understood as a priestly sacrifice, the 'new Pasch', instituted by Christ, should also (or rather *a fortiori*) be understood as a sacrificial offering. He went beyond the normal ritual of the Passover to introduce gestures and sayings that revealed his priestly intention to offer himself as victim in self-sacrifice.

Second, the Council of Trent recognized the Eucharist to be the 'clean', sacrificial 'oblation' foretold by Malachi: 'This is the clean oblation which cannot be defiled by any unworthiness or malice on the part of those who offer it, and which the Lord foretold through Malachi would be offered in all places as a clean oblation to his name.' As an oracle from 'the Lord of hosts' the prophet (some time after 500 BC) left a famous statement about the worship offered by Gentiles: 'from the rising of the sun to its setting my name is great among the nations, and in every place incense is offered to my name and a pure offering; for my name is great among the nations' (Mal. 1: 11). Malachi was clearly outraged by the current corrupt practices of Jewish priests and hence was ready to contrast them very unfavourably with what was happening among 'the nations'. The Jewish priesthood was failing in its vocation by misleading the people, and corrupting the worship of God (Mal. 1: 6–2: 9; 3: 3–4).[10]

---

[8] R. J. Daly, *Christian Sacrifice: The Judaeo-Christian Background Before Origen* (Washington, DC: Catholic University of America Press, 1978), 395, n. 10.

[9] J. M. Scholer, *Proleptic Priests: Priesthood in the Epistle to the Hebrews* (Sheffield: Sheffield Academic Press, 1991), 68.

[10] The words in Trent's decree that 'any unworthiness and malice on the part of those who offer it [the clean oblation]' reflected Malachi's judgement on the Jewish (not the Gentile) priests. But in the context of the Reformation controversies the

Looking at 'the nations' around the world, the prophet saw them not only reverencing the name of YHWH but also making pure sacrificial offerings to him in their worship. Whether they were aware of this or not, the cult of the Gentiles 'in every place' entailed true reverence for the God of Israel and a 'pure offering' to his name. It is hard to imagine a more positive view of the religious faith and cultic practices of 'the others' who were Malachi's contemporaries. Nevertheless, given the eschatological emphasis of the Book of Malachi as a whole, the prophet may have intended 'the future establishment of the kingship of God over all the earth'.[11] In this context we should recall Zephaniah, a prophet who was active around 630, and so earlier than Malachi, and who announced the *future* conversion of the nations and did so in terms of cultic worship: 'From beyond the rivers of Ethiopia my suppliants, my scattered ones, shall bring my offering' (Zeph. 3: 10).

Fairly quickly in their story, Christians were to apply Malachi 1: 11 to the Eucharist, its sacrificial dimension, and its celebration by various communities of believers meeting from east to west ('from the rising of the sun to its setting'). Thus, apropos of the Sunday celebration of the Eucharist, the anonymous author of the *Didache* (from around AD 100), when instructing some early community, connected the purity of this sacrifice (Malachi's 'pure offering') with reconciliation within the community: 'On the Lord's own day gather together, break bread and give thanks, having first confessed your sins so that your *sacrifice* may be pure. Let no one who has a quarrel with a companion join you until they have been reconciled, so that your *sacrifice* may not be defiled.' The text then adds: 'For this is the *sacrifice* concerning which the Lord said: "In every place and time offer me a pure *sacrifice*, for ... my name is marvelous among the nations"' (no. 14; italics ours).[12] About a century later Irenaeus of Lyons called on the same passage from Malachi to defend his faith in the Eucharist as the 'pure sacrifice' for all nations (*Adversus Haereses*, 4. 17. 4). The verse from the prophet became a classical text for expounding the sacrament and its sacrificial character.

Council affirmed, more or less explicitly, that, despite the 'unworthiness' and even 'malice' of some (many?) Catholic priests, the Eucharist they offered remained 'a clean oblation'.

[11] A. E. Hill, *Malachi* (New York: Doubleday, 1998), 219.

[12] See K. Niederwimmer, *The Didache* (Minneapolis: Fortress Press, 1998), 194–9.

Hence the decree from Trent attached itself to a long-standing interpretative tradition by understanding the verse from Malachi to prefigure 'the clean oblation' or sacrificial offering that was/is the Eucharist instituted by Christ at the Last Supper. Yet the Council did not allege that Christ himself had the prophecy of Malachi in mind when he 'instituted' the Eucharist to leave the Church 'a visible sacrifice'. Rather, the decree simply pointed to the Eucharist and said: 'this is the clean oblation' foretold by Malachi. Contemporary exegesis, by highlighting the future thrust of the prophet's oracle, may make it easier to imagine that the verse in some sense foreshadows the Eucharistic worship of Christians.

In putting a case for the sacrificial nature of the Eucharist, Trent appealed in the third instance to 1 Corinthians: 'The apostle Paul also refers clearly to it [the Eucharist as sacrifice] when . . . he says that those who have been defiled by partaking of the table of the devils cannot be partakers of the table of the Lord. By "table" he understands "altar" in both cases.' Horrified by the thought that his fellow Christians in Corinth who share in the Eucharist might also share in pagan sacrifices, Paul insists: 'you cannot partake of the table (*trapezēs*) of the Lord and the table (*trapezēs*) of demons' (1 Cor. 10: 21). In the context he has just mentioned Jewish sacrifices in the Jerusalem Temple (not yet destroyed at that time): 'Consider the people of Israel. Are not those who eat the sacrifices sharers in the altar (*thusiastēriou*)?' (1 Cor. 10: 18). He sets this alongside what pagans do in the temples of Corinth: 'they sacrifice to demons and not to God' (1 Cor. 10: 20). 'Altar' and 'table' seem to be used here as synonyms. Even if they are not strict equivalents, Paul obviously compares the Eucharistic meal with Jewish and pagan sacrifices. Since the Eucharist derives from what Christ did at the Last Supper, Paul implies that the Eucharist, instituted by Christ on the night before he died, was/is a sacrifice. We argued that more fully in Chapter 2 above.

The first three—and, especially, the first and third—biblical arguments in support of recognizing the sacrificial value of the Eucharist stand up reasonably well. But what of the fourth argument? Here Trent appealed very widely to all kinds of sacrifices, offered within Judaism ('under the regime of the [Jewish] law') and among the nations or at least prior to the Mosaic Law ('under the regime of nature'), that it is considered to have *prefigured* the sacrifice initiated by

the Last Supper: 'this [Christ's self-sacrifice] is the oblation prefigured by various types of sacrifices under the regime of nature and of the law. For it includes all the good that was signified by those former sacrifices; it is their fulfillment and perfection.' As examples of sacrifices offered 'under the regime of nature' and not yet 'under the regime of the law', the Council had in mind 'various types of sacrifice', a generous range that presumably should be understood to include the sacrificial offering made by Abel (Gen. 4: 4), a sacrifice offered by Noah (Gen. 8: 20), the offerings made by Abram (journeying immediately after his call and not yet renamed 'Abraham') (Gen. 12: 7–8), and the testing of Abraham through the command to sacrifice Isaac, his heir on whom the future of the chosen people depended (Gen. 22: 1–19).

The sacrifice offered by Abel may seem a particularly happy example in the context of this book. The Letter to the Hebrews named Abel first on its list of heroes and heroines of faith, noting that God approved of Abel's gifts and that through his faith Abel 'still speaks' (Heb. 11: 4). The letter comes back to Abel. While acknowledging his bloody death and what it has to say, the author of Hebrews emphasizes the superiority of Jesus' priestly offering that mediated the new covenant and 'speaks a better word'—presumably of forgiveness and cleansing: '[you have come] to Jesus, the mediator of a new covenant, and to the sprinkled blood that speaks a better word than the blood of Abel' (Heb. 12: 24).[13] This new truth, about Jesus' priestly mission, stands in some continuity with, or at least discloses some analogy to, the sacrifice of Abel but surpasses it ('speaks a better word').

Nevertheless, one can hardly claim that the violent death of Abel clearly prefigured the self-sacrifice initiated by Christ through the Eucharist that he instituted—still less that the offerings made by Noah and Abraham did so. Perhaps one can and should argue this way: the 'various types of sacrifice under the regime of nature and of the law' yield some analogy, even if not necessarily a close analogy, to the sacrifice to which Christ committed himself at the Last Supper and consummated on Calvary. Anything that was good in those ancient sacrifices found its subsequent, higher counterpart in Christ's self-sacrifice.

---

[13] See C. R. Koester, *Hebrews* (New York: Doubleday, 2001), 414–16, 546.

While the Letter to the Hebrews insists on the real novelty brought by Christ's priesthood, it does not propose this new truth as totally and utterly new. Unless the Levitical priesthood and, in particular, the ceremony of the Day of Expiation had supplied, for instance, a sacrificial and ritual language, Hebrews could not have talked the way it did about Christ's once-and-for-all sacrifice. Furthermore, along-side the radical discontinuity between the exercise of priesthood under the Old Law and Christ's priesthood, Hebrews accepted some continuity: for instance, in qualifications for priesthood (e.g. Heb. 5: 1–4), in the way that 'every high priest is appointed to offer gifts and sacrifices' (Heb. 8: 3), and in the general principle that the forgiveness of sins requires 'the shedding of blood' (Heb. 9: 22). For all its emphasis on novelty that reached its climax in the claim that the new covenant brought by Christ's sacrifice made the first covenant 'obsolete' (Heb. 8: 13), Hebrews allowed for some (limited) continuity with the prior pattern of divine arrangements about priesthood and about its exercise in the offering of sacrifice. Seen in retrospect, those arrangements prepared the way, at least partially, for Christ's high priesthood. That way of stating matters may follow the thrust of Hebrews better than ideas about Christ's sacrifice 'ful-filling' and 'perfecting' previous sacrifices and 'including' all the good they signified.

All in all, this fourth argument from prior forms of sacrifice, found at the end of chapter 1 of Trent's decree, lends only a rather general credibility to the conclusion that Christ instituted a new and perma-nent form of sacrifice at the Last Supper.

The decree on 'the most holy sacrifice of the Mass' moves ahead in chapter 2 to affirm that the visible sacrifice is 'truly propitiatory (*propitiatorium*)'.[14] In teaching that, Trent first emphasizes that 'in this divine sacrifice which is celebrated in the Mass the same Christ

---

[14] What we cite from ch. 2 is found in DzH 1743; ND 1548. One 'canon' that follows in the decree and that corresponds to this chapter adds several items not contained as such in the chapter—expressed in the form of anathemas directed against the views of unnamed Reformers (but obviously including Luther and Calvin) and condemning anyone who 'says that the sacrifice of the Mass is *merely* an offering of praise and thanksgiving, or that it is a *simple* commemoration of the sacrifice accomplished on the cross, or that it benefits only those who communicate' (DzH 1753; ND 1557; italics ours).

who offered himself once in a *bloody* manner on the altar of the cross is contained and is offered in an *unbloody* manner' (italics ours). Any difference between Calvary and the Mass touches only the 'manner of offering': 'the victim is one and the same: the same [Christ] now offers through the ministry of priests, who then offered himself on the cross; only the manner of offering is different. The fruits of this oblation (the bloody one, that is) are received in abundance through this unbloody oblation.'

Calvin, incidentally, recognized how 'the papists' maintained that the Mass was 'not something new or different from the sacrifice of Christ but the same thing.'[15] Yet he rejected 'the practice of daily sacrifice' as 'wholly inconsistent with and foreign to the priesthood of Christ'.[16] First, it meant that Christ was 'offered by other hands' (even if Trent said that Christ 'now offers through the ministry of priests'). Second, it attempted to repeat the sacrifice of Christ that was 'offered once and for all', even if the papists 'chatter[ed] about the sacrifice [of the Mass] being the same' as that offered by Christ. Third, it involved 'nonsense' by claiming (against the witness of Hebrews that 'there is no sacrifice without blood and death') that the manner of offering Christ's sacrifice at Mass was 'bloodless'. Hebrews, however, states that 'there is no [sacrificial] forgiveness of sins without the shedding of blood' (Heb. 9: 22), and does not maintain that there is no sacrifice *tout court* without blood and death. Yet, in fairness to Calvin, he made this third statement only after correctly observing that 'the papists . . . maintain that their Mass is a sacrifice for the atonement of the sins of the living and the dead'.[17] The issue between him and 'the papists' became: could one accept a sacrifice for the forgiveness of sins and for the atonement/ expiation of sins that perpetuated, applied, and under visible signs rendered present a bloody sacrifice but that in itself involved an unbloody manner of offering?

Calvin (and Luther) will return below when we analyse further chapter 2 of the decree on the holy sacrifice of the Mass. Trent, as we

---

[15] J. Calvin, *The Epistle of Paul the Apostle to the Hebrews*, trans. W. B. Johnston (Edinburgh: Oliver & Boyd, 1963), 139, after commenting on Heb. 10: 18.
[16] Ibid. 137, commenting on Heb. 10: 11.
[17] Ibid. 139.

saw above, speaks of Christ as having offered himself on 'the altar of the cross'; he was 'the victim' of this sacrifice, which he 'now offers through the ministry of priests'. Given the theme of this book, we regret that Trent did not complete its set of terms, 'sacrifice', 'altar', and 'victim', by explicitly stating that Christ himself was and remains 'priest' or 'high priest'. But what did/does Christ's once-and-for-all sacrifice effect? Without exploring and defining the full scope of this sacrifice, the decree calls it a 'truly propitiatory' sacrifice by which God the Father was 'appeased (*placatus*)'; he then 'grants grace and the gifts of repentance' and 'pardons wrong-doings and sin, even grave ones'. After briefly interpreting Christ's sacrifice as 'propiti-atory' and effective in 'appeasing' or 'placating' God (and so placating the divine anger), Trent presses on to introduce three further terms in the course of defending the sacrifice of the Mass: 'it is rightly offered . . . not only for the sins, *punishments, satisfaction* and other necessities of the faithful who are alive but also for those who have died in Christ but are not yet wholly *purified* (purgati)' (italics ours). First, the terminology of 'satisfaction' reaches back, as we saw in Chapter 6, through Aquinas to Anselm. There we also noted, sec-ondly, how Anselm explicitly ruled out the idea of God 'punishing' sinful human beings, let alone God punishing his own Son in their place. Aquinas, however, introduced—albeit briefly—the notion of Christ's sacrifice 'placating' God and thus helped to prepare the way for those who fully espoused the idea of Christ being punished in the place of sinners and so propitiating an angry God by paying a redemptive ransom. Thirdly, talk of sinners being 'purified' or 'cleansed' from the guilt or 'stain' of their sins finds plenty of biblical support, not least in Hebrews (e.g. Heb. 9: 14). What would the Reformers make of such language?

Calvin and Luther challenged the whole notion of the sacrifice of the Mass being offered in that way for the living and the dead. Apropos of the once-and-for-all sacrifice of Christ and its effects, however, Calvin, as we saw, endorsed the traditional language of 'satisfaction' being offered for sin. More significantly, he and Luther supported and developed, as we showed in the previous chapter, the language about Christ's sacrifice 'appeasing' or 'propitiating' an angry God, who then grants grace and forgiveness to sinners. Once

again we can refer the reader to the case that one of us has developed against espousing such a penal substitution view.[18]

Trent, to be sure, speaks only once of God being 'appeased' or 'placated', and in the corresponding 'canon' does not use this term. There it calls the Mass 'a propitiatory sacrifice . . . offered for the living and the dead, for sins, punishments and satisfaction' (DzH 1753; ND 1557). More precision might have led the Council to name the Mass as being 'an expiatory sacrifice'. 'Expiation', 'purification', and 'cleansing' seem to us the terms to employ in this context. They avoid the more or less inevitable understanding that a 'propitiatory sacrifice' involves 'appeasing' the divine anger—a notion that can hardly be reconciled with the New Testament's stress on the initiative of divine love in the drama of human redemption (e.g. John 3: 16; Rom. 5: 8). It is only very occasionally that fathers of the Church use the language of propitiation. Origen, for instance, in his *Homilies on Leviticus*, when referring to Christ's words, 'this is my blood that will be poured out for many for the remission of sins' (Matt. 26: 28), remarks: 'his blood makes God favourable (*propitium*) to you and reconciles you to the Father' (9. 10; see ibid. 13. 3).

Raymond Moloney makes a generous case in support of Trent's naming 'propitiation' among the principal effects of the Eucharist.[19] What we missed in this defence was any reference to the language of 'expiation', 'purification', and 'cleansing'. Moloney seems to imply that maintaining the sacrificial value of the redemption effected by Christ (and coming through redemption's presence in the Eucharist) involves maintaining its 'propitiatory' value. But 'sacrifice' and 'propitiation' do not stand or fall together. The language of 'sacrifice' should be maintained, but it should be qualified as an 'expiatory sacrifice'. Even if the Christian tradition has not always clearly distinguished 'expiation' from 'propitiation', the New Testament support for using the former term and dropping the latter seems very strong.[20]

[18] G. O'Collins, *Jesus Our Redeemer* (Oxford: Oxford University Press, 2007), 133–60.

[19] R. Moloney, *The Eucharist* (London: Geoffrey Chapman, 1995), 217–20, 221–2, 240. Yet earlier Moloney acknowledges the distinction to be drawn between 'propitiation' and 'expiation' (ibid. 26).

[20] O'Collins, *Jesus Our Redeemer*, 15–18.

Before completing the decree on the sacrifice of the Mass, Trent faced some of the secondary complaints of the Reformers, which we recalled in the last chapter: for instance, Luther's call to celebrate the liturgy in the vernacular and to proclaim out loud (and no longer in a whisper) the Eucharistic Prayer. Trent defended 'the low voice' in which 'the words of consecration' were recited and rejected the proposal that the 'Mass should be celebrated only in the vernacular' (DzH 1759; ND 1563). Such changes were to come, but only 400 years later, when the Second Vatican Council introduced a wide use of the vernacular and an audible recital (or singing) of the Eucharistic Prayer. Both of these practices, in any case, had for centuries already characterized the worship of Eastern-rite Christians, including those in union with the Bishop of Rome.

The Decree on the Sacrament of Order

A year after responding to the Reformers with its decree on the sacrifice of the Mass, the Council of Trent issued a decree on the sacrament of orders. For many of the Reformers, the uniqueness of Christ's priesthood left room only for the common priesthood of all baptized Christians. There was no ministerial priesthood that was conferred through ordination. To preside over the worship of Christian communities and, in particular, over the celebration of the Eucharist, leaders did not need any special sacramental power; their ministry came through delegation by the community.

This decree, promulgated on 15 July 1563, gave the Council fathers a chance of commenting on Christ's priesthood and drawing conclusions from their teaching about his priesthood. But the decree never explicitly addressed the priesthood of Christ, even though it took up things related to the subject.

First, chapter 1 begins with a firm statement about the correlation between priesthood and sacrifice, a theme that goes back through Aquinas and Augustine to Hebrews: 'sacrifice and priesthood are by the ordinance of God so united that both have existed [together] under every law.' The Council might have paused here to reflect on the union between sacrifice and priesthood in the person of Christ. Instead, it draws at once a key conclusion that concerns ministerial

priesthood: since 'the Catholic Church has received from the institution of Christ the holy, *visible* sacrifice of the Eucharist, it must also
be acknowledged that there exists in the Church a new, visible, and
external priesthood'—a priesthood 'instituted by the same Lord our
Saviour' (DzH 1764; ND 1707; italics ours). The language of 'visible
and external priesthood' recurs in the corresponding canon (DzH
1771; ND 1714). In this way the 1563 decree builds directly on the
1562 decree: since Christ instituted a new form of sacrifice, he must
also have instituted a new form of priesthood.

Applying to ministerial priesthood some sacramental terminology,
'visible' and 'external', recalls the language used in the 1562 decree on
the sacrifice of the Mass: as 'a visible sacrifice (as human nature
demands)' and the 'new Pasch' to 'be offered by the Church through
her priests under *visible* signs' (DzH 1740–1; ND 1546; italics ours).[21]
The language applied to priesthood matches that applied to sacrifice,
and vice versa. Both are visible and external, but also point to the
invisible, hidden, and internal realm, which featured (see previous
chapter) in the accounts Luther and Calvin offered of Christ's spiritual kingship and priesthood. The sacramental theology of the
Catholic Church, exemplified paradigmatically by Thomas Aquinas,
highlighted the visible and external signs and at times needed to be
reminded of the invisible, hidden, and spiritual realities.[22]

The crux of the 1563 decree on holy orders came in chapter 4:
'The Ecclesiastical Hierarchy and Ordination'. The Council rejected

---

[21] See also in the 1562 decree the defence of 'ceremonies, vestments, and [other]
external signs which the Catholic Church uses in the celebration of Masses' (DzH
1757; ND 1561; italics ours). This canon corresponds to ch. 5 of that decree: 'Since
the nature of human beings is such that it cannot easily be raised to meditate on
divine things without external supports, holy Mother Church ... has made use of
ceremonies such as mystical blessings, lights, incense, vestments and many other
things of this kind ..., whereby both the majesty of so great a sacrifice might be
commended, and the minds of the faithful excited by these *visible* signs of religion
and piety to the contemplation of the most sublime matters which lie *hidden* in this
sacrifice' (DzH 1746; not included in ND; italics ours).

[22] In an antiphon he wrote for the Feast of Corpus Christi, Thomas achieved a
lovely balance between the external and the internal: '*O sacrum convivium in quo
Christus sumitur; recolitur memoria passionis eius; mens impletur gratia; et futurae
gloriae nobis pignus datur*' ('O sacred banquet in which Christ is received; his suffering
is remembered; [our] mind is filled with grace; and we receive a pledge of the glory
that is to be ours').

holding that the only way of sharing in Christ's priesthood was through the common priesthood of all believers: 'if Christians [the Reformers] should assert that all Christians are without distinction priests of the New Testament, or that all are to be equally endowed with the same spiritual power, they seem to be doing nothing else than upset the Church's hierarchy, which is like an army with banners' [Song of Solomon 6: 3], as if, contrary to the teaching of St Paul, 'all were apostles, all prophets, all evangelists, all pastors, all doctors [1 Cor. 12: 29; Eph. 4: 11]' (DzH 1767; ND 1710). The Council fathers did not reject here the priesthood of believers, nor could they do so, since this common priesthood of all the baptized was based on the New Testament and had been maintained by Christian tradition (see Aquinas in Chapter 6 above). But, in the context of challenges from the Reformers, they were intent on ministerial ordination and the hierarchy as essential for the Church's survival and vitality. They dedicated the rest of chapter 4 to describing clerical offices, especially the office and role of ordained bishops and priests. Trent did not deny the common priesthood of the baptized, but missed a chance of expounding in detail what it is and how it differs from the ministerial priesthood.

Similarly, the stress the Reformers placed on the preaching of the Word (see previous chapter above) led the Council to react and leave that priestly function (of Christ and his ministers) more or less out of the picture. They mentioned it, but only to condemn those who held that priests 'who have once been rightly ordained can again become lay persons if they do not exercise the ministry of the Word of God' (DzH 1767; ND 1710). The Council fathers did not want to denigrate the Word of God, but could not see their way to affirm positively that preaching and teaching are true priestly functions, found primarily and pre-eminently in the public ministry of Jesus himself. The first of the 'canons' that followed chapter 4 anathematized any who claimed 'that there is in the New Testament no visible and external priesthood, or that there is no power of consecrating and offering the true body and blood of the Lord and of remitting and retaining sins, but only the office and bare ministry of preaching the Gospel, or that those who do not preach are not priests at all' (DzH 1771; ND 1714). Since Trent saw the Reformers to be one-sidedly stressing the preaching of the Word, the Council reacted by emphasizing a 'visible and

external priesthood', tied to the offering of the Eucharist and the administration of the sacrament of penance. This was to confine ministerial priesthood to the powers of consecrating bread and wine and absolving sins. The prophetic/preaching role of priests was overlooked, and their kingly role reduced to 'the power of the keys' in penance, with no mention of their shepherding and leading the flock.

One can argue that, at this point in history, defending the cultic and 'judicial' function of the ministerial priesthood was more important than setting out an adequate or even comprehensive account of the ordained ministry. In fact the Council of Trent, in its decree on the sacrament of order, proposed at the start a limited agenda, 'to condemn the errors of our time' (DzH 1763; ND 1706)—or, in other words, to defend a 'sacrificing priesthood' against the Reformers' attacks and not to expound a full doctrine of ministerial priesthood. This meant, however, that the priestly ministry of preaching was barely acknowledged by the Council of Trent. A fuller recognition of the priestly character of preaching would come slowly in the Roman Catholic Church's teaching, theology, and legislation for seminary training, and would flower fully only at the Second Vatican Council.

THE FRENCH SCHOOL

Given Trent's insistence on the sacrificial character of the Eucharist, to be celebrated by ordained priests who share in a 'new, visible, and external priesthood' instituted by Christ, the Catholic renewal of the ministerial priesthood focused on the celebration of the Eucharistic sacrifice and only slowly began to draw inspiration, for a wider and deeper view of priesthood, from the example of Christ's own priesthood. More immediately, the Council's teaching on ministerial priesthood led to reforms in the preparation and education of the clergy.

But, 'since the Council had not indicated how seminaries should be structured and run', Aidan Nichols writes, 'their creation was anything but smooth'. He adds: 'as with the picture of the ideal

bishop, while Trent had provided valuable cues, it did not offer a fully fledged presbyteral spirituality: the portrait of the spiritual priest, clothed with ministerial holiness, remained to be painted. Whereas Charles Borromeo . . . was a pioneer in episcopal solicitude for the formation of the presbyterate, the making of this portrait had to await the post-Tridentine "French School".[23] When it emerged in the seventeenth century, this school of spirituality contributed massively to the training of spiritual priests, formed through imitating Christ, the model of priesthood.

The seventeenth century witnessed the continuing rise of France as a nation. Bérulle, Condren, Olier, Eudes, and others[24] shaped a spiritual and ecclesiastical renaissance in the context of a political and cultural burgeoning that culminated in the reign of the 'Sun King', Louis XIV (1638–1715; ruler from 1661). The political reality and stability of seventeenth-century France provided a relatively tranquil laboratory for the reforming activity of priestly leaders, who aimed to renew the clergy in France and beyond. In 1611 Bérulle founded the French Oratory, with the training of priests as one of this institute's chief activities; by 1631, two years after his death, there were seventy-one houses of this branch of the Oratory.[25] In 1625 Vincent de Paul created the Congregation of the Mission (usually called Lazarists or Vincentians), an institute that took as its work both priestly formation and missions to the poor and marginalized. Olier began the Society of Saint-Sulpice, and by the time of his death in 1657 he had opened eight seminaries in France, including the original one, transferred after one year to Saint-Sulpice in Paris. He contributed much to the formation of ministerial priests over the next 300 years—a formation founded on a vision of Christ the priest. Eudes, who began as an

---

[23] A. Nichols, *Holy Order: The Apostolic Ministry from the New Testament to the Second Vatican Council* (Dublin: Veritas Publications, 1990), 106.

[24] Any list of the 'others' should include Blessed Agnès de Langeac (d. 1634), St Claude de la Colombière (d. 1692), St Francis de Sales (d. 1622), St Jane Frances de Chantal (d. 1641), St Louise de Marillac (d. 1660), Venerable Madeleine du Bois de Fontaines (d. 1637), Venerable Madeleine de Saint-Joseph (the first French prioress of the Great Carmel in Paris, d. 1637), St Margaret Mary Alacoque (d. 1690), Blessed Marie of the Incarnation (= Mme Acarie, d. 1618), and St Vincent de Paul (d. 1660), with St Louis-Marie Grignion de Montfort (d. 1716) and St John-Baptist de la Salle (who studied at Saint-Sulpice and died in 1719) closing the list.

[25] See 'Oratorians', *ODCC* 1193–4.

Oratorian, founded the Congregation of Jesus and Mary (later called 'Eudists'), with priestly formation and missions as its work. From the late nineteenth century, and especially after the work of Henri Bremond (d. 1933), the current of spirituality inspired by Bérulle came to be called 'the French School' of spirituality.[26]

As has sometimes been noted, these spiritual developments in France enjoyed parallels in scientific breakthroughs that happened in other European countries. William Harvey (d. 1657) discovered the circulation of the blood and the heart's role in it. His medical discovery was 'matched' by the spirituality of the Sacred Heart of Jesus, spread not only by Margaret Mary Alacoque and Claude de la Colombière but also by John Eudes. Through his astronomical observations, Galileo Galilei (d. 1642) supported the Copernican revolution: the earth moves around the sun and not vice versa. The French School of spirituality promoted a Christ-centred spirituality that put Jesus and not human beings at the centre.[27] It was a Christocentrism that valued his priesthood as Christ's highest dignity.

Pierre de Bérulle[28]

Bérulle, and later his fellow Parisian, Vincent de Paul, called for a spiritual reform of France in general, and of the clergy in particular.

---

[26] See R. Deville, *The French School of Spirituality: An Introduction and Reader*, trans. A. Cunningham (Pittsburgh: Duquesne University Press, 1994); Y. Krumenacker, *L'École française de spiritualité. Des mystiques, des fondateurs, des courants, et leurs interprètes* (Paris: Cerf, 1999); W. M. Thompson (ed.) and L. M. Glendon (trans.), *Bérulle and the French School: Selected Writings* (Mahwah, NJ: Paulist Press, 1989). See also H. Bremond, *A Literary History of Religious Thought in France*, iii (London: SPCK, 1936); Bremond dedicates most of this volume of nearly 600 pages to Bérulle, Condren, Olier, and Eudes.

[27] Copernicus caught the imagination of Bérulle, who wrote: 'An excellent mind of this age claimed that the sun and not the earth is at the centre of the universe. He maintained that it is stationary, and that the earth . . . moves in relation to the sun.' 'This new opinion', he added, 'is useful and should be followed in the science of salvation' (*Discourse on the State and Grandeurs of Jesus*, 2/2; trans. Thompson, *Bérulle and the French School*, 116).

[28] For bibliographical information see 'Bérulle, Pierre de (1575–1629)', *ODCC* 196.

Bérulle could have made his own the challenge that Vincent de Paul directed to the priests of his time: 'we wonder if all the troubles we see in the world ought not to be attributed to priests... What sacrifice, gentlemen, would you not offer to God in order to work for the reform of the clergy, so that they could live according to the exalted dignity of their state. By means of this effort the Church would be able to rise out of the opprobrium and desolation in which she finds herself.'[29]

For Bérulle, the heart of the matter was the sanctification of the clergy and not any merely disciplinary reform. Playing on one of the meanings of the Greek word (*klēros*, or 'inheritance') from which 'clergy' came, he suggested that this showed 'that they have no possession on earth and that the only wealth Jesus Christ has left them is this possession of heaven and this sharing in himself: that is to say, in his holiness, light, authority, adoring, and receiving authority from the Father, light from the Son and holiness from the Holy Spirit.'[30] When he erected an Oratory at Saint-Sulpice in 1610, Bérulle instilled in his recruits the need to refuse benefices and ecclesiastical honours and to return to the spirit of poverty of the early Church (see e.g. Acts 4: 32). He understood the original holiness of the clergy in terms of three gifts (authority, holiness, and light) and in a Trinitarian sense: 'At that time the clergy bore nobly the mark of God's authority, holiness, and light: three beautiful jewels in the priestly crown, joined together by God's design for his anointed ones, his priests and his Church... God preserved within this same order authority, holiness, and doctrine, uniting these three perfections in the priestly order in honour and imitation of the holy Trinity.'[31]

Bérulle's call for a renewal of the ministerial priesthood was deeply Trinitarian and thoroughly centred on Christ the High Priest. Ministerial priesthood should move around the eternal High Priest, just as the earth moves around the sun. What features emerge in this

---

[29] St Vincent de Paul, *Entretiens spirituels aux missionaires* (Paris: Seuil, 1960), 501–2.

[30] From 'A Letter on the Priesthood', *Correspondence de Bérulle*, ed. J. Dagens, i (Paris: Desclée de Brouwer, 1937), 617–18; trans. Thompson, *Bérulle and the French School*, 184.

[31] Ibid.

portrait of Christ's priesthood? Going beyond the Letter to the Hebrews, which highlighted Christ's perfect obedience and service (e.g. Heb. 10: 7), Bérulle adds adoration and love to picture Christ as an 'infinite adorer', ready 'to render service and infinite love':

> From all eternity there had been a God infinitely adorable, but still there had not been an *infinite adorer*. There had been a God infinitely worthy of being loved and served, but no man nor infinite servant able to render an infinite service and love. You are now, O Jesus, this adorer, this man, this servant, infinite in power, in being, [and] in dignity, so that you can fully satisfy this need and render this divine homage.[32]

For Bérulle, in the role of priest Christ was concerned with God the Father, adoring him and offering him supreme homage. In his other roles—for instance, as king, pastor, and judge—Christ was directed towards his Church, and was concerned to save and nourish human beings, as well as to judge them.

Bérulle distinguished the 'direction' of Christ's role as priest from the 'direction' of his other roles, but did not separate them. The incarnation revealed and initiated a divine 'chain' of love: 'the charity of the Father and the Son toward humanity' and 'the unity' of 'Jesus Christ with us in the Eucharist'.[33] In his priestly love, Christ instituted this sacrament 'to bind himself to our souls and to draw them into the plenitude of the divinity that dwells in him'.[34]

As regards ministerial priesthood, Bérulle stressed that 'it requires a particular relationship with Jesus Christ our Lord to whom we are conjoined in this ministry in a special manner'.[35] Personally he committed himself to perpetual service of Christ the High Priest, who had shown himself so united with human beings through his earthly life and heavenly glory: 'I join myself to you by the bond of perpetual servitude, in honour of the holy and sacred bond that you have with us on earth and in heaven, in the life of grace and glory'.[36]

---

[32] *The State and Grandeurs of Jesus*, 2/13; trans. Thompson, *Bérulle and The French School*, 126; italics ours.

[33] Ibid. 6/4; trans. Thompson, *Bérulle and the French School*, 140.

[34] *Oeuvres de piété*, 37; quoted Krumenacker, *L'École française*, 201.

[35] Ibid. 309 *bis*; quoted Krumenacker, *L'École française*, 202.

[36] *The State and Grandeurs of Jesus*, 2/6; trans. Thompson, *Bérulle and the French School*, 121.

Through the incarnation Christ had joined himself to humanity in 'a bond of love, a rare and singular love'. Addressing Christ, Bérulle continues: 'It is a holy and sacred bond, which joins your person to our nature; a bond that forms a new being, a new state, a new order; a bond that makes a new man and a new Adam. When I say a new man, I mean not simply a just man or a holy man, not an angelic or divine man, but a Man-God who sustains, rules, and delights heaven and earth.'[37] Like many other writers, Bérulle found Christ's loving bond with humanity and God supremely expressed in the high-priestly prayer that constitutes John 17. He understood this prayer to ask that all human beings should be sacrificially 'consumed' and drawn into the very life of God: 'he [Christ] begged for the grace that we might all be consumed in the supreme unity', which 'he shares eternally with the Father'.[38]

In an eloquent passage, Bérulle presents the union in Christ of divinity and humanity, a union that made him the effective priestly mediator between God and human beings: 'God is man and man is God. God is man, clothing himself with our humanity. Man is God, subsisting and living in the Godhead. In the world there is a *mediator* between God and men, who is man in order to undergo death men have merited. He is God to overcome death, which men could not defeat, and to offer them his life and eternity.' In tones worthy of Augustine of Hippo, Bérulle spells out four paradoxical aspects of the redemption effected by the divine-human Mediator: 'It is the only Son of God who is this *mediator*, who became man for men and who, through a wondrous love and power, [1] exalted us by humbling himself, [2] glorified us by suffering, [3] divinized us by becoming human, and [4] rendered us eternal by dying.' Astonished by the deep truth of human salvation and, incidentally, not forgetting the theme from Hebrews about Christ's permanent priestly intercession, Bérulle exclaims: 'How great is this mystery, which begins on earth and ends in heaven where Jesus is at the right hand of the Father! How great is this mystery, which joins for all eternity earth with heaven and God with man!'[39]

---

[37] Ibid.

[38] Ibid. 3/10; trans. Thompson, *Bérulle and the French School*, 130–1.

[39] Ibid. 7/9; trans. Thompson, *Bérulle and the French School*, 142; italics ours.

Like some other classic Christian authors (see e.g. John Chrysostom and John Calvin above), Bérulle understood Christ's priesthood to begin with the incarnation. But, unlike them, he pictured the
initial exercise of this priesthood as taking place in the 'temple' of
Mary's womb: 'He [Jesus] is in her as in a *temple* where he praises and
adores God; where he *offers* his respects to the eternal Father, not only
for himself but for every creature. It is a holy and sacred *temple* where
Jesus dwells, the true *ark* of the true *covenant*.' After this language of
'temple', 'offering', and 'ark of the covenant', Bérulle expands the
priestly imagery by adding 'altar', 'host', 'offering sacrifice', and 'oblation': 'The heart of the Virgin is the first *altar* on which Jesus *offered*
his heart, body, and spirit as a *host* of perpetual praise . . . his first
sacrifice, making the first and perpetual *oblation* of himself, through
which . . . we are all made holy.'[40] Without explicitly using here the
term 'priest', Bérulle applies to Jesus the classic terminology of
priestly activity.

Charles de Condren

After the death of Cardinal Bérulle in 1629, he was succeeded as
superior-general of the Oratory by Charles Du Bois de Condren.[41]
Through his *Idée du sacerdoce et du sacrifice de Jesus-Christ*,[42] Condren continued the teaching of his predecessor, with a strong devotion to the mysteries of the Incarnate Christ but now with even more
emphasis on his sacrifice and his being victim.

---

[40] *The State and Grandeurs of Jesus*, 28/1; trans. Thompson, *Bérulle and the French
School*, 161; italics ours. Bérulle presupposes here the view of Thomas Aquinas that,
from the first moment of his conception, Christ enjoyed in his human mind the vision
of God granted to the saints in heaven. After being endorsed for centuries by Roman
Catholic theologians and (marginally and in the first half of the twentieth century) by
official Catholic teaching, this view has been widely abandoned. See G. O'Collins,
Christology: A Biblical, Historical, and Systematic Study of Jesus (2nd edn., Oxford: Oxford
University Press, 2009), 208, 211, 266–9; id., *Incarnation* (London: Continuum, 2002),
82–4.

[41] For bibliographical information see 'Condren, Charles de (1588–1641)', ODCC
397.

[42] C. de Condren, *The Eternal Sacrifice*, trans. A. J. Monteith (London: Thomas
Baker, 1906). This posthumous work was put together by his disciples and first
published in 1677.

Condren stressed how God, 'the sole object' of human adoration, the One to 'whom alone sacrifice can be offered', is 'pure spirit'. Hence adoration and sacrifice should be 'spiritual'. Sacrifice, he declared, 'is the most perfect form of adoration, the holiest and most worthy of God'.[43] We find that adoration paradigmatically exemplified in the unique sacrifice of Jesus Christ the High Priest.

Condren distinguished four phases in the one sacrifice of Christ ('consecration' in the incarnation, 'immolation' on the cross, 'consummation' or 'burning', and communion in returning to God) that—in the words of Hebrews 10: 14—'made perfect' those whom he 'has sanctified'. He stated: Jesus Christ, 'by one sole oblation, taken in its fullness, and by one only sacrifice, of which [1] the consecration began with the mystery of the incarnation to continue forever, [2] the immolation took place on the cross, [3] the consummation and [4] communion at the resurrection—by this one sacrifice Jesus Christ has perfected forever those whom he has sanctified'.[44] The one purpose of Christ's sacrifice was 'that all the elect, his members' would form with him 'the eternal holocaust which the divine fire of the Holy Spirit will consume without destroying on the altar of the Divine Word, in the temple of God, the bosom of the Father'.[45] In this one sacrifice that achieved the redemption and sanctification of human beings, 'what is greatest and most worthy' was Christ's 'entrance into heaven bearing his own *victim* [himself] for the perfection and consummation of our salvation'.[46]

In this vision of Christ's one sacrifice 'for us (*pro nobis*)', his priesthood is always connected with his being victim—from the first 'mystery' of the incarnation and right through the other 'mysteries' of his life, death, resurrection, and ascension into eternal glory: 'the sanctification of Jesus Christ as *victim* was accomplished

---

[43] Ibid 31 (part 1, ch. 2; hereafter 1/2).

[44] Ibid. 118–19 (1/11). Condren draws on the Old Testament to propose also a five-part scheme for a perfect sacrifice: 'to have a true idea of the Christian sacrifice, it is necessary to know that there were five conditions necessary to make a sacrifice of the law a perfect sacrifice, or five parts which composed it...The first is the sanctification or consecration of the victim; the second, the oblation of the victim; the third, the slaying or immolation; the fourth, the burning or consummation; the fifth, the communion': ibid. 67 (1/6).

[45] Ibid. 179 (2/8).   [46] Ibid. 119 (1/11).

in the incarnation, in which mystery the Saviour was sanctified and consecrated by God himself... What is peculiar to Jesus Christ is this: by the same mystery in which he was consecrated and sanctified to be the *victim* of God, he was also consecrated as Priest for eternity.' Condren adds at once that leitmotif of Hebrews: 'you are a priest forever according to the order of Melchizedek.'[47] Yet his emphasis is: 'you are a victim forever.' Christ is eternal victim and eternal priest, rather than first priest and then victim.

Hebrews, while it does not exclude the notion of Christ being eternal victim, developed, as we saw in Chapter 3, the theme of Christ exercising forever his priesthood as eternal intercessor. The imagery supplied by the Genesis story about Melchizedek and the verse about him in Psalm 110 convey no sense of Melchizedek as personally being a victim.

This vision of Christ as eternal Priest *and* eternal Victim, shared by Condren and other members of the French School, saw the various 'mysteries' of Christ (from his incarnation, through his life, ministry, and death, to his resurrection and ascension into glory) as finding their supreme expression in 'the risen Christ, eternal priest and eternal victim of his perfect sacrifice'. In the 'heavenly consummation of Christ's sacrifice', his 'state of priesthood' continues forever in heaven.[48] The language of 'eternal sacrificial victim' and 'Christ the Victim' transposes into a later idiom the vision of 'the Lamb who was slain' that dominates the heavenly imagery of the Book of Revelation (see Chapter 2 above).

'State' figured characteristically in the vocabulary of the members of the French School. By 'state' or 'states' they meant those permanent conditions and interior dispositions in the life of Jesus—for instance, his willingness to be sacrificed—that informed the exterior 'mysteries' or events/acts of Christ's whole story and gave them value and power. They understood the incarnation to constitute Christ not only in the 'state' of 'infinite adorer' or 'infinite servant' of the Father (see Bérulle above) but also in the 'state' of priesthood and victim-

---

[47] *The Eternal Sacrifice*, 81–2 (1/8); italics ours.
[48] E. A. Walsh, *The Priesthood in the Writings of the French School: Bérulle, De Condren, Olier* (Washington, DC: Catholic University of America Press, 1949), pp. xiv–xv.

hood. That 'state' began when the Word of God assumed the human condition and continues forever in his risen glory.[49]

In the French School's vision, Christ remains for ever at the right hand of his Father, as eternal priest, victim, and source of life for the mystical body of which he is the head. In heaven he enjoys the final and active glory of his priesthood. The rhetoric of 'forever priest' and 'forever victim' flowered with Olier.

But, before moving to Olier, let us add something about the link Condren identified between Christ's one sacrifice and the Eucharist. It is important to note that he insisted that there is only 'one and the same' oblation made by Christ; 'that oblation first made in the bosom of his most holy Mother at the moment of his incarnation' was 'repeated and manifested in the Temple [Luke 2: 41–51], perfected on the cross, continued in the Mass, and destined to exist eternally in heaven'. But there are differences in the external manifestation of this one oblation or internal disposition: 'in the incarnation it was hidden in the Blessed Virgin; in the Temple veiled under his childhood, on the cross under a murder; in the Mass it is clothed with signs, while in heaven it is without veil, without signs, in glory.'[50] Anything that is perceived externally—for instance, in the 'signs' of the Mass—makes efficacious sense only in the light of the internal disposition, which is the 'real' sacrifice. Not surprisingly, Condren cites Augustine and Aquinas in support of this position: 'If we would know sacrifice, we must believe that what we see is not sacrifice or the reality of the things contained in it, but that, as St Augustine says and St Thomas after him, visible sacrifice is only the sign and figure of the invisible [sacrifice].'[51]

As regards the Eucharist, Condren maintains that it 'applies' rather than 'repeats' the sacrifice of the cross. Following the Council of Trent, he speaks of 'the bloody sacrifice' being offered in another, 'unbloody manner': 'the Mass does not apply an effect of the sacrifice of the cross but the sacrifice itself.' Yet 'it is the same sacrifice as that of the cross, the same victim being therein offered. It would,

---

[49] On 'states' see Thompson, *Bérulle and the French School*, 37–8, 186.

[50] *The Eternal Sacrifice*, 120 (1/11).

[51] Ibid. 35 (1/2); he refers to Augustine, *The City of God*, 10. 5; and Aquinas, *STh*, 2a2ae. 81. 7 resp.; 3a. 22. 2 resp.

nevertheless, be incorrect to say that the sacrifice of the cross is repeated in the Mass.' Rather, 'the same [sacrifice] is offered in a different, unbloody manner, in order that we may participate and communicate in the bloody sacrifice'.[52]

For Condren, the Mass is 'the same sacrifice' as that of the cross because it 'contains' the cross and makes present Christ 'immolated on the cross'. On the altar at Mass Christ 'is offered' or 'offers himself' in 'memory' of his once being 'immolated on the cross'. Condren declares:

The sacrifice of the Mass is the same as that of the cross, inasmuch as the one contains the other. For it is Jesus Christ immolated on the cross who is present on the altar after the consecration, and is there offered as having been immolated [on the cross] for us. [On the altar] he has in the Mass the state of death, which the Jews inflicted upon him in his crucifixion, inasmuch as he there offers himself as [having been] once immolated on the cross. It is in memory and in virtue of that immolation that he is offered [on the altar] by the Church.

How does the Mass 'clothe in signs' Christ's offering himself on the altar 'as having been once immolated on the cross'? Like other Catholics (but not the Council of Trent), Condren sees the death of Christ 'represented' by the separate consecration of bread and wine: 'This state of immolation and death' is shown and represented [on the altar] by the mysterious separation of his body and blood under the different species of bread and wine, separately consecrated.'[53]

Jean-Jacques Olier

Deeply influenced by Vincent de Paul and Charles de Condren, Olier conducted missions in various parts of France. He then settled down to his main vocation, the training of priests through his foundation of the Society and seminary of Saint-Sulpice.[54]

---

[52] *The Eternal Sacrifice*, 114–15 (1/11).
[53] Ibid. 106–7 (1/10).
[54] See 'Olier, Jean-Jacques (1608–57)', *ODCC* 1189, and 'Saint-Sulpice, Society of', ibid. 1454.

For Olier, permanently offering sacrifice, and not merely making intercession, qualifies the heavenly life of Christ and its impact on the Church on earth: 'there is sacrifice in heaven, because heaven is most of all the place of perfect religion and of the highest worship that can be rendered to God. By right, sacrifice should be offered there, and offered unceasingly, because it is there that religion suffers no interruption.' Along with this 'deduction' from the principle that heaven is 'the place of perfect religion' and 'the highest worship' offered to God, Olier associates Christ's eternal offering of sacrifice with a central theme of Hebrews: 'Our Lord, having been made priest for all eternity according to the order of Melchizedek was constituted by God, his Father, *to offer him sacrifice forever.* Thus it is that our Lord is the priest of his holy sacrifice, in which he offers himself and his Church as a holocaust to God in the odour of sweetness. He himself is the priest and victim.'[55] In short, the glorified Christ remains a perpetual sacrifice and an eternal victim.

Like Bérulle and Condren, Olier understood the self-offering of Christ to have begun with the incarnation, an offering secretly made in the womb of the Virgin and publicly made at the presentation in the Temple (Luke 2: 22–38): 'On coming into the world, Our Lord in the womb of the Blessed Virgin at once offered himself as victim to God his Father, as on an altar, to be one day immolated and consumed to the glory of his divine majesty.' Olier added that, since this initial offering was 'secret and unknown' to human beings, and since 'the Son of God had come to make it public', he went 'into the Temple a short while after his birth' and presented 'himself publicly to God the Father by the hands of his mother and St Joseph. It was at this time that he gave external expression to the religion that he had poured secretly into both these acts, in order to form an august sacrifice, one worthy of such adorable majesty.'[56]

For good measure, Olier adds that, at the very moment of his conception and 'coming into the world' on 'the holy day of the incarnation', Christ not only dedicated himself to the Father but

---

[55] *L'Esprit des cérémonies de la messe: explication des cérémonies de la grand' messe de paroisse selon l'usage romain* (Perpignon: Forum Diffusion, 2004), preface; trans. Walsh, *The Priesthood*, 21.

[56] Ibid. 6/2; trans. Walsh, *The Priesthood*, 49–50.

also offered 'with himself all the faithful' to be God's 'living victims'. They were to 'suffer one day death' in Christ's 'spirit of sacrifice, so as to enter afterwards into heaven' with Christ 'as consummated victims'. Thus, in the womb of Mary, the incarnate Son also 'vowed', 'consecrated', and 'willed to sacrifice' with himself 'all his members'. He intended 'that one day he would consummate them together, and make of them *one victim* for the eternal glory of God in heaven'.[57] Over the centuries other Christians have endorsed a hope for a heavenly union with Christ. Thus, Julian of Norwich declared in chapter 51 of her *Showings*: 'Jesus is in all who will be saved, and all who will be saved are in Jesus.'[58] The third Eucharistic Prayer hints at the same hope in the prayer that 'we, who are nourished by his body and blood, may be filled with the Holy Spirit, and become one body, one spirit in Christ'. But neither Julian nor this Eucharistic Prayer expressed the desire in terms of becoming one, eternal victim with Christ.

Olier, however, could express his vision of Christ's intention more broadly and understand it to include adoration and praise and not merely victimhood. The final design of Christ was, he stated, 'to make of all human beings but one adorer, to make of all their voices but one voice of praise, and to make of all their hearts but one victim in himself, who is the universal and unique adorer of God, his Father'.[59]

Through the unfolding mysteries of his story, Christ manifested exteriorly his permanent, unchanging self-oblation. A sacrificial disposition characterized every stage of his life, leaving a supreme example for ordained priests and all the baptized to follow. The will to be offered was the internal sacrifice, revealed publicly in the external sacrifice. The interior disposition to adore, sacrifice, and return to the Father, disclosed from the incarnation to Christ's permanent existence in heaven as priest and victim, shaped the core of the spiritual message of Olier and the French School in general. That message recalls Augustine's view of the reality of sacrifice (see Chapter 5 above) and the Reformers' call for an interior

[57] *L'Esprit des cérémonies*, 2/2 and 6/2; trans. Walsh, *The Priesthood*, 90.
[58] *Showings*, trans. E. College and J. Walsh (New York: Paulist Press, 1978), 276.
[59] *L'Esprit des cérémonies*, 8/3; trans. Walsh, *The Priesthood*, 92.

spirituality that left no room for external cultic activity that lacked heart.

With a harsh judgement on 'the Jews', Olier contrasted mere external sacrifices with internal, self-immolation: 'Jesus was not satisfied with empty show and a false, hypocritical religion like that of the Jews, who, only because they had to, offered external and useless things. For they failed to immolate themselves in reality, a thing which the very nature of the victim demanded, for it was but a figure of an internal immolation.' Olier looked back to the story of Cain as a classic example of empty sacrifice that lacked a self-offering: 'He offered only fruits and inanimate creatures, without offering himself... in the sacrifice due to God, the one who offered the sacrifice should have been the principal victim.'[60]

Olier expounded his view of sacrifice for all Christians. The call to share through self-sacrificing holiness in the priesthood of Christ extended to every one of his baptized followers. 'All Christians', Olier wrote, 'are priests in faith and in the hidden life of the Spirit. They are all priests in Jesus Christ. They are called to live in a spirit of sacrifice because the Spirit of Christ dwells in all the faithful in order to exercise his priesthood and spread his sacrifice.'[61]

Olier described the life of all Christians in terms of self-sacrifice, the cross, and proclaiming the word—a language that Luther could also have used (see Chapter 7 above): 'like a sacrificial victim of Christ, the community sees the cross as the best altar on which it strives every day to present its sacrifice, either by fighting valiantly for Christ against the world, the flesh, and the devil, or by proclaiming Christ himself at every moment in word and example.'[62] As regards the clergy and those preparing for the ordained priesthood, Olier likewise treated sacrifice as an all-encompassing commitment and not merely a liturgical function. Ministerial priests should be more than cultic performers. Christ himself exercised his own priesthood in a perpetual sacrifice. Even if the notion of the unborn Christ

---

[60] Ibid. 7/5; trans. Walsh, *The Priesthood*, 41.

[61] J.-J. Olier, ed. F. Amiot, *Catéchisme chrétien pour la vie intérieure et Journée chrétienne* (Paris: Le Rameau, 1954), 193.

[62] J.-J. Olier, *To Live for God in Christ Jesus: An Anthology of the Writings of Jean-Jacques Olier*, ed. M. Dupuy, trans. L. B. Terrien (Paris: Compagnie de Saint Sulpice, 1995), 126.

consciously sacrificing himself in his mother's womb and presenting himself publicly in the Temple when only a few weeks old—quite apart from theological issues over his human consciousness—seems odd to contemporary sensibility, an insight remains: a true, internal sacrificial impulse was present right through his life and in all his activities. In his baroque way, Olier developed the theme of the Letter to the Hebrews: 'When Christ came into the world, he said: "See, God, I come to do your will"' (Heb. 10: 5, 7).

As much as, or even more than, Hebrews, Olier valued the consummation of Christ's sacrifice brought by his ascension into heaven, 'the place of perfect religion' and 'the highest worship that can be offered to God' (see above). As priest *and* victim, Christ returned to God and remains forever in communion with him. On 'the day of the ascension' the Father 'received his Son into his bosom and consumed him in himself, a thing he had already begun to do on the day of the resurrection'.[63] 'These mysteries which began at one time', Olier added,

continue always. They are the mysteries of eternity, and are therefore permanent and always the same. The Father is always consuming the Son in himself, as he did on the day of the resurrection, even though he does not continue to raise him from the flesh, for he is no longer in the flesh. He continues to receive his Son into his bosom, and to bear him within himself, even though he does not lift him from the earth as he did on the day of the ascension.[64]

Once again this baroque exuberance goes beyond the sober imagery of Hebrews about Christ 'sitting at the right hand of God' (Heb. 1: 3; 10: 12). Where Hebrews pictures Christ as forever making intercession for human beings (Heb. 7: 25), Olier (and Condren) portray the risen Christ as the Victim forever being consumed in sacrifice.

Like Calvin, Olier cherished the mystery of the ascension, even representing it as the day on which Christ was proclaimed priest forever: 'on the day of his ascension' the 'character (*qualité*) of priest was conferred upon him with splendour, because his Father made

---

[63] With his language of being 'consumed', Olier thinks of the Old Testament priests allowing fire to consume completely the victims they had immolated and so make the sacrifice perfect.

[64] *L'Esprit des cérémonies*, 8/2; trans. Walsh, *The Priesthood*, 55.

him sit at his right hand' and 'declared to him with a solemn oath that he was priest for all eternity'.[65] Having 'merited' the Holy Spirit and been 'proclaimed the sovereign priest of the Church', Christ 'received the power of distributing his gifts' and began to make use of that power by giving the Spirit.[66] Thus Olier brought together the themes of the glorious Christ as high priest and giver of the Holy Spirit.

The image of Christ as victim being eternally 'consumed' led Olier to set the bar very high in what he expected from ordained priests. Christ was entirely 'consumed in God and made holy with God's own holiness, in order to be worthy to enter into him and to dwell as his [God's] perpetual victim in his bosom, as in a temple'. The 'state and disposition of the priest' is or should be just that: 'the state of Jesus Christ risen.' God 'calls all priests to this state, and desires to consume them all interiorly. He desires to separate their hearts from all the inclinations of the flesh, in order to make them live uniquely in Jesus Christ, his Son, risen for his glory.'[67]

His vision of the Father 'receiving' the Son through the mysteries of the resurrection and ascension meant that Olier, like Hebrews, never wavered in acknowledging Christ's humanity to be at the heart of his priesthood. The mysteries of his resurrection and ascension involved Christ being gloriously transformed in his humanity, so that he could be forever 'received' into 'the bosom' of the Father and exercise his eternal role as priest and victim. That transformation made possible what Hebrews pictured as the passage 'through the veil' (see Heb. 10: 20) into the heavenly sanctuary.

But a significant difference remains. Hebrews uses *active* terms in portraying Christ's movement to God: he 'has passed through the heavens' (Heb. 4: 14), he 'has entered the inner shrine' (Heb. 6: 20; see 9: 12), and so he 'opened for us' a 'new and living way' to God (Heb. 10: 20). Olier uses language of Christ being 'raised', 'lifted', 'received', and 'consumed' (see above). This *passive* terminology can picture the resurrection as a sign that God is 'satisfied' (appeased?),

[65] J.-J. Olier, ed. L. Tronson, *Traité des saints ordres* (Paris: La Colombe, 1953), 232 (3/5).
[66] *L'Esprit des cérémonies*, 7/3; trans. Walsh, *The Priesthood*, 20–1.
[67] Ibid. 1/2; trans. Walsh, *The Priesthood*, 96–7.

has 'accepted' the sacrifice of his Son, and wants to witness that he is now 'reconciled' with his Son by 'giving him' again life and 'embracing' him. 'Without the resurrection', Olier states, 'we have no sign of [God's] reconciliation [with his Son], we have no testimony that God has accepted the sacrifice of his Son . . . The fact that his only Son has risen declares that the Father is satisfied, and that he has given the true testimony of his reconciliation by giving him his own life, and by embracing him in his bosom.'[68] Such language seems to turn the Son into a passive protagonist and approach the picture Luther drew of the climax of redemption (see Chapter 7 above). It is a language that does not easily fit the witness of Hebrews (see what we recalled from Hebrews in Chapters 3 and 7 above).

Appealing to the demands of 'perfect religion', Olier speaks of Christ as 'destroying' himself and even 'utterly annihilating' himself, and then 'returning' to the Father and being 'reunited' with him. This way of putting things may have 'the merit' of presenting Christ in a more active light, but it also seems to imply that Christ's death was an act of suicide—something that Hebrews does not say (see Chapter 4 above). In Olier's words, 'the religion of Jesus Christ was a perfect religion, because he annihilated himself utterly in his Father, and in this way returned to God completely, as religion demands. In order to have a perfect sacrifice, the victim must return to God. It is not enough for the creature to be separated from itself; it must be reunited with its proper origin.' Having said that, Olier goes back at once to language that again suggests a passive role for Christ in redemption: 'God is not all fully satisfied or content, nor are his requirements for religion entirely accomplished until he has taken his creature back into himself, and made it return to his bosom, so that it can take up again the place from which it went forth.'[69]

Olier also differed from, or rather went beyond, Hebrews by writing of 'these mysteries of eternity' as being mirrored and symbolized in the celebration of the Eucharist. He took the elevation of the consecrated elements to be a sign of Christ completing his sacrifice in the ascension:

---

[68] *L'Esprit des cérémonies*, 7/5; trans.Walsh, *The Priesthood*, 68.
[69] *Traité des saints ordres*, 232–3 (3/5).

The elevation of the body and blood of Our Lord . . . indicates a completion of sacrifice. For of old when the victim was lifted up to heaven in the flame, it was the sign of a more fundamental reality: namely, that the victim was returning to heaven from whence it came, to enter in and to be again united with its divine principle. In the ancient sacrifices this was a figure of the most holy ascension.[70]

This approach carried consequences in the way Olier presented the offering of the sacrifice. He recognized a tight link between (1) the priest who on earth offers the sacrifice in union with Christ and (2) Christ who in heaven offers the sacrifice of himself and of all the saints already in glory. Olier wrote: 'As he offers the sacrifice, the priest . . . offers it in unity with the power and spirit of Jesus Christ, who is the same in this sacrifice [on earth] as in heaven where he offers the sacrifice of himself and of all the saints with him.' This account of the sacrificial offering in the Eucharist made the ordained priest a figure who moves between earth and heaven: 'the priest is lifted in spirit into heaven, where Jesus Christ is offering himself, and at the same time [the priest] remains on earth making there the same sacrifice he [Christ] makes in heaven.' In heaven Christ also offers all the saints to the Father, while the priest on earth, inasmuch as he is 'in' Christ, also joins in offering the saints: 'Jesus Christ is in all the saints whom he offers to God, his Father, and the priest on earth is also in Jesus Christ, with whom he offers all the saints in glory.'[71] One might see Olier's way of linking the permanent sacrifice in heaven with the Eucharistic sacrifice on earth as a gloss on the Lord's Prayer that is directed to Christ himself: 'Thy sacrifice be continued on earth as it is in heaven.'

Olier proposed a rich account of what is involved for the Church in the sacrifice of the Mass: it expresses 'the purpose of the Church and of its duties towards God. All that is due to the glory of God from the beginning of the world to the end is comprised in this sacrifice.' Olier's sense of Christ's presence at the Eucharist included, but moved beyond, his presence in the consecrated elements:

---

[70] *L'Esprit des cérémonies*, 7/2; trans. Walsh, *The Priesthood*, 63.
[71] Ibid., preface; trans. Walsh, *The Priesthood*, 85–6.

'Jesus Christ, already offered to God, is *present* there [at the Mass] in all his members and in his entire mystery. This complete mystery is the *whole Christ*, . . . Jesus Christ with all the faithful, with this great body so widespread and so multiplied, one Jesus, dwelling in his members.'[72]

This language both recalls Augustine and anticipates teaching from the Second Vatican Council. In Chapter 5 we summarized what Augustine said about 'the whole Christ (*totus Christus*)', both Head and Body, and the priestly, sacrificial functions that Christ performed and performs as Head of the Body that is the Church. In its constitution on the sacred liturgy, Vatican II understood 'every liturgical celebration' to be 'an action of Christ the Priest and of his Body, which is the Church' (*Sacrosanctum Concilium*, 7). As regards the presence of Christ in the Eucharist, Vatican II enumerated four modes of that presence: (1) 'in the person of his minister'; (2) 'in the Eucharistic species'; (3) 'in his word since it is he himself who speaks when the holy scriptures are read'; and (4) in the assembled faithful praying and singing together (ibid.).

Before leaving Olier, we need to recall a question raised by *The Treatise on Holy Orders*, published in 1676, nineteen years after his death, and prepared by the third Sulpician superior-general, Louis Tronson. The book purported to be 'according to the writings and the spirit of Jean-Jacques Olier' (subtitle), but it seems to have been shaped, at least in part, by Tronson's stress on a clerical, cultic, and rule-oriented understanding of priesthood, shaped by a negative, world-denying, almost Jansenistic spirituality. The book left behind somewhat Olier's pastoral, mystical, and voluntary vision. Where Olier recognized that all the baptized are called in Christ to a life of self-sacrificing holiness, Tronson saw priestly holiness within a special cultic framework and omitted any reference to the priesthood of all the faithful. In his vision, clerical holiness differed essentially from the holiness of ordinary Christians. Even if Tronson reworked the teaching of Olier, the *Treatise* 'did help to centre in many ways the theology of priest [priesthood?] on Jesus Christ himself. The sacrament of order was, to some degree at least, seen as the very sacrament

---

[72] *L'Esprit des cérémonies*, 9/1; trans. Walsh, *The Priesthood*, 103.

of the ministry of Jesus.'[73] In the light of problems raised by the reworking of the *Treatise*, we have cited it sparingly and with caution.

St John Eudes

Originally an Oratorian, Eudes withdrew to found the Congregation of Jesus and Mary, an institute of priests consecrated to 'the hearts of Jesus and Mary' and dedicated to running seminaries.[74] In the light of criticisms made by the Reformers, it is notable that for Eudes (as for Olier and other members of the French School) one of the principal functions of priesthood was preaching the Word of God. He pointed out that Jesus, the model for priests, spent his public life in preaching and after his resurrection gave his apostles the mission to announce the good news to the whole world. Through preaching, priests show themselves to be 'the veritable mouthpieces of the Eternal Father, the ambassadors of the Son of God'.[75]

Those selected by Jesus, the supreme High Priest, form his associates in the one-and-only priesthood, centred on the one Priest, Jesus himself. They are to be not only 'prophets of his holy teaching' but also 'kings of his empire'. Eudes saw ministerial priests as 'living images' of 'the Sovereign Priest, Jesus Christ', being 'clothed with the very priesthood conferred on him by his eternal Father, and one with him as all members are one with their Head'.[76] Like Calvin and others, Eudes linked closely the functions of king and priest. He told the clergy: 'You are clothed and adorned with a kingly priesthood. You are priests and kings, as Jesus Christ himself is the Supreme Priest and King.'[77] He added: 'your royalty is not temporal but eternal, a participation in the royalty of Jesus Christ.'[78]

---

[73] K. B. Osborne, *Priesthood: A History of the Ordained Ministry in the Roman Catholic Church* (Mahwah, NJ: Paulist Press, 1989), 288. On the reworking of the *Treatise* by Tronson, see Thompson, *Bérulle and the French School*, 60–1.

[74] See 'Eudes, St John (1601–80)', *ODCC* 574–5.

[75] J. Eudes, *The Priest: His Dignity and Obligations*, trans. W. L. Murphy (New York: Kenedy, 1947), 74.

[76] Ibid., p. xxv.

[77] Ibid. 2.

[78] Ibid. 3.

Eudes used such language to remind clergy that their kingly dignity did not mean earthly power but rather a potential for servant leadership with imperishable, heavenly results. He wanted their interior dispositions to be such that their priesthood shone through everything—not only through their celebrating the sacrifice of the Mass at the altar and preaching the Word of God from the pulpit, but also through all that they said and did: 'Let the world see in your actions, your walk, your person, your gestures, your attire, your daily habits, the reflection of your interior life, which will prove beyond doubt that you are a priest, not only at the altar and in the pulpit, but [also] in every place and in everything you do, think, and say.'[79]

Like Thomas Aquinas, Eudes composed a Mass (with an accompanying office), but his was a Mass dedicated to 'the Priesthood of Jesus Christ'. Adopted by the priests of Saint-Sulpice around 1660, by the Benedictines of the Blessed Sacrament, and by several dioceses (including Rouen), the Mass continued to be celebrated until the middle of the nineteenth century, when it fell into disuse at a time when the full and uniform usage of the Roman Liturgy was accepted. The fine sequence of twenty-five strophes shows where the emphasis lies. The priesthood of Christ appears when he is called 'Founder of priests (*sacerdotum fundator*)' and 'High Priest (*Sacerdos maximus*)'. But the concern of Eudes is with the holiness and dignity of ministerial priests, called 'envoys of the Divinity (*legati Numinis*)', 'brothers of the kind Virgin (*fratres almae Virginis*)', and 'fathers of the faithful (*patres fidelium*)'. The sequence contains no reference, or no clear reference, to the celebration of the Eucharist, while stressing the preaching and teaching role of priests, who, as 'teachers of the nations (*doctores gentium*)' and 'trumpets of the High Prince (*Summi tubae Principis*)', 'should herald Christ Jesus (*Christum Jesum praedicent*)'.[80]

Along with the Mass written by Eudes, we should recall several litanies of Christ as Priest and Victim composed in France during the seventeenth and eighteenth centuries.[81] During his pontificate

---

[79] *The Priest*, 83.

[80] 'The Mass of the Feast of the Priesthood of Jesus Christ' is reproduced in ibid. 272–9.

[81] J. Evenon, 'Les Litanies du Christ prêtre et victime', *Ephemerides Liturgicae*, 119 (2005), 25–51.

(1978–2005) John Paul II was to quote from these litanies. A book he published on the occasion of the fiftieth anniversary of his own priestly ordination included as an appendix (in Latin with an English translation) a 'Litany of Our Lord Jesus Christ Priest and Victim', with its sixty-three petitions drawn almost entirely from the Letter to the Hebrews.[82]

CONCLUSIONS

This chapter has brought together the teaching of the Council of Trent (sixteenth century) and works of three leading representatives of the French School (seventeenth century) on Christ's priesthood and human participation in that priesthood. As we saw, Trent promulgated four documents that concerned priesthood but explicitly mentioned the priesthood of Christ only in the decree 'on the Most Holy Sacrifice of the Mass'. Bérulle, Condren, Olier, and other key figures in the French School dedicated themselves in word and deed to the reform of the clergy. In doing so, they had much to say about the high priesthood of Christ, which was, for instance, the central theme of an entire, posthumously published book by Condren. The French School left what is arguably the most sustained amount of reflection on Christ, priest and victim, in the history of Christianity—admittedly, largely as pastoral and spiritual exhortations rather than as essays in systematic theology.

The Reformers—and, in particular, Luther (as we saw in the last chapter)—longed for the spiritual transformation of the clergy. The Oratorians (Bérulle and Condren), the Sulpicians (founded by Olier), the Vincentians (Vincent de Paul), and other religious institutes animated just such a transformation. After the death of Bérulle, leadership in seminary training passed to Olier. These eminent members of the French School, as we showed above, also emphasized the preaching and teaching role of the clergy, the ministry of the Word which Luther stressed and which had formed an essential part

---

[82] John Paul II, *Gift* and *Mystery* (New York: Doubleday, 1997).

of the priesthood exercised by Jesus himself.[83] The French School (see Olier above) likewise respected the common priesthood of all the faithful, a New Testament theme strongly defended by Luther and other Reformers.

Bérulle, Condren, Olier, and other members of the French School showed a keen sense of the self-sacrificing nature of Christ's priesthood, which made him victim as well as priest—a self-sacrificing dedication to be followed by those who share in his priesthood. 'Priests and pastors', Olier declared, 'should have a very high degree of patience because, in Christ Jesus and with Christ Jesus, they are both priests and victims for the sins of the world. Jesus Christ wished to be the victim of his sacrifice. He became the host-victim for all people.' From this Olier drew the conclusion:

Since priests are like sacraments and representations of him who lives in them to continue his priesthood and whom he clothes with his external conduct and his interior dispositions, ... he wishes furthermore they be interiorly rooted in the spirit and dispositions of a host-victim in order to suffer, endure, do penance, in short, to immolate themselves for the glory of God and the salvation of the people.[84]

We return to the theme of priesthood and suffering in subsequent chapters.

The Council of Trent had legislated for the founding of seminaries as vital for an adequate preparation of the clergy and their spiritual renewal. Apropos of the priestly ministry of the Word, Trent offered very little teaching. The cultic function of priests as celebrants of the Eucharist and as ministers of absolution in the sacrament of penance remained paramount concerns for the Council. It never set itself to produce a comprehensive vision of Christ's priesthood and his followers' participation in it. This meant also that it had almost nothing to say about the priesthood of all the baptized.

---

[83] The Letter to the Hebrews is the key New Testament text on Christ's priesthood. But, since it does not address the public ministry of Jesus, it leaves out of consideration the priestly function of that ministry.

[84] J.-J. Olier, ed. F. Amiot, *Introduction à la vie et aux vertus chrétiennes* and *Pietas Seminarii* (Paris: Le Rameau, 1954), 9/2; trans. Thompson, *Bérulle and the French School*, 246.

In the sixteenth century, and especially in the aftermath of the Council, seminaries were set up (e.g. in Rome, Milan, Douai, and Valladolid), but in France that took time. One had to wait for Bérulle and others in the early seventeenth century to initiate the proper training of the French clergy (also as ministers of the Word), as well as for some recognition of the common priesthood of all the faithful. Sulpician and Vincentian seminaries then spread beyond France to other European countries (including Poland), North America, Africa, and elsewhere. The French School—in particular, through Olier and the Sulpicians—had a long-lasting impact on the preparation of ministerial priests in the Catholic Church. Over half of the bishops who attended the Second Vatican Council (1962–5) had received Sulpician or Sulpician-inspired training.

9

Newman and Others on Christ's Priesthood

After gathering a rich harvest from the French School, we scouted around more widely in the seventeenth and eighteenth centuries for further insights into the priesthood of Christ. But any results we drew from the work of official teachers, theologians, spiritual writers, poets, composers, and other Christians proved increasingly thin.

George Herbert (1593–1633), for instance, wrote about Christ as King and filled poems with images taken from the cross and death of Christ, but offered very little about Christ as Priest. In 'The Church Militant' he did write of 'Christ's three offices' as Priest, Prophet, and King, but only briefly and to grieve over these offices being perverted by sin (ll. 171–4, 177–80, 187–8). In his hymn, 'The Name of Jesus', John Newton (1725–1807)—best known for writing 'Amazing Grace'—included one verse that uses titles of Christ to open up prayer:

> Jesus! My Shepherd, Husband, Friend,
> My Prophet, Priest, and King;
> My Lord, my Life, my Way, my End,
> Accept the praise I bring.

The repeated 'my', especially through the fourth line, gives the verse a powerfully personal sense. Newton names Jesus as 'Priest', yet does not pause to reflect on what 'my Priest' might mean as one of the three elements within Christ's threefold office. The same is true for the hymn composed by Bishop Christopher Wordsworth (1807–85), 'Songs of thankfulness and praise': 'at Jordan's stream' Christ was made 'manifest' as 'prophet, priest and king supreme'. The threefold office is recalled but not developed.

The wealth of reflection from the French School encouraged us to probe the history of spirituality elsewhere. The two volumes of Bishop Gordon Mursell's *English Spirituality*[1] looked like a good place to start. While the themes of the cross and the Eucharist appeared here and there, the author had nothing to report on Christ's priesthood from any spiritual writers in England down the centuries, right to the end to the second millennium. Three bishops collaborated in producing *Love's Redeeming Work*. This long reader in Anglican spirituality provided much that was a gripping read, and yet only a little for the theme of our study.[2] Whatever the reasons, the priesthood of Christ has remained presupposed or even widely overlooked in the history of Christian reflection and writing, whether spiritual, poetic, pastoral, or theological.

Here John Henry Newman (1801–90) proves a refreshing exception. What he said and wrote about the priesthood of Christ and, in particular, his triple office as priest, prophet, and king helped prepare the way for later theology and official teaching on the triple office. Hence we open this chapter with Newman's seminal work before moving to several theologians of the twentieth century, the teaching of the Second Vatican Council (1962–5), and beyond. The triple office, expounded by Calvin and endorsed by Newman, flowered in what Vatican II taught about the priesthood of all the baptized and the ministerial priesthood.

In that unfolding story other factors played their role: for instance, a variety of contributions to a Christ-centred focus in theology (e.g. from Karl Barth, especially the later Barth) and biblical studies; developments in liturgical theory and practice, which (for Roman Catholics) were expressed and nourished by such magisterial milestones as the 1947 encyclical of Pope Pius XII, *Mediator Dei*, and Vatican II's 1963 constitution on the sacred liturgy, *Sacrosanctum Concilium*; the thought of Yves Congar (1904–93) on the baptized Christians' participation in Christ's office of priest, prophet, and

---

[1] London: SPCK, 2001.
[2] G. Rowell, K. Stevenson, and R. Williams (eds.), *Love's Redeeming Work: The Anglican Quest for Holiness* (Oxford: Oxford University Press, 2001); Christ's priesthood appears in a few passages, taken from Bishop Jeremy Taylor, Bishop Samuel Seabury, and some others.

king; and ecumenical developments, in particular those that came
through the work of the Faith and Order Commission, which first
met in 1927 and which published various valuable texts, including
the 1982 document *Baptism, Eucharist and Ministry* that we discussed in the Preface.

JOHN HENRY NEWMAN

What did Newman propose about the priesthood of Christ, either by
itself or in the triple office of priest, prophet, and king, and about
participation in that priesthood through baptism and ordination?[3]
His fullest treatment of the triple office came in the preface to the *Via
Media*, a two-volume collection that Newman gathered from what he
had written as an Anglican in 1833–45 and that he published as a
Roman Catholic in 1877, in the aftermath of the First Vatican
Council (1869–70). The first volume of *Via Media* was a third edition
of his *Lectures on the Prophetical Office of the Church* (first published
in 1837); the second volume consisted of various tracts and letters.
The preface that Newman wrote to the *Via Media* was 'his last great
contribution towards a theology of the Church',[4] and spelled out his
mature application to the Church of the office of priest, prophet, and
king. Let us recall first of all what Newman had already left behind on
that subject in many sermons and tracts. One might add the three
famous words that open his poem 'Lead, kindly light'; some find in
them an unconscious correspondence to the kingly, priestly, and
prophetic office, respectively.

---

[3] For Newman's life and work, see I. Ker, *John Henry Newman: A Biography*
(Oxford: Oxford University Press, paperback edn. 1990); and S. Gilley, *Newman
and His Age* (London: Darton, Longman & Todd, 1990). For Newman on the triple
office of Christ, see S. D. Otellini, 'The Threefold Office of Bishop', ch. 3 of his
Newman on the Episcopacy (Rome: Gregorian University, 1986), and M. T. Yakaitis,
The Office of Priest, Prophet, and King in the Thought of John Henry Newman (Rome:
Gregorian University, 1990).
[4] Ker, *John Henry Newman*, 701; see ibid. 139–44, 701–7.

Newman's Earlier Use of the Triple Office

The progress of Newman's own thought in the area of Christ's triple office offers a kind of personal microcosm of the kind of process he detected in the Church at large and wrote about, above all, in *Essay on the Development of Christian Doctrine* (1845). The process of personal maturation ran for over fifty years. We detect it beginning in a sermon preached on 31 October 1824 at St Clement's Church, Oxford, soon after being ordained, when he referred briefly to the triple office of Christ: 'He is our Prophet, Priest, and King unto those who believe.'[5]

But at this stage in his theological development Newman focused more on the kingly office of Christ (and his kingdom) than on his prophetic and priestly office. We find him preaching a sermon (no. 160) on 4 April 1827 entitled 'On the Mediatorial Kingdom of Christ'. He began as follows: 'It is my intention this morning to enter somewhat at length into a consideration of the nature of that kingdom which Christ received from his Father on his resurrection: his Mediatorial Kingdom.' Reflecting on this sermon and responses it provoked, Newman added, with reference to the triple office, a note to his text: 'The chief parts of Christ's office as Mediator between God and man' are 'usually treated by divines under three heads.'[6]

In another sermon (no. 175), preached at St Mary the Virgin, Oxford, on 7 September 1828, Newman risked departing from the Creed ('his kingdom will have no end') and the eternal nature of Christ's priesthood (the Letter to the Hebrews and subsequent tradition) by remarking: 'It is plainly evident that the Mediatorial Kingdom of Christ is not eternal—it had a beginning, it will have an end—but for a time. It was established for a particular purpose, a recovery of a sinful race.'[7] We can agree that the end of human history

---

[5] 'We Preach Christ Crucified', Sermon 29, unpublished MS at Birmingham Oratory (hereafter Oratory), B.3.iv.a, 20; quoted Yakaitis, *Office*, 12.

[6] Unpublished MS at Oratory, A.8.1; quoted by Yakaitis, *Office*, 17. As Yakaitis points out (ibid. 19), Newman drew here on Bishop Joseph Butler, *The Analogy of Religion Natural and Revealed* (1736; London: J. M. Dent, 1906), 174.

[7] Unpublished MS at Oratory, B.3.iv.a. ('The Mediator'), Sermon 175, 19; quoted by Yakaitis, *Office*, 21.

will bring a closure to the 'recovery of a sinful race'. Since there will be no more sinners to be recovered, this purpose will cease in practice and cannot be eternal. Nevertheless, in his glorified humanity the risen Christ remains the One through whom human beings will enjoy divine life forever. As Karl Rahner puts it, 'the Word—by the fact that he is man and insofar as he is this—is the necessary and permanent *mediator* of all salvation, not merely at some time in the past but now and for all eternity.'[8] In that sense the risen Christ will remain the High Priest forever, 'according to the order of Melchizedek' (Hebrews) or immortal priest and victim (Condren and Olier). Yet, by distinguishing 'God's universal kingdom' (and, presumably, eternal kingdom) from Christ's 'mediatorial kingdom' or role in human history as the Mediator who rescues and redeems sinners, Newman might justify his affirmation that Christ's 'mediatorial kingdom' will have an end.

When using the language of 'mediation', Newman accepted that innumerable biblical and later figures could be called 'mediators' between God and human beings; they differ from Christ because they convey 'to us' but do not gain 'for us' the 'favour of God'. In a sermon preached at St Mary the Virgin on 12 October 1828, he said about Christ:

His mediation differs from that of all other mediators whether in the systems of grace or providence. Moses and the prophets, the Jewish and Christian Churches, our parents, friends, and superiors, mediators as they are in one sense between God and men, do not convey to us spiritual blessings. But the One, Supreme, Accepted Mediator, our Saviour Christ, not only conveys to us the favour of God but [also] has gained it for us.[9]

In another sermon preached at St Mary the Virgin, on 16 September 1828, Newman was clear that Christ 'owed' his triple (mediatorial) office of priest, prophet, and king to the incarnation, through

---

[8] K. Rahner, 'The Eternal Significance of the Humanity of Jesus for Our Relationship with God', *Theological Investigations*, iii (London: Darton, Longman & Todd, 1967), 35–46, at 45; italics ours. See G. O'Collins, *Incarnation* (London: Continuum, 2002), 40–1.

[9] 'On the Atonement (considered generally)' (Sermon 178), unpublished MS at Oratory, B.3.iv.a., 1; quoted Yakaitis, *Office*, 27; corrected.

which he 'was made man for us sinners'. The incarnation meant that
'offices and acts are attributed to him, which are not attributed to the
Father'.[10] Here Newman joined a long tradition (going back through
Calvin and Chrysostom to Hebrews) that recognized that it was the
humanity Christ assumed which made it possible for him to exercise
his priesthood.

Preaching on Christian ministry moved Newman to express himself on Christ's priesthood and the ordained ministers who become
'partakers' in this 'high office'.[11] Three years later, in a sermon
preached on 14 December 1834, Newman described ministers of
the gospel as Christ's 'substitutes', and looked back to the original
apostles: 'he [Christ] expressly made them his substitutes to the
world at large.' Through 'standing in Christ's place', they were 'exalted by an office far above any divine messengers before them'. The
'sacred treasures committed to their custody' were 'those peculiar
spiritual blessings which flow from Christ as a Saviour, as a Prophet,
Priest, and King'. He remains 'the sole Source of spiritual blessing
to our guilty race'; his apostles and subsequent ministers are his
'substitutes', but have only an 'instrumental and representative'
function.[12]

Newman was not indifferent to the fact that people at large 'believe
only so far as they can see and understand'. They 'are witnesses of
the process and effects of instructing and ruling' (the exercise of
the prophetic and kingly office), but not of 'what may be called the
ministry of reconciliation' (the exercise of the priestly office). Hence
they find it easier to 'accept Christ's ministers as representatives of his
prophetic and regal authority' than to accept them as representatives
'of his priestly authority'. Calling the triple office imparted to the
ministers of the gospel three 'portions' of Christ's own 'anointing',

[10] 'On the Christian Scheme of Mediation as Connected with Natural and Jewish
Systems' (Sermon 176); unpublished MS at Oratory, B.3.iv.a. ('The Mediator');
quoted Yakaitis, *Office*, 24.
[11] 'On the Ministerial Order as an Existing Divine Institution' (Sermon 323),
preached at Christ Church Cathedral, 18 Dec. 1831, at the ordination of Thomas
Mozley (a former pupil, whose brother married one of Newman's sisters), unpublished MS at Oratory B.3.iv.a. ('The Mediator'); quoted Yakaitis, *Office*, 36.
[12] 'The Christian Ministry', Sermon 25 in *Parochial and Plain Sermons*, ii (London:
Rivingtons, 1884), 300–19, at 301–4.

Newman acknowledged that his fellow Anglicans could readily accommodate a ministry that inherited 'two portions' of Christ's anointing (the prophetic and kingly 'portions'). It was 'the third' or priestly 'portion' that created difficulties. Hence Newman concentrated on the question of 'possessing the third: not, however, with a view to proving it, but rather of removing such antecedent difficulties as are likely to prejudice the mind against it'.[13]

Newman proceeded to list six points in describing the priestly office of ministers in the Church. (1) As founders of Christ's Church, the apostles had a unique commission that ended with them. Nevertheless, (2) the 'gifts' of Christ continued for subsequent ministers, since he had promised his presence. (3) The priesthood of Christ continues today through the working of the Holy Spirit. That priesthood is (4) sacramental, (5) Eucharistic, and (6) intercessory.[14]

In an 1834 sermon on 'The Indwelling Spirit' and subtitled 'For the Feast of Pentecost', Newman reflected on the reception and working of the Holy Spirit, the means by which the offices of baptismal and ministerial priesthood are imparted and continue—a theme reiterated, as we will see later, by Tom Torrance. Newman recalled how Christ, *before* entering his ministry, 'received the consecration of the Holy Spirit for our sakes'. The Spirit came to Christ 'from God', and 'passed' from Christ 'to us'. Newman interpreted accordingly the Pauline phrase 'Spirit of Christ'. The Holy Spirit 'is not simply called . . . the Spirit of God but the Spirit of Christ, [so] that we might clearly understand that he comes to us from' Christ.[15] We should not ignore a significant item affirmed almost in passing by Newman. It is not merely that, like Hebrews 9: 14, he appreciated the consecration for his priestly role that Christ received from the Holy Spirit. Following the Gospel accounts of Christ's baptism and Acts 10: 38, Newman saw how that consecration for the priestly role *preceded* the public ministry of Jesus—a happy reminder that Jesus' preaching and activity for the kingdom formed an essential part of the exercise of his priestly ministry.

---

[13] Sermon 25, in *Parochial and Plain Sermons*, 305.
[14] Ibid. 306–7.
[15] Sermon 19, in ibid. 217–31, at 220.

In his *Lectures on the Doctrine of Justification* (first published in 1838), Newman might have introduced the theme of sharing in Christ's triple office. But, somewhat like the Council of Trent in its 1547 decree on justification, Newman did not have much to state explicitly about the triple office and, in particular, about Christ's priesthood.

Of Christ's priestly office, Newman wrote: 'before he came, there were many priests who had infirmity, offering sacrifices year by year continually, but now there is but One High Priest.' Apropos of the kingly office, he stated: 'before, there were judges, kings, and rulers of various ranks, but now there is but One King of kings and Lord of lords in his Kingdom.' With reference to the prophetic office, Newman combined it with the other two offices: 'There were mediators many, and prophets many, and atonements many. But now all is superseded by One, in whom all offices merge, who has absorbed into himself all principality, power, might, dominion, and every name that is named.'[16]

Newman summed up matters by declaring that Christ is the 'one proper Priest, Prophet, and King'. When he prepared these lectures for a third edition in 1874, Newman qualified this final remark by adding a footnote: 'It is true that there is *one* Priest and one Sacrifice under the Gospel, but this is because the Priests of the Gospel are one with Christ, not because they are *improperly* called Priests.' In support of this addition, he quoted a few words from the *Roman Catechism* (2. 84), published in 1566 after the Council of Trent closed: 'Christ and priests are one priest (*Christus et sacerdotes sunt unus sacerdos*)'.[17]

Nevertheless, Newman also associated the triple office with the baptized faithful, recognizing, in particular, that the Lord shared with them his priestly work as intercessor. In a sermon preached on 22 February 1835, he declared: '[The Christian] is made after the pattern and in the fullness of Christ—he is what Christ is. Christ intercedes above, and he intercedes below.' Newman understood this privileged gift of interceding for others to result from the passion of the Lord:

---

[16] *Lectures on the Doctrine of Justification* (3rd edn., London: Longmans, Green & Co., 1874), 197–8.
[17] Ibid. 198.

'He died to bestow upon him [the Christian] that privilege which implies or involves all others, and brings him into nearest resemblance to himself, the privilege of intercession. This, I say, is the Christian's especial prerogative.' This 'privilege of intercession' makes the Christian resemble Christ in his permanent *priestly* intercession at the right hand of the Father (Rom. 8: 34; Heb. 7: 25). Yet Newman described the Christian who makes such intercession not as a priest but as 'a prophet', and even 'a confidential, familiar friend' of the Son of God.[18]

In a sermon preached on 29 November 1840, Newman described the risen and ascended Christ as 'ever near us, ever at hand'; he 'is the only Ruler and Priest in his Church, dispensing gifts, and has appointed none to supersede him'. In a way that recalled Augustine (see Chapter 5 above), Newman insisted that Christ is always the primary, albeit invisible, priest who performs baptisms, blessings, and 'all acts of his Church'; the ministerial priests are merely 'outward signs' of Christ. Newman declared: 'Christ's priests have no priesthood but his. They are merely his shadows and organs; they are his outward signs; and what they do, he does. When they baptize, he is baptizing; when they bless, he is blessing. He is in all acts of his Church, and one of its acts is not more truly his act than another, for all are his.'[19]

The following month Newman preached on Christmas Day a sermon entitled 'The Three Offices of Christ', the full flowering of his thought on the topic. He began by pointing out that those who prefigured Christ in the Old Testament exhibited traits associated with one or two functions of Christ's threefold 'mediatorial office' but never all three functions: 'Melchizedek, for instance, was a priest and a king, but not a prophet. David was a prophet and a king, but not a priest. Jeremiah was priest and prophet, but not a king. Christ was Prophet, Priest and King.'[20]

---

[18] 'Intercession', Sermon 24 in *Parochial and Plain Sermons*, iii (London: Rivingtons, 1881), 350–66, at 362–3.

[19] 'Waiting for Christ', Sermon 17 in *Parochial and Plain Sermons*, vi (London: Longmans, Green & Co., 1901), 234–54, at 242.

[20] 'The Three Offices of Christ', Sermon 5 in *Sermons Bearing on Subjects of the Day* (London: Longmans, Green & Co., 1918), 52–62, at 52.

Newman understood the triple office to represent the 'three principal conditions of mankind'. Using a term that, whether he was aware of this or not, recalled the French School (see previous chapter), he identified three 'states' of life with each office: the states of those who suffer, work, and think/study. Since Jesus lived each state, we can see in each human state the outlines of his triple office: 'Endurance, active life, thought—these are the three perhaps principal states in which men find themselves. Christ undertook them all.' Suffering (as priest), working (as king), and thinking (as prophet) can occur at any stage in the story of human beings. Hence Newman then applied 'state' to the chronological development of Christ: 'he lived through all states of man's life up to a perfect man (infancy, childhood, boyhood, youth, [and] maturity), that he might be a pattern of them all.' Here the humanity of Christ emerged as utterly central in Newman's understanding of his mediatorship. The paradoxes that characterized Christ's human life served to focus the triple office of (1) priest, (2) prophet, and (3) king:

When our Lord came on earth in our nature, he combined together offices and duties most dissimilar. [1] He suffered, yet he triumphed. [2] He thought and spoke, yet he acted. He was humble and despised, yet he was a teacher. [3] He has at once a life of hardship like the shepherds, yet is wise and royal as the eastern sages who came to do honour to his birth.[21]

Pondering further Christ's three offices, Newman presented them in a Trinitarian key: 'in these offices he also represents to us the Holy Trinity; for in his own proper character he is a Priest, and as to his kingdom he has it from the Father, and as to his prophetical office he exercises it by the Spirit.' Newman was even ready to assign one of the offices to each person of the Trinity: 'The Father is the King, the Son the Priest, and the Holy Ghost the Prophet.'[22] Newman could have appealed to the three articles of the Creed, with the Father as the 'almighty Maker/Creator of heaven and earth', the Son who 'suffered death' and 'rose again', and the Holy Spirit who 'has spoken through the prophets'.

[21] Ibid. 53–4.
[22] Ibid. 55.

In this same sermon Newman pressed on to recognize how both ordained ministers and all the baptized share in the triple office of Christ. First, Christ willed that members of the 'ministerial order' would be his 'representatives and instruments' in embodying and disclosing (what otherwise would be 'incompatible') his prophetical, priestly, and regal functions. 'He left behind him', Newman declared,

those who should take his place, a ministerial order, who are his representatives and instruments, and they, though earthen vessels [2 Cor. 4: 7], show forth according to their measure these three characters—the prophetical, priestly, and regal—combining in themselves qualities and functions which, except under the Gospel, are almost incompatible the one with the other.

Second, citing appropriate New Testament passages, Newman pointed to the kingly, priestly, and prophetic offices of all the faithful: 'all his [Christ's] followers in some sense bear all three offices, as Scripture is not slow to declare. In one place it is said that Christ has "made us kings and priests unto God and his Father" [Rev. 1: 6], in another, "Ye have an unction from the Holy One, and ye know all things" [1 John 2: 20].'[23]

To portray the offices of king, priest, and prophet, Newman introduced three familiar figures from the worldly scene: the earthly king, the soldier, and the philosopher. He explained how it was that a self-sacrificing soldier suggested the priestly office: '[The soldier] not only is strong, but he is [also] weak. He does and he suffers. He succeeds through a risk. Half his time is on the field of battle, and half of it on the bed of pain. And he does this for the sake of others; he defends us by it; we are indebted to him; we gain by his loss; we are at peace by his warfare.' Newman appreciated also the usual negative features in the popular image of a soldier: 'His office is wanting in dignity, and accordingly we associate it with the notion of brute force, and with arbitrariness, and imperiousness, and violence, and sternness.' The 'soldiering' involved in Christ's priestly office is different: 'Christ and his ministers are bloodless conquerors.'[24] Undoubtedly, Newman was aware that his language about the soldier being 'strong' and 'weak' found some scriptural backing in what

---

[23] Sermon 5, in *Sermons Bearing on Subjects*, 55–6.
[24] Ibid. 57–8.

St Paul's wrote about Christ being 'crucified in weakness but living by the power of God' (2 Cor. 13: 4). Yet we should observe that Paul did not apply his paradox of weakness/power to the exercise of Christ's priesthood. Newman was probably also aware of the wonderful medieval tradition about Christ as the young warrior whose suffering and death redeemed human beings and brought them peace.[25] But here too we should recall that the imagery of that tradition persistently pictured Christ as a kingly hero and not precisely as a priest.

All in all, Newman's Christmas Day sermon on 'The Three Offices of Christ' was a stunning tour de force. He compared and contrasted those three offices with representative figures in the Old Testament. He firmly associated Christ's humanity and 'the states' of his human life with his work as Mediator, and also read the triple office in a Trinitarian key. He recognized how ordained ministers and all the faithful share, albeit differently, in the three offices of Christ, even if he did not take time out to explore the different manner of participation in the priesthood of Christ. Finally, Newman introduced three familiar figures from human life—and, in particular, 'the soldier'— to picture imaginatively the paradoxical nature of the priesthood exercised by Christ and his ministers.

A few weeks later, on 17 January 1841, Newman returned to Christ's triple office when preaching on 'The Season of Epiphany'. He applied eight titles to what was manifested in the story of Christ—from the episode in the Temple at 12 years of age right through to Christ's second coming. 'When he is with the doctors in the Temple [Luke 2: 41–52], he is manifested as a *prophet*; in turning the water into wine [John 2: 1–12] as a *priest*; in his miracles of healing as a bounteous Lord; . . . in his rebuking the sea [Mark 4: 35–41] as a *Sovereign* whose word is law; in the parable of the wheat and tares [Matt. 13: 24–30] as a guardian and ruler; [and] in his second coming as a lawgiver and judge.'[26] Here Newman explicitly threaded 'prophet' and 'priest' into this summary of Christ's story; 'king' was there equivalently under the titles of 'Lord', 'Sovereign',

---

[25] See G. O'Collins, *Jesus Our Redeemer: A Christian Approach to Salvation* (Oxford: Oxford University Press, 2007), 123–6.

[26] 'The Season of Epiphany', Sermon 6 in *Parochial and Plain Sermons*, vii (London: Longmans, Green & Co., 1901), 74–85, at 77; italics ours.

'guardian', and 'ruler'. While it makes easy sense to interpret Jesus as a boy manifesting prophetic wisdom in the Temple, what can we make of his being called 'priest' in the Cana episode? There is more than a hint here of what Jesus was to say in priestly fashion over the cup of wine at the Last Supper: 'This cup is the new covenant in my blood' (1 Cor. 11: 25). One should also note how Newman ascribed the 'miracles of healing' to Christ as 'bounteous Lord'. Back in Chapter 1 we put the case for interpreting in a priestly key these miracles of Jesus (and not merely John's story of the water being made wine at Cana).

In the same sermon Newman moved to touch on the liturgical duties involved in the priesthood of all the faithful, who through baptism become 'worshippers and ministers in the temple'. He pointed to 'the privileges and the duties of the new people' of God, whom Christ 'has formed to show forth his praise'. Christians 'are at once the temple of Christ, and his worshippers and ministers in the temple'.[27] Faith in Christ and baptism entail the new people of God in worship, praise, and liturgical ministry.

Newman's Use of the Triple Office After 1845

After Newman entered full communion with the Roman Catholic Church in 1845, the theme of the triple office surfaced periodically. In a sermon outline from 27 November 1849 he made two notes on the priestly office of Christ: 'he sits as our one Mediator and Intercessor' (Rom. 8: 34) and 'his intercession consists in presenting his human nature' (Heb. 7: 24–5).[28] That same year he began preaching the sermons that turned into *Discourses Addressed to Mixed Congregations*. When reflecting on King Solomon and his prayer when dedicating the Temple, Newman observed that a reference to 'His [God's] commandments, and His ceremonies, and His judgements' (1 Kgs 8: 58) corresponds to the prophetic, priestly, and kingly offices of Christ. But any prefiguring of Christ 'comes up short': Solomon

---

[27] Sermon 6, in *Parochial and Plain Sermons*, 78.
[28] *Sermon Notes of John Henry Cardinal Newman 1849–1878* (London: Longmans, Green & Co., 1914), 304.

prefigured 'the coming Saviour' as king and prophet but not as 'suffering' priest.[29] That observation echoed what Newman had preached on Christmas Day 1840 about King David prefiguring Christ as prophet and king, but not as priest (see above).

On 6 April 1851, when Newman chose to preach on the priesthood of Christ, he dwelt on a theme dear to Luther (see Chapter 7): Christ's priestly service for sinners. 'What is a priest?' Newman asked. 'See how much it implies: first the need for reconciliation; it has at once to do with sin; it presupposes sin. When then our Lord is known to come as a priest, see how the whole face of the world is changed.' Newman underlined the universal character of Christ's priestly service: 'the Son of God offers for the whole world, and that offering is himself. He who is high as eternity, whose arms stretch through infinity, is lifted up on the cross for the sins of the world.' Here Newman was clearer than the Letter to the Hebrews about the universal scope of the beneficiaries of Christ's priestly sacrifice (see Chapter 4). Like Hebrews, Newman took up the language about Christ being 'a priest forever according to the order of Melchizedek', but, unlike Hebrews, he applied it to the permanent sacrifice of the Mass: it is not 'done and over; it lasts'.[30]

In the aftermath of the First Vatican Council's definition of papal primacy and infallibility, William Gladstone questioned the possibility of Catholics in England being loyal to their country. In a 1874 response to the prime minister, Newman famously portrayed conscience as taking precedence over any authority, papal or secular. He expressed this precedence by making use of the scheme of the triple office: 'Conscience is the aboriginal Vicar of Christ, a prophet in its informations, a monarch in its peremptoriness, a priest in its blessings and anathemas, and, even though the eternal priesthood

---

[29] 'Perseverance in Grace', in *Discourses Addressed to Mixed Congregations* (London: Longman, Green & Co., 1913), 124–44, at 137–8. Where the Authorized Version of 1611 (which Newman had used up to his entering into full communion with the Catholic Church) translated the phrase from Solomon's prayer as 'his commandments, and his judgments and his statutes', Newman now quoted the wording from the (Catholic) Douai Reims translation (1609). In the New Revised Standard Version (1989) there is no reference to priestly ceremonies: 'his commandments, his statutes, and his ordinances'.

[30] 'On the Priesthood of Christ', in *Sermon Notes*, 69–70.

throughout the Church could cease to be, in it the sacerdotal principle would remain and would have a sway.'[31] Here Newman presented the triple office as if it were a spiritual genetic code that pre-existed any institutional structures, with 'the sacerdotal principle', in particular, forming an intrinsic character of the Christian soul.

Lastly, when updating and correcting in the 1870s what he had written from 1833 to 1845, Newman was aware that there could be tension between the three offices of Christ when they found their counterpart in the life of the Church herself. He grappled with the difficult relationship between 'devotion', 'philosophy', and 'polity', experienced in the Church during the pontificate and, in particular, the last years of Pius IX (pope 1846–78). Writing to Frederic Lord Blachford on 3 June 1874, three years before he published the 'Preface to the *Via Media*', Newman said:

I have long wished to write an essay, but I never shall, I think, on the conflicting interests, and therefore difficulties of the Catholic Church, because she is at once, first a *devotion* [priestly office], secondly a *philosophy* [prophetic office], thirdly a *polity* [kingly office]. Just now, as I suppose at many other times, the devotional sentiment and the political embarrass the philosophical instinct. However, she has prospered and has made [her] way, in spite of this, for 1800 years and will still.[32]

In the 'Preface' he explained how the three offices of 'prophet, priest, and king' that belong supremely to Christ applied also to 'his very self below', the Church. Yet the Church shared these offices 'after his pattern' and 'in human measure'. That meant viewing Christianity as a philosophy (prophetic office), a religious rite (priestly office), and as a political power (kingly office). Newman correlated the three offices with the creedal characteristics of the Church as, respectively, 'apostolic', 'holy', and 'one and catholic'. Finally, he associated each office with some special 'centre of action': 'the schools' (prophetic

[31] 'A Letter Addressed to His Grace, the Duke of Norfolk on Occasion of Mr Gladstone's Recent Expostulation', in J. H. Newman, *Certain Difficulties Felt by Anglicans in Catholic Teaching Considered*, ii (London: Longmans, Green & Co., 1891), 171–378, at 248–9.

[32] *The Letters and Diaries of John Henry Newman*, xxvii (Oxford: Clarendon Press, 1975), 70.

office), 'pastor and flock' (priestly office), and 'papacy and curia' (kingly office).[33]

Newman understood these offices to have developed in a particular order, beginning with Christ himself and the early history of the Church. The process began with worship or the priestly office, was followed by theology or the prophetic office, and was completed by ecclesiastical 'polity' or the kingly office.[34] Newman drew attention to the tensions involved in the exercise of these offices: 'Each of the three has its separate scope and direction; each has its own interests to promote and further; each has to find room for the claims of the other two; and each will find its own line of action influenced and modified by the others, nay, sometimes in a particular case the necessity of the others converted into a rule of duty for itself.'[35]

This sampling of what Newman wrote in the 'Preface' to the *Via Media* illustrates how his primary concern in the 1870s was to apply the scheme of the three offices to the Church, rather than explore their application to Christ. As we will see below, their ecclesial application would prove fruitful at the Second Vatican Council a century later.

To sum up Newman's contribution on the three offices of Christ himself: Newman wrote more on the prophetic and kingly offices of Christ, and it is easy to see why. His 1837 *Lectures on the Prophetical Office of the Church* witnessed to his concern with that office. The kingly office caught his attention as he dealt with the question of authority in the Church and came to terms with joining a community headed by a papal 'monarch'. Apropos of Christ's priestly office, he reiterated in a new context themes we find earlier in the Christian tradition: for instance, the humanity of Christ as a necessary precondition for his priesthood (e.g. Hebrews, Chrysostom, and Calvin), and Christ as the real, if invisible, minister of all the sacraments (Augustine).

---

[33] *Via Media*, i (3rd edn., London: Longmans, Green & Co, 1918), pp. xxxix–xli.

[34] This reading of a historical sequence in the deployment of the three offices obviously invites some qualifications. The prophetic proclamation of the good news of Christ's resurrection from the dead surely came first. Otherwise there would have been no believers to share in the priestly worship.

[35] *Via Media*, i. p. xlii.

Yet there are also some fresh accents in Newman's presentation of Christ's priesthood. Unlike the Council of Trent, he treated that office along with the other two (Christ as prophet and as king). Unlike many predecessors, he also underlined the suffering nature of Christ's self-sacrificing priesthood and its implications for those who share in it. When treating the priestly office exercised by bishops, Newman proposed suffering for the sake of Christ as an essential feature of their apostolic witness. In the very first of the *Tracts for the Times* (9 September 1833) he expressed a wish for bishops to be blessed in this way: 'we could not wish them a more blessed termination of their course than the spoiling of their goods and martyrdom.' Two months later, in *Tract* no. 10 (4 November 1833), he repeated even more emphatically his wish that bishops could witness to Christ through suffering and martyrdom.[36] In the next chapter we return to suffering as a distinctive characteristic that deserves more attention. Lastly, Newman's insight about the laity sharing in the threefold office of Christ—and, in particular, the prophetic office—showed itself in his remarkable essay of 1859, *On Consulting the Faithful in Matters of Doctrine.*[37]

KARL BARTH AND THOMAS TORRANCE

Once we move to the twentieth century, we find some major theologians in the Calvinist tradition reflecting on the priesthood of Christ. As one might expect, Karl Barth (1886–1968) had something to say on the theme in his *Church Dogmatics*.

When handling the doctrine of reconciliation, Karl Barth dedicated pages to 'the glory of the Mediator' and 'his mediatorial work' 'among and in and through us'.[38] 'The glory of the Mediator' glossed the language used by Hebrews, which had presented Christ's priestly

[36] J. H. Newman *et al.*, *Tracts for the Times*, i (London: Rivington, 1838); see further Otellini, *Newman on the Episcopacy*, 123–6.

[37] Ed. John Coulson (London: Sheed & Ward, 1961).

[38] K. Barth, *Church Dogmatics*, IV/3/1, ed. G. W. Bromiley and T. F. Torrance (Edinburgh: T. & T. Clark, 1961), 278; hereafter references will be made within the text.

work as that of 'the Mediator of a new/better covenant' (Heb. 8: 6; 9: 15; 12: 24). At times, Barth joined Hebrews in calling Christ our 'High-priest' (pp. 282, 283) or simply 'the Priest' (p. 308).

As regards the full *'munus triplex'* of Christ as priest, king, *and prophet,* Barth reported early intimations in patristic authors of the fourth and fifth centuries. But he valued, above all, the firm emergence of the threefold office that came with later editions of Calvin's *Institutes,* in his 1538 *Catechism,* which proposed only the offices of king and priest, and in his 1541 *Geneva Catechism,* which added the office of prophet.[39] Barth recalled as well the *Heidelberg Catechism* of 1563 (question 31) that reflected much of the Reformer's thought.[40] By recognizing that Christ enjoyed the fullness of the Holy Spirit, Calvin could clearly propose the *'munus triplex'.* Barth, for good measure, also pointed out where the threefold office made its appearance not only in the *Roman Catechism* of 1566 but also in the work of a nineteenth-century Catholic theologian M. J. Scheeben (1835–88) (pp. 13–14).[41]

The relevant passage in the *Roman Catechism* declares: 'To adorn and illustrate his Church, there are three eminent offices and func-

---

[39] On Calvin's presentation of Christ's triple office, see P. Gisel, *Le Christ de Calvin* (Paris: Desclée, 1990), 131–50. In expounding 'and in Jesus Christ' of the Apostles' Creed, Calvin explained how Christ was anointed as king, priest, and prophet by the Father (pp. 20–1); on the development of the triple office in Calvin's catechisms and its future impact, see I. J. Hesselink, *Calvin's First Catechism: A Commentary* (Louisville, Ky.: Westminster John Knox Press, 1997), 118–21, 216–17. On the triple office in the Geneva *Catechism* and the *Heidelberg Catechism,* see J. Rohls, *Reformed Confessions: From Zurich to Barmen,* trans. J. Hoffmeyer (Louisville, Ky.: Westminster John Knox Press, 1998), 100–1.
[40] The *Heidelberg Catechism* replies to question 31: 'He [Christ] is ordained by God the Father and anointed with the Holy Spirit to be our chief Prophet and Teacher, fully revealing to us the secret purpose and will of God concerning our redemption; to be our only High Priest, having redeemed us by the one sacrifice of his body and ever interceding for us with the Father; and to be our eternal King, governing us by his Word and Spirit, and defending and sustaining us in the redemption he has won for us.' This catechism is found e.g. in A. C. Cochrane (ed.), *Reformed Confessions of the 16th Century* (London: SCM Press, 1966), 305–31, at 310.
[41] M. J. Scheeben, *Handbuch der katholischen Dogmatik. Erlösungslehre,* v/2, in *Gesammelte Schriften,* vi/2 (Freiburg: Herder, 1954), 226–306. Scheeben writes here of Christ as priest, prophet, and king, but devotes most pages (pp. 239–304) to his priestly office.

tions of our Lord Jesus Christ, those of Redeemer, Patron, and Judge . . . the human was redeemed by his passion and death . . . by his ascension into heaven, he has also undertaken for ever the advocacy and patronage of our cause . . . on the last day, Christ the Lord will judge all mankind' (1. 8. 1).[42]

It was Calvin's insight into Christ's '*munus triplex*' that Barth treasured. In general, when expounding the doctrine of reconciliation, Barth invested much more time in unpacking 'the new and particular feature of reconciliation in its form as revelation'—that is, 'the being and action of Christ in his prophetic office' (p. 281). As the Mediator and Guarantor of reconciliation, Christ exercised his prophetic office (*munus propheticum*) as 'the true Witness', the title Barth gave to the whole volume. Not unsurprisingly, the longest section in the volume was dedicated to the Mediator as 'the Light of Life' (pp. 38–165), which developed the theme of reconciliation as revelation. As a unique prophet (p. 49), Christ worked as 'Reconciler, Saviour and Mediator' (p. 47), and his entire life was light, truth, and revelation (p. 79). In short, his reconciling work took place as 'prophetic Word' (p. 86). Barth was ready to name Christ as 'High-Priest and King' (pp. 107, 282, 283, 308). Occasionally he associated the three offices, as when he stated that 'Jesus Christ is not only the High-Priest and King but also the Prophet, Herald and Proclaimer of this accomplishment [reconciliation]' (p. 165). But it was Barth's student, T. F. Torrance (1913–2007), who gave more substance to the triple office and much more to Christ's human priesthood.

Torrance, steeped as he was in the writings of Barth, felt at home with language about Christ as 'Mediator'. In lectures delivered originally in 1982 and published as *The Mediation of Christ*, Torrance spent a chapter on 'The Person of the Mediator'.[43] In this book references to priesthood were made in the context of the Old

---

[42] Trans. J. A. McHugh and C. J. Callan (New York: Wagner, 1934; republished several times). Neither here nor elsewhere did the *Roman Catechism* call Christ a 'prophet'; it called him 'king' (4. 11. 8 and 9) and 'priest'. Apropos of the sacrifice of the Mass, it stated: 'the priest is one and the same, Christ the Lord; for the ministers who offer sacrifice . . . consecrate his body and blood, not in their own [person], but in the person of Christ' (2. 4. 75).

[43] T. F. Torrance, *The Mediation of Christ* (Edinburgh: T. & T. Clark, rev. edn., 1992), 47–72.

Testament's 'priestly people' and their sacrificial system.[44] In an earlier work,[45] Torrance had examined 'the three-fold office of Christ in
ascension'. As we saw at the end of Chapter 6, he found in the
ascension more to say than Thomas Aquinas about the ongoing
priestly ministry of Christ.

But it was in a collection of lectures, largely given in ecumenical
contexts and originally published in 1975, that Torrance articulated
at length the mediatorial work of Christ's human priesthood.[46] When
elucidating the identity and work of Christ as priest, he engaged fully
with the Gospel accounts of the Last Supper, with the Letter to the
Hebrews, and with the Eucharist in the life of the Church. Through
his 'self-consecration' and 'high priestly intercession' at the Last
Supper, Torrance explained, Jesus intended that his disciples should
be 'presented to the Father through his own self-offering on their
behalf' (p. 106). Along with the Gospel accounts of the institution of
the Eucharist, the teaching of Hebrews illuminates 'the nature and
mission of Christ Jesus as the Apostle and High Priest of our confession' (Heb. 3: 1) and his work as the unique 'Priest and Mediator'.
Offering himself 'without blemish' to the Father through the power
of the Holy Spirit (Heb. 9: 14), he 'has consecrated for us a new and
living way into the holiest [sanctuary] through the veil of his flesh'
(Heb. 10: 19–20), and so through Christ 'we may come boldly to the
throne of grace' (Heb. 4: 16) (pp. 107, 108, 110).

Synthesizing thus the witness of Hebrews and the Gospels and
respecting the mission of the Holy Spirit allowed Torrance to understand the Eucharist as the priestly presence of the sacrificial self-
offering of the incarnate, crucified, risen, and ascended Christ—a
sacrificial self-offering in which the faithful share. The Eucharist 'is
Christ himself who is really present pouring out his Spirit upon us,
drawing us into the power of his vicarious life, in death and resurrection, and uniting us with his self-oblation and self-presentation
before the face of the Father where he ever lives to make intercession

[44] Ibid. 30, 75.
[45] T. F. Torrance, *Space, Time and Resurrection* (Edinburgh: Handsel Press, 1976),
112–22.
[46] T. F. Torrance, *Theology in Reconciliation: Essays Toward Evangelical and Catholic Unity in East and West* (Eugene, Oreg.: Wipf & Stock, 1996); hereafter references
will be made within the text.

for us.' Thus the Eucharist is 'what it is' because of its 'grounding' in 'what God in Christ has done, does do, and will do for us in his Spirit' (p. 107). In the celebration of the Eucharist Christ acts by 'assimilating us in mind and will to himself and lifting us up in the closest union with himself in the identity of himself as Offerer and Offering to the presence of the Father' (p. 118).

Five convictions play crucial roles in Torrance's view of Christ's priestly presence in the celebration of the Eucharist. First, he sets that presence within 'the whole economy' of Christ having become man 'for our sake' (p. 111). In his priestly activity Christ became 'God's place within the space-time of this world' (p. 120), and that activity includes everything from the incarnation through to the ascension into heavenly glory.

Second, he follows and vigorously develops Augustine's vision of Christ's continuing activity in the celebration of the sacraments. The Eucharist is what Christ does to us and for us, not anything that we do to Christ. 'It is Christ himself', Torrance writes, 'who constitutes the living content, reality and power of the Eucharist' and 'who gives meaning and efficacy to its celebration in the Church by being savingly and creatively present in his mediatorial agency' (p. 109). In his identity as the perfect 'Priest and Victim, Offerer and Offering' (p. 134), Christ continues to present us to the Father on the grounds of his one 'all-sufficient sacrifice' (p. 111).

Torrance returns again and again to this theme of Christ's presence in the Eucharist: 'when the Church worships, praises and adores the Father through Christ and celebrates the Eucharist in his name, it is Christ himself who worships, praises and adores the Father in and through his members, taking up, moulding and sanctifying the prayers of his people.' This priestly presence of Christ invests with power the Church's prayers for the world: 'when the Church at the Eucharist intercedes in his name for all mankind, it is Christ himself who intercedes in them' (p. 134).[47]

---

[47] In another work Torrance attended to Christ's post-ascension prophetic activity manifested in the Church's ministry of the Word (*Space, Time and Resurrection*, 119–21): when the Church proclaims, it is Christ who proclaims. Torrance appealed here to Mark 16: 20: 'they [the eleven] went out and proclaimed the good news everywhere, while the Lord worked with them.'

Third, Torrance shows himself admirably Trinitarian in his appreciation of the Eucharistic worship. It is 'essentially a participation' in the heavenly worship which Jesus the 'ascended High Priest renders to the Father in the oblation of his endless life'. It is 'worship in the same Spirit *by whom* we are made one with the Son as he is one with the Father, *in whom* we have access to the Father, and *through whom* we are taken up into the eternal communion of the Father, the Son and the Holy Spirit' (p. 110; italics ours). For Torrance, the Eucharist is an utterly Trinitarian narrative. As he states, 'we worship and pray to the Father in such a way that it is Christ himself who is the real content of our worship and prayer', and 'in the Spirit the prayer that ascends from us to the Father is a form of the self-offering of Christ himself' (p. 209).

Fourth, the living power and presence of Christ at the celebration of the Eucharist provide Torrance with grounds for speaking repeatedly of the 'eucharistic sacrifice' (pp. 112, 133, 134). As the living reality of Christ's priestly self-oblation, worship, and intercession, the Eucharist makes present his 'all-sufficient sacrifice'. To exclude talk of the 'eucharistic sacrifice' would be to call into question any vision of Christ's powerful presence as 'Offerer and Offering' at the Eucharist. To justify his position, Torrance also appeals to what Paul wrote in 1 Corinthians 10: 16 about the Eucharist as sacrifice: 'the bread which we break and the cup of blessing which we bless are communion (*koinonia*) in the body and blood of Christ, and the Eucharistic offering of Christ to the Father which we make through him is communion (*koinonia*) in his own sacrificial self-offering to God the Father' (p. 119).

Fifth, Torrance joins the mainstream tradition by insisting on humanity as the necessary prerequisite for Christ's priesthood: 'Christ worshipped as man' (p. 113).[48] Here Torrance strongly endorses the conclusions Josef Jungmann reached about a certain 'liturgical monophysitism' that emerged towards the end of the fourth century.[49] Reacting to the Arians, who denied Christ's true divinity and attributed

---

[48] This recalls a theme from Bérulle and Condren about Christ as the perfect 'adorer' of the Father.

[49] See J. A. Jungmann, *The Place of Christ in Liturgical Prayer*, trans. A. Peeler (London: Geoffrey Chapman, 1965).

to him only a mediating role between the Creator and his creatures, those who composed liturgical texts both in the East and in the West progressively reduced the place given to the human priesthood of Christ. This diminished place for 'the human mediation of prayer through Jesus Christ' evoked a theological error: namely, that of those 'Monophysites' who so stressed the divinity of Christ as to let it 'swallow up' his genuine humanity. Up to that period the Church adored Christ 'equally with the Father and the Holy Spirit', but 'with great unanimity kept to the rule of turning to God the Father, in liturgical prayer, through Christ the [human] High Priest' (p. 115).[50] Now, 'stress upon the deity of Christ, in reaction to Arianism, prompted incorporation into the liturgies of formal prayers to Christ who as Lord receives our prayers and as Mediator bestows divine gifts upon us'. Thus, 'prayer motivated by Christ' tended to 'displace prayer through the human priesthood of Jesus', who was himself regarded 'as a [surely 'the'?] worshipper of God'. In subsequent developments, liturgical prayers 'addressed directly to Christ as God' had 'the effect of thrusting him up into the awful mystery of Godhead, with the result that the humanity and mediatorship of Christ recede more and more into the background' (pp. 115–16).

Torrance notes two practical results arising from this change. First, the 'poor creature at worship is confronted immediately with the overwhelming majesty of almighty God'. Thus, 'the fearful gap between the eternal God and sinful man, instead of being bridged in the priesthood of a Jesus touched with the feeling of all our infirmities, seems to be wider than ever' (p. 116). Second, officiating priests tended to take the place of Christ himself—a development that was less than happy (p. 287).

Torrance not only shows great regard for the meticulous research of Jungmann (see p. 287) but also manages, through a wide know-

---

[50] In his 1943 encyclical *Mystici Corporis* ('The Mystical Body'), Pope Pius XII expressed the same two points and in the same way—by echoing the Creed and referring to liturgical practice. On the one hand, 'it is necessary for all Christians to know and understand clearly that the man Christ Jesus is truly the Son of God, and himself true God'; on the other hand, '[liturgical] prayers are usually addressed to the eternal Father through his only begotten Son, especially in the Eucharistic sacrifice where Christ, being both Priest and Victim, discharges in a special manner his office of Mediator' (ND 1215).

ledge of the fathers of the Church, to expand our vision of the fateful starting-point for the 'Monophysite' developments in liturgy. Strong opposition to an Arian rejection of Christ's divinity led Apollinarius of Laodicea (d. *c.* 390) to the other extreme and 'demolished' the integrity of Christ's human agency. For Apollinarius, the all-encompassing divine Word took the place in Jesus of any human, rational soul. 'A refined form of Apollinarianism' challenged the reality of Christ as the High Priest, 'praying and worshipping in our place and on our behalf'. That error brought a 'seriously deficient' understanding of the Eucharist, because it lost the early 'emphasis upon Christ praying and worshipping as one of us' and 'on our behalf'. Apollinarians, ancient and modern, forget that 'our worship of God the Father is with, in and through the [human] mind of Jesus Christ his Son' (pp. 116–17; see pp. 139–214). They fail to accept that Christ is God come as fully human, so as to act as our High Priest from the side of humanity *towards the father* and not merely to act from the side of the Father *towards humanity.*

Thus, wherever the full humanity is reduced or ignored, any true appreciation of the priesthood of Christ will also be lost. His genuine humanity is integral to the exercise of his priesthood. Torrance joined forces with Jungmann to expose a major cause for a diminished view of Christ's self-sacrificing priesthood that has persisted for centuries.

When making his notable contributions to a Christian understanding of Christ's priesthood, Torrance repeatedly engaged in dialogue with the teaching of the Second Vatican Council (e.g. pp. 54 and 59–65) and with the ecumenical initiatives developed by Yves Congar (p. 59). To complete this chapter, we turn to the work of Congar and Vatican II, where Congar proved himself to be among the leading theological contributors.

CONGAR AND VATICAN II

Some, like Aidan Nichols, have drawn a more or less straight line from Newman, through Yves Congar (1904–95), to the way Vatican II (1962–5) deployed the triple office of Christ in its 1964 document on the Church, *Lumen Gentium* ('Light of the Nations'; hereafter *LG*)

and two subsequent, connected documents of 1965: on the apostolate
of lay people, *Apostolicam Actuositatem* ('Apostolic Activity'; hereafter
AA), and on the ministry and life of priests, *Presbyterorum Ordinis*
('The Order of Priests'; hereafter *PO*).[51] Unquestionably, there is some
truth in the 'line from Newman' thesis. Congar referred to him several
times in a landmark volume of 1953 on lay people in the Church,[52]
prepared French translations of Newman's writings on the Church,
and followed him in understanding the Church to 'perform the three
offices of Christ as prophet, priest and King'.[53] Nevertheless, the thesis
needs qualifications that concern both the run-up to Vatican II and
Congar's input during the four years of the Council itself.[54]

Yves Congar on the Threefold Office

Other authors, both official and theological, helped create a context
that would facilitate in the 1960s the passage of the '*triplex munus*'
into the Council's documents. In a widely read book that expounded
the ministerial priesthood and the priesthood of all the baptized,[55]
Joseph Lécuyer drew not only on biblical and patristic sources but
also on two papal encyclicals: the first by Pius XI on 'the Catholic
priesthood (*Ad Catholici Sacerdotii*)' of 1935, and the second by Pius

[51] A. Nichols, *Yves Congar* (London: Geoffrey Chapman, 1989), 73. Nichols's
judgements would surely have been modified, as we shall see, if the diary Congar
wrote during the Council had been available earlier: *Mon journal du concile*, 2 vols.
(Paris: Cerf, 2002). See J. Wicks, 'Yves Congar's Doctrinal Service of the People of
God', *Gregorianum*, 84 (2003), 499–550, at 515.

[52] Y. Congar, *Jalons pour une théologie du laïcat* (Paris: Cerf, 1953); trans.
D. Attwater as *Lay People in the Church: A Study for a Theology of the Laity* (London:
Bloomsbury, 1957).

[53] J. Coulson, 'Newman's Hour: The Significance of Newman's Thought, and its
Application Today', *Heythrop Journal*, 22 (1981), 394–406, at 396.

[54] Some detected a long-term influence from Aquinas's use of the triple office (see
Ch. 6 above), others thought rather of Calvin's influence. Thus George Tavard wrote:
'John Calvin . . . related the tasks of ministry to the threefold functions of Christ as
priest, prophet and king, that he saw in the light of the Old Testament. This typology
passed into all later Calvinism through the Heidelberg Catechism (Q. and A. 31).
It . . . was used at Vatican II as a key to the task of bishops, priests, and laity' ('The
Ordained Ministry: Where Does It Fit?', in *Doctrine and Life*, 38 (1988), 518–19.

[55] J. Lécuyer, *Le Sacerdoce dans le mystère du Christ* (Paris: Cerf, 1957); trans.
L. C. Sheppard as *What Is a Priest?* (London: Burns & Oates, 1959).

XII on liturgical worship, 'The Mediator of God (*Mediator Dei*)' of 1947. Both encyclicals distinguished the ministerial priesthood from the priesthood of all believers. The first announced a new, 'votive' Mass in honour of Jesus Christ the eternal High Priest, a Mass that survived the liturgical changes Vatican II inaugurated and is still to be found in the 1970 Missal of Paul VI.[56] The second encyclical contained a vivid picture of the incarnate Word of God initiating his priestly work by leading off a worldwide hymn of praise to God: 'The Word of God, when he assumed a human nature, introduced [past tense] into this land of exile the hymn that in heaven is sung [present tense] throughout all ages. He unites the whole community of humankind with himself and associates it with him in singing this divine canticle of praise' (ND 1225). These words from *Mediator Dei* evoke something of the Book of Revelation's vision of earthly liturgy being matched (and surpassed) by heavenly liturgy, and adds a further picture: at his incarnation the Son of God led off a cosmic hymn, and that hymn of divine praise will never end. We return below to this passage.

In his 1953 book Congar dedicated well over a third of the volume, chapters 4, 5, and 6, to the way lay people share in the priestly, kingly, and prophetical (in that order) functions of Christ. A further book on the laity, coming from another author who would also play a major role at Vatican II, Gérard Philips, appeared in 1962, the year the Council began: *Pour une christianisme adulte*. Philips expounded the three functions of the laity in chapter 3: 'A Priestly, Prophetic, Royal People.'[57]

When the Council met in the autumn of 1962, a preparatory text 'On the Church (*De Ecclesia*)' (in which chapter 1 spoke of the bishops being adorned with the 'offices of preacher, priest, and king', and chapter 6, for which Philips was largely responsible, referred to the common priesthood of the faithful) was sharply criticized in the final days of the First Session (1–6 December 1962). Even

---

[56] In 1925 Pius XI, along with his first encyclical ('Quas primas') that he dedicated to the kingship of Christ, instituted the feast of 'Christ the King', which is still celebrated but now on the last Sunday before the First Sunday of Advent.

[57] Trans. E. Kane as *Achieving Christian Maturity* (Dublin: Gill, 1966), 65–93.

before that, in October 1962, Cardinal Leo Jozef Suenens had asked Philips to 'revise, complete, and improve' the schema on the Church.[58] The preparatory schema was removed, and over several months (February–May 1963) a new text was prepared on the basis of a revised text authored by Philips.[59] For some weeks in the spring of 1963 Congar also worked on the revision. The new draft was mailed to the bishops in the middle of the year, well before they were to begin the Second Session in October 1963. In that revised 'schema' the triple office of the bishops was further developed in what became chapter 3 of *LG* ('The Church is Hierarchical'), and the priestly, prophetic, and kingly role of all the baptized introduced, above all, in chapter 4 ('The Laity'). Philips played a major role in these developments.[60] But what of Congar?

In his diary entry for 7 December 1965 Congar listed what he had contributed—either as initial drafter of texts or as editor of emendations subsequently proposed by the bishops—to eight of the sixteen documents issued by the Council. He mentioned that, as regards *LG*, he had contributed to chapter 1 and to numbers 9, 13, 16, and 17 in chapter 2 ('The People of God'). He made no claim to have drafted number 10 (that calls Christ 'High Priest' and distinguishes between the common priesthood of the faithful and the ministerial priesthood), number 11 (that deals with the priestly nature of all the baptized), or number 12 (that deals with their prophetic office). Likewise, apropos of chapter 3 (on the hierarchical nature of the Church), Congar made no claim to have been involved in drafting numbers 25–7 (that deal, respectively, with the teaching/prophetic role of the bishops, their priestly role in worship, and their pastoral/kingly role in leadership). Finally, as regards chapter 4 (on 'the laity'),

---

[58] G. Ruggieri, 'Beyond an Ecclesiology of Polemics: The Debate on the Church', in G. Alberigo and J. A. Komonchak (eds.), *The History of Vatican II*, ii (Maryknoll, NY: Orbis Books, 1997), 281–357, 282–4.

[59] J. Grootaers, 'The Drama Continues Between the Acts: The "Second Preparation" and its Opponents', in ibid. 359–514, at 399–410.

[60] Two years after the Council closed, Philips published *L'Église et son mystère au IIᵉ Concile du Vatican: histoire, texte et commentaire de la Constitution 'Lumen Gentium'*, 2 vols. (Paris: Desclée, 1967). Philips treats the threefold office of the bishops (i. 254–7) and, at greater length, that of the laity (ii. 31–48).

he did not claim to have drafted numbers 34–6 (that deal, respect-ively, with the priestly, prophetic, and kingly role of lay people).[61]

In that same diary entry Congar did not mention *AA*, a decree that twice acknowledges how all the baptized share in 'the priestly, pro-phetical, and kingly office of Christ' (no. 2; see no. 10). That sharing in the threefold office of Christ becomes the basis for what the decree has to say about the apostolate of the laity. Seemingly, Congar had little or nothing to do, at least directly, with the drafting and emend-ing of *AA*.

Apropos of the '*munus triplex*', Congar's hand is most visible in the decree *PO*. He drafted the text (with the help of Joseph Lécuyer and Willy Onclin), was involved in the revisions, and composed the moving conclusion (no. 22). In this document on the ministry and life of priests, numbers 4–6 take up and spell out in detail what the introduction states: 'through the sacred ordination and mission that they receive from the bishops, priests are promoted to the service of Christ the *Teacher, Priest* and *King*' (no. 1; italics ours). Number 4 details what is involved in priests being 'ministers of God's Word'; number 5 sets out what is entailed in their being priestly 'ministers of the sacraments and the Eucharist'; and number 6 describes their role as kingly 'rulers of God's people' and 'pastors of the Church'. Even though, a decade before Vatican II opened, Congar had built the threefold office of Christ into his seminal book on the *laity*, his major contribution at the Council on the '*munus triplex*' came rather in the decree on the ministry and life of *priests*.[62] Apparently he had nothing directly to do with the teaching on the threefold office of the laity to be found either in chapter 4 of *LG* or throughout *AA*.

Congar proved to be a twentieth-century bridge that helped bring Newman's reflections on Christ's office as priest, prophet, and king into the teaching of Vatican II. Yet, while rating highly the contribu-tions of Newman, we should not ignore the long-term impact of a threefold ecclesiological scheme that emerged in Roman Catholic

---

[61] Congar, *Mon journal du concile*, ii. 511.

[62] On the preparation and content of PO, see J. Frisque and Y. Congar (eds.), *Les Prêtres, formation, ministère et vie* (Paris: Cerf, 1968). For further documentation on the genesis of passages on the '*munus triplex*' in *LG*, *AA*, and *PO*, see G. Alberigo and J. A. Komonchak (eds.), *History of Vatican II*, 5 vols. (Maryknoll, NY: Orbis Books, 1995–2006).

circles towards the end of the nineteenth century and applied only to hierarchy. In the work of a leading canonist, George Phillips (1804–72), and in a dogmatic constitution on the Church prepared for the First Vatican Council (1769–70) but never voted on (since the arrival of the Italian army forced the Council to close abruptly), we find the triple scheme of '*magisterium, ministerium et regimen* (teaching, ministry, and government)'. This language emerged when it became clear (for example through the work of Phillips, who published seven volumes on ecclesiastical law), that teaching (= the exercise of the prophetic office) could not be properly interpreted as an act of sacred orders (= the exercise of the priestly office) or an act of jurisdiction (= the exercise of the kingly office).[63]

Vatican II on the Threefold Office

Before concluding this chapter, we want to recall some passages from *LG*, *AA*, and *PO*. Before doing so, however, the first document to be promulgated by Vatican II needs to be mentioned: the 1963 'Constitution on the Sacred Liturgy', *Sacrosanctum Concilium* ('The Sacred Council'; hereafter *SC*). Two themes should be retrieved.

First, in language that evokes Augustine and Torrance, the Council declares that the liturgy 'is rightly seen as an exercise of the priestly office of Jesus Christ'; 'every liturgical action' is 'an action of Christ the Priest and of his Body, which is the Church'. Right in that same context the constitution quotes Augustine: 'by his power he [Christ the Priest] is present in the sacraments, so that when anybody baptizes, it is really Christ himself who baptizes' (*SC* 7; see Augustine in Chapter 5 above). Then follows a lyrical list of the multifaceted modes of Christ's priestly presence in the liturgy—and, especially, at the Eucharist (ibid.)—that could have come from Torrance. Yet he, Luther, and other Reformers would doubtless have preferred to have listed right there a central form of Christ's active and permanent

---

[63] In this context we should not forget what Barth (see above) documented: the presence of the 'threefold office of Christ' in the 1566 *Roman Catechism* and in the work of the nineteenth-century Catholic theologian Matthias Scheeben.

presence that is mentioned only later: 'in the liturgy God speaks to his people, and Christ is still proclaiming his Gospel' (*SC* 33).

Second, without adding a reference (seemingly an oversight), *SC* quotes the passage from *Mediator Dei* that we cited above, significantly replacing 'the Word of God' by a title that evokes Hebrews, 'the High Priest of the New and Eternal Covenant': 'Jesus Christ, the High Priest of the New and Eternal Covenant, when he assumed a human nature, introduced into this land of exile the hymn that in heaven is sung throughout all ages. He unites the whole community of humankind with himself and associates it with him in singing this divine canticle of praise' (*SC* 83). Earlier, the same constitution has taught that the risen Christ is present 'when the Church prays and *sings*' (*SC* 7; italics ours). Now the document sums up this singing as one 'divine canticle of praise', led by the incarnate 'Cantor' himself, who joins all the human race in singing this heavenly hymn that he brought to earth. Thus the High Priest of the New and Eternal Covenant continues his priestly work through the Church, which is 'ceaselessly engaged in praising the Lord [presumably understood as God the Father] and interceding for the salvation of the entire world' (*SC* 83).

In a way that carries forward what we heard from Augustine, Torrance, and others, Vatican II is saying here: 'The Church intercedes for the entire world; Christ intercedes for the whole world. The Church sings the praises of God; Christ sings the praises of God. The human race praises God; Christ praises God.'[64]

In his *Expositions of the Psalms*, Augustine said: 'it is the one Saviour of his [mystical] body, our Lord Jesus Christ, Son of God, who prays for us, who prays in us, and who is prayed to by us. He prays for us as our priest; he prays in us as our head; he is prayed to by us as our God. Let us therefore recognize in him our voice and in us his voice' (85. 1). Augustine understood the Psalms, in particular, to be the voice of the whole Christ, head and body/members.

---

[64] In picturing Christ as the Choir Master of a universal hymn of praise, this passage in *SC* 83 evokes and builds on (1) the work of praising God by the Old Testament priests in the Temple, 'the house of the Lord' (Ps. 134; 135); and (2) the 'sacrifice of praise' inculcated by Hebrews (Heb. 13: 15–16).

Vatican II gives us a modern and extended version of this image. Christ in his priestly role is understood as having inaugurated, through his incarnation, the final singing of the divine praises on earth. He is pictured not as offering a sacrifice in a sanctuary (see Hebrews) but as associating with himself not merely those who come to know and believe in him but also the whole human community, and doing so to form a cosmic chorus of which he is obviously the leader. The passage in *SC* 83 strikingly portrays the active, priestly presence of Christ in and with all human beings. The unity of the whole human race in him, which began with the incarnation, must be understood to be strengthened through the resurrection. Finally, it will be perfected when human beings reach 'the halls of heaven' and join the celestial choir. This picture of Christ the priestly and cosmic Choir Master serves to symbolize the union of all, baptized and non-baptized alike. Even those who have not yet heard his name are mysteriously but truly in the hands of Christ the Priest and Choir Master of the world. He constantly presents humanity's cause and praise to the Creator.

Promulgated a year after *SC*, *LG* names Christ as 'Teacher, Shepherd and Priest' (no. 21) or, using one equivalent title in his threefold office, as 'Teacher, King, and Priest' of the 'new and universal' people of God (no. 13). Distinguishing 'the common priesthood of the faithful' from 'the ministerial or hierarchical priesthood', *LG* adds that 'each in its own proper way shares in the one priesthood of Christ', which is a 'royal priesthood' (no. 10). *LG* completes the threefold scheme when it moves on to say that 'the holy People of God shares also in Christ's prophetic office' (no. 12).

Given its scope as a constitution on the Church, *LG* did not set itself to explore and define the priesthood of Christ himself. It was concerned rather to illustrate in detail how others participated in his priestly, prophetic, and kingly office. Nevertheless, before doing that, in language which Augustine, Torrance, and others would have endorsed, it sets out the living presence and continuous activity of 'the Lord Jesus Christ': in 'the person of the bishops, to whom the priests render assistance', this 'supreme High Priest is present in the midst of the faithful. Though seated at the right hand of God the Father, he is not absent.' But, through the service of the bishops, he 'preaches [present tense] the Word of God to all peoples, administers [present

tense] ceaselessly' the 'sacraments of faith', and 'directs and guides [present tense] the people of the New Testament on their journey towards eternal beatitude' (no. 21). This vision of Christ as the ever-active prophet, priest, and shepherd/king shapes what the Council wishes to say about the bishops as 'teachers of doctrine, ministers of sacred worship, and holders of office in government' (no. 20).

The document invests further time in unpacking the prophetic, priestly, and kingly ministry of *bishops*: as, first, preachers, teachers, and 'heralds of the faith' (no. 25); as, second, 'stewards of the grace' of the fullness of priesthood (no. 26); and as, third, 'vicars and legates of Christ' who 'govern the particular churches assigned to them' (no. 27). The text then applies the threefold office to *priests*: 'after the image of Christ, the supreme and eternal priest (Heb. 5: 1–10; 7: 24; 9: 11–28), they are consecrated in order to preach the Gospel and shepherd the faithful as well as to celebrate divine worship' (no. 28). Where the bishops are pictured in their prophetic, priestly, and kingly roles, the order is varied, at least here, for priests: they 'preach', 'shepherd', and 'celebrate divine worship'.

Finally, chapter 4 elaborates the threefold office of the laity as priests, prophets, and kings (in that order). First of all, 'Christ Jesus, the supreme and eternal Priest', 'intimately joins' the laity to 'his life and mission', and gives them 'a share in his priestly office' to offer spiritual worship in the Holy Spirit 'for the glory of the Father and the salvation of the world' (no. 34). Second, Christ, 'the great prophet who proclaimed the kingdom of the Father', now 'fulfills this prophetic office not only by the hierarchy who teach in his name . . . but also by the laity'. He 'establishes them as witnesses' and 'powerful heralds of the faith' (no. 35). Third, 'the Lord also desires that his kingdom be spread by the lay faithful'—the kingly office of the laity that is developed at even more length than their priestly and prophetic office (no. 36).

In its fourth and final session the Second Vatican Council promulgated two decrees, first *AA* in November 1965 and then *PO* in December 1965, which developed *LG* by spelling out in specific detail what sharing in the threefold office of Christ entailed in the lives of lay persons and priests, respectively. Never before in the history of Roman Catholicism had a general council published documents dedicated to the life and ministry of lay people and priests. Never

before had a council attended to the royal priesthood (and prophetic office) conferred on all the baptized. Even if the Council of Trent (see Chapter 8 above) had something to teach about the ordained priest-hood in its decrees on the Mass and the sacrament of order, *PO* (along with what we have already gleaned from *LG*) went beyond the limited view of priesthood offered by Trent. Most importantly, it insisted that preaching the Word is an essential and, indeed, primary obligation of ministerial priests.

Thus far this book has gathered from the Scriptures and tradition relevant witness to the way Christ exercised and exercises his priest-hood and to the way he shares it with his followers, both in the ministerial priesthood and the priesthood of all the baptized. On the basis of all that witness we now address the two central questions of this book: What are the characteristics of Christ's priesthood? And how is it shared or should it be shared?

10

Twelve Theses on Christ's Priesthood

Chapters 5 to 9 of this book have shown how little official teaching and theological reflection on Christ's priesthood developed over two thousand years of Christianity. His priesthood was taken for granted and rarely became controversial. Even when controversies emerged, as they did at the Reformation, they focused on those who shared in Christ's priesthood rather than on his priesthood in itself. The most sustained period of reflection on his priestly office came in the seventeenth century. But, even then, the French School concentrated on the spiritual life of all those who shared in the self-sacrificing priesthood of Christ, whether through baptism or through ministerial ordination.

Regularly, even if not always, those who did contribute something to a deepening understanding of Christ's priesthood had all commented on the Letter to the Hebrews (Origen, Chrysostom, Aquinas, Luther, and Calvin). This letter (or, more accurately, homily) is, unquestionably *the* key source for understanding and interpreting the priesthood of Christ. Yet over the centuries Hebrews has not drawn the kind of attention that Christians gave to the Gospels, Romans, and other books of the New Testament. One might speak of a 'marginalizing' of Hebrews, a marginalizing that was associated with, and even encouraged, a diminished interest in the priesthood of Christ.

Given this widespread and chronic reticence about Christ's priesthood, we thought it best to be crisply clear about where we stand and set out our conclusions in the form of theses. Some of the theses that follow will be relatively uncontroversial, others more controversial. But in all cases we will provide our motives for proposing them.

THESIS 1

The Jewish matrix and some New Testament books other than Hebrews are indispensable sources for those who explore the priesthood of Christ. As regards the Jewish matrix that must enter any adequate appreciation of Christ's priesthood, we should first recall (from Chapter 2 above) such passages from Paul as 1 Corinthians 5: 7 ('Christ, our paschal lamb, has been sacrificed'), 1 Corinthians 10: 18 (about the sacrifices that were still going on in the Jerusalem Temple), and Romans 3: 25 (the sacrificial ceremony on the Day of Expiation). Some knowledge of Jewish sources is indispensable for grasping what Paul intends to say. Add too the priestly and sacrificial vision of the whole Church founded by Christ that 1 Peter proposes and that cannot be adequately grasped without reference to relevant passages in Exodus and Isaiah. As we saw also in Chapter 2, the heavenly liturgy in the Book of Revelation which centres on the Lamb is patterned on ceremonies celebrated in the Jerusalem Temple. A reading of Revelation that ignores these ceremonies and Old Testament sources for the vivid language which this apocalyptic book employs will go seriously astray in grasping its message about Christ, Victim and Priest.

The Letter to the Hebrews highlights the impact of Christ's priestly activity in rendering 'obsolete' the 'old covenant', with its priesthood and practices (Heb. 8: 13). Nevertheless, to illuminate Christ's priesthood Hebrews itself draws liberally on Jewish priestly and Temple imagery, as well as picking up very positively the figure of Melchizedek. It also endorses some Old Testament principles about priesthood: for instance, that being 'taken from among human beings' is an indispensable qualification for being appointed a priest by God (Heb. 5: 1), and that priesthood and sacrifice are essentially connected (Heb. 8: 3).

Despite this sense of some continuity with the past, Hebrews is bent on expounding the novelty of Christ's high priesthood. He radically changed the nature of priesthood: by replacing a past of many priests in becoming 'the one proper Priest' (Newman), and, as we shall see, by bringing a massive revision in what sacrifice means. In this context we must note the persistent temptation to play down the discontinuity and return to a Levitical-style priesthood, or at least to press excessively into service themes from the priesthood of Aaron

when delineating the ministerial priesthood derived from Christ. We saw (in Chapter 5) this trend setting in as early as 1 Clement. In the sixteenth century the Reformers zealously denounced ways in which Catholic priesthood had returned to Levitical styles and practices. Serious reflection on the Letter to the Hebrews should have checked these abuses.

At the same time, the author of Hebrews never makes or implies the claim: 'read my text and you will know everything you need to know about Christ's priesthood and about sharing in it through universal and ministerial priesthood.' Along with its elaborated vision of Christ the new High Priest entering the heavenly sanctuary with his own blood (to expiate sins and establish the new covenant), and in his risen glory continuing to intercede for humanity, Hebrews evokes (without developing fully or even to some extent) other key themes in the narrative of that priesthood: the divine kingdom preached by Jesus; his institution of the Eucharist (probably); his crucifixion (certainly; see Heb. 6: 6; 12: 2). The Last Supper and the crucifixion (followed by his glorious resurrection) enter the story as defining moments in the narrative of Christ's priesthood. We need the Gospels (and, to some extent, Paul) to fill out those moments for us, just as we rely on the Gospels to know and appreciate the years of Jesus' public ministry, which can and should be read in a priestly key as well as in a prophetic/teaching key. The Gospels, even if briefly, present the risen Christ as sending (and empowering through the Spirit) chosen representatives among his followers to carry that prophetic/priestly/kingly ministry out to the whole world (e.g. Matt. 28: 19–20). Thus, we must call not only on Hebrews but also on other books of the New Testament to form and fashion an adequate version of Christ's priesthood. Hebrews is required but not sufficient reading for the central theme of this book.

THESIS 2

The Son of God became a priest, or rather the High Priest, when he took on the human condition.

From the time of Hebrews right down to the twentieth century (e.g. Chrysostom, Augustine, Aquinas, Calvin, Newman, and Torrance), Christian theologians have repeatedly insisted that the Son of God would not have exercised his priestly office unless he had truly taken on the integral human condition. His humanity was essential to his priesthood.

Augustine developed this theme though his image of Christ as 'the humble doctor': becoming the Priest for the human family involved Christ in a radical self-humbling. Torrance distinguished between (1) the Church rightly recognizing Christ's divine identity by adoring him 'equally with the Father and the Holy Spirit', and (2) a misguided reaction to Arianism that gave rise to liturgical texts that reduced the place given to the human priesthood of Christ. Any such excessive reactions in defence of Christ's true divinity at the expense of his humanity entail losing a proper appreciation of his priesthood. That priesthood stands or falls with his being fully and truly human.

THESIS 3

The priesthood of Christ and its exercise began with the incarnation.
We saw in Chapter 4 how Hebrews understood Christ's priesthood to embrace his entire life—from his coming into the world to do God's will (Heb. 10: 5–7) and living a 'holy, blameless, and undefiled' life (7: 26) during all 'the days of his flesh' (5: 7). To be sure, for Hebrews the death, resurrection, and glorification of Christ characterized essentially his priesthood. But this did not mean that everything which came before, above all his public ministry, was a mere prelude to the *real* exercise of his priesthood. The priestly narrative of Hebrews embraced the whole story, right from Christ's first coming into the world. His priesthood began with incarnation (so e.g. Chrysostom and Calvin).

In Chapter 8 we quoted some vivid, even baroque, language from Bérulle, Condren, and Olier about the exercise of Christ's priesthood starting within the 'temple' of Mary's womb. As Bérulle put it, 'the heart of the Virgin is the first altar on which Jesus offered his heart, body, and spirit as a host of perpetual praise . . . making the first

perpetual oblation of himself, through which . . . we are all made holy'. This was to presuppose that Christ's human mind was actualized in a unique way from the first moment of his conception—a view endorsed by Roman Catholics for many centuries but widely abandoned in the course of the twentieth century. Nevertheless, we endorse a central truth that was maintained by the French School with its own imagery: Christ was a priest (or rather the Priest) from the beginning of his human existence, and did not first become a priest only at some later stage: for instance, at the Last Supper, at his crucifixion, or even only at his glorious ascension.

THESIS 4

In his public ministry Jesus exercised a priestly ministry.
As we argued in Chapter 1, the prophetic teaching and miraculous activity of Jesus during his public ministry should also be recognized as priestly. After the Holy Spirit descended on him at his baptism, Jesus inaugurated his work of evangelization. Right from the time of the New Testament (Acts 10: 38), that descent of the Spirit was understood to be an anointing for a mission, which should be understood not only in a prophetic and kingly key but also in a priestly key. (In our next thesis we will present something on the way in which the three 'offices' of Christ mutually condition each other.)

In our Preface we reported ten points about the priesthood of Christ that can be drawn from the presentation of that priesthood in two landmark documents published in 1982: *Baptism, Eucharist and Ministry* from the Faith and Order Commission of the World Council of Churches, and the *Final Report* from the Anglican–Roman Catholic International Commission. Neither *BEM* nor the *Final Report* listed the public ministry of Jesus as an essential feature in the exercise of his priesthood. This was a serious omission, and somewhat puzzling when one recalls (1) the vehement criticisms that came from the Reformers against the priests of their day for neglecting the ministry of the Word, and (2) the primary place given to preaching in Vatican II's account of the priestly ministry (see Chapter 9 above). This sixteenth-century challenge and the

twentieth-century response should have alerted those responsible for composing *BEM* and the *Final Report* to the relevance of Jesus' public ministry for any complete view of his priesthood.

The public ministry of Jesus entered essentially into the exercise of his priesthood (see e.g. Origen, Luther, and the French School). His total dedication to the cause of God's kingdom substantiated what the Letter to the Hebrews said in summing up the priestly work of the incarnate Son: he came to do God's will (Heb. 10: 7). Jesus' role as teacher/preacher exemplified what Jeremiah and other Old Testament witnesses had said about *instructing* God's people as a distinguishing feature of priesthood (see Chapter 1 above). It also anticipated Paul's preaching the good news, which the apostle understood to be a priestly, liturgical ministry (Rom. 15: 16). Since Paul interpreted his ministry of proclamation as a priestly service (see Chapter 2 above), *a fortiori* we should say this also about Jesus' proclamation of God's kingdom.

Right from his first chapter, Mark (and then the later evangelists) understood that being active in proclaiming/teaching was inseparable from Jesus' being active in healing and other miraculous activity. Since Jesus' teaching was priestly, so too was his activity as healer. Teaching and healing were two distinguishable but inseparable expressions of his priestly identity and activity. By preaching, healing, and forgiving sins, Jesus built up a 'community of the faithful', those who accepted his message of God's kingdom that was already breaking into the world.

One can summarize much of the public ministry of Jesus by speaking of him as feeding people at 'two tables'. Centuries later Augustine, when commenting on the Lord's Prayer, identified 'our daily bread' as both our daily material needs and our daily spiritual bread, with the latter including both the Word of God and the Eucharist. In this double perspective of the 'Bread of Life', Christ sustains his followers for time and eternity (John 6: 25–65).[1] Augustine initiated an enduring tradition of interpretation, which would find expression and endorsement at the Second Vatican Council: 'Christians draw nourishment through the Word of God from the

---

[1] *Commentary on the Lord's Sermon on the Mount*, trans. D. J. Kavanagh (Washington, DC: Catholic University of America Press, 1951), 135.

double table of holy Scripture and the Eucharist' (*PO* 18).[2] This theme finds its counterpart or 'early intimation' (to use Newman's language about the development of doctrine) in the ministry of Jesus. His priestly outreach to people took a double form: he both fed them with his teaching and shared his presence with them by joining them for meals. Those meals, especially his eating with the sinful and disreputable, characterized Jesus' priestly ministry (e.g. Mark 2: 13–17 parr.; Luke 19: 1–10).

The most vivid picture of Jesus nourishing people at a 'double table' comes from the stories of the feeding of five thousand (Mark 6: 30–44 parr.) and then of four thousand hungry people (Mark 8: 1–10 par.). The former group seem to have been predominantly Jewish and the latter predominantly Gentile—a way of expressing how Jesus' mission went out to all people.[3] In the first story Jesus 'taught' (Mark 6: 34), 'healed' the sick (Matt. 14: 14), or both taught and healed (Luke 9: 11) before feeding them. In the second story, situated in Gentile territory (the Decapolis), a 'great crowd' (Mark 8: 1; see Matt. 15: 30) was drawn to Jesus by his healing and teaching activity. What he does in feeding people on both occasions foreshadows the Last Supper and the institution of the Eucharist (see Chapter 1 above). During his ministry and at its end, Jesus nourishes people in a 'double' and priestly way.

THESIS 5

The three 'offices' of Jesus are distinguishable but inseparable.
The last chapter documented the way Newman came to appreciate how the priesthood of Christ must be understood with his other two 'offices', and vice versa. Earlier (Chapter 7) we saw how, in Luther's thought, Christ's kingship was seamlessly linked with his priest-

---

[2] This theme of the 'double table' is expressed more fully in Vatican II's Dogmatic Constitution on Divine Revelation, *Dei Verbum* ('The Word of God'), 21; see also the decree on the renewal of religious life, *Perfectae Caritatis* ('Perfect Charity'), 6.
[3] See G. O'Collins, *Salvation For All: God's Other Peoples* (Oxford: Oxford University Press, 2008), 82–3. On the two feeding stories, see J. P. Meier, *A Marginal Jew: Rethinking the Historical Jesus*, ii (New York: Doubleday, 1994), 950–66, 1022–38.

hood,[4] and how Calvin elaborated more effectively the doctrine of the threefold office, with Christ being inseparably priest, shepherd/ king, *and* prophet/teacher—a development treasured and endorsed in the twentieth century by Karl Barth.

The canon of the New Testament includes an entire book on the priesthood of Christ (Hebrews). Even if there are no corresponding books on Christ as prophet and/or on Christ as king, the New Testament thoroughly justifies acknowledging the prophetic and kingly office of Christ. In Chapter 1 we drew together from the Gospels the reasons for recognizing Jesus to be prophet and king, albeit in his own way. To that evidence one might add some witness from other New Testament books.

For example, Revelation, when evoking the divine victory over the Antichrist and his empire, tells its readers that the Lamb who was slain will conquer them, because 'he is Lord of lords and King of kings' (Rev. 17: 14). Those royal titles recur a little later, when we learn that the rider at the head of the heavenly armies bears not only the name of 'the Word of God' (Rev. 19: 13) but also that of 'King of kings and Lord of lords' (Rev. 19: 16). By associating the 'Word of God', who presumably bears a divine message and witnesses to the truth of God, closely with the 'King of kings', Revelation in its own dramatic way connects Christ's prophetic and kingly roles.[5] This same book has already connected these roles in its opening chapter by calling Christ 'the faithful witness' and 'the ruler of the kings of the earth' (Rev. 1: 5). This 'faithful witness' testifies to the truth, and so is also named as 'the faithful and true witness'

---

[4] A fascinating modern counterpart to this intimate association Luther recognized between Christ's kingship and priesthood is found in the Feast of Christ the King instituted by Pope Pius XI in 1925. Addressing God the Father, the preface says: 'You anointed Jesus Christ, your only Son, with the oil of gladness, as the eternal priest and universal king. As priest he offered his life on the altar of the cross and redeemed the human race by this one perfect sacrifice of peace. As king he claims dominion over all creation, that he may present to you, his almighty Father an eternal and universal kingdom: a kingdom of truth and life, a kingdom of holiness and grace, a kingdom of justice, love, and peace.' Christ is being celebrated as King, but the preface (and, to some extent, the prayer over the gifts and the prayer after communion), without any special pleading, also attend to the priesthood of Christ.

[5] Some think here of the picture in Wisd. 18: 15 of God's 'stern warrior', the all-powerful word who leaps down from heaven to slay the first-born of the Egyptians. But see G. B. Caird, *The Revelation of St John the Divine* (2nd edn., London: A. & C. Black, 1984), 244.

(Rev. 3: 14). Once again, a close association of Christ's prophetic and kingly roles crops up in the text of Revelation.

It is Hebrews that supplies full warrant for naming Christ 'priest', although, as we have seen in Chapters 1 and 2, other books of the New Testament witness, at least implicitly, to his priestly office. Revelation, as we showed in Chapter 2, pictures a kind of heavenly victimhood of Christ through the figure of the Lamb who was slain, but does not call him 'priest'. It comes very close to doing so, however, when it speaks of him as having 'freed us [or possibly 'washed us'] by his blood' (Rev. 1: 5). A love that drove him to accept a sacrificial victimhood is prominent here, but the active (rather than passive) role of Christ in the sacrifice is to the fore: 'he freed/washed us.' This amounts to calling Christ simultaneously 'priest' and 'victim'.

The New Testament testifies, then, to Jesus as priest, prophet, and king, with 'king' being easily the commonest of these three titles. Only eight titles of Jesus occur more than twenty times in the New Testament, and 'king' comes in seventh with thirty-eight occurrences. 'Priest', 'prophet', and 'king' find a home, then, among the many distinctive names or titles with which the New Testament designates Jesus, and belong among the earliest answers to the question: 'who/what do you say that I am?' (see Mark 8: 27–9 parr.). The sheer number of his titles (well over one hundred in the New Testament) bears eloquent witness to the fact that no one title exhausts the personal mystery of Christ and his redemptive work.[6]

It is crushingly obvious that, for the authors of the New Testament, 'priest', 'prophet', and 'king' are not disconnected but are strictly interrelated in articulating a threefold dimension of Christ's ministry and redemptive work. These three titles and the 'offices' to which they refer mutually condition each other. Christ's priestly role is also prophetic and kingly; his prophetic role is also priestly and kingly; his kingly role is also prophetic and priestly.

---

[6] The Letter to the Hebrews calls Jesus 'priest' six times and 'high priest' ten times. For further leads and statistics on the titles of Jesus in the New Testament, see G. O'Collins, 'Images of Jesus and Modern Theology', in S. E. Porter *et al.* (eds), *Images of Christ Ancient and Modern* (Sheffield: Sheffield Academic Press, 1997), 128–43; id., 'Images of Jesus: Reappropriating Titular Christology', *Theology Digest*, 44 (1997), 303–18; id., 'Jesus as Lord and Teacher', in J. C. Cavadini and L. Holt (eds.), *Who Do You Say That I Am? Confessing the Mystery of Christ* (Notre Dame, Ind.: University of Notre Dame Press, 2004), 51–61.

THESIS 6

The priesthood of Christ involved him not only in being tried and tested
but also in becoming vulnerable to lethal persecution.
By speaking merely of his 'sacrifice', *BEM* and the *Final Report* were
content to use an umbrella term to recall Christ's sufferings, but did
not pause to recognize, as Hebrews does, how extreme vulnerability
belonged to the 'job description' of Christ's priesthood. By becoming
a human priest, the incarnate Son of God made himself vulnerable to
suffering and violent death (Heb. 5: 7–8). Becoming a priest involved
becoming a victim—a new and disturbing aspect of Christ's priesthood. This becoming personally the victim took him quite beyond
the job description not only of Levitical priests (who sacrificed
animals as victims) but also of Melchizedek (who offered some
bread and wine and was held up by Hebrews as foreshadowing
Jesus the High Priest to come). *BEM* and the *Final Report* rightly
invoke 'sacrifice' when sketching the nature of Christ's priesthood.
But they would have followed Hebrews more closely if they had also
mentioned that Christ accepted in faith the suffering destiny involved
in realizing to the full his own priesthood—a theme cherished by the
French School.

   In preparing for the picture of Jesus whose own faith led him to
endure the shame and extreme pain of death by crucifixion (Heb. 12:
2),[7] Hebrews introduces a long roll-call of heroes and heroines of
faith. Right from the opening example of Abel, it is clear that faith
regularly made these men and women vulnerable to suffering, per-

---

[7] When the author writes of Jesus as 'the pioneer and perfecter of faith', he means
Jesus' own faith, as commentators almost unanimously recognize. C. R. Koester
writes: Jesus 'takes faith to its goal, going where others have not yet gone. He is the
source and model of faith for others ... Jesus pioneers and completes faith by fully
trusting God and remaining faithful to God in a way' that others are to follow
(*Hebrews* (New York: Doubleday, 2001), 523). Curiously, a number of outstanding
translations, like the New Jerusalem Bible of 1985 and the New Revised Standard
Version of 1989, insert an 'our' that is not found in the original Greek text and
translate accordingly: 'the pioneer and perfecter of our faith' (NRSV) and 'Jesus, who
leads us in our faith and brings it to perfection' (NJB). See G. O'Collins, *Christology:
A Biblical, Historical, and Systematic Study of Jesus* (2nd edn., Oxford: Oxford
University Press, 2009), 262–80.

secution, and even violent death. Hebrews notes that many of these persons of faith were tortured, mocked, flogged, and imprisoned (Heb. 11: 35–6), as well as mentioning three ways in which some of them died: 'they were stoned to death, they were sawn in two, they were killed by the sword' (11: 37). In this list of heroes and heroines of faith we find one royal name, King David (11: 32), a general reference to 'the prophets' (also vs. 32), but no priests as such, even if several of those listed (like Abel, Noah, Abraham, and King David himself) did on occasion perform some cultic, priestly action (see Chapter 1 above).

The Gospels report that Jesus recognized that a prophetic vocation might well involve suffering and even violent death: 'Jerusalem, Jerusalem, the city that kills the prophets and stones those who are sent to it!' (Matt. 23: 37 par.; see also Matt. 23: 34 par.). Jesus is also remembered as having mentioned the killing of Zechariah (Matt. 23: 35 par.), a priest who, by command of King Joash, was stoned to death 'in the court of the house of the Lord' (2 Chron. 24: 20–2). There are good grounds for taking these statements as stemming substantially from Jesus, and thus concluding to what should be a relatively uncontroversial position: Jesus himself acknowledged the dangers that attended a prophetic and priestly vocation.[8] He clearly thought of himself and his mission *also* in prophetic terms (Mark 6: 4 parr.). That he understood his vocation *also* in priestly terms appears a reasonable conclusion from the narratives of the Last Supper (see next thesis). He seems *also* to have in some sense thought of himself in kingly terms. We might base this conclusion on such passages as his interchange with James and John when they ask to sit on Jesus' right hand and left in his coming royal glory (Mark 10: 35–45 parr.). Jesus' ominous reply about what his kingship will involve, the 'cup' that he will drink and the 'baptism' with which he will be baptized, more than hint at the suffering to come. It will culminate with his being crucified on the charge of being a dangerous royal pretender (Mark 15: 26). That charge suggests that Jesus had given an impression of claiming, at least implicitly, some kind of royal authority. Where the charge affixed to the cross indicated that Pontius Pilate

---

[8] See J. Nolland, *The Gospel of Matthew* (Grand Rapids, Mich.: Eerdmans, 2005), 942, 945–8, 950–1.

thought of that kingship as a threat to public order, Jesus himself understood his kingship in terms of service and suffering.[9]

Unquestionably, we cannot draw from the historical witness of the Gospels a picture of Jesus clearly enunciating his threefold office as priest, prophet, and king. But there are good reasons for concluding that (1) he understood his mission in terms of prophetic, kingly, and priestly functions, and (2) knew the deadly risks inherent in these functions (for further details see Chapter 1). In particular, as we shall argue in the next thesis, he knew the exercise of his priesthood to involve him in suffering and a violent death. At the Last Supper he dramatized what Hebrews expressed about the utter vulnerability of his priestly vocation.

THESIS 7

At the Last Supper, when instituting the Eucharist as a sacrificial meal, Jesus committed himself through a cultic, priestly act to his self-sacrificing death.

Here we come to the first of the three supremely defining moments in the narrative of Christ's priesthood: the Last Supper, the crucifixion, and the resurrection into glory. This thesis bristles with controversial points—not least over two central issues, the first more general and the second more particular.

First, what is 'sacrifice', and is it still viable language for Christians? Many people find the idea of the sacrifice of a human being and, especially, of a totally innocent human being strange and even morally repulsive, especially when it is presented as 'placating' an angry, 'bloodthirsty' God. Nico Schreurs makes the claim: 'sacrifices in general and blood sacrifices, in particular, disgust most of our contemporaries.'[10] Years earlier, J. S. Whale pointed out how for many people the very idea of such sacrifices is 'revolting' and both 'morally

---

[9] See O'Collins, *Christology,* 67–80.

[10] N. Schreurs, 'A Non-Sacrificial Interpretation of Christian Redemption', in T. Merrigan and J. Haers (eds.), *The Myriad Christ: Plurality and the Quest for Unity in Contemporary Christology* (Leuven: Leuven University Press, 2000), 551.

and aesthetically disgusting'.[11] In the Western world and beyond, the language of sacrifice seems irreconcilable with contemporary 'ideals' of self-realization and self-fulfilment, the 'good life' promoted by endless advertisements and TV soap operas. Add too that political rhetoric about dying for one's country which has been employed for two thousand years or more—not least by unscrupulous modern leaders. For the sake of power, wealth, and prestige, they have debased the language of sacrifice and self-sacrifice and led millions to their death. Perhaps the sharpest criticisms levelled at sacrificial interpretations of the Last Supper and Christ's death have come from contemporary feminism. Some feminist theologians point out how some traditional presentations of Christ the innocent victim sacrificing himself to atone for the sins of others have been misused to legitimate the sufferings of innumerable women. They have been encouraged to endure all kinds of violent injustice and victimization by imitating the self-sacrificial love and redemptive death of Christ.[12]

One can understand why, for various reasons, Ernst Käsemann and others have wanted to abandon the whole notion of sacrifice.[13] And yet this would mean also refusing to follow the Letter to the Hebrews and the mainstream Christian tradition in naming Christ as 'priest'. From Hebrews and Chrysostom, right down to Torrance and beyond, calling Christ 'priest' stands or falls with the correlative reality of sacrifice. If we give up speaking of sacrificial self-offering, we should also drop the language of his priesthood. Undoubtedly the language of sacrifice has at times been massively misused, but the witness of Hebrews and other New Testament authors makes it a normative way of characterizing Christ's death and resurrection. Below we return to appropriate ways of using sacrificial language.

---

[11] J. S. Whale, *Victor and Victim* (Cambridge: Cambridge University Press, 1960), 42.

[12] See e.g. M. Grey, *Redeeming the Dream: Feminism, Redemption and Christian Tradition* (London: SPCK, 1989); R. R. Ruether, *Introducing Redemption in Christian Feminism* (Sheffield: Sheffield Academic Press, 1998).

[13] E. Käsemann, *Jesus Means Freedom*, trans. G. Krodel (Philadelphia: Fortress Press, 1970), 114. In his *Le Salut par la croix dans la théologie contemporaine (1930–85)* (Paris: Cerf, 1988), Michel Deneken puts the case for simply banishing 'sacrifice' from Christian vocabulary.

But, second, can we apply the language of sacrifice to what Christ committed himself to at the Last Supper? Did Christ's institution of the Eucharist take a sacrificial form (so, for example, Cyprian, Chrysostom, and the Council of Trent)? Or, through his words and gestures at the Last Supper, did Christ leave his followers a 'testament' or 'covenant' (Luther), a loving 'remembrance' of the sacrifice made on Calvary (Calvin)? Obviously traditional Catholicism and traditional Protestantism collide at this point. Should our interpretation of what Christ did for his followers and bequeathed to them on the night before he died lead us to speak of 'the sacrifice of the Mass', or to use rather the 'meal' language involved in speaking of 'the sacrament of the Lord's Supper'? The 'sacrifice' language entails speaking of an ordained priest 'offering the sacrifice of the Mass', whereas the 'meal' language entails speaking of an ordained minister (or simply someone designated by the community) 'presiding at the Lord's Supper'.

Maintaining 'Sacrifice'

There is much about sacrifice and, in particular, cultic sacrifice in the Old Testament, even if it nowhere offers a rationale for sacrifice. In general, publicly recognized priests offered, ritually and in the name of the people, sacrifices in some kind of sacred setting. These authorized priests served God at an altar and performed cultic, sacrificial acts on behalf of the community. Sacrifices took three forms: (1) gift-offerings of praise and thanksgiving, (2) sin-offerings, and (3) communion-offerings or covenantal sacrifices involving a communion meal.[14]

The Old Testament also used the language of sacrifice in a wider sense, as being a matter of inner dispositions and praiseworthy behaviour. Thus, Psalm 51 appears to have ended originally by proposing a 'contrite heart' as 'the sacrifice pleasing to God'

---

[14] Along with the references provided in Ch. 1, see also G. A. Anderson and H.-J. Klauck, 'Sacrifice and Sacrificial Offerings', *ABD* v. 871–91; I. Bradley, *The Power of Sacrifice* (London: Darton, Longman & Todd, 1995); P. Gerlitz *et al.*, 'Opfer', *TRE* xxv. 251–99; and G. O'Collins, *Jesus Our Redeemer: A Christian Approach to Salvation* (Oxford: Oxford University Press, 2007), 156–72.

(vs. 17). A later addition (from the time of the Babylonian captivity or shortly thereafter) aimed to modify what seemed an anti-cultic sentiment and to bring the psalm into line with liturgical ritual. It asked God to 'rebuild the walls of Jerusalem. Then you will delight in right sacrifice, in burnt offerings and whole burnt offerings; then bulls will be offered on your altar' (vv. 18–19). But the wider, non-cultic sense of sacrifice would also persist.

In any case, the Old Testament taught (see Chapter 1) that external rituals were worthless without (1) the corresponding interior dispositions, and (2) compassionate behaviour. One psalm acknowledged that doing God's will counts for more than any formal sacrifices of thanksgiving (Ps. 40: 6–8); these verses would be quoted and endorsed by Hebrews 10: 5–7. Matthew would explain Jesus' practice of forgiveness by having him quote Hosea 6: 6 and so challenge conventional ideas about divine forgiveness and sacrificial sin-offerings: 'I desire mercy and not sacrifice' (Matt. 9: 13; see also 12: 7). A wise scribe was to react to Jesus' teaching on love towards God and neighbour by declaring that practising such love 'is more important than all burnt offerings and sacrifices' (Mark 12: 33 parr.). The prophet Micah provided an Old Testament warrant for such a position: rather than all manner of burnt offerings and other sacrifices, what God expects of his people is 'to do justice, and to love kindness, and to walk humbly with your God' (Mic. 6: 6–8).

St Paul, as we saw in Chapter 2, used the terminology of sacrifice in both a cultic (e.g. 1 Cor. 5: 7) and a non-cultic way. Gordon Fee illustrates how the apostle's use of the imagery of *blood* shows how he understood Christ's death in a cultic, sacrificial way.[15] The non-cultic sense was to the fore when he appealed to the Christians of Rome: 'present your bodies (= your selves) as a living sacrifice, holy and acceptable to God, which is your spiritual [or 'reasonable'] worship' (Rom. 12: 1). The apostle called on believers to live self-sacrificing lives. Sacrifice was not merely something that had happened on their behalf; it was something in which they should be intimately involved,

---

[15] G. D. Fee, 'Paul and the Metaphors of Salvation', in S. T. Davis, D. Kendall, and G. O'Collins (eds.), *The Redemption* (Oxford: Oxford University Press, 2004), 43–67, at 55–60.

even to the point of self-surrender to a new, demanding form of existence in the sight of God.

Augustine of Hippo also took up the theme of sacrifice in both ways. On the one hand, he declared: 'he [Christ] is a priest in that he offered himself as a holocaust for expiating and purging away our sins' (*Sermo*, 198. 5).[16] On the other hand, Augustine stressed the interior relationship of love, without which the mere external performance of ritual would never bring the desired communion with God: 'all the divine precepts', which 'refer to sacrifices either in the service of the tabernacle [in the desert] or of the temple [in Jerusalem]', are to be understood symbolically 'to refer to the love of God and neighbour. For "on these two commandments depend the whole Law and the Prophets" [Matt. 20: 40]' (*The City of God*, 10. 5). It was the interior disposition that gave value to the exterior, cultic actions: 'a sacrifice is the visible sacrament or sacred sign of an invisible sacrifice' (ibid.). The external sacrificial gift must symbolize the inner, invisible sacrifice—a conviction strongly endorsed not only by the Reformers but also by others writing earlier (e.g. Origen) and later (the French School).

In the light of Psalm 51, Thomas Aquinas endorsed a broad, non-cultic account of sacrifice: 'whatever is offered to God in order to raise the human spirit to him, may be called a sacrifice' (*STh*. 3a. 22. 2). Yet in the very same article Aquinas proposed a more cultic reading of sacrifice, or at least of the sacrifice of Christ, who was 'a perfect victim, being at the same time victim for sin, victim for a peace-offering, and a holocaust'.

Like many others before and after him, Aquinas drew here on the Letter to the Hebrews. That extensive treatment of Christ as 'high priest according to the order of Melchizedek' (Heb. 5: 10; 6: 20), as we saw in Chapter 3, lavishly used imagery from sacrificial rituals prescribed for the Levitical priesthood, with the aim of showing both (1) the superiority of Christ's own priesthood and (2) the superiority of the sacrifice Christ offered once and for all (Heb. 5: 10; 6: 20). At the same time, Hebrews recalled that Christ did not die in a sacred setting but in a profane place, with his bloody death on a cross

---

[16] *Sermons* III/11. *Newly Discovered Sermons*, trans. E. Hill (Hyde Park, NY: New City Press, 1997), 219.

occurring 'outside the city gate' (Heb. 13: 11–13). Despite the pervasive cultic imagery, Hebrews ended with a non-cultic version of the sacrifice of Christ, priest and victim.

The Letter to the Hebrews encourages eight convictions about Christ's priesthood and the strictly related reality of sacrifice.

(1) We should not simply apply to his sacrifice and priesthood models we have drawn from elsewhere. We would miss much of what Christ did and does as priest, if we try to describe and explain it *even* along the lines of the Levitical priesthood which, according to tradition, had been developed by Moses at the command of God. There is something radically new about the sacrifice and priesthood of Christ. We should evaluate priesthood and sacrifice in the light of Christ, and not vice versa. The author of Hebrews approached Christ's death and resurrection in the light of existing notions of sacrifice, only to reinterpret dramatically these inherited images and views.[17]

Both in the ancient world and later, sacrifice was normally understood as human beings in a cultic setting surrendering something valuable to God (especially a victim who was slain), with a view to bringing about communion with God and changing the participants who took part in the shared feast. Hebrews, however, while presenting Christ as a sacrificial victim in his death, explicitly denied that this death took place in a cultic setting (see above) and at best only hinted at a sacred feast shared by believers (Heb. 13: 9–10). The most startling difference, however, from any 'conventional' understanding of sacrifice, a difference which Hebrews and other New Testament books illustrate, is that it was not human beings who went to God with their gift(s) or victim(s); it was God who provided the means for the sacrifice to take place (e.g. Rom. 3: 25; see Chapter 2 above).

---

[17] Apropos of the modern situation, Robert Daly criticizes those who approach the sacrifice of Christ in the light of conventional theories: 'We have usually started at the wrong end. We should have tried to learn from the Christ-event what it was Christians were trying to express when, at first quite hesitantly, in earliest Christianity they began to speak of the Christ-event . . . as sacrificial; instead, we went to look at the practice of different religions in the world, drawing up a general definition of sacrifice, and then seeing if it were applicable to Christ. The usual definition drawn from the history of religions or cultural anthropology is reasonable enough in itself— but when made to apply to Christ, it is disastrously inadequate': 'Sacrifice Unveiled or Sacrifice Revisited: Trinitarian and Liturgical Perspectives', *Theological Studies*, 64 (2003), 24–42, at 25.

As Hebrews put it, 'in these last days' God provided his Son for the priestly work of 'purification for sins' (Heb. 1: 1–3). The normal roles were reversed: in this sacrificial process the primary initiative was with God and not with human beings. In the words of Edward Kilmartin:

Sacrifice is not, in the *first* place, an activity of human beings directed to God and, in the *second* place, something that reaches its goal in the response of divine acceptance and bestowal of divine blessing on the cultic community. Rather, sacrifice in the New Testament understanding . . . is, in the *first* place, the self-offering of the Father in the gift of the Son, and, in the *second* place, the unique response of the Son in his humanity to the Father, and, in the *third* place, the self-offering of believers in union with Christ by which they share in his covenant relation with the Father.[18]

(2) Whatever Christ did by way of external sacrifice symbolized and expressed his interior self-giving to the Father. Far from being centred on himself, Christ related in love and obedience to God the Father and was ready for painful self-renunciation; he had come to do God's will (Heb. 10: 7, 9). The interior dispositions of Christ made all the difference (see e.g. the French School in Chapter 8).

(3) His whole life was a continual free gift of himself (or sacrifice) to God and others. The compassionate service of others described by the Gospels filled out the obedient self-giving through which the Letter to the Hebrews sums up the human life of Jesus (Heb. 2: 17–18; 5: 1–3). A spirit of sacrifice characterized the entire human existence of the Son of God, from his incarnation through to completing his work of 'purification for sins' and sitting at the right hand of God (Heb. 1: 1–3). It would be a mistake to limit Christ's sacrificial performance to his death and exaltation. The self-giving of his life moved seamlessly into his self-giving at death.

(4) This self-sacrifice should not be understood as if Jesus were a penal substitute, who was punished in the place of sinners and so appeased an angry God. We saw in Chapter 6 how Aquinas opened the door for others to develop this interpretation of sacrifice by calling it 'something which is done to render God due honour with

---

[18] E. Kilmartin, *The Eucharist in the West: History and Theology*, ed. R. J. Daly (Collegeville, Minn.: Liturgical Press, 1998), 381–2; italics ours.

a view to *placating* him' (*STh.* 3a. 48. 3 resp.; italics ours). Luther, Calvin, Catholic preachers such as J. B. Bossuet, and other Christians took to an extreme this view of Christ being punished for sinners and even as a sinner—a morally repulsive view that Hebrews and other New Testament witnesses do not support.[19]

(5) The Letter to the Hebrews, our longest New Testament sacrificial treatment of Christ's death and exaltation, strongly emphasizes something different: the sacrificial death of Jesus purified or *expiated* the defilement of sin. Even then, Hebrews does not reduce the impact of his sacrifice to a cleansing from the 'pollution' of sin. It *also* interprets that sacrifice as sealing a new covenantal relationship between God and human beings (e.g. Heb. 9: 15; 12: 24). We return below to what Christ's sacrifice did both towards expiating sin and bringing a new covenant of love.

(6) Christ's loving acceptance of his passion leads to a further, key element in his priestly sacrifice. Physical pain and other forms of suffering simply as such do not atone for sins and effect human redemption. 'Suffering as such', Aquinas argues, 'is not meritorious.' Only insofar as someone 'suffers willingly' can suffering become 'meritorious' (*STh.* 3a. 48. 1 ad 1). Only because Christ 'suffered out of love' was his death a 'sacrifice' (3a. 48. 4 ad 3).

(7) This sixth point ties in closely with a further conviction: the sheer quantity of suffering that Jesus was to endure in his atrocious death does not decide the value of his self-sacrifice. The Letter to the Hebrews invokes his sufferings (Heb. 5: 7–8) but, unlike Mel Gibson in his film *The Passion of Christ* (2004) and many before him, makes no attempt to highlight the amount of those sufferings, apart from the horrendous, central fact of his dying by crucifixion (Heb. 6: 6). Gibson concentrated on the physical suffering endured by Christ, in order to bring out the enormity of human sin. But the sheer amount of that sacrificial suffering is far less important than the identity of the One who suffered to save a world enormously damaged by sin; that identity is underlined by Hebrews right from its opening verse.

(8) A final reflection in support of reading sacrificially the death (and resurrection) of Christ takes us beyond Hebrews to the Gospel

---

[19] For a rebuttal of the penal substitution theory of Christ's sacrifice, see O'Collins, *Jesus Our Redeemer*, 133–60.

narratives. In responding to two major objections ('Did Jesus commit suicide?' and 'How could God collaborate in the slaying of his
Son?'), we understand the death of Jesus to have come about through
a mysterious convergence of divine love and human malice. Calvary
was the inevitable consequence of Jesus' commitment to his mission
and the service of others, a commitment that he refused to abandon,
even though his words and actions placed him on collision-course
with those in power. By continuing his ministry, going to Jerusalem
for his last Passover, and facing his opponents, Jesus indirectly
brought about the fatal situation. In that sense *he willed his death
by accepting it* rather than by deliberately and directly courting it. He
paid the price for his loving project of bringing life to the world. Thus
we can see how the self-sacrificing death of Jesus was not due to his
positive and direct will (or to that of his Father), but to the abuse of
human freedom on the part of religious and political leaders whose
interests were threatened by the uncompromising message of Jesus.[20]

The Last Supper a Sacrificial Meal?

It is one thing to join Hebrews in holding that the death and exaltation of
Christ was a unique, once-and-for-all sacrifice. It is another to maintain
the sacrificial nature of what Christ did and said at the Last Supper—not
least because any position here will shape one's understanding of the
Eucharist. Let us begin with a more general consideration.

(1) It is hardly controversial to speak either of the self-sacrificing
nature of Christ's life or of his accepting for others, through the
words and gestures he used, a last, deadly confrontation with those in
power. In that sense, the Last Supper integrated into his mission a
final act of service. In death, as in life, he served and sacrificed himself
for others and for the kingdom of God (Mark 14: 25 parr.).

(2) Then, as we noted in Chapter 8, by the time of Jesus the festival
of the Passover had long been given a sacrificial significance. In
Philo's view of universal priesthood, the whole nation functioned

---

[20] See further O'Collins, *Jesus Our Redeemer*, 169–71, as well as what John writes
about the role of Caiaphas in Jesus' death (Ch. 1 above), and what Ch. 4 above says
about the claim that Jesus committed suicide.

as priests when celebrating the Passover. To claim that Jesus (and his companions at the Last Supper) did something sacrificial would not have appeared strange talk in first-century Judaism.

What happened at the Last Supper was, of course, no normal celebration of the Passover: it maintained, strengthened, and personalized the sacrificial significance. Jesus went beyond the normal ritual to introduce gestures and sayings that revealed his priestly intention to offer himself as a self-sacrificing victim. He wanted the breaking of the bread, identified as his body, and the pouring out of his blood to image forth the sacrificial surrender of his life, the priestly action of total self-giving that was about to take place in his violent death.

Through the words and gestures of the 'institution narrative' (Mark 14: 22–4 parr.; 1 Cor. 11: 23–5), Jesus offered a covenant sacrifice—a cultic, priestly act that he wished to be continued as a central practice in the community which he had gathered. Wolfhart Pannenberg sums up the significance of what happened: 'meal and sacrifice go together at the Lord's Supper, just as the covenant sacrifice and covenant meal did in Israel.'[21] As we noted in Chapter 9, Tom Torrance calls the Eucharist 'the Eucharistic sacrifice', and logically does so on the basis of what he says about the Last Supper: through his 'self-consecration' and 'high priestly intercession', Jesus intended that his disciples should be 'presented to the Father through his own self-offering on their behalf'.[22]

Unlike Paul and the three Synoptic Gospels, John does not report the institution of the Eucharist at the Last Supper. Nevertheless, one finds clear Eucharistic references in Jesus' discourse about 'my flesh for the life of the world' and the invitation to 'eat my flesh and drink my blood' (John 6: 51–8). By 'becoming flesh' and assuming a complete human nature (John 1: 14), the incarnate Logos could offer himself in death and so surrender his own physical existence 'for the life of the world'. The reality of Jesus' sacrificial death is expressed through the distinction between the 'flesh' to be eaten and

---

[21] W. Pannenberg, *Systematic Theology*, trans. G. W. Bromiley, iii (Grand Rapids, Mich.: Eerdmans, 1998), 319. See further the section on the Last Supper in Ch. 1 above.

[22] T. F. Torrance, *Theology in Reconciliation: Essays Toward Evangelical and Catholic Unity in East and West* (Eugene, Oreg.: Wipf & Stock Publishers, 1996), 106.

the 'blood' to be drunk: 'eating the flesh and drinking the blood entail that the flesh has been broken and the blood shed.'[23] In the discourse on the Bread of Life, John's Gospel provides its own precious commentary on what Jesus' institution of the Eucharist intended.

In Chapter 7 we documented the strong resistance of the Reformers to a sacrificial interpretation of the Last Supper. In the historical circumstances, this opposition of Luther and Calvin was understandable. The belief that priestly sacrifice had been made and mandated by Christ at the Last Supper had led not only to life-giving Eucharistic practice but also to the abuses of 'multiple Masses' and 'private Masses', as we also recalled in Chapter 7. The Reformers called for Eucharistic celebrations at which the faithful regularly communicated and also did so by receiving from the chalice.

The title and subtitle of Torrance's book (see n. 22 above) bring to mind easily what has happened 'on both sides', so to speak. On the 'Catholic' side the faithful have come to participate much more in the celebration of the Eucharist and to communicate regularly whenever they do so. By mandating the celebration of the Eucharist in the vernacular and a wide availability of 'Communion under two kinds', the bishops of the Catholic Church have, in fact, said 'yes' to two changes that Luther earnestly desired. The call of the Reformers and members of Roman Catholic religious institutes to hear and preach the Word of God was also heard in Vatican II's document on the Eucharist. The faithful assembled for the Eucharist should not only be 'nourished at the table of the Lord's Body' but also 'instructed by the Word of God' (*SC* 48).[24]

On the 'Protestant' side, twentieth-century biblical scholars led the way in recognizing the sacrificial implications of a key phrase from the institution narrative: 'do this in *memory* of me'. For the ancient Israelites, 'memorial (*zikkaron*)' was a sacrificial word: a victim burned on the altar was called a 'memorial' or 'reminder'.[25] A new appreciation of the sacrificial significance of 'memorial (*anamnesis*)' and of its counterpart in the words of Jesus (Luke 22: 19; 1 Cor. 11:

---

[23] A. T. Lincoln, *The Gospel According to John* (London: Continuum, 2005), 232.

[24] On the 'double table' of word and sacrament, see Thesis 4 above.

[25] On the significance of 'memory/memorial' for clarifying the sacrificial dimension of the Last Supper, see R. Moloney, *The Eucharist* (London: Geoffrey Chapman, 1995), 42–9.

24–5) found its place in such landmark ecumenical documents as *BEM* and the *Final Report*.[26]

From the 1920s Romano Guardini and others encouraged Catholics to think of the Eucharist as a sacrificial meal and not simply as a sacrifice.[27] Protestant scholars like Pannenberg and Torrance exemplify the shift by heirs of the Reformation in their readiness to recognize how 'meal and sacrifice' go 'together' at the celebration of the Last Supper and in the 'Eucharistic sacrifice' of the Church.[28] Observing this shift still leaves us, however, with a crucial question to be faced in the next chapter: what is the relationship between the Eucharist celebrated by the Christian priests and the sacrificial self-offering of Christ at the Last Supper? But before closing this chapter, we must state five further theses.

THESIS 8

Christ's priestly self-offering at the Last Supper was consummated in the sacrifice of Calvary and its acceptance through his resurrection and exaltation.

This thesis evokes the Letter to the Hebrews and its language about the high-priestly sacrifice of Christ being completed and made perfect when he was raised and exalted to glory and life everlasting in the presence of God. Commenting on the language of 'completion' or 'perfection' that pervades Hebrews, Christopher Koester states: 'Jesus is made complete by his death and exaltation to glory, so that he now serves as high priest forever at God's right hand.'[29] Through his

---

[26] On 'anamnesis' see *BEM* 115–16 ('Eucharist', 5–13); Anglican–Roman Catholic International Commission, *The Final Report* (London: SPCK, 1982), 18–20;

[27] See J. Ratzinger, 'Is the Eucharist a Sacrifice?', *Concilium*, 4/3 (1967), 35–40.

[28] This change allows *BEM* to speak not only of the 'eucharistic meal', 11, 12 ('Eucharist', 2, 12–14) but also of the Eucharist as a 'sacrifice of praise', 10 ('Eucharist', 4).

[29] Koester, *Hebrews*, 123.

suffering, death, and glorification, Jesus has been perfected in his priesthood and its exercise. His death on the cross and glorious resurrection was not only the highest exercise of his priesthood but also brought it to fulfilment—in his definitive life with God.

Eternally interceding now for those still to be brought to completion through the fulfilment of the divine promises, Christ the High Priest presents forever on their behalf to the Father his sacrificial self-offering (see e.g. the French School and Torrance). The 'pioneer/leader' in the project of salvation, Christ 'sanctifies' others, as God the Father 'brings them to glory' (Heb. 2: 10–11). The faithful can see in the suffering and exaltation of their High Priest how God's purposes for them will be realized (Heb. 12: 2).

THESIS 9

The priestly work of Christ brought redemption in three forms: deliverance from evil, purification from the defilement of sin, and loving communion with God in the new covenant.

(1) To have communion with God, human beings must be delivered from the power of death and the devil. Hebrews first speaks briefly of Christ destroying 'the one who has the power of death: that is, the devil' (Heb. 2: 14). In pictorial detail, the letter spells out what this deliverance from evil and sharing in Christ's glory (2: 10) entails. Through being brought to everlasting life in God's presence, those redeemed by Christ will 'enter God's rest' (4: 9–10), join the company of angels (12: 23), and take part in the festal gathering in the heavenly Jerusalem (12: 22). The deliverance *from* evil means deliverance *for* eternal salvation.

(2) Christ's priestly sacrifice was also expiatory and proved itself so in a unique way. The one priestly sacrifice of Christ did something the Levitical priests could not achieve by their repeated sacrifices: it 'cleansed consciences' from sin (Heb. 9: 14; 10: 14, 22). Where the language of deliverance seems less controversial,[30] talk of 'expiation'

---

[30] On 'Redemption as Deliverance from Evil', see O'Collins, *Jesus Our Redeemer*, 116–32.

can encounter difficulty and be misunderstood, above all by being taken as equivalent to 'propitiation'. To introduce the topic, we need to notice that, whereas redemption as victorious deliverance enjoys a broader sense of overcoming not only sin but also Satan, death, and evil in all its forms, expiation concerns sin and its results. It would make no sense to talk of 'expiating death' or 'expiating Satan'. Hebrews directs our gaze to the great Day of Expiation, 'Yom Kippur', which illustrates classically how sin and expiation are correlative. Any interpretation of the expiatory work of Christ's priesthood depends on what we make of the damage brought about by those breakdowns in relations with God, our neighbour, and the created world that constitute sin.[31]

Sin, in all its various manifestations, disrupts the life and fabric of the universe. Wrongdoing damages the sinner and produces evil effects in one's basic relationship with God and in social relationships with other human beings. God is always ready to pardon sinners who allow themselves to be touched by divine grace, acknowledge their guilt, and ask for forgiveness. But God cannot treat an evil past and the lasting damage done by sin as if they were not there. Otherwise, as Anselm of Canterbury pointed out, 'those who sin and those who do not sin would be in the same position before God' (*Cur Deus Homo*, 1. 12). Anselm rightly argued that 'it is impossible for God to be merciful in this way' (ibid. 1. 24). First, sinners themselves need to be changed, to face (sometimes painful) readjustment, and to be rehabilitated. Second, some things—at times, many things—must be repaired and set right. The moral order, damaged by sin, needs to be reordered and purified. This is where expiation comes into play.

The author of Hebrews, like other early Christians, felt at home with the Old Testament language of purifying the contamination caused by sin. Their symbol world included cleansing with blood among the ritual ways of dealing with the evil results of sin. They could appreciate that the sacrificial death of Jesus was 'the means of expiating' these effects through 'his blood' (Rom. 3: 25). As Hebrews put it, the blood of Christ, the High Priest who entered once and for

---

[31] On sin, see ibid. 43–80.

all in the heavenly sanctuary, purifies sinners (Heb. 9: 11–14); his self-sacrificing death wipes away the pollution caused by sin.

Many people in advanced industrial societies, including many Christians, find such language distasteful. Yet they might be reminded of what Mary Douglas argued in a 1993 work: there is a universal feeling that sin somehow defiles human beings.[32] Years earlier she had studied the widespread sense of purity and defilement, pointing out that behind the Code of Holiness in Leviticus and its persistent distinction between clean and unclean lay a common concern for order and completeness. 'Holiness', she wrote, 'means keeping distinct the categories of creation. It therefore involves correct definition, discrimination and order.'[33] The pollution of sin brings dangerous disorder and fragmentation; things must be brought back to harmony and wholeness. Drawing on Douglas, Colin Gunton concluded that 'we shall . . . begin to understand the nature of sacrifice when we come to see its function in the removal of uncleanness which pollutes the good creation'.[34]

(3) Talking of the personal causality of priestly love that instituted a new covenant and communion with God might seem to introduce language that takes us away from the Letter to the Hebrews. Yet that text does portray Christ the High Priest actively mediating a new covenantal relationship with God, which brings a final, festal gathering in 'the city of the living God' (Heb. 12: 22–4). But what of Christ's priestly love? Hebrews invokes love when exhorting Christians to a life of faith, hope, and love (Heb. 10: 22–4), but needs to be enriched by drawing on John (e.g. John 3: 16–17) and Paul (e.g. Rom. 5: 8) for the theme of divine love.

The redemption effected through Christ's priesthood has revealed and communicated the divine love to human kind. The tri-personal God has created the conditions in which our response can be made. One can speak then about the 'empowering', creative quality of the divine love that is embodied in Christ the High Priest and that draws

---

[32] M. Douglas, *In the Wilderness: The Doctrine of Defilement in the Book of Numbers* (Sheffield: Sheffield Academic Press, 1993).

[33] M. Douglas, *Purity and Danger* (Harmondsworth: Penguin, 1970), 53; see also D. P. Wright and H. Hübner, 'Unclean and Clean', *ABD* vi. 729–45.

[34] C. E. Gunton, *The Actuality of Atonement: A Study of Metaphor, Rationality and the Christian Tradition* (Edinburgh: T. & T. Clark, 1988), 119.

men and women to respond freely in love. They are enabled to love by being loved. Human love has the power to generate love; ever so much more does the divine love, at work in the priestly activity of Christ, possess the power to generate love. Hebrews, through its rich language and pictures, presents Christ as vividly and powerfully actualizing God's redeeming love.[35]

THESIS 10

The priesthood of Christ continues forever, since he eternally intercedes for the world and blesses the world, offers himself through the Holy Spirit to the Father, continues to pour out the Holy Spirit upon the Church and the world, acts on earth as primary minister in all the Church's preaching and sacramental life, and in heaven remains for ever the Mediator through whom the blessed enjoy the vision of God and the risen life of glory.

This unpacking of the activities of Christ as High Priest has five parts; let us take them up in turn.

(1) That the exalted Christ exercises forever his priesthood by continuing to intercede for the world comes straight out of the New Testament (e.g. Rom. 8: 34; Heb. 7: 25). That such priestly intercession should be characterized as 'blessing' picks up language from Ephesians about God 'blessing us in/by Christ with every spiritual blessing' (Eph. 1: 3). As we saw at the end of Chapter 6, Torrance speaks happily of an 'eternal benediction' being mediated by the exalted Christ, who remains forever the mediator of heavenly blessings and benefits.

(2) In Chapter 5 we cited Augustine on the eternal self-offering of Christ: 'as our Priest risen from the dead and established in heaven, Christ now offers sacrifice on our behalf'. Condren, Olier, and other notable Christian witnesses followed suit in understanding Christ's priestly intercession to be an eternal self-offering. They could appeal to the Book of Revelation and its picture of the heavenly liturgy, with

---

[35] On the transforming, priestly love of Christ, see further O'Collins, *Jesus Our Redeemer*, 181–99.

the Victim, the Lamb who was slain, forever facing the presence of God (Chapter 2 above). That this eternal self-offering of Christ the High Priest takes place 'through the Holy Spirit to the Father' develops, in general, the theme of Christ being consecrated by the Holy Spirit for his whole mission (Acts 10: 38; see Luke 3: 22; 4: 14) and, in particular, the view of those commentators who understand Hebrews 9: 14 to intend something more than a vague reference to the spiritual (lower-case) aspects of Christ's self-sacrifice: the Holy Spirit enabled Christ to make a perfect (and eternal) self-offering to the Father (see Chapter 3 above). Condren and Olier spoke vividly of the fire of the Holy Spirit eternally consuming the sacrifice through which the exalted Christ remains forever Victim and Priest. Through the Spirit the heavenly consummation of Christ's sacrifice continues for all eternity.

Apropos of the Eucharistic self-offering of Christ, Torrance expressed vigorously its essentially Trinitarian nature. The last chapter quoted his words about participation in the Eucharist: 'we worship and pray to the Father in such a way that it is Christ himself who is the real content of our worship and prayer'; and 'in the Spirit the prayer that ascends from us to the Father is a form of the self-offering of Christ himself'.

(3) Olier, as we saw in Chapter 8, pictured Christ the eternal High Priest as continuing to send the Holy Spirit into the Church and the world. The Johannine testimony to the Holy Spirit supports this, when Jesus says: 'When the Paraclete comes whom I will send you from the Father, the Spirit of truth who proceeds from the Father, that One will bear witness to me' (John 15: 26). The evangelist associates the Spirit not only with witnessing to Jesus but also with new birth and life (3: 5–8; 4: 10, 14; 7: 37–9), with truth and teaching (14: 16–17, 26; 16: 13–15), and with mission and the forgiveness of sins (20: 22–3). Such witnessing, giving new life, teaching the truth, and commissioning on the part of the Spirit are ongoing activities that involve a constant sending by the eternal High Priest.

Thus the Spirit universalizes the priestly work of Jesus (Torrance, in Chapter 9 above). Here we can deploy the theme of presence. The universal presence of the Spirit accompanies and enacts the presence of the exalted Christ which is a universal presence. Since the Co-Sender of the Spirit (the risen Christ) is always inseparably there with

the Sent (the Holy Spirit),[36] and since Christ is present everywhere and in every human life, the Spirit must also be present everywhere and in every human life. Here, to avoid misunderstanding, we should add at once: people do not have to be aware of living in the presence of Christ and the Holy Spirit for this to be the case. *Being present* does not, as such, imply *being known to be present*. Torrance's helpful language about the Holy Spirit universalizing the priestly work of Christ implies a universal presence of the Spirit and Christ.[37]

(4) To hold that the eternal High Priest incessantly acts as the primary, invisible minister in the preaching and sacramental life of the Church obviously makes more precise what is left more general in the New Testament. The Gospel of Matthew closes with the risen Christ's command to evangelize and baptize all nations and with the promise, 'I will be with you always' (Matt. 28: 19–20). But Christ does not particularize matters by promising: 'When you preach, I will be with you always as the invisible preacher; when you baptize, I will be with you always as the invisible minister.' The longer ending to Mark pictures Christ being 'taken into heaven and sitting down at the right hand of God' after commissioning 'the eleven' to preach and baptize everywhere. They, then, 'went out and proclaimed the good news everywhere, while the Lord worked with them and confirmed the message by the signs that accompanied it' (Mark 16: 19–20). Like Matthew, the author of this additional ending to Mark witnesses to the belief and experience of early Christians: the exalted Christ was not absent but dynamically present in their mission to preach and baptize.

The Book of Acts, without expressly qualifying the activity as priestly, tells the story of Jesus being with those who preached the Gospel, working with them, and confirming what they did in his service through the power of the Holy Spirit. In the Lucan scheme, the risen Jesus needs to be withdrawn from the visible scene before the Holy Spirit comes. But the ascension does not mean that Jesus has gone away, as if he were on a very long sabbatical leave in another universe. He remains dynamically, if invisibly, present in and to the life of the Church. Here distinctions may seem to become a little

---

[36] See O'Collins, *Salvation For All*, 142–60.

[37] On this universal presence of Christ and the Spirit, see further ibid. 207–29.

blurred. Luke can move from cases of faithful guidance by the risen and ascended Lord (Acts 9: 10–16; 18: 9–10; 22: 17–21) to cases of guidance by the Holy Spirit (Acts 8: 29; 10: 19; 16: 6), without distinguishing clearly between them. He reports at least once guidance by 'the Spirit of Jesus' (Acts 16: 7), in parallelism with 'the Holy Spirit' (Acts 16: 6). Does Luke mean here the Holy Spirit who comes from Jesus, the Spirit who somehow is Jesus, or the Spirit who brings us to Jesus? As regards the initial outpouring of the Spirit, Luke distinguishes Jesus as divine Co-Sender from the divine Spirit who is sent or poured out (Luke 24: 49; Acts 2: 33). But when witnessing to the spread and life of the Christian community, Luke often refers to the powerful guidance of Jesus and that of the Spirit in a seemingly undifferentiated manner. Both are constantly present 'in, with, and under' the ministry of the Church.

Luke's narrative puts flesh and blood on what the Letter to the Hebrews states about human beings being enabled through Christ the High Priest to approach God's 'throne of grace' (Heb. 4: 16). One might risk summing up what Hebrews conveys about the place and means of salvation: 'Outside Christ the High Priest and his ongoing priestly self-offering and intercession there is no salvation.' To avoid misunderstanding, one should add at once: 'But there is no way to be "outside Christ" and no zone beyond him and his priestly activity.'

It was Augustine (see Chapter 5 above) who classically expressed in debate with the Donatists his faith in Christ as the real, albeit invisible, minister of every baptism, no matter who was the visible minister of baptism. Later, Augustine's principle was extended to the Eucharist, the administration of other sacraments, preaching, and the celebration of the divine office. In the last chapter we quoted Vatican II's Constitution on the Divine Liturgy on the multifaceted presence of Christ in the celebration of the liturgy, preaching the Word, and praying the divine office.[38]

Few have witnessed more powerfully than Tom Torrance to the active, priestly presence of Christ whenever the Eucharist is celebrated. In Chapter 9 we cited Torrance's emphatic words: 'when the

---

[38] See K. Rahner, 'The Presence of the Lord in the Christian Community at Worship', trans. D. Bourke, *Theological Investigations*, x (London: Darton, Longman & Todd, 1973), 71–83.

Church worships, praises and adores the Father through Christ and celebrates the Eucharist in his name, it is Christ himself [in the Spirit] who worships, praises and adores the Father in and through his members, taking up, moulding and sanctifying the prayers of the people.'

(5) The fifth item in our summary of the permanent exercise of Christ's priesthood concerns his role as the Mediator for the blessed in heaven. Adapting the words of the Creed, we can say: 'His priesthood will have no end.' In his glorified humanity Christ will remain eternally the Agent (or rather joint Agent with the Holy Spirit) through whom human beings will be raised and enjoy divine life forever. In an essay on 'The Eternal Significance of the Humanity of Jesus for our Relationship with God', Karl Rahner put it this way: 'the Word—by the fact that he is man and insofar as he is this—is the necessary and permanent mediator of all salvation, not merely at some time in the past but now and *for all eternity*.'[39]

Augustine was second to none when it came to this eternal priestly mediation of Christ and to applying the image of head and body (see Chapter 5 above) to the final presence of all in Christ. He summoned Christians to their future life: 'Be united in him [Christ] alone, be one reality alone, be one person alone (*in uno estote, unum estote, unus estote*)' (*In Ioannis Evangelium*, 12. 9). From incorporation in Christ, Augustine moved to picture a profound solidarity with him, and even to a personal assimilation. Augustine, while expounding the resurrection of individuals to eternal life,[40] also insisted that they will be drawn in the closest imaginable way into the reality of Christ: 'and there will be one Christ loving himself (*et erit unus Christus amans seipsum*)' (*In Epistolam Iohannis*, 10. 3).

Augustine also expressed the final communion of life through Christ's priestly mediation in terms of praise: 'there we shall praise; we shall all be one, in him [Christ] who is One, oriented towards the One [the Father]; for then, though many, we shall not be scattered

---

[39] K. Rahner, *Theological Investigations*, trans. K.-H. Kruger and B. Kruger, iii (London: Darton, Longman & Todd, 1967), 35–46, at 45; italics ours.

[40] See G. O'Collins, 'Augustine On the Resurrection', in F. LeMoine and C. Kleinhenz (eds.), *Saint Augustine the Bishop: A Book of Essays* (New York: Garland, 1994), 65–75.

(*ibi laudabimus, omnes unus in uno ad unum erimus; quia deinceps multi dispersi non erimus*)' (*Enarrationes in Psalmos*, 147. 28). Addressing the triune God, Augustine also wrote: 'and without ceasing we shall say one thing, praising You [the Trinity] in unison, even ourselves being also made one in You [the Trinity] (*et sine fine dicemus unum laudantes te in unum, et in te facti etiam nos unum*)' (*De Trinitate*, 15. 28. 51).

THESIS 11

At all stages (in his incarnation, ministry, death, and risen glory) the priesthood of Christ is essentially Trinitarian.
This thesis draws together what the previous thesis has stated under (2) and (3). No New Testament writer goes beyond Luke in his vision of the Trinitarian face of the whole story of Jesus: from his conception through the power of the Holy Spirit through to his sending (with the Father) of the Holy Spirit at the first Pentecost. The Spirit-bearer becomes the Spirit-giver (Luke).

The Letter to the Hebrews, *the* New Testament witness to the priesthood of Christ, is also thoroughly 'Trinitarian'—not least by its biblical quotations. It treats the Scriptures not as the written word of God but as the spoken word of the tripersonal God. Where St Paul introduces quotations from the Scriptures with such rubrics as 'it is written' (e.g. Rom. 9: 13, 33; 11: 8), 'the Scripture says' (e.g. Gal. 4: 30), and 'Moses says' or 'David says' (e.g. Rom. 10: 19; 11: 9), Hebrews puts biblical texts into the mouth of either God (the Father) (e.g. Heb. 1: 5) or of the Son (e.g. 2: 12) or of the Holy Spirit (e.g. 3: 7–11). It is rare that anyone else is allowed to speak the words of Scripture, as Moses does in Hebrews 9: 19–20. Hebrews draws on the biblical texts for a Trinitarian doctrine—one might say, drama— in which the Father speaks to the Son and to us in the Son, the Son addresses the Father, and the Holy Spirit bears witness to us. Thus Hebrews expounds Christ's priesthood within a kind of Trinitarian drama.

As we showed in Chapter 8, Bérulle, Condren, and Olier understood Christ's priestly self-offering to the Father to have begun with

the incarnation, even before he was born into the world. Their vision of the various 'states' in Christ's priestly history included the Father from the outset. This portrayal of Christ's priestly existence became clearly Trinitarian when the Holy Spirit entered their vision of the consummation of Christ's sacrifice brought by his resurrection from the dead and ascension into heaven.

THESIS 12

While the priesthood of Christ is unique, it is also participated in, albeit differently, by all the baptized and by ordained ministers.
This final thesis serves to introduce what will be presented and developed fully in the final chapter.

We might press on and add further theses about Christ's priesthood, responding, for instance, to the question: was he, as priest-victim, the substitute and/or representative of sinful human beings? Or are substitution and representation unsatisfactory, 'extrinsic' terms? Would it be better to use the language of 'communion', 'incorporation', and 'solidarity'? Such language finds support in the way Hebrews insists on Christ's priestly solidarity with those to whom he was sent (e.g. Heb. 2: 17–18; 3: 1; 4: 15). But these and other questions can be dealt with more satisfactorily in the coming chapter.

11

Sharing Christ's Priesthood

In the third century St Cyprian of Carthage wrote: 'that which Christ is, we Christians shall become (*quod est Christus, erimus Christiani*)' (*De Idolorum Vanitate*, 15). This dictum bears application to the threefold office of Christ: what Christ is as priest, prophet, and king, Christians become. But what, in particular, does sharing in Christ's priesthood entail for the baptized faithful and for ordained ministers? We can approach these questions through the teaching of Samuel Seabury (1729–96), the first bishop of the Episcopal Church in the United States.

Seabury wrote of Christ 'as a priest' offering 'himself as a sacrifice to God in the mystery of the Eucharist: that is, under the symbols of bread and wine; and he commanded his apostles to do as he had done. If his offering were a sacrifice, theirs was also. His sacrifice was original, theirs commemorative. His was meritorious through his merit who offered it; theirs drew all its merit from the relation it had to his sacrifice and [priestly] appointment.'

After clarifying the sacrificial nature of the Eucharist, Bishop Seabury logically proceeded to expound the priestly implications of Christ's command to his apostles 'to celebrate the Holy Eucharist in remembrance of him': he 'communicated his own priesthood to them in such measure and degree as he saw necessary for his church—to qualify them to be his representatives' and 'to offer the Christian sacrifice'.

As for the non-ordained faithful, 'such portion of Christ's priesthood is given to them as qualifies them to join in offering the Christian sacrifice and to partake of it with the priests of the church'. Hence, Seabury went on to say, 'the whole body of Christians' is 'said

to be made not only *kings* to reign with Christ in glory hereafter but [also] *priests* unto God [Rev. 5: 10; 20: 6]'. He added at once that from this priestly dignity it does not follow that 'private Christians have a right or power to consecrate the Eucharist: that right or power being by the institution itself confined to the apostles and their successors and those empowered by them'.[1]

At least in this passage, Seabury developed a view of ministerial priesthood which centred on the cultic powers of offering and consecrating the Eucharist and which remained silent about priests being also called to preach the Word and act as good pastors to the faithful—two themes developed, albeit differently, by the Reformers and Vatican II. What he held about sacrificing bishops and priests sharing in Christ's priesthood in a 'measure and degree' that differed from 'the portion of Christ's priesthood' given to 'the whole body of Christians' coincided with the teaching of the Council of Trent. Seabury went beyond Trent by expressly recognizing, as Vatican II would also do, the kingly and priestly dignity of all the baptized.

What Seabury wrote can set up the central issue for this chapter: granted that all the baptized share in Christ's priesthood, is there some special, ordained priesthood beyond that 'portion'? Or are all Christians endowed with equal spiritual privileges, powers, and responsibilities—as priests, kings/shepherds, and prophets? As we saw in Chapter 7, the Reformers insisted that all the baptized are priests, in order to deny any 'special', priestly ministry derived from Christ. Let us begin with some relatively uncontroversial theses.

THESIS 1

All the baptized share in the dignity and responsibility of Christ's triple office; they are all priests, prophets/teachers, and kings/shepherds.

In Chapter 2 we recalled how Romans and 1 Peter used priestly language for the Christian faithful. The priestly and kingly dignity

---

[1] S. Seabury, 'Discourses on Several Subjects' (1793), quoted in G. Rowell, K. Stevenson, and R. Williams (eds.), *Love's Redeeming Work: The Anglican Quest for Holiness* (Oxford: Oxford University Press, 2001), 326–7.

promised to the Israelites (Exod. 19: 6; Isa. 61: 6) was extended to all the baptized (Rev. 1: 6; 5: 10). Hebrews understood Christ's priestly self-sacrifice to have initiated sacrifices of praise and good works among his followers (Heb. 13: 15–16).

We saw in Chapter 5 how Origen pictured the ideal Christian life as sharing in the high-priestly holiness of Christ. Chrysostom stressed the priestly holiness required of all the baptized. All believers should share in the priesthood of Christ through acts of virtue and the suitable interior dispositions that should accompany them, the priestly self-sacrifice of daily life. Augustine picked up the New Testament language about the royal priesthood of all the baptized. We could move on and cite other Christian witnesses down the centuries who appreciated how baptism conveys a share in Christ's priestly and kingly office. That baptism also brings a share in Christ's prophetic office may seem less clear. Significantly, Seabury, at least in the passages quoted above, acknowledged the priestly and kingly dignity of all the baptized but had nothing to say about their sharing in Christ's prophetic function.

Revelation portrayed faithful Christians in royal and priestly terms (Rev. 1: 6; 2: 26, 3: 21; 5: 10; 20: 6). The author of that book was understood to exercise a prophetic gift (1: 3; 22: 7, 10, 18–19). But did Revelation also regard the whole Church as a prophetic commu-nity, one that prophetically mediated between God and the rest of humanity? The book contains at least one passage where it takes 'prophets' more broadly and, seemingly, as equivalent to 'saints', God's 'servants', and those who 'fear' his 'name' (Rev. 11: 18). Paul interpreted prophecy to be the special, charismatic endowment of a select number of Christians (1 Cor. 14: 1–33; see Rom. 12: 6; Eph. 4: 11), one of the greatest gifts that he listed as second only to that of being an apostle (1 Cor. 12: 28–9). The prophets were those whose intelligible preaching built up the Church in faith by explaining the mysteries of God. A Deutero-Pauline letter presented apostles and prophets as figures of the past, foundation-stones with Christ as the corner-stone (Eph. 2: 20; see 3: 5).

Luke, however, took a broader view of prophetic utterance, taking up words of the prophet Joel about all the people in Judea and applying them to the Spirit being poured out on all human beings (even if the immediate need was to explain the phenomenon of the

disciples speaking in foreign tongues). It was in universal terms that he understood the promise to have been fulfilled that prophecy would be revived in the 'last days' (Acts 2: 14–21).[2] Like Paul (1 Cor. 12: 13), Luke assumed that all Christians received the Holy Spirit (Acts 10: 44–8), and he closely linked prophecy with the reception of the Spirit. As much as anyone, Luke could be considered the scriptural patron of the belief that all the baptized share in the prophetic office of Christ. In any case, if they share in the priestly and kingly office of Christ, they should be expected to share in his (inseparable) prophetic office.

Add too the basic Christian conviction, expressed vividly by Paul and John, that faith and baptism entail being incorporated in Christ and becoming living members of his Body that is the Church. Precisely because they participate so intimately in his life, the faithful participate in his priestly, prophetic, and kingly functions. Many Christian communities express this sharing of all the faithful in the threefold office of Christ through anointing them at baptism and confirmation, and using prayers that articulate their new dignity and responsibility as priests, prophets, and kings/shepherds.

Obviously the faithful express their *priestly* identity at the celebration of the Eucharist when they remember and join themselves to the self-offering of Christ. But they also live out their priesthood whenever they become the means through which Christ blesses and sanctifies others: for instance, as husbands and wives and mothers and fathers. They perform their *prophetic* function whenever, at home, in schools, and at their workplace, they witness to their faith in Christ. In a special way, all Christian parents, teachers, writers, and artists are called to live out their prophetic office. They show their *kingly* responsibility and freedom by promoting the reign of Christ and by serving/leading others in the spirit of the ideal king that Isaiah vividly pictured (Isa. 11: 1–9). Few have expressed better than Luther (see Chapter 7 above) the royal freedom and responsibility of all the baptized. But, nearly five centuries later, we need to add a major and vitally important item to the scope of this kingship as he envisaged it: namely, responsible stewardship towards our fragile

---

[2] See J. A. Fitzmyer, *The Acts of the Apostles* (New York: Doubleday, 1998), 252–4.

earth. Caring for our planet features among the essential 'royal' duties of all the baptized.

The Letter to the Hebrews ended by evoking the priestly sacrifices of praise and good works that should mark the existence of the faithful (see above). In the light of other New Testament sources, we should remark that they have also been anointed by the Holy Spirit (e.g. 1 John 2: 20) and sent by Christ on a threefold mission of priestly, prophetic, and royal witness in building up the community and reaching out to the world.

THESIS 2

The triple office of all the baptized and, in particular, their priesthood, possesses a certain priority over the participation in Christ's triple office shared by those in the ordained ministry.

During his public ministry, Jesus called the Twelve from an *already* existing community of disciples. In a similar, if not exactly parallel, way those to be ordained for ministry are called in and from the wider community. From the ranks of the faithful, they are chosen to be ordained, and to be missioned for their ministry. In this sense, all the baptized, who constitute the new people of God, enjoy a certain precedence in the dignity of their priestly, prophetic, and kingly office. No one can enter the ministry of the ordained without being previously baptized; no one should enter the ministry of the ordained without being recognized as a devoted disciple of Jesus.

As Roman Catholics, we agree with what the Anglican–Roman Catholic International Commission wrote: the ministry of the ordained 'is not an extension of the common Christian priesthood but belongs to another realm of the gifts of the Spirit'.[3] The Second Vatican Council had earlier described this distinction between the ministerial priesthood and the priesthood of all the faithful as one of kind and not merely one of degree, adding, 'each in its own proper way shares in the one priesthood of Christ' (*LG* 10). To this we might

---

[3] ARCIC, *The Final Report* (London: SPCK, 1982), 36.

add: it is by precedence that the priesthood of all the faithful shares in the one priesthood of Christ, since baptism precedes any priestly ordination. No Christian community would ordain those who had not yet been baptized and so do not yet share in a primary way in the priesthood of Christ. It is always from among the members of the priestly faithful that those to be ordained are called. In their ordained ministry they are to serve the priestly faithful; they come *from* them and function *for* them.

To adopt the language of 1 Peter (see Chapter 2 above), all the faithful are the 'living stones' that make up the new, spiritual Temple which is the whole Body of Christ; as priests in that Temple they offer themselves as spiritual sacrifices together with Christ the High Priest. There is only one priesthood, one sacrifice, and one Temple. In their own idiom the French School proposed something very similar: the whole Christian life and the life of all Christians form a priestly act, united with the priestly self-sacrifice of Christ himself. To talk this way is obviously to give a certain priority to the priesthood of all the faithful.

Augustine does not expressly invoke the priesthood of all the faithful, but he speaks of their common sacrifice, as the one Body of Christ offered in 'the sacrament of the altar'. 'This', he writes, 'is the sacrifice of Christians: while many, they are one body in Christ. This is also celebrated by the Church in the sacrament of the altar, so well known to the faithful, wherein it is shown to the Church that she herself is offered in the thing which she offers (*hoc est sacrificium Christianorum: multi unum corpus in Christo. Quod etiam, sacramento altaris fidelibus noto, frequentat ecclesia, ubi ei demonstratur, quod in ea re quam offert, ipsa offeratur)*' (*The City of God*, 10. 6). Without mentioning either the priesthood of the baptized or that of ordained priests who minister at the altar, Augustine prioritizes the common self-offering of the whole priestly Church when writing thus of the Eucharist.

We might summarize the basic responsibility that the priesthood of the faithful entails. Through their sharing in the priesthood of Christ, all baptized Christians are called to offer themselves in the Holy Spirit as a living sacrifice to God and to intercede for the Church and the salvation of the whole world.

THESIS 3

The three offices of all the faithful will often be in tension and sometimes in conflict, but should always be set towards resolution and harmony.

In Chapter 9 we recalled a particular insight offered by John Henry Newman about tensions that could emerge through the Church sharing in the threefold office of Christ. In particular, he wrote about the 'conflicting interests' and 'difficulties' he detected in the exercise of the priestly, prophetic, and kingly offices during the later years of the pontificate of Blessed Pius IX.

In 1 Corinthians 12 Paul wrote about the variety of spiritual gifts enjoyed by the Christian community in Corinth and about tensions that could arise through the exercise of these different charisms. The gifts should all serve the common good; diversity should not be at the expense of unity. One might understand Newman to have transposed into the key of the triple office the possible and actual tensions that Paul detected in the exercise of various charisms.

Many readers, without lapsing into harsh judgements, should be able to remember situations where tensions arose between Christians who embodied different emphases in exercising the threefold dignity received through faith and baptism. The more prophetic bent of some can lead to conflict with others of a more priestly or kingly/ pastoral bent. Or the priestly aptitude of some can create issues with others of more pastoral/kingly instinct. Whatever the diversity, it should be harmonized for the good of all.

THESIS 4

The priesthood of all the faithful, along with their prophetic and kingly/ pastoral office, involves not only being tried and tested but also becoming vulnerable to persecution and lethal hostility.

This thesis, which matches our sixth thesis in Chapter 10 about vulnerability and suffering characterizing the exercise of Christ's own triple office, rests on abundant New Testament witness. Jesus himself warned of persecution that his followers would undergo

(e.g. Matt. 10: 17, 23). 1 Peter, which calls the faithful a 'royal' and 'holy' priesthood (1 Pet. 2: 5, 9), was written to encourage them in their sufferings. The Book of Revelation, which represents Christians in royal and priestly terms, engages right from the start with the trials and afflictions they must undergo (e.g. Rev. 2: 2–3, 9–10). The Letter to the Hebrews, before applying sacrificial, priestly language to Christian existence (Heb. 12: 28: 13: 15–16), gathers example after example of the suffering and even death that the life of faith entails (11: 1–12: 2).

Baptism is the central expression of what it is to *become* a Christian and so share in the priesthood of Christ. The Eucharist is the central expression of what it is to *be* a Christian and exercise that priesthood.[4] Baptism, along with the priestly identity it confers, involves being assimilated to the suffering and death of Christ (Rom. 6: 3–4). The Eucharist, inasmuch as it means 'proclaiming the death of Christ until he comes' (1 Cor. 11: 26), can be described as a self-involving appropriation of the cross of Christ or a sharing in Christ's death in order to share in his life. The event of the cross constitutes the corporate and individual identity of Christians and shapes the exercise of their common priesthood.

THESIS 5

It was not only at the Last Supper but also earlier (during his ministry) and later (after his resurrection) that Christ called and 'established' some of his disciples as priestly ministers who would share in a special way in his priesthood for the service of his community and the world. Christ, the supreme embodiment of priesthood, exercised his priesthood *before* the Last Supper (see Chapter 1 above on the Gospels, and

---

[4] In *BEM* the Faith and Order Commission of the World Council of Churches called the Eucharist 'the central act of the Church's worship' ('Eucharist', 1). In the Constitution on the Sacred Liturgy, Vatican II described the Eucharist as 'the summit towards which the activity of the Church is directed' and 'the fountain from which all her power flows' (*SC* 10).

Thesis 4 in Chapter 10) and in his risen glory *after* his suffering and death (see Chapter 3 above on Hebrews, and Thesis 10 in Chapter 10). Likewise, *before* the Last Supper he called from the wider group of disciples a core group of Twelve and, through a trial mission, associated them with his priestly work of preaching and healing (Mark 3: 13–19; 6: 7–13 parr.). *After* his resurrection, as Matthew 28, Luke 24, John 20–1, and Acts 1 illustrate, he definitively commissioned and sent them, as well as (with the Father) empowering them with the Holy Spirit for their mission.

In the sixteenth century the Council of Trent taught that Christ's institution of ministerial priesthood coincided with his institution of the sacrifice of the Mass (DzH 1740, 1752, 1764; ND 1546, 1556, 1707). But it did not teach that the institution of ministerial priesthood coincided *totally* with Christ's institution of the Eucharist. If the core group of the Twelve are taken to embody initially the ministerial priesthood, did Christ 'establish' them in that role merely during a few minutes at the Last Supper and even merely with the words 'do this in remembrance of me'? To be sure, the Last Supper was a (or even the) defining moment in their being initiated into a priestly office by Christ. But all the moments, which make up the full story of his sharing with them his priesthood, included what came before the Last Supper and what followed afterwards. Only an impoverished view of their ministerial initiation would ignore what Christ shared and did with the Twelve earlier and later than their final meal together.

Trent, as we saw in Chapter 7, in defending the sacrificial nature of the Eucharist, concentrated on the cultic side of priesthood and remained silent about the inseparable prophetic and pastoral offices. By expounding a richer view of priesthood as including preaching the Word of God and pastoral ministry, Vatican II set the ordained ministry in a context which included, but went beyond, cultic ministry (see Chapter 9 above). This richer view of priesthood requires us to rethink seriously the series of events through which Christ inducted a select group of his disciples into sharing in his priesthood.

What, then, of those who succeed the Twelve and the wider group of New Testament apostles (e.g. Paul) by sharing in Christ's priesthood through an ordained ministry?

THESIS 6

Through the invocation of the Holy Spirit and the laying on of hands, priests are ordained to share in a special way in the priesthood of Christ. With this thesis we move to the ordained ministry and to controversial positions which should be founded on the New Testament, to the extent that this is possible. Like all the baptized, the ordained share in the priesthood of Christ but do so differently. Both contribute, but in their own way, to building up the Body of Christ and serving the world.

Commenting on Hebrews, Christopher Koester maintains that 'it is clear' that the letter 'assumes that Christ's heavenly ministry (*leitourgia*; 8: 2, 6) undergirds earthly Christian worship (*latreuein*; 12: 28) and that his self-sacrifice gives rise to sacrifices of praise and good works among his followers (13: 15–16)'. Koester ends by saying: 'a place remains for leadership in the community of faith (13: 7, 17). But Hebrews does not call these leaders "priests".'[5] Koester might have added that Hebrews does not specify whether these 'leaders' (no matter what they are called) presided at Christian worship and, above all, at the Eucharist. Nor does the letter clarify just how these leaders became leaders.

Paul (1 Cor. 11: 23–6) shows that the Eucharist was the central act of Christian worship. Yet neither he nor anyone else in the New Testament identifies clearly those who presided at the Eucharist and how they came to perform that role.[6] Paul and further witnesses use, however, some more particular terms than the very generic 'leaders (*hēgoumenoi*)' when reporting leadership roles in established churches and how Christians were appointed to such roles.

Admittedly, in his earliest letter Paul speaks vaguely of those who 'preside (*proistamenoi*)' in the Church (1 Thess. 5: 12). But, writing

---

[5] C. R. Koester, *Hebrews* (New York: Doubleday, 2001), 380. It is worth noting, more broadly, that the New Testament never applies priestly language to Christian leaders as such—except for Rom. 15: 16 (see Ch. 2 above).

[6] Acts 20: 7–12 provides the only case where we can identify the person who presided and preached (at length!) at a Sunday Eucharist: Paul himself. On this passage see J. A. Fitzmyer, *The Acts of the Apostles*, 667–9.

to the Philippians, Paul addresses 'overseers (*episcopoi*)' and their 'helpers (*diakonoi*)', terms that are often translated, somewhat anachronistically as 'bishops' and 'deacons' (Phil. 1: 1).[7] But how they originated, what rites made them into 'overseers' and 'helpers', and what they did is left obscure. In another letter he notes that, within the whole Body of Christ, God has appointed apostles, prophets, teachers, workers of miracles, healers, helpers, administrators, and speakers in various 'kinds of tongues' (1 Cor. 12: 8–12, 28–30; see Rom. 12: 4–8).[8] These eight ministries in 1 Corinthians 12: 28 become five in another list of ministries for building up the Body of Christ: 'The gifts he [Christ] gave were that some would be apostles, some prophets, some evangelists, some pastors and teachers' (Eph. 4: 11). The list now includes the 'evangelists' or official messengers/preachers of the good news (see Rom. 10: 8–17).

'Prophets' are mentioned not only by Paul but also by Luke, who records details of their activity in the emerging Church (Acts 11: 27; 13: 1; 15: 32; 21: 10). At least for Paul, 'prophets' seem to have been something like inspired or gifted preachers.

The Acts of the Apostles also reports 'elders/presbyters', who along with 'the apostles' lead the Jerusalem church under James (Acts 11: 30; 15: 2, 4, 6, 22–3; 16: 4). Used of authority figures in Judaism, 'elders' came to designate officials in Christian communities, without Luke or anyone else indicating how that happened. Early in Acts, Paul and Barnabas are said by Luke to have installed 'elders' in local churches (Acts 14: 23). Yet neither in the certainly authentic letters of Paul nor in the Deutero-Paulines does the apostle ever speak of 'presbyters' as such in the churches to which he writes, let alone install such persons. When Paul visits Jerusalem for the last time he meets 'all the elders' and James, but neither 'apostles' nor 'the Twelve' are mentioned (Acts 21: 18).

Earlier, Acts 6: 1–6 has reported the appointment of seven to 'serve (*diakonein*)' in administering the Jerusalem church. One of them (Stephen), however, works wonders and acts as an outstanding speaker (6: 8–10) before being put on trial and martyred.

---

[7] In Rom. 16: 1 Paul names Phoebe as a 'deacon/helper'.

[8] On 'prophets', 'teachers', and other ministries in Paul's letters, see J. D. G. Dunn, *The Theology of Paul the Apostle* (London: T. & T. Clark, 2003), 580–93.

Another (Philip) becomes a wandering preacher and miracle-worker (8: 4–40).

The foundation of many local churches by apostles and others brought a shift in leadership, when pastors (called 'overseers', 'elders (*presbuteroi*)', and 'helpers' or 'deacons') took over from the missionary apostles, the other 'evangelists', and the founders, among whom had been the 'pillars' of Galatians 2: 9. A range of New Testament sources reflects this movement from missionary to settled pastoral leaders (e.g. along with Phil. 1: 1; Acts 20: 17, 28; 1 Pet. 5: 1–4; the Pastoral Letters to Timothy and Titus). Nevertheless, many details about the appointment of these pastors, their leadership functions, and their relationship to the travelling missionaries remain obscure.

The Pastoral Letters, when recording a more developed organization of ministries, speak of 'overseers' or 'bishops' and their qualifications (1 Tim. 3: 1–7; see Titus 1: 7–9), of 'the elders' or 'presbyters' to be appointed by Titus in 'every town' of Crete (Titus 1: 5–6; see 1 Tim. 5: 17–20), and of the qualities of 'deacons' (1 Tim. 3: 8–10, 12–13), and apparently also of deaconesses (1 Tim. 3: 14). At least in Titus 1: 5–7, 'overseers' and 'elders' seem to be overlapping and almost synonymous categories. Luke also seems to take 'presbyters' and 'overseers' as equivalent (Acts 20: 17, 28). There is some indication of succession in teaching authority (2 Tim. 2: 2). Much is conveyed about the teaching, preaching, defence of sound doctrine, administration, and family behaviour expected from leaders. But apart from some passing regulations concerning worship (1 Tim. 2: 1–2, 8) and several references to the 'laying on of hands' (1 Tim. 5: 22; see 4: 14; 2 Tim. 1: 6), nothing further is said about the liturgical life of the community and, for instance, about the roles taken by these leaders (or others) in baptizing, celebrating the Eucharist, and instituting others as their successors in leadership functions.[9]

All in all, the New Testament, while witnessing to some organized ministry and structured leadership, yields no standard terminology for ministerial leaders and no fully clear pattern about how they

---

[9] On various officials in the early Church, see Fitzmyer, *The Acts of the Apostles*: on 'apostles' (pp. 196–7), 'bishops/overseers' (pp. 678–9), 'deacons' (p. 345), 'elders/presbyters' (pp. 482–3, 535), 'prophets' (p. 481), and 'teachers' (p. 496).

functioned. To the extent that we can glimpse something about their appointment, commissioning, or 'ordination' (to speak somewhat anachronistically), it seems to have occurred through the 'imposition' of hands and an invocation of the Holy Spirit (e.g. Acts 13: 3; 14: 23; 1 Tim. 4: 14; 2 Tim. 1: 6). The threefold ministry of leadership in the Pastoral Letters ('overseers/bishops', 'elders/presbyters', and 'deacons') offers an early intimation of the threefold leadership ('bishop', 'presbyters', and 'deacons') that emerged in the second century—a ministry for which they would be ordained through invoking the Holy Spirit and imposing hands.[10]

During the first centuries, as we saw in Chapter 5, the application of 'priest' (*hiereus* in Greek and *sacerdos* in Latin) was not uniform. Origen attached the term to those whom Ignatius of Antioch called 'presbyters', whereas Cyprian of Carthage usually applied *sacerdos* only to bishops. Augustine, as we noted, applied *sacerdos* occasionally to bishops and merely now and then to 'simple' priests. Normally he used the term only of Christ himself. We return below to this phenomenon of 'reticence' in the use of the term 'priest' for both ordained ministers and Christ himself.

THESIS 7

Those who are ordained to priestly ministry are called by Christ in the Church and through the Church.
Here Roman Catholics, Orthodox, Anglicans, and some other Christians part ways with those who understand ordained ministers to be simply delegates of the community. In this view, ordination to ministry derives its authority and substance by delegation from the priesthood of the baptized. Ministers, in this view, are called by the community and not precisely by Christ.

Nowadays, at Catholic and some other ordinations to priestly ministry, the faithful are expected to express their approval of the

---

[10] On all this see *BEM* 21–5 ('Ministry', 7–25); G. O'Collins and D. Kendall, 'Leadership and the Church's Origins', in *The Bible for Theology* (Mahwah, NJ: Paulist Press, 1997), 101–16.

candidates for priestly ministry through applause and other signs of acceptance. Nevertheless, after someone responsible for their preparation has presented the candidates, the ordaining bishop accepts and calls them. This call is understood as follows: just as God chose and called Jesus to be the High Priest (Letter to the Hebrews), Jesus in turn chose and called his apostolic representatives (the Gospels). They in turn, enlightened and empowered by the Holy Spirit, chose and called overseers/bishops to succeed them. The bishops continue to be responsible, in the name of Christ and with the help of the Holy Spirit, for the choice and call of those to be ordained bishops, priests, and deacons.

As Ignatius of Antioch expressed matters succinctly in the early second century, bishops do not owe their ministry to the Christian people but to the 'Father and the Lord Jesus Christ' (see Chapter 5 above). In *BEM*, the Faith and Order Commission wrote similarly: 'Christ continues through the Holy Spirit to choose and call persons into the ordained ministry.'[11]

THESIS 8

Those ordained to the priestly ministry are called to promote the unity of Christian communities, their continuity in the faith 'that comes to us from the apostles', and their pilgrimage towards the heavenly kingdom. This thesis sets the ordained ministry, its sharing in the one priesthood of Christ, and its service within a broader mission and context that includes but extends beyond presiding at public worship.

Those ordained are not only presiders at the Eucharist but also preachers of the Word and pastors of the people. Through their prophetic activity as preachers/teachers and their 'kingly' activity as pastors, ordained priests play a major (but obviously not unique)

---

[11] 'Ministry', 11. A few years later the Commission commented on this passage: 'for the sake of the ongoing life and mission of the Church there must be persons, called by God, sent by Christ, and assisted by the Holy Spirit and recognized by the people of God, to preach the word, to celebrate the sacraments, to bring together and guide the Christian community in faith, hope and love' (*Baptism, Eucharist and Ministry 1982–1990* (Geneva: WCC Publications, 1990), 121).

leadership role in promoting communion among the faithful, guiding them to their final goal, and preserving and actualizing the life-giving revelation that comes from Christ and his apostles, as well as sharing with all people the good news that is Jesus himself.

In their inseparable, if distinguishable, roles as priests, prophets, and kings, ordained ministers are called to be Christ's instruments who face, so to speak, in three directions. As prophetic teachers they are to maintain continuity with the apostolic past; as priests they visibly actualize Christ's powerful presence through the Holy Spirit; and as pastors they lead the faithful towards God's future kingdom.

Just as with the priesthood of all the faithful, so the priesthood of the ordained must be set in the wider framework of the three offices and their exercise. Thesis 2 above about the baptized faithful finds its counterpart in this thesis about the ordained.

THESIS 9

Ordained to act in the person of the invisible Christ, priests act and intercede for others as his visible representatives.

Augustine, as we noted in Chapter 5, understood the Church's ministers to be visible signs of the invisible but dynamically present priesthood of Christ—sacraments of Christ, the Head of the body that is the Church.

In 1964 Vatican II linked the pastoral work of priests to the Shepherd and Head (*LG* 28). In a subsequent document of 1965 the Council returned to this thought and portrayed priests as being 'configured to Christ the Priest in such a way that they are able to act in the person of Christ, the Head' (*PO* 2; see also 6) and as 'servants of the Head' (*PO* 12).

THESIS 10

Participation in Christ's priesthood through ministerial ordination may be misused through evil conduct but can never be retracted or undone.

Whether we speak of an 'indelible mark', a 'sacramental character', or simply of the permanent nature of ordination, this thesis in effect states: 'once a priest, always a priest.'

In Chapter 6 we summarized what Aquinas wanted to say about the 'indelible mark' brought by sharing in Christ's priesthood through baptism and then by sharing in that priesthood through ministerial ordination. In both cases a related but different participation in Christ's priesthood left an enduring 'stamp' or 'character' on the person baptized or ordained. Just as Christ's priesthood is eternal, Aquinas argued, so too is the priesthood of those baptized and those ordained. One cannot be either baptized or ordained a second time.

THESIS 11

The special sharing by the ordained in the priesthood of Christ involves a further call to a life of holiness.

Right from Paul (and his themes of the spiritual 'worship' and 'ministry' exercised in daily life) and 1 Peter (see Chapter 1 above), the royal priesthood of the baptized was understood to call them to live out a holy existence. Paul and Hebrews, in particular, extended cultic language to picture the 'priestly' existence of all Christians. In later centuries Chrysostom was second to none in emphasizing the priestly holiness in daily life expected of all Christians.

Yet sharing in Christ's priesthood through ministerial ordination involves a further call to holiness. Origen, the French School, and other Christian witnesses down the centuries have insisted on the spiritual, self-sacrificing qualities required of ministerial priests. The Reformers, Vincent de Paul, and others have expressed their sorrow and indignation over the unworthy lives of many priests and bishops.

In particular, presiding at the celebration of the Eucharist puts priests into an intimate and self-involving role in proclaiming the Lord's death and resurrection. At the Eucharist all the faithful, to be sure, are called to identify with Christ who gave himself for others. Yet the presiding priests are summoned in a special way to manifest a true consistency between their cultic activity and their human lives.

Their identity at the altar should be seamlessly linked to a manifestly holy identity in daily life.

As we noted in Chapter 9, Yves Congar played a major role in preparing Vatican II's decree on the ministry and life of priests. Writing shortly after the Council closed, he firmly set out the self-giving that the Eucharist requires from priests and people: 'The Eucharist of the New Testament is not a rite that could exist apart from our giving ourselves to God and to one another, in order to form one body of sacrifice in Jesus Christ, who was delivered for us.' He drew the logical conclusion: 'However beautiful, ritually, the celebration may be, if it does not include the effective spiritual sacrifice of human beings [it] is not really and truly the sacrifice of the New Testament.' In the same vein, Congar added: 'we do not discharge our duty to God by offering him in sacrifice "some thing", however precious or costly, if it is anything, or even everything, except *our selves*.' For 'the one thing God desires from us' is 'our heart, our selves, living persons made in his image'.[12]

Congar put his finger here on the persistent temptation for priests to indulge and be satisfied with ritualism. Gestures, words, and what accompanies them can become more important than interior devotion and loving service to others. In the New Testament and the works of early Christian writers, 'liturgy (*leitourgia*)' referred both to Christian worship and to the obligation to meet the material needs of others. The double usage of this term suggests the essential bond between worship and social action through the service of the needy and suffering.[13]

Finally, Augustine and Luther are at their best on this theme. As we documented in Chapter 5, Augustine emphasized that the external rituals performed by priests should be matched by the inner obedience and sacrifice of their lifestyle. True sacrifice, for Augustine, was always found in a life given to God in faith and love. Luther puts matters more vividly. Introducing a specific detail from the rite of

---

[12] Y. Congar, *Priest and Layman*, trans. P. J. Hepburne-Scott (London: Darton, Longman & Todd, 1967), 79–80, 92–3; trans. corrected.

[13] See G. O'Collins, *Living Vatican II: The 21st Council for the 21st Century* (Mahwah, NJ: Paulist Press, 2006), 59–60; and S. R. Holman, *The Beggars Are Dying: Beggars and Bishops in Roman Cappadocia* (New York: Oxford University Press, 2001).

priestly ordination, he draws out the pastoral implications of being anointed and writes: 'beyond other Christians, they [priests] are anointed on their fingers, not so much for the purpose of being worthy to touch the sacrament of the body of Christ as to deal gently with the matter of the same sacrament: that is, with the people of Christ.'[14]

With this image we arrive at our final thesis, and the question: how do ordained priests participate in Christ's priesthood when they celebrate the Eucharist? Unquestionably, there are less controversial issues that belong here: for instance, about the 'invocation (*epiclesis*)' of the Holy Spirit at the Eucharist and the Trinitarian nature of the Eucharist. In *BEM* the Faith and Order Commission dealt clearly and helpfully with both matters. In its *Report on the Process and its Responses*, the Commission drew matters together: 'in the Holy Spirit, Christ comes to us, clothed in his mighty acts, and gathers us in his self-offering to the Father.'[15] This same *Report* delineated and rejected two extreme views of what happens at the Eucharist: 'the Lord's Supper is neither the occasion of a simple recollection of Christ and his death, nor yet a repetition of Calvary.'[16] If so, what then is the Eucharist in its essential link with the once-and-for-all, sacrificial, self-giving of Christ?

THESIS 12

In the celebration of the Eucharist ordained priests are visible signs of the invisible Christ, Priest and Victim or Offerer and Offering, whose unique and sufficient sacrifice, accomplished once and for all in his life, death, and resurrection, continues to be present and operative on behalf of the whole human race.

The heart of this thesis is the Augustinian-style distinction between the 'visible signs' (the ministerial priests) and the 'invisible Christ',

---

[14] *Lectures on Hebrews* (Heb. 5: 1), in *LW* xxix. 170.
[15] Faith and Order Commission, *Baptism, Eucharist and Ministry 1982–1990*, 116.
[16] Ibid. 115.

perpetually present and active through the Holy Spirit in his priestly work at the sacrificial meal that is the Eucharist.

In the founding event of his sacrifice that would define forever the Christian story, Jesus established a new covenant with God, which he visibly articulated at the Last Supper and ratified through his death and resurrection. Through instituting the Eucharist as the perpetual, living, and effective commemoration of his sacrifice in which he would remain dynamically present, he could draw into his own self-offering all later generations of believers.

This is to recognize that the Eucharist is neither a mere 'memorial' of Christ's sacrifice nor simply a communion in the 'benefits' Christ has brought to human beings. His benefits, whether at the Eucharist or beyond, are 'unavailable without his person' and his personal presence.[17]

In their *Final Report*, ARCIC joined all those who insist that the Eucharist is not 'a repetition of the historical sacrifice', and added: 'it is a sacrifice in a sacramental sense'.[18] Both points invite comment. If 'repetition' is false or at least hopelessly misleading, so too is another 're-' word: 're-presentation'. That can too easily suggest that somehow Christ's self-sacrifice was not being constantly presented to the Father. If we speak of a case being 're-presented' before a court, we imply that it was presented earlier and now, after a certain lapse of time, is being presented again. As regards the Eucharist being 'a sacrifice in a sacramental sense', it might be better to speak here of a 'sacramental form'. Following some insights from Tom Torrance, George Hunsinger writes of the action of the Eucharist not being 'another action than that which Christ has already accomplished on our behalf'. It is 'the very same action' performed by Christ but now in a 'sacramental form'.[19]

At every Eucharist Christ is the Offerer, the One who invisibly but truly presides at the visible, sacramental celebration of his once-and-for-all sacrifice. He takes up into his self-offering the visible priest

---

[17] G. Hunsinger, *The Eucharist and Ecumenism* (New York: Cambridge University Press, 2008), 16.

[18] *Final Report*, 2 and 20.

[19] Hunsinger, *Eucharist and Ecumenism*, 17; he quotes T. F. Torrance, *Conflict and Agreement in the Church*, ii (London: Lutterworth, 1960), 152.

and the assembled faithful. He is then the One who in the Eucharistic meal shares himself with all the faithful. The ordained priests act 'in the person of Christ'—not in the sense of replacing him or substituting for him but in the sense of acting as visible signs of his invisible and dynamic presence as the Offerer and the Offering. The visible priest presides at the Eucharistic ceremony, but it is Christ who perpetually offers his sacrifice. One might adapt Augustine and say: Peter presides, Christ offers. Paul presides, Christ offers.

The presence of Christ, the High Priest and Head of the Church, is made visible not only through the assembled faithful but also through his ministerial priests. Yet we should never forget that statement we quoted in Chapter 6 from Thomas Aquinas: 'only Christ is the true priest, the others being only his ministers' (*Super Epistolam ad Hebreos*, 8. 4). We may gloss this statement and say: only the invisible Christ is the true priest; the others, while visible, are only his ministers. Addressing God the Father, the ancient Roman Canon or First Eucharistic Prayer speaks of 'your people and your ministers (*servi*)'. Significantly, it reserves the title of 'your priest' to the figure of Melchizedek.

EPILOGUE

We could obviously press on and add further theses: for instance, about (1) tensions that arise between the exercise of the priesthood of the baptized and the ordained priesthood; (2) about the suffering and vulnerability involved in being ordained to the priesthood; and (3) about the role of the Holy Spirit in baptism/confirmation and in ordination to the priesthood (or to the episcopacy and diaconate). Both at baptism and at ordination the Holy Spirit is invoked, but differently, just as the Spirit is involved, albeit differently, in the exercise of the universal priesthood and in that of the ministerial priesthood.

The stated aim of this book has been to facilitate a better understanding of Christ's unique priesthood. Yet, as we have demonstrated, 'Christ the High Priest' or simply 'Christ the Priest' has not been a title that has flourished within the Christian story. The Creed

of 381, accepted and used by all Christians, has privileged three other titles: 'Christ (Messiah)', 'Lord', and 'Son of God'. Down through the centuries 'Saviour' (used of Jesus sixteen times in the New Testament) and 'Redeemer' (curiously, never applied to him in the New Testament) have also proved enduringly valuable Christological titles. Jesus' title as 'priest', along with the theme of his priesthood, has been somewhat marginalized down through the centuries, just as the major biblical document on his priesthood, the Letter to the Hebrews, has also suffered a certain marginalization.

The priesthood of Christ should be drawn into the mainstream of theological, pastoral, and prayerful reflection. His priesthood will prove revelatory and transformative for those who wish to appreciate more deeply and deploy more effectively the graces of universal priesthood and ordained priesthood. Without a much richer understanding of Christ's priesthood, will it be possible to energize and mobilize more fruitfully the ministries of the baptized and the ordained?

In practice, such understanding, energizing, and mobilizing will come mainly through the impact of Christian faith's primary language: biblical and liturgical texts, music, painting, sculpture, and architecture. Such verbal, musical, and 'material' expressions *show* the high-priestly actions of Christ rather than attempting to *explain* them. These primary expressions communicate meanings directly and appeal to the imagination and the heart. From the beginning of Christianity, for example, the fourth 'Servant Song' (Isa. 52: 13–53: 12), which pictures someone whose cruel suffering brings blessings to many, has functioned to show directly rather than explain intellectually what the priestly death of Jesus means. Any account of the primary religious language that has 'shown' his priesthood down through the centuries must include at the very least the Letter to the Hebrews, the constant celebration of the Eucharist and the other sacraments, the liturgy of Holy Week, and representations of the crucifixion. They all exemplify the primacy of 'showing' over 'telling' for those who wish to be touched by the priesthood of Christ. To be sure, we need the second-level language of theological reflection and clarification, but it cannot take the place of the primary religious language and its 'showing'. Let us conclude with one example of such primary language.

In the apse of San Clemente in Rome a monumental mosaic brings together visually into an integrated unity things that would otherwise have remained separate and scattered. At the centre is Christ on his cross, inaugurating all the movements in the mosaic. As the source of all else, especially the life of the vine and its branches, the thin wood of the cross communicates vibrant existence to the thriving world of the whole mosaic. Christ is the 'source of eternal salvation' (Heb. 5: 9) and a vital dynamism characterizes that salvation.

The cross is a throne of victory and triumph. From the top of the mosaic a hand emerges from the sanctuary of heaven and crowns the cross with a laurel wreath. God has accepted the priestly sacrifice of Christ. At the foot of the cross a small snake slithers away—to represent evil being banished by that sacrifice.

The rich vitality of the salvation effected by Christ the High Priest is expressed not only by the lively doves placed along the cross and the two deer drinking water at the foot of the cross, but also by the panorama of a redeemed world: a woman feeding her chickens, a bird nourishing its young, a man tasting wine, and cherubs gambolling with joy. The richness and variety of these scenes point to Christ the High Priest gathering all creation to himself and presenting it to the Father.

At the bottom of the apse two processions of sheep, six leaving from the town of Bethlehem and six from the city of Jerusalem, meet in the middle under the cross. They recall, respectively, the place where the High Priest was born 'in these last days' (Heb. 1: 2) and the place of his death and resurrection, where he 'entered the inner shrine behind the curtain' (Heb. 6: 19). Bethlehem features a set of descending stairs and Jerusalem features a window opening on an ascending stairway: the descent and ascent, respectively, of Christ's incarnation, passion, and priestly exaltation to 'the presence of God on our behalf' (Heb. 9: 24).

Vibrant activity fills the apse of San Clemente. Life flows out from the cross and, in turn, all life is gathered together by the cross—to become a supreme gift of praise offered to the Father by Christ the eternal High Priest.

Select Bibliography

Note: The first four chapters contain references to commentaries and other relevant, secondary literature on the biblical material; subsequent chapters include the appropriate references to the fathers of the Church, Thomas Aquinas, Martin Luther, John Calvin, members of the French School, John Henry Newman, Karl Barth, Tom Torrance, Yves Congar, and others.

Althaus, P., *The Theology of Martin Luther*, trans. R. C. Schultz (Philadelphia: Fortress Press, 1966).

Attridge, H. W., *The Epistle to the Hebrews* (Philadelphia: Fortress Press, 1989).

Bacchi, L. F., *The Theology of Ordained Ministry in the Letters of Augustine of Hippo* (San Francisco: International Scholars Publications, 1988).

Balthasar, H. U. von, 'The Priest of the New Covenant', in *Explorations in Theology*, vol. 4, *Spirit and Institution*, trans. E. T. Oakes (San Francisco: Ignatius Press, 1995), 353–81.

Beard, M. and North, J., *Pagan Priests: Religion and Power in the Ancient World* (London: Duckworth, 1990).

Botte, B. *et al.*, *The Sacrament of Holy Orders* (London: Aquin Press, 1962).

Calvin, J., *The Institutes of the Christian Religion*, trans. F. L. Battles and J. T. McNeill, 2 vols. (Philadelphia: Westminster Press, 1960).

Cody, A., *Heavenly Sanctuary and Liturgy in the Epistle to the Hebrews* (St Meinrad, Ind.: Grail Publications, 1960).

—— *A History of Old Testament Priesthood* (Rome: Biblical Institute, 1969).

Congar, L., *Lay People in the Church*, trans. D. Attwater (rev. edn., London: Geoffrey Chapman, 1965).

—— 'Sur la trilogie: prophéte-roi-prêtre', *Revue des Sciences Philosophiques et Théologiques*, 67 (1983), 97–115.

Coulson, J., 'Newman's Hour: The Significance of Newman's Thought and its Application Today', *Heythrop Journal*, 22 (1981), 394–406.

Crehan, J. H., 'Priesthood, Kingship, and Prophecy', *Theological Studies*, 42 (1981), 216–31.

Deville, R., *The French School of Spirituality: An Introduction and a Reader*, trans. A. Cunningham (Pittsburgh: Duquesne University Press, 1994).

Drilling, P. J., 'The Priest, Prophet and King Trilogy: Elements of Its Meaning in *Lumen Gentium* and for Today', *Église et Théologie*, 19 (1988), 179–206.

Dubin, P., *Le Sacerdoce royal des fidèles dans la tradition anciennne et moderne* (Paris: Desclée, De Brouwer, & Cie, 1950).

Fiorenza, E. S., *Priester für Gott. Studien zum Herrschafts- und Priestermotiv in der Apokalypse* (Münster: Aschendorff, 1972).

Fuchs, J., 'Origines d'une trilogie ecclésiologique à l'epoque rationaliste de la théologie', *Revue des Sciences Philosophiques et Théologiques*, 53 (1969), 185–211.

Gisel, P., *Le Christ de Calvin* (Paris: Desclée, 1990).

Goergen, D. J. and Garido, A. (eds.), *The Theology of the Priesthood* (Collegeville, Minn.: Liturgical Press, 2000).

Guyette, F., 'Jesus as Prophet, Priest, and King: John Wesley and the Renewal of an Ancient Tradition', *Wesleyan Theological Journal*, 40 (2005), 88–101.

Houssiau A. and Mondet, J.-P., *Le Sacerdoce du Christ et de ses serviteurs selon les pères d'église* (Louvain-La-Neuve: Centre d'Histoire des Religions, 1990).

Hunsinger, G., *The Eucharist and Ecumenism* (New York: Cambridge University Press, 2008).

Koester, C. R., *Hebrews* (New York: Doubleday, 2001).

Krumenacker, Y. *L'École française de spiritualité* (Paris: Cerf, 1999).

Lécuyer, J., *What is a Priest?*, trans. L. C. Sheppard (London: Burns & Oates, 1959).

Marmion, Blessed Columba, *Christ—The Ideal of the Priest*, trans. M. Dillon (London: Sands & Co., 1952).

Osborne, K. B., *Priesthood: A History of the Ordained Ministry in the Roman Catholic Church* (Mahwah, NJ: Paulist Press, 1989).

Rosato, P., 'Priesthood of the Baptized and Priesthood of the Ordained', *Gregorianum*, 68 (1987), 215–66.

Schick, L., *Das dreifache Amt Christi und der Kirche* (Frankfurt: Peter Lang, 1982).

Scholer, J. *Proleptic Priests: Priesthood in the Epistle to the Hebrews* (Sheffield: Sheffield University Press, 1991).

Sherman, R., *King, Priest, and Prophet: A Trinitarian Theology of Atonement* (New York and London: T. & T. Clark International, 2004).

Thompson, W. M. (ed.) and Glendon, L. M. (trans.), *Bérulle and the French School: Selected Writings* (Mahwah, NJ: Paulist Press, 1989).

Torrance, T. F., *The Mediation of Christ* (rev. edn., Edinburgh: T. & T. Clark, 1992).

—— *Theology in Reconciliation: Essays Toward Evangelical and Catholic Unity in East and West* (Eugene, Oreg.: Wipf & Stock Publishers, 1996).

Vanhoye, A., *Old Testament Priests and the New Priest*, trans. B. Orchard (Petersham, Mass.: St Bede's Publications, 1986).

Wood, S. K. (ed.), *Ordering the Baptismal Priesthood* (Collegeville, Minn.: Liturgical Press, 2003).

Yakaitis, M. T., *The Office of Priest, Prophet, and King in the Thought of John Henry Newman* (Rome: Gregorian University, 1990).

Zahringer, D., *Das kirchliche Priestertum nach hl. Augustinus* (Paderborn: Schöningh Verlag, 1931).

Index of Names

Biblical Index

10: 6 15
10: 10–13 15
16: 12–13 2

2 Samuel
2: 4 2
2: 7 2

1 Kings
8: 1–65 2
8: 58 218
17–19 15
18: 17–40 7
18: 38 82
19: 16 2n.
22: 5–23 15

2 Kings
2–8 15

1 Chronicles
24: 10 8

2 Chronicles
24: 20–22 249

Ezra
7: 1–5 4

Job
33: 23–6 32

Psalms
2: 2 2
2: 7 2
22 26, 143
27: 5 141
40: 6–8 253
46: 4 2
50: 8–15 5
50: 13–14 37
50: 14 56
50: 23 5, 37, 56
51 252, 254
51: 17 5, 37, 253

51: 18–19 253
51: 19 117, 129n.
63: 7 141n.
69: 4 106
89: 35–7 150
91: 4 141
95 90, 152
105: 15 2n.
110 46, 190
110: 1 45, 46
110: 4 2, 51, 52, 74, 122n.
134 235n.
135 235n.
141: 2 5, 37

Tobit
4: 7–11 5
12: 15 32

Sirach
35: 1–4 5
35: 1–6 32
45: 6–25 3
45: 17 3
48: 8 2n.

Song of Songs
6: 3 181
8: 5 146

Wisdom
18: 15 246

Isaiah
1: 11–17 4
1: 25 74
6: 2–3 40
9: 6 109, 110
11: 1–9 275
22: 22 110
22: 24 110
28: 7 4
52: 13–53: 12 292

53 143
53: 4–12 110n.
53: 6 110
56: 6–7 5
58: 6 14
61: 1–2 2n., 14
61: 6 38, 161, 274
66: 18 5
66: 21 5

Jeremiah
18: 18 3
26: 7–11 4
31: 31–3 21
31: 33–4 54

Ezekiel
1: 1–3 7
40–8 39n.

Daniel
1: 3–6 82n.
9: 24 149
10: 5 39n.

Hosea
4: 8 73, 74
6: 6 5, 94, 253

Zephaniah
3: 10 172

Amos
5: 21–7 4
7: 10–17 4

Micah
6: 6–8 253

Haggai
1: 1 4
1: 12 4
1: 14 4
2: 2 4
2: 4 4